Greenfinger

GREENFINGER

The Rise of Michael Green and Carlton Communications

RAYMOND SNODDY

faber and faber
LONDON · BOSTON

To my parents, Mary L. Snoddy and
the late Matthew Snoddy

First published in 1996
by Faber and Faber Limited
3 Queen Square London WC1N 3AU

Photoset by Parker Typesetting Service Ltd, Leicester
Printed in England by Clays Ltd, St Ives plc

© Raymond Snoddy, 1996

Raymond Snoddy is hereby identified as author
of this work in accordance with Section 77
of the Copyright, Designs and Patents Act 1988

A CIP record for this book
is available from the British Library

ISBN 0–571–17374–8

1000814481

2 4 6 8 10 9 7 5 3 1

Contents

Illustrations

Preface

This book came to be written because of a growing fascination with how a complete outsider managed to force his way by sheer determination to the centre stage in the British television industry while still managing to remain virtually unknown. The rise of Michael Green and Carlton Communications is one of the great untold business adventure stories, the story with everything – money, charm, ruthlessness and success. And yet profile writers have often been reduced to recycling old cuttings and listing those who declined to speak to them about Michael Green. As media correspondent of the *Financial Times* I have covered the affairs of Michael Green and Carlton since he first shocked the world of ITV in 1985 with his audacious bid for Thames Television, and this book draws on many meetings and conversations with the Carlton chairman since that period.

Writing a book about a living figure, even one who has put himself into the public domain by becoming a media owner, carries with it a special responsibility. Such subjects should have the right to put their point of view if they choose to exercise it. After initial conversations Michael Green decided that he did not want anyone to write a book about him. The issue was sufficiently important to him to take time out on 31 December 1993 – the day before the launch of Carlton Television – for lunch at the Connaught to explain why he, or more precisely his wife Tessa, did not want such a book written. Green suggested that Tessa should be taken to lunch to see whether her mind could be changed. It could not. Over lunch at Orso, Tessa Green explained that the problem was people might believe what was in a book and that it was much easier to control what appeared in newspaper or magazine articles. Later, at a chance meeting at a dinner for a visiting Faber and Faber American author, Tessa expressed surprise that this book was still going ahead.

'I thought we had squashed that,' she said. This then is a wholly unsought and unauthorized book, with all the resulting advantages and disadvantages. Access to the Green family has not been possible, and piecing together the early days of both Michael Green and Carlton has been like detective work. Some friends, such as the BBC executive Alan Yentob, asked for permission to contribute and it was granted. With others the answer was 'No'. Michael

Green, for example, prevented his close friend Gerald Ratner from giving an interview. Ratner, who was initially happy to talk, explained: 'Michael says that if I don't speak to you maybe the book won't get finished, and even if it gets finished maybe it won't be any good.'

Thanks are due to many people who contributed with advice and interviews to what turned out to be a lengthy and complex task. Not all of the 150 people interviewed are in a position to have their contribution publicly acknowledged. I am particularly grateful to Richard Dunn, the former managing director of Thames; Peter Ibbotson, the former director of communications at Carlton Television who came up with the title *Greenfinger* over a creative lunch at the Ivy restaurant; and to my friend and former *Financial Times* colleague Jason Crisp, now a stockbroker. Among the many other people who helped with interviews and comments are: Rod Allen, Jarvis Astaire, Mary Baker, Brian Basham, John Beedle, Sir Tim Bell, Chaim Bermant, Dorothy Berwin, Alex Bernstein, Frank Biondi, John Birt, Sir Christopher Bland, Roland Bottomley, Geoff Bowan, Ray Brassington, John Burbidge, Bob Cole, Michael Colenso, Giles Coode-Adams, Aldwyn Cooper, Lawrence Connelly, Michael Cox, Patrick Cox, Richard Davis, Keith Dawson, Charles Denton, Robert Deveraux, Greg Dyke, Keith Edelman, David Elstein, Quentin Faulk, James Gatward, Bob Gavron, Michael Gifford, David Glencross, Terry Goldberg, Michael Grade, Colin Green, Lord Griffiths, Graham Grist, Ray Hawkins, Richard Hooper, Janice Hughes, John Jackson, David Jeffers, Barry Johnstone, Peter Kleeman, Steven Leahy, Sue Lewis, Charles Levison, Arthur Levy, Stuart Lipton, Mike Luckwell, Dennis Marks, David Mellor, Sir Peter Michael, Roy Moore, Rupert Murdoch, Max Nachman, Sir David Nicholas, Katherine Pelly, John Perriss, David Puttnam, Tony O'Reilly, Tim Renton, Jessica Reif, Michael Rice, Gerry Robinson, Sir George Russell, Colin Sanders, Naomi Sargent, Willie Scullion, Nicholas Serota, Paula Shea, Rabbi Cyril Shine, Michael Sorkin, Martin Sorrell, Sir Colin Southgate, Sue Summers, Richard Taylor, John Thomson, Lord Young, John Waterlow, David Wells, Lady Wolfson, Nigel Wray, Alan Yentob and Stephen Zimmerman.

Thanks are also due to Matthew Evans, chairman of Faber, who was enthusiastic about the book from the outset; to my copy-editor Bob Davenport; to my agent Arthur Goodhart, who is also an editor by any other name; to Sue Pritchard, who produced transcripts quickly and well; and to Kevin Cahill and Chris Willis for their knowledge of Companies House.

Michael Green, it should be noted, was always able to distinguish with good grace between the work of the media correspondent of the *Financial Times* and the author of a book he did not want.

My greatest gratitude is reserved for my wife Diana and children Julia and Oliver, who once again had to endure the long weekends of work, which is the inevitable lot of authors who also work on daily newspapers.

Introduction

Hanover Square, just round the corner from the bustle of Oxford Circus, is a natural home for some of the better-known estate agents, branches of up-market banks, *Vogue* magazine and obscure public companies with well-polished brass plates. From the south side of the square St George Street leads into the heart of Mayfair. On the right-hand side of the street there is an elegant, white double-fronted Georgian house which stands out from the rest as if it could still be a gentleman's residence. Unlike all the others, the building has no name-plate on its door. It is only when a visitor has reached the black period doors of the entrance, a few steps away from the pavement, that there is any clue to the identity of the person or company inside. To the left of the door there is a simple buzzer with a single word in letters half an inch high – Carlton.

For more than eight years 15 St George Street has been the headquarters of Carlton Communications – one of the top 100 British companies and a company which owns a bigger slice of British commercial television than any other. It is also the spiritual home of Michael Green, chairman of Carlton and the man who in less than thirty years has created from nothing one of the UK's largest media empires.

In the foyer attractive young women on the busy switchboard say 'Hello Carlton' hundreds of times a day. On the way to the lift a visitor notices metallic sculpture and on the wall an old Technicolor poster of the film *Coney Island*, starring George Montgomery and Betty Grable.

Michael Green's office, at the rear of the building on the third floor, looks out over some of the most expensive rooftops in London. It is uncluttered, modest in size and minimalist in tone. There are very few clues to the personality and lifestyle of its occupant. The polished wooden desk is small by the standards of those seeking to use scale to underline power, and it is unnaturally tidy. Perched on white plinths there are a television set tuned to ITV, with the sound turned down, and a Reuters share-price monitor which shows the changing fortunes of the Carlton share price. On a third plinth there is a sculpted head. Taped to the side is a colour snapshot of Green's two daughters from his first marriage and two sons from his second. It is the only personal touch. The mementoes that some bosses litter around their lairs to say 'I am human too' are largely missing.

The most dramatic features are the pictures that dominate the white walls of the room. Over the years they have changed several times. For a long time the dominant image was a famous photograph of a coal-miner by the American photographer Richard Avedon. In 1990 Green was photographed alongside the image for a profile in the now defunct *Business* magazine which appeared under the headline 'The Modest Media Magnate'. In the picture the slight, pink, figure of Michael Green – who just about reaches average height – wearing a conventional business suit and a coy smile, contrasted in a jarring way with the black-and-white image of the strong, burly, unsmiling miner whose face is stained by coal dust. 'The important thing about that photo for me is that here's a guy who actually works for a living,' Green told the author Jeffrey Robinson without any apparent irony.

Although the symbolism of work is still on display, the miner has long gone from Green's office and has been replaced by much more expensive contemporary art. Behind his desk there is a painting featuring a traffic 'Stop!' sign, two spades and a sledgehammer. To his left is a stylized city and industrial scene and in front an enormous American canvas – *Roxy Arcade*.

Michael Green invariably works in his shirtsleeves with his black shoes kicked off and lying under the desk. There is no hint of the flamboyant media mogul. He is the very archetype of those whom young television producers disparagingly refer to as 'the suits' – those who ultimately control their lives. The smell of expensive cigars is in the air, and the next Diet Coke is not very far away. There is no sofa in the office: Michael Green receives visitors sitting behind his desk.

On the desk is his most formidable business weapon – the telephone – which he uses to spread charm, ambush staff, and make demands on his long-serving PA, Beverley. But most of all Michael Green uses the telephone to gossip, to banter, to exchange information on the rapidly changing media business with some of its most illustrious players. If he wants to find out what is going on at the BBC he has only to ask his friends Sir Christopher Bland, the chairman, John Birt, the director-general, or Alan Yentob, who is in charge of all BBC production. Channel 4 is run by his friend Michael Grade, who has often provided advice.

If he has an inquiry about newspapers, Green can call his friends Conrad Black, owner of the Telegraph group, or Max Hastings, editor of the London *Evening Standard*. The film industry? Then there is his friend Sir David Puttnam. Green is also a friend of Lord Weinstock, managing director of

GEC. International media tycoons such as Rupert Murdoch, chairman of The News Corporation, and John Malone, president of Tele-Communications Inc., America's largest cable company, take his calls, as do the heads of the Hollywood studios. Lord Hollick, chief executive of United News and Media, and Gerry Robinson, chairman of the Granada group, are more rivals than friends but they too are part of the ever-active media-mogul network for whom information is not just power but also money.

Michael Green is also often included in the ranks of the 'north London mafia', the group of successful businessmen who include his close friends Charles and Maurice Saatchi, who used to run the world's largest advertising agency, Martin Sorrell of the advertising and marketing group WPP, and, another close Green friend, Gerald Ratner, the jeweller – and, of course, Grade and Yentob. The phrase irritates members of the 'mafia' because it is so obviously an euphemism for 'Jewish' and because it is trotted out glibly almost as an explanation for success rather than just a contributory factor – as if contacts and back-scratching were all, and hard work and judgement had nothing to do with it.

In Michael Green's case he even disputes the geography. He has always been much more West End and Mayfair than north London. Although as a businessman Green has travelled a long way – from a £2,000 overdraft facility to a company capitalized at £3 billion in 1996 when convertible stock is included – he has rarely moved away from a few square miles in the centre of London, from his early days in a flat off Baker Street to his present grand home just off Park Lane. Even the Carlton headquarters in St George Street is just round the corner from where in the 1960s, in Conduit Street, Michael Green and his brother, David, ran a tiny direct-mail company called Tangent, serving the needs of the growing number of Jewish estate agents.

The story of Michael Green and Carlton is a remarkable one by any standards. The teenager with three O-levels who built up Tangent and later Carlton with his brother says he is now worth more than £100 million and is one of the UK's most highly paid businessmen, earning more than £1 million a year when bonuses and benefits are included. But the importance of Michael Green lies not just in his wealth. In the league table of the rich he is really only in the Phil Collins or Michael Heseltine class and trails behind Lord Sainsbury or Matthew Harding, the reinsurance specialist famous for his battles to control Chelsea Football Club. The importance of Michael Green lies in his influence over what we see on our television screens. Michael Green controls – and although his shareholding in Carlton is now small he really does control – the two largest ITV companies: Carlton

Television in London and Central Independent Television in Birmingham and Nottingham. Carlton has a large stake in Independent Television News, of which Green is a former chairman. He is also a shareholder in Meridian, the south-of-England broadcaster, and Good Morning Television, the commercial breakfast station.

Green's appetite for acquiring television companies and launching new channels is undiminished. Yet, despite his growing power and influence, he remains the unknown media tycoon, and the story of how a tiny direct-mail company with revenues of a few thousand pounds was turned into one of the UK's leading media groups has never been told in detail.

There are many anecdotes about Michael Green the man, but they tend to be contradictory and merely add to the enigma. When a young investment manager at Norwich Union whom Green respected died suddenly of a heart attack, the Carlton chairman went to the trouble of finding out his mother's address and sent a letter of condolence saying the Norwich Union man had been one of the most talented investment managers he had ever met. But there have been other, very different, incidents when Green has unleashed obscenities at junior and senior colleagues alike. 'He is the sort of man who makes secretaries cry,' said one senior businessman.

Yet his powerful personality impresses even those who would prefer to despise him. 'Michael has an almost tangible charisma. And I know that there have been times when I thought, "God I hate this bloke." And yet when I've been in his presence I've thought, "I want him to like me,"' one former Carlton executive says.

Another glimpse of the character of Michael Green the businessman can be gained from a incident that occurred on the morning of Monday 11 February 1991, just after 10 a.m., as the Carlton chairman paced up and down outside the Billy Wright Room at Central's Birmingham headquarters where the board was meeting. Green was being elected to the board, but he had to wait until the relevant item on the agenda had been reached before he could take part. First the Central chairman, the late David Justam, had to deal with matters arising from the last meeting. Discussion dragged on longer than expected, and outside the door as he waited to be called Green got more and more impatient.

Suddenly, twenty minutes after the meeting began, the door of the Billy Wright Room burst open and there was Green. The startled chairman explained as patiently as he could that they were not quite ready for him yet. Green stood there as the other board members shuffled their papers in embarrassment, then said, 'Well I hope you won't keep me waiting long.'

Justam said he would let Green know.

For Michael Green the incident was like water off a duck's back, and within ten minutes of finally being elected to the Central board he was playing a full part in the proceedings as if he had always been a member.

'He is a very unusual businessman who does not conform to the rules guiding other people. His *modus operandi* is to destabilize and unsettle ordered situations, and he pays no attention to normal protocol or even politeness. He is the John McEnroe of business – disruptive, arguing with the umpire, trying to get the rules changed,' said one of those present.

The incident gives just a hint of an impatient, complex, driven man.

This book is devoted to unravelling the story of how Michael Green managed to build Carlton Communications and to trying to answer the question even senior broadcasters still ask in puzzlement: 'Who is Michael Green?'

Chapter 1

Out of the Ukraine

The only thing that is certain about Michael Green's origins is that all four of his grandparents came from Kiev, in what is now the Ukraine. In common with hundreds of thousands of others, they were part of the wave of emigration that saw more than 1 million Jews leave the tsarist empire between 1870 and the start of the First World War. About 120,000 settled in Britain, many arriving in the East End of London with nothing.

Some tsars were more liberal than others and relatively tolerant towards the Jewish community, but during the course of the nineteenth century there was a slow tightening of controls and growing restrictions. The hope was that, if life was made sufficiently unpleasant for the Jews, more and more would convert to Christianity.

Only certain categories of Jews were permitted to travel or live outside the Pale of Settlement – twenty-five western provinces of Russia, including the Ukraine, stretching from the Baltic to the Black Sea. They ranged from discharged soldiers (Jews were conscripted into the Russian army, although it was very difficult for them to rise above the rank of private because they were banned from military college) to graduates, 'useful merchants', mechanics, distillers, brewers and artists.

As Paul Johnson has described it, 'Visitors from the West were shocked to see troops of frightened Jews being driven through the streets by police posses in the early hours of the morning, the result of the *oblavas* or night raids. The police were entitled to break into a house during the night using any force necessary and demand documentary proof of residence rights of everyone, irrespective of age or sex.' The main factor relieving the general gloom was the corruption of tsarist officials – many different permits and travel documents could be obtained if the bribes were large enough.

Life became worse for the Jewish community in Russia after the assassination in March 1881 of the relatively liberal Alexander II. The assassination, with the supposed involvement of a young Jewish woman, was followed by anti-Jewish riots and massacres. In May there were bloody pogroms in Kiev and Odessa, and before the year was out nearly 200 Jewish communities across the Pale had suffered serious violence, ranging from murder and arson to rape. However, there is considerable evidence from contemporary reports that the inability to earn a living was as important a motive for the subsequent mass migration as was sporadic violence.

In 1890, when Jews were expelled from Moscow and Kiev, a new wave of emigration got under way. But would-be emigrants first had to get out of Russia. Passports were difficult and expensive to obtain legitimately, and were not given at all to potential conscripts. This meant that many had to bribe officials to get the documents they needed or pay corrupt shipping agents to be smuggled out of the country. When they reached embarkation ports such as Bremen, Hamburg or Rotterdam they were often exploited again, and theft of baggage and exorbitant lodging-house rates were common.

For many the difficulties only began at the completion of a long journey culminating in a three-day voyage across the North Sea. The fortunate had relatives waiting at the English dockside, but for most there was an uncertain welcome from the established and largely prosperous Jewish community already in Britain. In Lloyd P. Gartner's words, 'A motley mass of waterfront sharks and thieves lay in wait to despoil the others of money and baggage, under the guise of "guides", "porters", and runners for lodging houses. More contemptible were the Jews who used their knowledge of Yiddish to win immigrants' confidence only to defraud them.'

The worst of the suffering – at least in London – was ameliorated by the Poor Jews' Temporary Shelter in the East End, funded by a number of wealthy Jews. It helped between 1,000 and 4,000 new arrivals a year to find somewhere to live and get a job, although immigrants could stay in the shelter for a maximum of only two weeks.

In 1888 the retired Chief Rabbi Nathan Alder, in a message to the Jews of eastern Europe, warned that many of those who had arrived in England were finding it very difficult to support themselves and their families and 'at times they contravene the will of their Maker on account of poverty and overwork, and violate the Sabbath and the Festivals'. The former Chief Rabbi added that, however rich or charitable it might be, the Jewish community simply could not support such an influx of poor refugees pouring into London. 'It is impossible, for any one city cannot support all the refugees of other countries, besides the poor who already reside in it. There are many who believe that all the cobblestones of London are precious stones, and that this is the place of gold. Woe and alas it is not so.'

The public mood in Britain's industrial cities was made worse by the fact that the years between 1870 and 1903 were marked by one economic depression after another. Fear of competition for jobs and the resulting downward pressure on wage rates encouraged anti-alien and anti-Semitic attitudes. Organizations such as the British Brothers League held rabble-rousing meetings in Mile End and Stepney in the East End, designed to exploit the strangeness of the new arrivals who were Yiddish-speaking, Orthodox and often poorly dressed. Newspaper coverage and opinion did little to ease tension. The London *Evening Standard* wrote in March 1903, 'The last two decades have seen the formation and spread of a careful series of provincial Jewries in the great trading and industrial centres of the Kingdom, characterized by all the dirt and nastiness, the squalor and crime, superstition and vice, which are the salient features of the Hebraic settlements in the Russian and Polish frontier districts.'

The fact that Jewish rates for both crime and unemployment were low did nothing to lessen the social and political pressure that led to the Aliens Act of 1905. This gave considerable power to officials and tribunals to prevent immigrants from landing, and, although they continued to arrive, the numbers of Jewish migrants were greatly reduced.

Most of those who came to England had to share crowded and often insanitary lodgings which sometimes doubled as workshops. There they had to toil long hours for poor pay for sweatshop owners, particularly in the garment-making industry. Although a high proportion of the new arrivals were self-employed and aspired to be employers themselves, many had to submit to what was known as the 'pig market' – the open-air hiring of labour that took place every Saturday in London's Whitechapel Road.

A survey of the occupations given by those helped by the Poor Jews' Temporary Shelter between 1895 and 1908 found that 29 per cent had made garments of some kind, 23 per cent were in trade and commerce, and 9 per cent made boots and shoes. Few such individuals have left many traces beyond fading family photographs and memories.

Despite the lack of detailed knowledge, it is clear that Michael Green's forebears – the great-grandparents, accompanied by their children, who made the difficult journey from Russia around the turn of the century – were in every respect typical of that huge wave of Jewish emigrants from eastern Europe that transformed the character of London's East End and the central areas of many other British cities.

There are still arguments among members of Green's family over their origins. Some aunts claim their ancestors were aristocrats; others that they were butchers. Green accepts that it is far more likely they were butchers rather than aristocrats, and indeed the family name of Greenspan – shortened to Green after the Second World War – is a well-known one in the trade of kosher butcher. Apart from butchery, members of the family earned their livings in the traditional Jewish trades of boot-making and selling, watch-making and garment manufacture.

Michael Green's paternal grandfather, Morris ('Morrie') Greenspan, was a boot-maker and was unable to read and write when on 16 January 1915, at the age of twenty-three, he married seventeen-year-old Sarah Taylor. The ceremony was held at Philpot Street Synagogue in Mile End, just off London's Commercial Road, not far from where they both lived at 14 Betts Street, in what was probably then a tenement building.

The fact that Morrie signed his wedding certificate with an 'X' suggests that when he arrived in England from the Ukraine he was old enough to go straight to work and did not have the opportunity to attend the special Jewish schools set up to educate the new arrivals.

Their son Harold was born on 5 November 1919, when the family lived at 86 Dean Street, in Soho. Morrie, who was clearly beginning to move up in the world, was already describing himself as a boot-dealer. By the time Michael Green's father, Cyril, was born, on 23 December 1924, the family had moved to 377 Brixton Road.

On Michael Green's maternal side, his grandfather Chaskal, or Charles, Goodman – the son of Jacob Goodman, a butcher – left school at fourteen and worked as a watchmaker's apprentice around the City Road and Clerkenwell areas of London before moving on to making dresses. When he married, on 1 August 1920 at the age of twenty-four, in the Borough New Synagogue in Southwark, he already described himself as 'a Costumier (Master)'. His twenty-three-year-old bride, Rebecca Finegold, whose father, Solomon, was a cloth merchant, was a costumier's shop assistant. Their daughter Irene – Michael Green's mother – was born on 3 November 1923. By then the East End had been left behind and the Goodmans lived at Templars Avenue, Golders Green, in north London.

The generation who had arrived as children from Kiev with their Yiddish- and Russian-speaking parents had by the 1920s got a firm foothold in British society and were beginning to make their way as modest businessmen.

'My great-grandparents, who I very vaguely remember – my parents would remember them well – lived all the time with my grandparents and spoke Russian and Yiddish, and to the day they died in London they could not read or write. They could recognize the bus – the number – but they didn't know what a 9 or a 31 was,' Michael Green recalls. When his great-grandmother died in London she was still unable to speak a word of English.

'On my mother's side they all went to the East End. They were in the dress business, and the big move was going from the East End to St John's Wood. The Jews had this ambition that you get out of the East End. They all started in the East End, and the big moment was when you managed to make enough money to take your family to the other side of London.' Green believes that the difference between where he started and where he is now is tiny compared with the achievement of his grandparents.

The experience of Morrie and Sarah Greenspan and Charles and Rebecca Goodman is typical of that of the first generation of east-European refugees and emigrants who came to Britain in the late nineteenth and early twentieth centuries. Their path was the typical one of their community – the move from skilled artisan to small businessman and, above all else, self-employment. It is a family background common to many British Jews who are now in leading positions in British business. As Martin Sorrell, chairman of WPP, describes it, 'All our grandparents had nothing.'

When Cyril Greenspan married Irene Goodman on 3 December 1944, at the St John's Wood Synagogue, Marylebone, all the East End addresses had been left behind. Cyril, who lived in Hendon, was described as a company director, even though, like his bride, a private secretary who lived in Swiss Cottage, he was only twenty. He was a dapper and well-dressed man, although not very well educated, and was always on the lookout for opportunities – trying one thing and, if it was not a success, moving on to the next. Irene was a short, lively young woman who appeared to be very determined. 'David is more like Cyril, and I think Michael has got shades of Irene, because Irene is a tough nut. There is no doubt about it,' says a family friend.

By the time Cyril and Irene's first child, David Brian, was born, on 14 February 1946, the family name had been changed to Green. It was not obvious why the change was necessary, but Cyril was anxious to get on in business and, with the horrors of the Second World War fresh in his mind, probably thought it was a sensible precaution to be less obviously Jewish. When their second son, Michael Philip, was born, on 2 December 1947 at a nursing-home in Avenue Road, Hampstead, Cyril was a dress manufacturer and the family were living at 60 Regency Lodge, Swiss Cottage – the same block of flats where Irene had lived before her marriage.

When Michael Green was six months old, Cyril and Irene decided to leave the drab postwar London of rationing and shortages and emigrate to Australia. Cyril went ahead to organize accommodation for his young family and travelled by seaplane from Southampton – a journey that took eight days.

Irene Green, her two young sons and a nanny left Liverpool on 17 June 1948 on the SS *Bulola* for the four-week voyage to Australia. During the journey Michael became seriously ill and developed a very high fever. The Catholic nanny feared that the baby would not survive, and she took it on herself to give him the last rites of the Catholic Church. He was so ill that his father met the boat at Perth and took him off to get proper medical attention. The others stayed on board until the final destination, Sydney.

The Greens lived first in Sydney but later moved to Melbourne. For a time it looked as if they were about to become new Australians, but Cyril and Irene did not like the Australian way of life and after two years they decided to return to England. Cyril later told colleagues that the business venture in Australia – a canning company – had not been a great success. The reason for the return to England probably also involved wanting to start again in a more familiar environment.

After his return to London in 1950 Cyril's luck changed. He met Max Nachman, who became his business partner – a relationship that transformed his fortunes and considerably improved the expectations of his young sons. Nachman – a precise, intelligent man who was fluent in a number of European languages – had received a college training in textile manufacture in his home town of Chemnitz in Saxony – a city known as the Manchester of the East. Nachman, who is Jewish, began visiting the UK in 1934 as a representative of a Chemnitz textile company. After witnessing Nazi storm troopers in action, raiding his family home and stealing his father's valuable stamp and coin collection, he decided to live permanently in the UK. It was a decision that probably saved his life.

Initially the young German represented a group of nine Continental textile companies in London, before working solely for a Viennese glove-maker for the princely sum of £7 a week. He was able to run his own motor car – still a rarity for a young man in pre-war London.

When the Second World War broke out Nachman volunteered for the British army. He was accepted, and he swore the oath of alliance just in time to avoid the fate of most German-speaking 'aliens' in Britain – detention. He was so determined to fight the Nazis that he had bought an early version of glass contact lenses to cure his short-sightedness and successfully fool the army medical examiners into believing his eyesight was A1. As a German citizen, however, the only regiment he was allowed to join was the Pioneers, whose troops did many of the hard, unglamorous jobs such as clearing rubble during the London Blitz.

After the war Nachman launched a shirt-manufacturing business in Manchester, but he decided to return to London with his equipment and set up a factory there, mainly because his wife was a Londoner and missed the capital. Following their return from Australia, Cyril and Irene Green met Nachman through a friendship with one of his brothers-in-law.

Cyril Green, who still had a modest amount of capital, was looking for a new business opportunity and already had a registered company – Cymark. Thus the two decided on a fifty-fifty joint shirt-making venture, with Green putting up £1,500 and the Cymark name and Nachman contributing his equipment and knowledge. They set up in a 6,000 square foot factory in Effra Road, Brixton, and were soon employing between thirty-five and forty people producing shirts which were sold initially through shops owned by Nachman's brothers-in-law.

The young Michael Green remembers being taken to the Cymark premises in Brixton with his brother on Saturday mornings. To the two small boys the factory seemed enormous. The young brothers had no doubt that one day they too would be making shirts, and that eventually the business would be theirs.

'I think I knew at a very early age that I was going to be a businessman,' recalls Michael Green. 'There was nothing in my background or my family that suggested that was not a good thing to do. My father was very much a businessman, not very well educated, a man who would open up the factory at 7 a.m. So you would see your father leave very early, you would see him come home late, you knew about the work ethic, and the conversation at dinner would be about business and making money.'

Nachman, who was very much a perfectionist, determined to produce shirts he could be proud of. Several times in the early 1950s he travelled to continental Europe, attending exhibitions and visiting factories in such cities as Milan, Paris and Zurich. He was looking for specific types of fabric to exploit the growing trend towards non-iron and easy-iron shirts. In particular he wanted to find a special kind of interlining for shirt collars which would be completely loose inside the collar and comfortable. It was the shirt-maker's equivalent of the pursuit of the Holy Grail. During a frustrating visit to Zurich in 1954 Nachman decided to try just one more factory from a list of names he had obtained from the Zurich Chamber of Commerce. One Friday afternoon he handed over a sample and waited for the usual shake of the head. Instead the manufacturer went away and came back with a roll of exactly the lining-material Nachman was looking for.

Back in Britain, Nachman combined the latest non-iron fabric from a mill in Lancashire with the new Swiss lining in the collars. Shortly after, he and his advertising agent then sat down one evening with his daughter's school dictionary in search of a name that would have the right connotations and be easily pronounced in foreign languages. Nachman spotted the word 'tern' – one of those well-travelled species of sea bird common from Europe to North America to the Arctic. As Tern shirts began to sell, the company even began to advertise nationally, and a stylish grey and yellow box was developed for the never-iron shirts. They were a great success, and Cymark began to grow.

'All of this was me. Cyril I relegated to be a factory manager in Brixton, to run around with a measure, checking,' says Nachman, whose relationship with Cyril Green had been deteriorating for some time, although the venture remained a fifty-fifty partnership.

By the mid-1950s Tern shirts with comfortable collars were on sale all over the UK, and Cymark started to attract attention from other manufacturers. In 1956 Max Nachman was contacted by Douglas Bertish, a director of the long-established family-owned shirt- and tie-maker M. Bertish & Co., which made shirts under the Consulate brand name. The company had been founded in Bristol in 1909, but ran into trouble between 1952 and 1955, suffering from production difficulties and large write-downs on unsold stock. In the year to December 1955 it made a loss of £6,992.

After talks, it was proposed that Cymark and M. Bertish should merge. In return for selling Cymark to M. Bertish, the two Cymark partners would get a total of 2,000 ordinary shares in the enlarged company. During the negotiations Nachman insisted that he should have a larger share of the new equity than Cyril Green, and eventually it was agreed that Green should have 760 shares and Nachman 1,240. Both held significant minority stakes in the new enlarged company, which was to keep the name M. Bertish & Co. Nachman and Douglas Bertish would become joint managing directors of the new enlarged company, while Cyril Green would continue to run the factory in Brixton.

After the merger was completed, in 1956, M. Bertish & Co., with Nachman and Bertish alternating as chairman, produced shirts under the Tern by Consulate and Tern Cosmopolitan brand names. Sales rose, and in the year to the end of January 1957 the merged company had profits of £30,267. But the name Cymark was buried in the historical small print – and with it much of Cyril's influence.

To begin with at least, Michael Green's schooldays were happy and privileged. His first preparatory school was Northbridge House in St John's Wood, a coeducational, non-denominational school where the boys wore blue caps and played cricket on Hampstead Heath. His fellow pupils included the Asher children – Jane, Claire and Peter – and the late Lord Delfont's daughter Susan.

Quentin Faulk, now a journalist specializing in the film industry and a former editor of the magazine *Screen International*, was a fellow pupil at Northbridge House. He and Michael Green were friends when they were aged ten or eleven. Faulk recalls visiting the smart Green flat at 28 Bickenhall Mansions, just off Baker Street, for tea. 'I remember this very ebullient kid – a rather cheeky little boy with an amusing face. Looking at the pictures one sees of him now in the papers, it was just a younger version of that,' says Faulk (who was already better at cricket than Green).

Richard Davis, now a magazine publisher, remembers meeting Michael Green at Northbridge House when they were about ten years old. They became friends because they shared a common approach to school – neither had the least interest in academic work and indeed wanted to do as little as possible. They were the class jokers – although in a strict school intent on inculcating good manners their misdemeanours never got beyond talking and fooling around at the back of the class. The usual punishment was to be sent together to stand outside the study of the headmaster, Mr Warwick-James, until he returned from teaching his class.

'We waited for the heavy-booted footsteps of Warwick-James to arrive, and he would always make comments like "Not you two again!" and first of all he would give you a hard slap around the back of your head. Then you would go into the study – either together or individually – and he would tell you what he thought. But that was all we really got,' Davis recalls.

Green and Davis were friends out of school as well, and Davis stayed overnight in the Bickenhall Mansions flat, where the two boys laughed and joked as Green slept in the bottom bunk bed and Davis in the top. Green would also travel out to Hendon on the bus to stay with his friend.

Even then Green had a distinctive mop of dark hair which was regularly treated with Brylcream, and at frequent intervals he would pull out his comb to restore the perfection of his quiff. He also had a sweet tooth. When Michael Green visited the Davis home, one the first things he did was to raid the cup-cakes and biscuits in the larder off the kitchen.

'We were the cheeky chappies,' says Davis, whose father, Robert, once a partner in a Regent Street hairdressing salon, knew Cyril and Irene socially. The two boys lost touch with each other when they were sent to different schools at a time when Northbridge House looked like closing (although it actually managed to reopen quickly in new premises).

Green went on to Hereward House in Strathbury Gardens, NW3, and began to shine there. He remembers being captain of cricket and football and a prefect. He clearly thought he was doing quite well as he got a first small taste of being in charge. He also managed to pass his common entrance examination – the test that needed to be passed to gain entrance to any public school with academic pretensions.

By contrast, David Green, who also went to Northbridge House, seems to have been less academic than his younger brother. David went to a boarding-school, Whittlebury School, near the Silverstone racetrack in Northampton-shire. Pupils did not have to pass the common entrance examination to be accepted at Whittlebury, which has since closed down, and Michael's old schoolfriend Richard Davis was dispatched to Whittlebury after flunking his common entrance examination. He went there even though his parents had first asked David Green his opinion of Whittlebury and had been told it was 'rubbish'.

Meanwhile business was good at the enlarged M. Bertish & Co. Partly as a result of the special collars and the national advertising campaign, the company was able to claim, 'Tern shirts are among the most popular on the market, being on sale in more than 2,500 retail outlets throughout the United Kingdom and also in many other parts of the world.' By the beginning of 1960 profits had reached £203,651 a year and the company was starting to think about floating on the London Stock Exchange.

However, the proposed flotation posed a difficult choice for Cyril Green. He could take out his money and start again, or he could remain with the growing company in what would almost certainly be an increasingly secondary role and watch as the partner he no longer got on with became more and more powerful.

In an early draft of the flotation prospectus for M. Bertish & Co. (which would later take on the name of its most famous product, Tern Consulate), Cyril appears as one of the directors, with the title 'production director' pencilled in against his name. But when the 'tombstone' advertisement marking the successful completion of the Stock Exchange flotation appeared in the *Financial Times* of Monday 5 December 1960 – showing a company with an authorized share capital of £500,000 in the form of 2 million five-shilling shares – Cyril Green's name had disappeared from the list of directors. Just before his thirty-sixth birthday, Cyril had decided to take the money and leave the company. It is unlikely that the other directors did much to dissuade him.

According to Nachman, Cyril irritated the directors by selling £20,000 worth of his shares soon after the stock started trading at 16s 9d. The directors had wanted to avoid selling shares in the early days of trading, to keep the price as high as possible. But Nachman could hardly complain too much about Cyril Green: he concedes that two of his brothers-in-law did the same thing. A total of 1.4 million shares were issued and made available for trading, which meant that the capitalization of M. Bertish at that point was more than £14 million at 1996 prices. Not long after, Nachman and Bertish bought Cyril's shares for around £220,000 – the equivalent in 1996 prices of £2.65 million – a splendid return on the initial investment of £1,500 and a decade of hard work.

The news that their father had sold out was revealed to the young brothers one morning over breakfast, and it appears to have had a startling and profound impact. 'I remember the unhappiest moment, when my father floated the company. It became public and he made a lot of money, and so we were now the equivalent of millionaires at a time when you could buy a house for £5,000. And then he sold out – within a few weeks he sold out. It was quite obvious that he and his partner had not got on for many, many years, which I didn't know,' Michael Green remembers. 'David and I just looked at each other and thought, "My God, this is our future, this is disastrous. What are we going to do?" We thought it was the worst thing in the world. We didn't understand the concept of him having a large amount of money, and we thought we would no longer have anywhere to go when we left school – we were so convinced that we were going into the business. So it was quite interesting how we must have been brought up at some level to believe that that was our destiny.'

David Green was approaching fifteen and his brother Michael was just thirteen when they saw their patrimony apparently disappearing before their eyes. Greater uncertainty and heartache was to follow. Not long afterwards Green's parents split up as Cyril walked out, family members say, because of a relationship with an au pair.

'Although I didn't and I wouldn't accuse my parents of behaving badly at all, you suddenly think, "Shit – I've got to do things myself." Your whole world is suddenly turned upside down,' says Green. He believes that on the whole the experience had positive aspects – though obviously not something anyone would wish for themselves – and that as a result he and his brother grew up more quickly. 'I can remember having had a good life, having lived in a wealthy home, having had all the things that a good background can give you; the insecurity of a divorce and a father walking out – and, in theory, at some level your inheritance having walked out, even though you were never short of anything. I think that twigged something else in my brain saying, "Hold it, Michael – you are going to go out and make money as soon as you possibly can,"' he says.

It is easy to exaggerate the effects of such shocks to explain the future. Not every schoolboy who goes through the trauma of his parents divorcing goes on to become a multimillionaire. There is, however, some pragmatic evidence that the loss of a parent through either death or divorce during childhood, or a marked loss in status, may act as a spur for businessmen and entrepreneurs in later life. Cary Cooper, management-psychology professor at the University of Manchester Institute of Science and Technology, has tried to isolate the driving force behind business high-flyers. In 64 per cent of his high-achievers he found the experience of loss in childhood – a considerably higher proportion than would have been expected.

In early 1962, at the age of fourteen, Michael Green joined Haberdashers' Aske's School, a middle-ranking public school with rising academic standards, set in spacious rural surroundings at Elstree in Hertfordshire. A largely day school, it had been founded in Hoxton in 1690, and moved to Hampstead in 1898 and to its present site in 1960.

Although the school was founded as a Christian school, by the 1960s many religions were catered for and, because of the large Jewish communities nearby, between 20 and 30 per cent of the pupils were Jewish at the time of Green's arrival. The school denies the common impression, even among former pupils, that there was ever a quota to limit the proportion of clever Jewish boys, who tended to figure disproportionately in the academic success of the school.

Apart from traditional subjects, there was considerable emphasis on theatre, music and art. Many old boys from the school – contemporaries or near-contemporaries of Green – have distinguished themselves in such fields. Nicholas Serota, who was school captain in 1964, has gone on to be director of the Tate Gallery. Dennis Marks was head of music and arts at BBC Television before becoming general director of English National Opera. David Elstein was director of programmes at Thames Television before taking on the same role at Sky Television. Haberdashers' contemporaries of Green who have gone on to have successful business careers include Martin Sorrell of WPP and Keith Edelman, now chief executive of the Storehouse retail group and a governor of the school.

Marks – a scholarship boy whose four grandparents also came from Kiev – remembers Green well. They got to know each other in 1962, when both appeared in the school production of Shakespeare's *Coriolanus*. Marks played one of the main parts, Menenius Agrippa, a friend of Coriolanus. Green was one of the marching spear-carriers, with not a word to say.

'I remember him as a sweet, charming, sensitive, shy fifteen- and sixteen-year old. If you had asked me which of my Haberdashers' contemporaries I would single out for becoming a major force in the business and media world, then I think one of the last people I would have thought of was Michael Green. He did not give any indication, any impression, of the hunger for influence and power which he clearly has now,' Marks says.

Green left little mark on Haberdashers' – no prizes or honours of any kind. Equally there is nothing to his detriment in the school records, except that his academic achievement was not even close to that expected at a school where many went to university and high-flyers such as Elstein – a descendant of rabbis – get exhibitions to Cambridge.

In July 1964 Green took his O-levels and managed to pass just two – English Literature and History. The following term he joined the resit class and added a third, English Language, and also made a start with A-level Economics. Remarkably for someone who is now noted for his ability to devour numbers and extract useful information from a balance sheet as if it were a novel, Green did not pass O-level Mathematics. Green explains the disparity simply: he could never see any point in quadratic equations, but numbers in a balance sheet are very practical things.

Despite his lack of conventional success, Green regards Haberdashers' as a very good school and blames no one but himself for apparently losing his way and having an unhappy time. He accepts that he failed to make the transition from being one of the top dogs at a small prep school to coping in a larger institution where there were many clever boys, and thinks his failure at Haberdashers' was partly to do with wanting to succeed and realizing he would not be able to because the competition was just too intense. 'I think it was to do with wanting to shine. If I was in a public school and there were lots of very clever people, the odds are I wasn't going to get to the top there, because there were too many bright people. I wasn't interested in being number six,' he says. Green remembers telling himself while at Haberdashers' never to think of his schooldays as the best days of his life, because once he left prep school he did not enjoy them at all.

Keith Dawson, who taught at Haberdashers' during Green's years and returned as headmaster after a spell in the state sector, is interested in the phenomenon of successful entrepreneurs whose formal academic qualifications are sometimes minimal. Entrepreneurs, Dawson notes, are usually individuals with strong individual flair and a tendency to find their own way around the system – indeed they buck the system by not taking no for an answer. It is a description that fits Michael Green perfectly. The Haberdashers' headmaster believes that Green knew where he was going and had already got the firm impression that academic qualifications were not necessary. 'At that time he took a course of action which was available and, you know, he had connections and off he went and did what he wanted. It is much more difficult now to do that,' adds Dawson, who notes that Green is friendly and supportive to the school today, despite never having been a conventional high-flyer.

When Green left Haberdashers' in December 1964, after only a few months of struggling with A-level Economics, he was a worry to his mother, Irene, who after her separation had become a mature student at the London School of Economics, where she took a degree in psychology, going on to practise as a child psychologist. She would have preferred her younger son to have continued studying and enter the professions – perhaps becoming a doctor – rather than leaving school with just three O-levels.

Other than knowing that he was too impatient to stay at school and wanted to get into business, Green had little idea what he was going to do. He was certain that he did not want to work in the retail industry – he had spent part of a summer holiday working in a shoe shop, and found the idea of having to wait for the customer to come to him too passive and frustrating. He was equally certain that making money out of property, as a number of his schoolfriends went on to do, was also, for him, too boring and undemanding. 'I knew I didn't want to go into the property business. Lots of contemporaries were estate agents or accountants, and I knew very clearly that I wanted a product that you could touch, feel – that was tangible. I saw lots of other people making money, but in for me not a very attractive business. The idea of buying and selling properties or any commodity did not hold any interest,' he recalls.

Financially his was a privileged background, although he was never totally mollycoddled and Green says his parents were firm in teaching him the rudimentary skills of budgeting. 'My parents gave me a bank account at an early age. Each year they would give me a set amount of money – it was not very much – and I was told that was all I was getting. I could spend it in a week, but it had to last me a year. From that I learned about budgeting, and I always did manage to keep some money in the bank and I never asked for more,' he told Judi Bevan and John Jay for their book, *The New Tycoons*.

Cyril Green also took a robust approach to finding employment for his young son. Michael Green tells the story of how he asked his father for help in finding his first job. He was handed a copy of the London *Evening Standard* and told to look in the classified advertisement columns.

It was his mother – clearly fed up and concerned that her younger son was doing nothing – who tried to help in a more practical way. She asked a friend, a physician, Dr Barrington Cooper of Devonshire Place, just off Harley Street, if he could find her footloose son a job – any job.

The doctor called his friend Michael Rice, a public-relations consultant who had once had strong ambitions to be a Conservative MP but who changed his mind because he suspected that he might be too fastidious for politics. Instead of trying to become an MP, Rice had decided to specialize in the PR aspects of foreign policy, representing a number of overseas governments in London, and on his real passion, archaeology.

'He [Dr Cooper] said, "Look I have a friend, a woman psychologist. She has a young son who is extremely bright, very difficult. She is sick and tired of the way he is behaving at home – fed up with him. She wants him to get out. Will you give him a job?"' Rice remembers.

The public-relations expert, who at the time ran one of the largest PR consultancies in London, agreed to take on the seventeen-year-old Michael Green as an office boy in the company's elegant premises at 39 Park Street, parallel to London's Park Lane.

Michael Rice Associates had its own photographic studio and commissioned corporate films. There were also close links with a number of advertising agencies and printing companies – in particular Lund Humphries, a Bradford fine-art printer and publisher – and with both the Egyptian and the Bahrain governments, although the consultancy also represented the ZIM shipping line of Israel. Making tea and coffee for the many visitors was an important part of the duties of the new office boy, who was paid around £3 a week.

Rice found Michael Green appealing. He had a quick intelligence and a confident manner without being arrogant. Socially the young office boy was even then seen by his contemporaries as an unusually serious figure. A close friend, Gerald Ratner, who was to build up and lose a family jewellery empire, had chosen a colonel's helmet and a shooting-stick as appropriate birthday presents for Michael's sixteenth birthday. 'He was always so serious, I enjoyed sending him up,' says Ratner, who has always been known for his sense of humour.

In the north-west-London Jewish social set, which included the brothers Charles and Maurice Saatchi, Michael Green was a party-goer. Although some saw him as a bit of a loner, and definitely very conservative for the swinging sixties, journalist Sue Summers remembers that at parties in his teenage years Michael Green was usually the one upstairs under a pile of coats with a girl.

At Michael Rice Associates Green was considered a perfectly adequate office boy and at least brushed up against a range of new skills. The company had moved a long way from conventional public relations and had developed considerable expertise in design, both for print and for the mounting of exhibitions. When he wasn't running messages or making tea, Green spent most of his time in the design studio in the basement, where artwork was prepared.

Green stayed only a matter of months in his first job. When he left, of his own volition, Michael Rice wondered whether all the Arab customers had been a factor at a time of rising tension in the Middle East. In fact Michael Green was simply leaving for another job and better prospects.

Chapter 2

The Frères Verts

Michael Green's second job was working for a small printer near London's Euston station. David, Osler and Frank was run by a rather unconventional businessman, an Indian called Anthony Nelson, who was an aspiring poet and appeared to be in printing partly, at least, so that he could publish his own work. His company also had a modest direct-mail operation.

One of Green's grandfathers was Nelson's landlord and was able to help him to get a job which, though unspectacular for a former Haberdashers' boy, would at least enable him to begin developing some business skills in a sector that was starting to interest him. The seventeen-year-old liked the idea of taking a blank page and turning it into a printed product.

'Being a guillotine operator was very strange, but I was enjoying it because I was making some money – although I had had help getting the job,' Green explains.

The fact that David, Osler and Frank was a small company meant that he had the opportunity to learn a number of rudimentary skills quite rapidly. While many of his old classmates were preparing for university, Green was becoming acquainted with the great crashing hot-metal machines that assembled lines of metal type. He was able to spend some time as a junior salesman, and every week he also had to pick up the cash for the staff wages. Because the company was sometimes close to going broke, he had to go to two different banks in the hope of raising enough cash to pay the wages. 'I learned very quickly how difficult private businesses were, and how close to the wind this lovely man sailed every single Friday when it was wages time,' Green says.

Michael Green stayed at David, Osler and Frank less than a year, before joining his brother in their own business in 1965. After his years at Whittlebury, David Green had begun selling a poor man's rival to the Dymo gun which punched out embossed plastic tape for use in filing and labelling. The plastic gun was sold by retailers such as W. H. Smith and Ryman. The little company was also involved in the selling of other office supplies.

J & D Stationers, set up by David Green and Joseph Jonkler, was incorporated on 12 January 1965. In July that year Jonkler resigned as a director and was replaced by Michael Green. The brothers were still living at home – 28 Bickenhall Mansions. In October the company changed its name to Tangent Systems – a change approved by the Board of Trade two months later. David Green was then nineteen and Michael seventeen.

'We had £500 between us, and yet we had the courage to go into business. I look back and I find it remarkable – absolutely staggering,' says Michael Green, who brought to the tiny business his rapidly acquired knowledge of the printing industry. In addition to the £500 – most of which went on office furniture – the brothers could also call on a £2,000 overdraft at the North Audley Street branch of Barclays Bank, guaranteed by their parents.

At Tangent, Michael Green acted as a broker, taking in orders for printing jobs and farming the work out to a number of different printers, alongside David Green's sales of what they called Tangent guns, the tape that went with them and other office supplies. 'It was small-scale, but at least you got your hands dirty. You were rushing around and you were in control. I was in control of my own destiny. If you did well you made some money,' Green says.

A near-contemporary, now a successful businessman, remembers going along to Tangent's offices in Soho for an interview for a job as a carbon-paper salesman in those early days. Rightly or wrongly, the interviewee formed the impression that the aim was to try to sell companies large quantities of carbon paper – more, perhaps, than their immediate needs. A line in telephone sales patter had already been carefully worked out. 'Somewhat shady, not illegal, not dishonest,' was the view of the young man, who decided to look for a job elsewhere.

Tangent may have been a tiny company, but the brothers quickly demonstrated that they intended to pursue their business careers with some style by moving on to premises above a shop at 21 Conduit Street, off Regent Street in London's West End – hardly the cheapest location for a fledgling venture.

Not long after, Green remembers going to the bank with the little company's accounts and asking for its overdraft limit to be raised. When Barclays asked him to go and get his parents' permission, the insulted young businessmen told them not to be ridiculous. The sales figures alone, he argued, justified lifting the overdraft limit. Green was so incensed at how he had been treated that he walked out of the Barclays branch, down North Audley Street to Berkeley Square, and into the Bank of Nova Scotia. There Tangent's overdraft was trebled without question, and it was many years before Barclays Bank had any further business from the Greens.

As they peddled print orders, office supplies and Tangent guns, the Green brothers were part of a new, more confident, Jewish generation. They were thoroughly established and were able to enjoy some of the financial security created by their parents. Sometimes they appeared more than a bit flash. Michael Green owned a spectacular AC Cobra, and David Green drove an Aston Martin. And, whatever happened to their business venture, it would never be a rags-to-riches story: there would always be a comfortable home to return to if thing went wrong.

From the outset the Green brothers were on the lookout for something new. So, when they visited a business-efficiency exhibition and noticed an auto-typing machine – a new device controlled by punched tape – they were intrigued. The Greens bought a number of the machines, installed them in their offices in Conduit Street, and became pioneers – in a small way – in the modernization of the direct-mail business.

The cumbersome machines looked like large electric typewriters. A pneumatic device on the side, which took the punched tape, bashed out the common text of the letters almost like a small printing-machine. Names and addresses were added by young typists who each sat controlling four or five of the machines. The technique was of particular use to estate agents, as it enabled them to send out apparently personal letters to potential clients along with property details. Unsurprisingly, most of the Greens' developing direct-mail business was with estate agents.

Stuart Lipton, who had a two-room estate agency next door, at 19 Conduit Street, and who got to know the Green brothers at the time, believes that the Greens were pioneers in the field. Until then estate agents had no cost-effective method of sending out large numbers of smart, personalized letters to potential clients. 'They were a cut above junk mail because they were individually typed, and that was the fascination of the technology,' says Lipton, who went on to become chief executive of the publicly quoted property company he created, Stanhope Properties.

A large number of Jewish estate agents were setting up in the 1960s, and they were all keen for business. It was another aspect of the generational change in the Jewish community. There was a lot of family pressure for children to become professionals and move away from what was disparagingly called 'the shmutter business' – the clothes trade – and estate agency provided a respectable opening for those who had neither the academic qualifications nor the patience to become doctors, dentists, lawyers or accountants.

The Tangent business developed, and soon boxes containing the letter-

heads of a growing number of Jewish estate agents littered the office floor in
Conduit Street. Accounts for the year to the end of March 1968 show pre-tax
profits of £8,720 – £5,234 after tax – to add to £509 unappropriated profit in
1967. The brothers paid themselves £3,500 each, but the book value of their
cars was no less than £8,909. Tangent had hire-purchase commitments of just
over £3,000 and a bank overdraft of £3,707. There was also a loan account of
£2,000 at V.I.P. Travel, the travel agency run by Irene Green and her new
husband, Willy Wilder. The brothers – who said they were 'reasonably
confident' about trading prospects for the coming year – were not paying
themselves a dividend, despite successful trading, because of the overdraft
and the hire-purchase agreements.

The business soon outgrew Conduit Street, so Tangent moved to larger
premises and an even more fashionable address – 39 Upper Brook Street,
Park Lane, near the American Embassy. The Green brothers started in the
basement but later also took over the ground floor. The building was elegant
and Victorian, but even then the Green style was uncompromisingly modern,
with Scandinavian furniture and lots of contemporary art – or, as one member
of staff described it, 'awful things stuffed on a bit of plywood: probably worth
a fortune, but bloody awful'.

The Green brothers shared a large office with a view of a small garden, just
as they now shared a flat in the Euston area. Yet the two brothers were very
different. David was the more physically solid, laid-back and probably the
nicer of the two. Michael Green, physically more slight, was always more
highly strung and fidgety. Although David was seen as the more go-ahead,
and sometimes even the tougher of the two, Michael Green was never the kid
merely hanging on to his elder brother's coat tails. Staff overheard noisy rows
conducted in the Greens' high-pitched voices, but in general people were
struck by how well the brothers usually got on and how complementary they
were.

Employees tended to be recruited from a friend of a friend, or by urging
part-time workers to join the staff, and many of them were clever, stylish
young women – such as Margie Glyn-Owen, who had done a bit of modelling
work and was David Green's PA. One such friend of a friend was June de
Moller, who came to Upper Brook Street in 1968 to do some temporary
secretarial work and stayed. Michael Green had immediately spotted the
apparent inconsistency – the temporary typist was wearing an expensive
Hermes silk scarf – and took an interest.

June de Moller had been educated at Roedean, the leading girls public
school, and had begun reading for the bar. However, her husband, André, was

a barrister, and one of those, she thought, was quite enough in any family. She found business interesting and challenging, and was soon running the auto-printing operation for the Green brothers as well as filling and sealing envelopes.

The next step forward for Tangent Systems happened partly by chance. It involved another piece of pioneering – applying computers to the direct-mail business. Tangent's direct-mail business was so tiny that it scarcely registered as part of the direct-mail industry, which was dominated by two large players: The Facsimile Letter Printing Company and, its main rival, British International Addressing, BIA.

The Facsimile Letter Printing Company, which had taken over other competitors such as the Direct Mail Centre, and BIA tended to match each other in particular markets. For instance, the Facsimile Letter company had worked for British European Airways (BEA) for thirty years, while BIA provided PanAm's direct-mail needs in the UK.

The Facsimile Letter company – founded and still owned by the Bartholomew family – had been an innovator in the past and had developed a system of printing letters so that they looked as if they had been typewritten. Monotype, the company specializing in typefaces for the printing industry, had supplied special 'typewriter' typefaces to print the letters on adapted Heidelberg presses. The use of silk ribbons and special inks to soften the impact contrived to create the illusion of receiving a personal typewritten letter. Facsimile employed about fifty typists to add names and addresses.

Computer technology was threatening to change the industry, and Lawrence Connelly, managing director of the Facsimile Letter company, was sent to the United States by BEA to investigate the use of computers in the direct-mail business. While there, he arranged a test mailing to the UK using the new American system. The mailing turned out to be disastrous, with most of the letters going to the wrong people, but one letter ended up in the hands of Michael Green – probably passed on by a client. Green was intrigued and called to arrange a meeting with Connelly. The meeting led to an experimental joint venture to test the concept under the name Connelly-Green Associates – 'linking one of the best known names in Direct Mail with a true pioneer in the World on computerized printing'. The 'computaletter' was not quite perfect yet, as a letter sent to Mr S. Snow in May 1970 at 'British Auropean [sic] Airways' demonstrated all too clearly. Connelly-Green gave two addresses: that of the Facsimile Letter company in Tooley Street and Tangent's Upper Brook Street offices.

The joint venture did not lead anywhere, but Tangent did buy a computer to replace the old 'steam-driven' typewriters and launched its own computerized direct service.

In June 1969 David Wells, who had just graduated from art college, came to work at Upper Brook Street to run the system. While a student, Wells had worked at Tangent on Saturdays, addressing letters to make a little money. 'It was the early days of direct mail. Michael Green was well ahead. He was one of the innovators of direct marketing – one of the first people to realize the potential,' Wells explains.

A letter sent out to a potential customer in 1970 gives a flavour of what the Greens were up to, and of the self-confidence – even chutzpah – of the young entrepreneur who, at the age of twenty-three, signed himself with a flourish as 'Michael Green, head of marketing at Tangent Mail, part of the Tangent Systems Group'. The company said its activities ranged from direct mail to list-broking (the selling of addresses) and associated printing, business systems and equipment.

The letter was addressed to 'Max Nachman, Tern Consulate, Tern Works, High Cross, Tottenham, London N15'. It read:

Dear Mr Nachman,

The letter you have in your hand was typed by a computer. It took one second and cost 11d. That includes virtually everything from the paper to the mailing.

Look at the personalized address, note how we can pick out your name, Mr Nachman, in the middle of a sentence. If you didn't know you would think this letter was written for you alone – that is precisely why our letters are read. They appeal to the individual.

We have over 500,000 names and addresses stored on tape and they are available to you, free. Think of the benefits to Tern Consulate Ltd – individually typed letters really do get read, you know because you have just read one.

Fill up the reply card and we will send you more information. Direct Mail means more sales.

At the bottom the young head of marketing added a handwritten note: 'P.S. I believe you know my father, Cyril Green!'

Not all the computerized letters were so word-perfect. One mass mailing sent out for a stockbroker should have referred to companies' shifting assets but instead said that they were 'shitting assets'. The fact that the mailing lists were largely lifted from telephone directories also meant that on occasion letters trying to sell lawnmowers were sent to people who lived on the tenth floor of high-rise flats.

Tangent carried out a mailing for a company called Safari Holiday Village, and for the standard of formality of the time it was a little racy. Strangers were addressed by their first name, and the letter went on in an equally familiar tone. The author of the letter said he did not know what the weather was like in Hendon or Hammersmith, but 'here in Tangier it's 90 degrees and we're basking in the sun'. It was, David Wells believes, the sort of communication that got junk mail the name of junk mail.

That year yet another very elegant young woman started showing up at the Upper Brook Street offices. Her name was Janet Wolfson. She was Michael Green's girlfriend, and for several months the office receptionist too.

Years earlier, attending his synagogue at Great Portland Street, Green had looked up to the women's gallery and had seen her as a twelve-year-old. He met her again when she was seventeen, in the kitchen of a friend's house at a party following the traditional family Friday-night supper. He asked her for a date the following Sunday.

To the other members of staff at Tangent, Janet Wolfson seemed an easy-going young woman – although it was clear she was far from being an ordinary receptionist. 'I remember driving up Great Portland Street with him [Michael Green] in this little wooden pick-up Mini that he used to drive, and I had no idea who Janet Wolfson was, or Isaac Wolfson either – never heard of them – and we were driving by this bloody great office block and he said, "That's Janet's grandfather's place." And I said, "Well, what is he – the caretaker or something?" ' said David Wells.

If anyone had bothered to take a detailed look at Tangent Systems in 1970 it would have seemed a very unremarkable company, except perhaps for the youth of its owners, their determination and their willingness to try new things. There was also a buzz about the place, with friends such as Gerald Ratner dropping in and frequent calls to others such as Charles Saatchi, who in the advertising world was creating a buzz of his own.

Michael Green was always looking for advice and ideas and was forever on the telephone sounding out friends and business contemporaries and absorbing information. He liked to hire and promote capable women, and had a marked taste for the stylish. It was noticeable to those there at the time, however, that he did not actually do much of the work himself. 'I have got to say I never actually saw Michael doing anything. Michael's big talent was knowing who could do what, bringing them in, making them work, putting people together and making things happen,' Wells recalls.

Tangent was now having a tougher time financially. Profits were not keeping up with sales. In the twelve months to March 1970 there was a net loss of £3,596 on turnover of £68,992. In contrast to the previous year, when

David and Michael Green paid themselves £2,000 each, the two young directors took no money out of the company. The directors' report, however, suggested that better prospects were on the way: 'The state of the Company's affairs at 31st March, 1970 was satisfactory, and the Directors are engaged on a new project which they are reasonably confident will prove successful during the current year.'

The 'new project' was The Facsimile Letter Printing Company, which, although it had survived two world wars and the depression of the 1930s, had now run into a difficult period financially. The chairman was Thomas Bartholomew – always known as Tony – who had trained as a compositor in the family firm and had worked there all his working life, apart from the Second World War, when as a reserve officer he had been quickly called up. By 1970 he was in his late fifties and seemed to be losing his interest and his grip.

While a thoroughly decent man, he was by then more passionate about the Honourable Artillery Company – the prestigious City of London branch of the Territorial Army – than about the detail of running the business. As can often happen with the second and third generation of family-owned firms – his grandfather had founded the company in 1906 – the hunger to succeed had gradually weakened and the response to change and competition was slower than required. Bartholomew's wife was also in poor health.

In 1970 Bartholomew seemed to colleagues to be disheartened by the company's disappointing performance that year and worried about its future. The company's 1970 accounts showed a loss of £31,722 on a turnover of £282,615. Its freehold property at 1 Braidwood Street, round the corner from the Tooley Street sales offices, near London Bridge on the south bank of the Thames, was listed in the accounts as being worth £24,838. But, as the property was being fully used for trading operations, the directors were of the view that 'a market valuation as compared with book value would be of no significance'.

Lawrence Connelly, the managing director, who had been with the company since 1949 and was due to take over full responsibility for running the company from Bartholomew, was not worried about the future. He knew that the asset base was strong, because he had been responsible for purchasing the freehold of the company's six-storey Braidwood Street factory. The premises were potentially worth much more than the £24,838 listed in the accounts. It was common knowledge that the area was ripe for development, and that was much more important than the loss in a bad year. Indeed in the May 1970 issue of *The Direct Mail Group News*, published monthly 'for the information and entertainment of the staff', there was the surprising news that a luxury hotel was going to be built on Mark Brown's Wharf, just down the road near Tower Bridge.

'This is a most interesting development; it seems hard to picture a luxury hotel amongst the wharves and warehouses of Bermondsey, but no doubt once a start is made other changes will follow and I dare say that in a few year's time the whole area will be completely unrecognisable – who knows it may become a second Mayfair,' wrote Bartholomew, who regarded being editor of the monthly staff newsletter as one of his most important tasks in a rather paternalistic company.

Because of the poor financial performance, Bartholomew became convinced that he needed a rescuer – someone to merge with and take the business forward as he increasingly took a back seat. The uncertainty spread to employees, who realized the company was not performing well, and some began to be concerned about their jobs. In contrast, Connelly believed that, because of the freehold building and the signs of impending development, the company could easily raise the sums of money needed to carry on as an independent enterprise: he rejected the idea that the company was run-down, in serious trouble or in need of a rescuer.

Connelly was, however, asked to draw up a short list of potential suitors for the company. To make up the list he added Tangent Systems.

'I produced three organizations that were anxious to do some sort of a deal with us. Green was one – and not one recommended by me, being a thoroughly lousy proposition. I knew Michael wanted the place because he wanted the property, but Tony decided to go in with Michael Green because Michael Green made all sorts of promises – he'd keep all the staff, nothing would change, Tony would go on as chairman. He did remain chairman for a short time,' says Connelly, a 4 per cent shareholder in the company.

'I resented Michael Green making all of this money out of what was rightfully my inheritance,' says Connelly – although he was not a member of the founding family and his only inheritance was the informal understanding that full managerial control would soon be his. Connelly believes that Green was very persuasive and very personable, and that Bartholomew – a thorough gentleman, though not much of a businessman – succumbed to the first significant business deployment of the Michael Green charm offensive. Connelly now admits he was very complacent and, as an experienced professional manager in his forties, failed to imagine how a serious business threat could possibly come from a raw twenty-three-year-old.

The first the staff knew that something was happening was when one day they saw a smartly dressed grey-haired man looking around the premises. It was Cyril Green, who had come to run an experienced eye over what would become his sons' first takeover.

Apart from the opportunity of applying computer skills to a loss-making company using old-fashioned technology, the Greens had definitely spotted the importance of the property the company owned. They called in their friend Lipton, the estate agent, to confirm what they already suspected: that the property in a potential redevelopment area was worth much more than the £24,838 value in the balance sheet and possibly more than the face value of the company itself.

'As I got to know him he asked me for advice. Michael spotted the opportunity [at Braidwood Street] and I went to look at it with him. I thought the area was probably going to be redeveloped and that there were assets hidden within the loss-making company,' Lipton recalls. Connelly claims the Greens got The Facsimile Letter Printing Company for 'a pittance', a fraction of what it was worth. It was their first significant deal.

At the beginning of 1971 Bartholomew held 1,854 shares in the company, Connelly 167, and two other directors had one share each, although a year earlier, when there was a total of 3,000 shares, other directors held significant stakes. The old directors, with the exception of Bartholomew, resigned collectively on 4 March 1971 and were replaced by David and Michael Green, who by then had moved home to the more fashionable address of 12 Park Lorne, Regent's Park, near Lord's Cricket Ground. By September that year Michael and David Green each held 2,499 shares in The Facsimile Letter Printing Company and Bartholomew owned just one share.

At the time of the change of ownership the company was already experiencing a major problem that stopped the direct-mail business in its tracks – the three-month Post Office strike that began in February 1971. The Greens rose to the challenge, helped by the fact that a lot of their business was still with central-London estate agents. David Wells was able to mobilize a small army of art students from his old college to carry out hand deliveries around London.

One of the first things the Greens did when they took over was to move in their automated letter-typing machines and the Tangent gun business and to close down the fifty-strong typing department, which was no longer necessary.

Connelly remained as managing director after the change of ownership, although today he believes that allowing himself to be persuaded to stay was a foolish mistake. He also encouraged others to stay too, on the grounds that he would be still be in charge. 'I had had all the promises that I could run it as managing director – I really would be managing director, with the power – and of course it was utter rubbish. I had no authority at all to do anything, and people were sacked,' says Connelly, who, together with part of the sales department, moved to Upper Brook Street, which now began to take on the feel of a company headquarters. Connelly says he found the atmosphere there, working so closely with the Green brothers, 'terrible'.

Connelly left the company after six months to set up a direct-mail division at the advertising agency Foote Cone and Belding. By then Michael Green had realized that computerized letter equipment might be a little ahead of the market, and tried – unsuccessfully – to sell it to Connelly. Connelly was happy to leave, but he had no doubt that Michael Green – a nervous and fidgety man, unable to stay still for a moment, always juggling with something and drinking Coca-Cola – would be a millionaire by the time he was thirty.

John Burbidge had worked at The Facsimile Letter Printing Company for thirteen years and was the buyer and warehouse manager when the Greens arrived. He decided it was time for him to move on. He was an ambitious young man, the future was uncertain and clearly a lot of redundancies were on the way, and, unlike Connelly, he had thought for some time that the company was dying. But Michael Green insisted that Burbidge was one of the ones he wanted to stay. The buyer said he would give him three months. Green pleaded for six months to prove he could turn the company round, and got it.

'I ended up managing director, and never looked back. Michael always gave people the opportunity. If they were willing to give the energy and the dedication to any company that I have seen him take over, he rewarded them with advancement of their careers – and financially,' says Burbidge.

Michael Green was also very persuasive in changing the mind of Sue Lewis, one of the company's top direct-mail sales executives. She had been on maternity leave having her daughter when the Greens had taken over, and she thought the birth marked, for her, the natural end of an era. She did not plan to return to work at the company. But Michael Green persuaded her to come and work in the Upper Brook Street headquarters, where she found that the atmosphere was often tense. 'Michael would upset everyone and blow his top, his cool, and David would have to go in and calm everyone down. It was deliberate. It was a game,' says Lewis, who saw it very much as a double act between the two brothers. She soon left Tangent to set up her own direct-marketing company.

In the early days of their new venture the Green brothers had considerable practical help from their father. He really would roll up his sleeves, take a broom, and sweep the floor if necessary, or help women employees lift work off benches. Cyril, then aged forty-seven, was full of energy and drive. Later – much to the surprise of some of the older printers in the company, who thought you needed to be a printer to run printing companies – he made a considerable success of being general manager in charge of printing operations. Cyril was a good general manager and added stability and experience to the venture.

Michael Green now suggests that a mixture of naïvety and cockiness meant that he did not feel at all awkward about being in charge of around 150 people who were all older than him. 'It is bizarre, but at the time I was not embarrassed. I don't want to pretend. I don't go to the pub drinking, pretending to be one of the mates. I was quite clearly the owner from a very early age, and I didn't want anyone to think otherwise. Although I also remember laughing with David and my secretary, saying, "I am still the youngest person we employ." I used to be the youngest person for years in the whole company,' says Green, who at the end of 1971 was twenty-four years old.

Despite the Post Office strike, in the nine months to September 1971 the merged company made a pre-tax profit of £29,898 and the accounts list a £60,162 profit on the sale of freehold property – the equivalent of £445,578 at 1996 prices. The brothers could have taken the profit and sold the rest of the business in the way of asset-strippers. Instead, following the sale of the freehold of Braidwood Street – which was indeed eventually knocked down, for the Hays Galleria development – operations were moved a mile away, to 18–19 Crimscott Street in Bermondsey.

In 1972 there was a further corporate restructuring. The Facsimile Letter Printing Company changed its name to the Direct Mail Centre, which became the group holding company, specializing in printing and direct-mail services. Tangent Systems – still selling the labelling devices – was a wholly owned subsidiary. As part of the restructuring, both the Greens brothers rolled their 1,300 shares in Tangent into the Direct Mail Centre. It meant they now each held 3,669 shares in the Direct Mail Centre and Bartholomew the remaining single share.

Although he already showed unusual maturity as a businessman, Michael Green was still going through phases and striking attitudes. For a time he wore long camel coats and smoked large green cigars. He never remotely became part of the youth culture of the 1960s and early '70s; instead he used part of his share of the money from the sale of the Braidwood Street premises to buy a secondhand black Rolls-Royce – a vehicle his mother Irene thought too funereal. It was the first of many Rolls-Royces and Bentleys owned by Green, who, although he has never been wildly extravagant and ostentatious, has never felt the common English need to understate his wealth.

At the same time as the Direct Mail Centre was expanding, the relationship with Janet Wolfson was becoming more serious. The Wolfson name was one of the most famous in the Anglo-Jewish community. It was Janet's grandfather, Sir Isaac Wolfson, who had created the family's great wealth. Born in the Gorbals in Glasgow, Isaac left school at fourteen and moved to London in 1920, intending to set up a mail-order business. Instead, in 1926, he joined what was then Universal Stores as a buyer. In 1931 the renamed Great Universal Stores went public, and a year later Isaac was appointed joint managing director. He later bought out the Rose brothers, who had founded the business. Wolfson, who read accounts as other people read thrillers, used the profits from the mail-order business – and profits were to rise year after year for nearly half a century – to become the UK's largest retailer.

In the early 1970s, when Green and Janet Wolfson were going out together, Gussie's – as Great Universal Stores was affectionately known – had more than 2,000 high-street shops, including Burberrys and Morrisons, the women's clothing specialist. It was also in everything from footwear, hotels and electrical goods to builder's merchants and a travel agency.

In 1971 GUS had pre-tax profits of £52.8 million and assets of more than £200 million. Sir Isaac Wolfson's granddaughter, Janet, was probably one of the richest young women in the UK, although many Wolfson millions were ploughed into good works, including the founding of colleges in Oxford and Cambridge, through his Wolfson Foundation set up in 1955 with £6 million worth of GUS shares.

By comparison with the Wolfsons Michael Green was a pauper. When Green first told Janet's mother, Lady Wolfson – a sparky lady who says exactly what she thinks – that he wanted to marry her daughter, the reply was blunt: 'But, Michael, you can't afford to keep her in tights.' That was about to change, and an important factor was the way the relationship with the Wolfsons opened up significant business opportunities for the Green brothers.

While Michael Green was going out with Janet Wolfson, three months before their marriage, the Wolfsons offered the Green brothers the chance to manage Carlton Photography and Design, a photographic studio based in Frederick Close, near Marble Arch, that primarily served advertising agencies and was owned by GUS. There was also an option to purchase if the relationship worked out satisfactorily.

Carlton Photography and Design had been founded by two Canadians after the First World War, as a freelance agency for artists. During the Second World War the company produced propaganda for the government, and soon after it employed as many as sixty-five artists and illustrators. By 1972 it had nine photographic studios, an art studio and a design department that could produce everything from magazine-page advertisements to complete booklets and catalogues. There were also studios in Manchester. One of its main contracts was providing the photographs for the all-important GUS mail-order catalogues.

It is inconceivable that the mighty GUS empire would have sold such an important asset to two unknown brothers in their early twenties if one of them had not been about to marry Janet Wolfson. It is equally certain that GUS would not have put the quality of its mail-order catalogue at risk by selling the company to incompetents.

The Direct Mail Centre was beginning to flourish, and the accounts for the year to the end of March 1973 show pre-tax profits of £100,204, net assets of £149,972 and £88,000 cash in the bank. The two directors were then paying themselves a total of £17,800. The accounts also state that the future prospects of the company were encouraging. The reason cited for the optimistic outlook was that the directors had exercised an option agreed on 10 July 1972 to purchase Carlton Photography and Design – or Carlton Studios, as it was generally known – effective from 1 April 1973. It was the first appearance of the Carlton name within the company.

Michael Green insists that the Direct Mail Centre was given no financial favours over the purchase of Carlton Studios and had to pay a top price of around £400,000, including a sum for goodwill. As a public company, GUS would have found it difficult to offer Carlton Studios at less than the market price even if it had wanted to, and the deal was subject to independent evaluation by outside accountants.

'I thought for a long time afterwards that we had grossly overpaid GUS, but it was our own money. We borrowed some from the bank and used some of our cash flow. But the point is it was an important deal for us because it got us into the photographic business,' says Green.

Michael Green is the first to acknowledge that he learned and gained from the Wolfson connection. 'Obviously, mixing with the Wolfsons, one was introduced to a lot of people, and I don't apologize for using any contacts I made. And I did use contacts – I would meet people and follow it up afterwards. Obviously they were interested in meeting me too – it was not a one-way process,' he says.

At such an early stage in his career Green may have been the one who benefited most from meeting captains of industry. Those he met through the Wolfsons included Arnold Weinstock – now Lord Weinstock, managing director of the GEC electronics and engineering group – and two cousins of the Wolfsons: the late Stuart Young, who became Green's accountant before going on to be chairman of the BBC, and his brother, David Young, now Lord Young, the former Trade and Industry Secretary.

If Green was feeling the burden of responsibility of being the co-owner of a growing company he did not allow it to show, and he managed to enjoy himself – particularly on Friday nights. On the evening when many Jews are at home having the Sabbath meal with their family, Charles Saatchi ran a regular poker game at his house in St John's Wood. It was a fairly serious game where the unwary could lose £1,000 in a single night. Michael Green was there quite often. A Saatchi employee who sometimes walked out with £700 or £800 at the end of the evening – more than his week's wages – found Michael Green and Charles Saatchi cautious and predictable poker players who tended to bet according to the value of their cards rather than trying to bluff with weak hands. The sessions eventually stopped because they were getting out of hand as the stakes got larger and larger.

The Greens – who were known in the Saatchi & Saatchi agency as the 'Frères Verts' – often turned up at lunchtime at the advertising agency, then in Golden Square, Soho, to play monopoly, chess or backgammon. If there was nothing much happening the games went on deep into the afternoon. Michael Green was a much more frequent visitor than David, because of his friendship with Charles Saatchi. The board-games were accompanied by wishful thinking and the hatching of new, usually madcap, schemes, for becoming seriously rich.

In the early 1970s Michael Green was settling into a way of life in which it was difficult to detect the boundaries between business, pleasure and even religion. He was brought up in the United Synagogue, which was mainstream Orthodox – almost the Jewish equivalent of the Church of England. In those days at least, the United, which had sixty congregations in London alone, was broad enough to accommodate a wide range of belief and observance (or the lack of it). It was the sort of establishment where the rule that you were supposed to walk to synagogue on the Sabbath was still in place but many worshippers thought nothing of parking their cars a street or two away before joining the more devout and walking the rest of the way.

The Green family had always – at least until Cyril and Irene's divorce – worshipped at the Central Synagogue in Great Portland Street, a synagogue of the prosperous and the would-be prosperous. It was founded in 1870 and

had been the synagogue of the Rothschilds; it was now the synagogue of the
Wolfsons. Sir Isaac Wolfson, who was painstakingly devout, was president of
the United Synagogue. In his day Sir Isaac was powerful enough virtually to
hand-pick the Chief Rabbi, who is the leader of the United Synagogue but
also claims a wider spiritual leadership in British Judaism. Those who aspired
to be suppliers to Great Universal Stores often found it beneficial to attend
the Central Synagogue, where Sir Isaac was warden for more than twenty
years.

The synagogue was destroyed in the Blitz in 1941 and rebuilt in 1955 in
what has been disparagingly called 'Rag-Trade Gothic'. Services are long and
usually informal, and during them men often talk among themselves –
sometimes about business. 'I would prefer it if they didn't talk, but as long as
they pray as well it's not such a terrible thing,' says Rabbi Cyril Shine, a
retired former rabbi of the Central Synagogue.

At the start of his business career Michael Green found synagogue, and the
contacts that could be made there, useful. A friend and businessman from the
early days remembers being asked by Green if he went to synagogue. When
the friend replied that he did not, Green advised him that he should. 'I do
more business in the synagogue than anywhere else,' said Green, perhaps
with a touch of bravado.

Rabbi Shine remembers Green as a boy. He officiated at his bar mitzvah –
the ceremony that marks the passage into adulthood of thirteen-year-old
Jewish boys. 'He was a very lively chap. I liked him anyway,' said the rabbi.
Michael Green was hardly religious at all, although he kept the festival days
such as New Year and the Day of Atonement and honoured, at least in
minimal terms, the traditions of the community he was born into. And for
many years his employees were not allowed to have German-made company
cars.

Green also pleased his parents by not 'marrying out' of the religion. Indeed
he was marrying into one of the most powerful families in the British Jewish
community – the equivalent of a middle-class commoner marrying into the
royal family.

Someone who knows the Wolfsons well believes they were not unhappy at
the prospect of having Michael Green as a son-in-law. The fact that he was
Jewish and from a good family with some money behind him, and had an
obvious determination to make considerably more, would all have helped.
Janet at the time was seen as a bit of a handful. She was lively and intelligent,
had an independent mind, and could have gone in a number of different
directions. Her parents were probably glad she married at all, never mind to a

Jew, when there is a long tradition of the offspring of the most illustrious Anglo-Jewry marrying out.

Chaim Bermant, a distinguished writer about the Jewish community and a long-time columnist of the *Jewish Chronicle* newspaper, believes that Leonard Wolfson would 'not have been averse to having someone like Michael Green as a son-in-law. He could have done much worse.'

On 12 October 1972 Michael Philip Green, a twenty-four-year-old company director, and Janet Frances Wolfson, a twenty-year-old spinster of no stated occupation, married under the *chuppah*, the portable canopy that is meant to represent God above and the importance of the family unit, in front of Leonard Wolfson and the rest of their families. It was a grand occasion at the synagogue, but not its most important wedding. 'There was a more significant wedding than that in the nineteenth century – a Rothschild wedding, when Prince Edward, who later became King Edward VII, was best man,' says Rabbi Shine, the man who married Michael and Janet Green.

Chapter 3

In the Print

In 1972 John Perriss started working for Garland-Compton, the UK arm of Compton, the large US advertising agency. In 1975 he found himself an employee of Saatchi & Saatchi-Garland-Compton, a company that was supposed to be a merger between the two groups. Although the Saatchi brothers owned only 36 per cent of the enlarged group, it was they who emerged on top. The brothers were running what was now London's fifth largest advertising agency, and everyone called it Saatchi & Saatchi.

For many years Perriss worked closely with Charles and Maurice Saatchi, who, like David and Michael Green, came from a comfortable, Jewish business background. Their father, Nathan Saatchi, had run a textile-importing business in Baghdad before buying cotton and woollen mills in Britain after the Second World War and moving his young family to Hampstead. Perriss was used to seeing the Green brothers hanging around the Saatchi offices, playing their lunchtime games of chess or backgammon. He also remembers the heart-sinking feeling he would experience when the telephone rang in his office and Charles Saatchi would say, 'I've got Michael Green with me. Can you just pop up?' It would mean another scheme was being hatched that would involve him in research – informal work for the Saatchis and their friends, rather than conventional tasks that the agency could bill for.

'There were always schemes. There were always things they were going to launch,' Perriss recalls. One of the impractical schemes, presumably prompted by the ownership of Carlton Studios, was to launch a new monthly photographic magazine to compete with the rather gauche nudes of *Amateur Photographer* and the tedious technical details of the more professionally orientated *British Journal of Photography*. The magazine would have gloss and class, and the would-be magazine owners hoped it would also make a lot of money. 'Put all our clients in. I have told Michael Green we will take the first six months' advertising in his new magazine,' Charles Saatchi told Perriss. The problem with this idea had to be explained: that none of their clients advertised in photographic magazines and, anyway, advertising agencies were supposed to get the best possible deals for their clients, rather than supporting risky publishing ventures dreamed up by friends. The idea for a new photographic magazine did not lead anywhere.

Another scheme thrown up by the Green-Saatchi 'entrepreneurs club' had a little more going for it. The Greens had stumbled across a small company on its way into receivership that had a large supply of eight-track tape-players and a stock of eight-track music cartridges to go with them. The sound quality was terrific. How about launching a music club? The Greens got very excited about the idea and communicated their enthusiasm to Charles Saatchi. At the Direct Mail Centre the Greens already had the staff and expertise to handle the mail-order side of things. What could be more natural than adding a music club – which anyway was just a mail-order business?

Maurice (left) and Charles Saatchi

The plan was that Saatchi & Saatchi would create and pay for the advertising to encourage people to join the club. Those who joined would get one of the eight-track players free of charge, and the club would make money by selling the music cartridges. Both sets of brothers would, of course, make a lot of money. The Stereo Tape Club of Great Britain was launched – and promptly fell flat on its face. In the battle between technical formats in the consumer-electronics market a winner nearly always emerges, and when that happens you can hardly give away the products of the losers. The bulky eight-track cartridge system was unable to compete with the growing dominance of the audio cassette.

The journey to fame and fortune was proving neither effortless nor uneventful, but the Greens were behaving like classic entrepreneurs, trying new ideas and, when they did not work, looking for other opportunities. The main Green business, the Direct Mail Centre group, was developing well. In the year to March 1974 turnover had reached £1.29 million and there was a pre-tax profit of £116,281, with the directors paying themselves a total of £23,000. That year there was a significant expansion of the printing business as the company bought a small printer, George & Chase, based at 256 Old Street in the City of London. All printing work was then centred on the Old Street premises, which meant that the factory at Crimscott Street, Bermondsey, was able to concentrate entirely on direct mail. The man who ran the Old Street operation, which had the capacity to turn out 580,000 A4 pieces of paper in four colours in a single day, was Cyril Green. Another part of the Greens' business was a company called Carltograph, based at Lancaster Street near the Elephant and Castle. A photographic printers which produced prints up to 20 feet in size, the company had a display department which made exhibition stands for companies such as ICI and British Steel Corporation. Carltograph was run by June de Moller.

A group was being assembled of companies which were able to share central services such as accountancy and administration and cross-promote each other. The revived *Group News* newsletter set out the strategy in November 1974: 'We take in one another's washing. Carlton send Direct Mail their client's printing inquiries and orders and recommend Direct Mail, while Direct Mail send Carlton orders for designing, photography and artwork and when the opportunity arises recommend the services of Carlton and Carltograph.'

The approach certainly helped to boost sales. In the year to March 1975 turnover leaped to £1.965 million, although pre-tax profits dropped to £77,674. The two directors paid themselves a total of £31,000.

A customer from those days – Janet Grant of AMR International, an American management-training and seminar group – found the Direct Mail Centre group of companies 'wonderful', partly because they were a one-stop shop offering direct mail, print and graphics. Above all, however, she felt they understood her business needs. There was an almost American feel to the service – they provided what the customer wanted, and seemed to understand the demands of international business. Grant, who rented space in Carlton's Frederick Close building, got to know Michael Green well and thought him a dynamic businessman.

As the company continued to develop on two fronts – printing and direct mail – new equipment was installed to insert materials automatically in envelopes at the new Direct Mail Centre plant. The staff there saw less of Michael Green and June de Moller, although they did keep an office at the plant and often spent time there in the mornings. John Burbidge, who was in charge of the Crimscott Street operations, remembers one afternoon when Green was playing backgammon in his office with de Moller and Felicity Mortimer, who was a sales list-broker. There was an urgent customer inquiry waiting to be dealt with, but other staff did not want to disturb Green and his backgammon-playing ladies. Finally an irritated Burbidge burst into the office. 'I said to him [Michael Green], "You have no right, even if you are managing director. We have a factory to run, and this lady has a sales query to sort out. She is holding all the staff up around here, and you shouldn't be encouraging it. I suggest she gets out of there now and sorts the problem out so that we can get on with the business."' Green accepted the criticism. The game came to a rapid end, and within a month Burbidge was promoted to managing director of the direct-mail operations.

Michael Green's visits to the Direct Mail Centre at Bermondsey from Tangent headquarters in Upper Brook Street seemed to become a little less frequent after one meeting in his ground-floor office. It was a hot day and Green had hung his jacket close to the window. As the meeting continued, an arm was seen to reach in through the window and snatch the jacket – complete with credit cards.

Direct Mail Centre managers say that Michael Green ran the business in a fair and honest manner, although he was tough and appeared to test people. If they met his exacting standards they became a member of the team. If they didn't the rejection was rapid and final, although usually when people departed they were reasonably compensated.

Green didn't take obvious pleasure in sacking people, but when it was necessary he did not hold back. One particular sacking, however, did not go well. There was a row, and Jo Black, a list-broking executive, was dismissed. She did not take it gracefully, and soon after there was what staff described as something resembling a gangster car chase down Borough High Street. It ended when the aggrieved lady's car bumped into the side of Green's Rolls-Royce. Green returned to his Bermondsey office and told staff to lock up, and said that if Jo Black turned up she was to be kept away from him.

The Green brothers continued to expand, and in the year to March 1976, for example, turnover increased to just over £3 million and pre-tax profits were £117,781. The following year revenue totalled £3.286 million and pre-tax profit grew to £179,421. During those years the company was being gradually transformed into an enterprise that was primarily involved in printing rather than direct mail.

The Direct Mail Centre added to George & Chase a much more substantial general printer with a reputation at the top end of the market: Mears Caldwell Hacker. The Greens had first bought a stake in the Clapham-based company by buying out one of the major shareholders, and then later acquired the rest of the company. The thing that appeared to interest them most about the company was that it had for many years printed the ICI annual report, and other clients included the BBC and Saatchi & Saatchi.

The acquisition of Mears Caldwell Hacker marked a shift away from direct mail to print. Direct mail, their previous specialization, seemed to interest them less and less, and they decided – wrongly, as it turned out – that it did not have much of a future. The effect of the printing acquisitions can be seen clearly in the group results, with turnover up to £8.58 million in the year to March 1978 and pre-tax profits of £557,340.

By then the company had been renamed Tangent Holdings, to reflect the move away from direct mail. The printing acquisition meant that Tangent was able to move the Direct Mail Centre to the Mears Caldwell Hacker premises in Clapham and sell Crimscott Street. The Tangent businesses were now located in what looked like a big shed, with a related list-broking operation located in a house in front.

As the Greens expanded in print, Burbidge decided it was time to set up his own operation and asked David Wells to join him as his partner. Michael Green conceded immediately to Burbidge that direct mail did not figure much in his future plans and was generous to the pair. They say Green not only offered advice but also gave them money to help set up their new direct-mail and marketing company, SR Communications, in Deptford, south London, without taking any stake in return.

Burbidge, though he may have had the occasional row with Michael Green, believes it was a privilege to work for him and is happy to concede that he learned a great deal about business that has been useful in his subsequent career.

Wells also absorbed important business lessons. He remembers a conversation with the young Green during a car journey which gave a clear insight into how the aspiring tycoon approached takeover targets. Green mentioned that he was looking at a particular company closely and was astonished by its quality. It was run well, and the owner took personal control of the petty cash – even deciding how many stamps the company should buy. That sounded like a very good prospect, thought Wells, and asked Green whether he was going to try to take it over. Absolutely not, was the instant reply. There was nothing to improve, so there was nothing in it for him.

Burbidge and Wells also acknowledge that Green's lessons included more than business and extended to expensive clothes, nice cars and good restaurants.

After ten years of working for Michael Green, Wells still struggles to sum up the often contradictory elements of his character. 'I think he is certainly ruthless. Maybe "ruthless" is the wrong word – he is determined, perhaps, but fair: a decent guy. And he could be incredibly arrogant. He could be incredibly rude when he put his mind to it. But by and large a decent guy – in fact, to have done as well as he has done, incredibly decent.'

In printing, the Greens had identified an industry that few could claim was well run, where the unions ran riot, and where family firms were coming under increasing pressure from foreign competition and changing technology. It was just the sort of industry where outsiders with modern business ideas could make a difference. And sometimes if you looked carefully there was an undervalued property buried in a loss-making printer. Inflation was rising, and not everyone had their property assets revalued as often as they should.

To John Waterlow, a member of the Waterlow printing family, which had printed everything from stamps to company reports since the nineteenth century, Michael Green was a member of the new breed of businessmen coming into the industry. Even though Green knew very little about printing, Waterlow thought he had more vision than most traditional printers.

In 1978 Michael Green heard that Lund Humphries, the Bradford-based fine-art printer, was on the market. It was a microcosm of many of the problems faced by the industry. The management were growing old gracefully, approaching retirement age together, and the owners had little direct interest in the company. Roland Bottomley, the managing director, was sixty-two, and his chairman, Anthony Bell, was five years older. Bottomley owned 12 per cent of Lund Humphries, and the other senior managers had a small stake, but by far the largest shareholder was the

Society of Authors, which had been left more than 80 per cent of the shares in the will of a former Lund Humphries chairman, Peter Gregory, who had died in 1959.

Bottomley says he found it difficult even to persuade anyone from the Society of Authors to travel to Bradford to visit the company, never mind discuss the management succession or complex issues such as finding a new direction for the firm in the hope it could be made to survive and prosper. He was convinced that Lund Humphries's traditional market was disappearing as Far East printers entered the fine-art market with high-quality printing at low prices. In 1976 information on the company had been sent out to corporate 'marriage-brokers' in the hope of finding someone to take the company over. Nothing had come of it, and Bottomley, who was determined to retire at the age of sixty-five, when he would have worked at the company for forty-nine years, was beginning to feel disheartened.

Then, unexpectedly, along came Michael Green, and to Bottomley the thirty-one-year-old seemed like a knight in shining armour. 'I was quite taken with him. First of all I was wary – you think, "Whiz-kids" and so on. He was most charming – disarming almost – and very frank about his hopes and his desires,' Bottomley recalls.

Tangent paid around £800,000 for Lund Humphries on 4 January 1979. The acquisition meant that more than 50 per cent of Tangent revenues were now coming from printing, and in its accounts for the year to March 1979 the company described itself as 'a private company specializing in printing and its related industries' – adding, with a touch of hyperbole, 'certainly one of the largest in the country'.

Tangent Holdings – renamed Tangent Industries – now employed just under 700 people in five main activities. By far the largest was printing, accounting for 53 per cent of sales. Exhibition display, which grew out of Carlton Photographic and Design, accounted for 15 per cent. Photography and bookbinding, through an acquisition called Leighton Straker, each contributed 12 per cent of revenues. Direct mail was now the smallest part of the company at 8 per cent.

Lund Humphries did unexpectedly well in its first year under Tangent's ownership. Unknown to Michael Green when he bought the company, an earlier astute investment in new equipment was about to produce larger profits than forecast. According to Bottomley, in the first year of Tangent ownership Lund Humphries made profits of around £200,000 – something that led some of his colleagues to wonder whether the company had been sold too cheaply.

Yet, despite the unexpectedly high profits from Lund Humphries, Michael Green did not turn out to be quite the knight in shining armour Bottomley had hoped for, mainly because the two men had very different agendas. The sixty-two-year-old had been looking for someone who would quickly come in and run the enterprise, plan a new strategic direction, and perhaps take the company into different sectors of the printing market. Michael Green, it soon became obvious, had other plans.

Over large helpings of Yorkshire pudding and steak-and-kidney pie in the unfamiliar surroundings of the Rock and Heifer pub near Bradford, the budding tycoon explained his ambitions to Bottomley. 'He told me then his hope was to get into radio and television – communications as a whole – and that was early 1979. He had all his ideas mapped out, although he wasn't quite sure how he would achieve them. He once told me he wanted to be Prime Minister. I told him he wouldn't,' recalls the no-nonsense Yorkshireman.

Green was equally honest about his interest in running, or rather his inability to run, printing or any other companies. The Lund Humphries managing director says Green admitted that he couldn't run companies directly, that he liked to stay in the background, and would Bottomley please carry on?

In September 1979 the importance of printing to Tangent Industries became even more marked when it took control of the City printing and publishing firm Metcalfe Cooper – yet another family company, in this case more than 100 years old, facing increasing difficulties.

Metcalfe Cooper was run by Christopher Cooper, a member of one of the founding families, who was in his fifties, appeared to be losing interest, and was thinking of early retirement. In 1973 the company had moved from Stratton Street, EC2, to new, purpose-built, six-storey freehold offices in East Road, near the junction of Old Street and City Road. Since the move, and perhaps partly because of the cost of the new building, the company was not prospering. In 1978 Metcalfe Cooper's turnover had been £2.5 million, but the company had made a loss.

The company had, not surprisingly, turned down a bid of £1 from Christopher Bland, then chairman of another City printing firm, Sir Joseph Causton & Sons. In Bland's view Metcalfe Cooper had far too large a staff of highly paid typesetters, and he had hoped by combining two indifferent printers to produce one good one. Instead Green beat him to the purchase: he had spotted the value of Metcalfe Cooper's building, New Roman House, and as a result he effectively got a printing business, albeit it a loss-making one, with a valuable building at a relatively modest price in an £1.24 million cash deal.

'Christopher Cooper was concerned that the company should be sold at a reasonable price to someone who would keep the business intact,' Green told *Printing World*. Green also told the trade magazine that he was particularly pleased with Metcalfe Cooper's publishing activities, which produced a quarter of the company's turnover and ranged from *Homefinder Magazine* and *Homes Overseas* to Wessex Publications, which produced tourist guides and maps. There was also an exhibition business. The new owner said he was sure the losses would be temporary and that the 230 Metcalfe Cooper printing workers would be retained.

For Green, the acquisition of Metcalfe Cooper looked like a good deal. Apart from the six-storey property, the company had a close relationship with Rothschild's, the merchant bank, and carried out a lot of financial printing work for it. In the past, financial printing had been very lucrative, because the customer was usually more concerned about speed, accuracy, security and delivery time than price, although by the beginning of the 1980s competition was starting to intensify in this specialized market.

Revenues from Metcalfe Cooper and Lund Humphries helped to boost Tangent's turnover to £11.45 million in the year to the end of March 1980. Pre-tax profits rose to £755,188, reduced by interest charges of £209,000 on money borrowed to help fund acquisitions. The results were accompanied by a warning that that the year ahead would not be easy. In the 1980 Tangent Industries annual report the Greens were self-confident enough to indulge in a state-of-the-industry analysis – almost certainly written by Michael Green. New media such as facsimile satellite transmission, video recording, Ceefax and Prestel were all competing in areas where print had once held sway, the analysis argued. 'Television and associated electronic media provide stiff competition to the printed product. Yet television programmes provide new avenues for publishers; computerized business systems create vast demands for printed materials. There is no foreseeable replacement for the book, brochure, photograph or carton,' the annual report insisted.

Although Michael Green's belief in print remained intact, his interest in publishing magazines did not take long to wane. Richard Davis, the 'cheeky chappie' from Northbridge House school, got an unexpected call from his old schoolfriend. Davis had done rather well in the intervening years and was the publisher of *What House?*, a leading magazine for home-buyers. Michael Green related how this company he had bought, Metcalfe Cooper, just happened to publish a magazine called *Homefinder*. In a rather patronizing way, he said he was prepared to do his old friend Davis a big favour and let him have the magazine at a really cheap price. Perhaps they could meet to discuss the possibility of a deal. But over lunch in a large dining-room at New Roman House the first question was not about magazines, or even about old times: Green wanted to know what sort of car Davis drove and how much money Davis's company was making. During the lunch – interrupted by a call from Charles Saatchi – Davis gathered that Green had a wife called Janet and two daughters, Rebecca and Catherine.

Later Michael Green took Davis in his convertible Rolls-Royce on a tour of the Tangent empire – from printing companies to the direct-mail business and on to Carlton Studios and Carlton Fox, a company which specialized in shop-fitting and constructing exhibition stands. All seemed eerily quiet. Very little was going on, except at Carlton Studios, where several fashion photographers were clicking away.

But Michael Green did do Davis a considerable favour by selling him *Homefinder* for only £30,000. Green's former schoolfriend built the magazine up, and in 1989 he sold it to Sterling Publishing for £300,000.

Meanwhile Lund Humphries was failing to live up to its initial promise. Ironically, Green backed Bottomley in a new idea that turned out to be a financially damaging one for the company – a move into web-offset printing. Lund Humphries's main strength had always been in high-quality sheet-fed printing rather than the more mass-market web-offset. To make the investment in the new press pay for itself, something like half the company's turnover would have to come from web-offset, but Lund Humphries was unknown at this end of the market and the orders failed to materialize. Bottomley accepts responsibility for what turned out to be 'a rather silly move' from which Lund Humphries started to lose money.

Under Tangent's ownership of Metcalfe Cooper, Christopher Cooper remained chairman until June 1981, when Michael Green merged the company with Mears Caldwell Hacker and became chairman and chief executive himself.

Bob Gavron, who built up St Ives, one of the relatively few British printing success stories of the 1970s and '80s, remembers meeting Green when Tangent was expanding its printing interests. He found Green to be one of those people you somehow find yourself on very friendly terms with almost immediately. Gavron, a grey-haired barrister with an agile mind, who took the unusual course of going into the printing industry rather than pursuing his legal career, was convinced that the arrival of Green would liven up the printing scene and make it more fun. Apart from those born into the printing industry, most print managers had been promoted from the shop floor and were usually more interested in machinery than in what goes on the printed page. Gavron, whose interests range widely in literature and opera, did not find many printers very bright. He thought it was easier to teach intelligent people to be printers than to teach printers to be intelligent.

Gavron says Green is one of the people he always looks forward to meeting, whether at the opera or over dinner. 'He is always lively, always cheerful, always very open. He is just one of those people, you know, you smile when you see him. He has got enormous charm, and you never quite know what he is going to say next. He is not predictable, and he is very quick, and he gets to the heart of the situation very fast,' Gavron believes.

When the Green brothers arrived at Metcalfe Cooper in a Rolls-Royce they looked 'flash', perhaps even a bit spivvy, and were obviously very different from the old management. The unions felt uneasy and threatened. But it was not the arrival of the Greens or the Rolls-Royce that caused the greatest surprise but who they brought with them – June de Moller, a very unusual phenomenon for the printing industry: a woman senior executive. 'She seemed to be the one that

June de Moller

pulled the strings and made things happen,' said Colin Green, a manager at Metcalfe Cooper when the Greens arrived, and no relation of the new owners.

The company had already started to explore computerized cold composition in a modest way and had installed examples of the latest technology in a small area of the typesetting department on the third floor of New Roman House. But it was not at all clear how it would be introduced or at what cost. Metcalfe

Cooper was a very strict closed shop with strong aggressive unions, complete with a well-known militant National Graphical Association organizer called Johnny Beck.

A short time after the Greens took over they announced that they were going to close down the increasingly antiquated hot-metal side of the business and move entirely to cold composition. They also introduced night shifts in every department to deal more efficiently with urgent overnight financial printing. 'They did it, and they did it very, very well. June de Moller negotiated with the unions, and they came to a series of agreements where they would retrain people. They also gave people options [for compensation],' says Colin Green, who was promoted to be manager of the photocomposition area. An extensive company-wide retraining programme was set up to complete the transition to computerized setting.

The Green brothers may have had ambitions to introduce modern management in the printing industry, but they were still plagued by the traditional inter-union rivalry between the NGA, representing the main skilled tradesmen, and the semi-skilled machine-minders of NATSOPA. Michael Green decided he wanted to get rid of NATSOPA and have only the NGA to negotiate with, yet discussions on terms were prolonged and looked as if they were heading for stalemate.

One night, in a radical and even provocative move which could have caused a walk-out, Michael Green went down to the machine-room on the ground floor and told the NATSOPA members in blunt language that he had had enough and insisted on a deal being signed. The unconventional action broke the deadlock and the NATSOPA members were made redundant, although the decisive factor was the size of the compensation package rather than Green's unconventional negotiating effort.

Colin Green was impressed with Green. 'He was always ahead of the game. If something was going to happen or there was a new area to get into, he seemed to be there,' said the printing manager.

Michael Green expected things to happen quickly – often very quickly. Little more than a week after the change-over to photocomposition, and before many of the hot-metal men had much of a chance to develop their new skills, an order was accepted for an overnight financial-printing job. The deadline was met.

Green was even prepared to confront Robert Maxwell, at the time one of the major figures involved in the reorganization and consolidation of the British printing industry after his takeover of the loss-making British Printing Corporation. Green poached one of Maxwell's executives, Nick Carter, to be the new managing director of Metcalfe Cooper. At the time, Carter was putting together a survival plan for Waterlow's London operations – part of the Maxwell empire. Characteristically, Maxwell threatened to sue the Green brothers for allegedly luring Carter from BPC, but the appointment went ahead. Although nearing retirement age, Carter made a significant contribution by enthusiastically embracing photocomposition and became so proficient that he was soon running small seminars to teach the compositors about the new technology.

The Carter connection may have led Maxwell to think of Michael Green when he wanted to sell Waterlow's London business. The two were close to a deal, but the sticking-point was reached when Maxwell insisted on keeping a minority stake in the company and remaining on the board. Green says he may have been only been in his early thirties then but he smelled danger and decided not to go ahead. It was the high point so far of Green's business career owning, if not actually always running, printing companies. Yet the print market was getting ever more competitive and there had to be a question mark over what sort of future there would be for a medium-sized, privately owned company in the face of aggressive predators such as St Ives, Norton Opax and even Maxwell's BPC. As the company was private, it had to fund its expansion by using cash flow, bank loans, ploughing back profits and selling properties, and this placed limits on the speed of growth. For all Green's youth and dynamism, and even though he, with his brother David and June de Moller, had modernized the company's print businesses and ran them well by contemporary printing-industry standards, time was probably running out for Tangent Industries.

One day Michael Green called John Perriss at Saatchi & Saatchi. The sardonic Perriss always tried to steel himself when, three or four times a year, the direct calls came from Green. Green was always after something that involved work, but even on the telephone Perriss usually found himself surrendering to the charm. This time the call was a little different. For the first time, Michael Green was inviting him to lunch.

On the appointed day, Green telephoned to say he would pick up his guest to take him to the La Braganza, a Wheeler's restaurant in Soho. Curious, Perriss asked Green where he was, only to be told that he was in his car. Perriss was impressed: it was the first call he had taken from a mobile phone. At the restaurant Green wanted an answer to only one question: 'How do I get into television?'

Chapter 4

Adam and the Ants

David and Michael Green had always made it clear that they wanted to float Tangent Industries on the Stock Exchange some day, and they had put a lot of effort into producing annual reports that looked good. Even when Tangent was a relatively small printing company the accounts and annual report were carefully illustrated and came complete with sophisticated graphics and bar charts demonstrating the breakdown of revenues by sector and how assets were accounted for. The annual reports, which gave more information than was legally necessary for a private company, were self-confident documents that a much larger publicly quoted company would have been happy to distribute.

'When you go public you have to show a five-year history, and I remember the accountants thinking it was a squeaky-clean five years: they had no problems. You can go back and find in the *Evening Standard* an article, probably eight or nine years before we floated, saying "Green For Go in 1980" and it said we were planning to float in 1980. We didn't float until 1983, but you can see it was years back that we had this idea of keeping our accounts clean and saying, "Here's our track record – we are going to be a public company," ' Michael Green remembers.

The Greens' intention was to go for a reverse takeover – a device used to get a rapid Stock Exchange quotation by acquiring a company that already has a quote. Apart from keeping bank and stockbroking charges to a minimum, reverse takeovers can allow relatively young companies to acquire a more substantial history and pedigree by in effect taking over an established quoted company and then changing its name. It might have been possible to take the perfectly respectable if rather dull medley of Tangent companies to the Stock Exchange, but it would have been difficult and the share price would have been unlikely to have attracted much of a premium.

The first target was a quoted Welsh printing and packaging group called David S. Smith, which was quite keen to complete a deal with the Greens. Smith's mainly printed cigarette cartons. Stuart Young of Hacker Young, Tangent's accountant, advised against going ahead with David S. Smith – perhaps because it would have tied Tangent totally into the printing industry.

One of the David S. Smith team who visited Michael Green's office at the time was struck by the dinner-jacket hanging on the back of the office door and thought that perhaps Green's ambitions might extend further than printing cigarette cartons.

Tangent's 1981 results, covering an eighteen-month period, show a considerable increase in turnover, to £19.2 million, although there was a sharp drop in pre-tax profit, to £147,774. The drop in profit partly reflected reorganization costs, which were taken on the profit-and-loss account rather than the company's balance sheet. Tangent Industries was still a healthy company, with assets of £4.5 million and £550,000 cash in the bank, but it hardly looked like a company that would fire the imagination of the Stock Exchange. Something had to be done to transform its sluggish image. A successful Stock Exchange float could yield an enormous prize. If the City likes a newly floated company the shares will rise, and a rising share price underpinned by confidence can convey an almost magical ability to acquire other companies without having to borrow money. You simply issue new shares, and if people believe the price is going to rise further they are happy to exchange tangible assets for such shares. It is a process that can come close to printing money.

Michael Green solved Tangent's image problem by combining his desire to float on the Stock Exchange with his growing ambition to get into television. It was Martin Richards, a solicitor at Tangent's legal representatives, Clifford Turner (later to become Clifford Chance), who alerted Green to a little company called Transvideo, owned by Arlen Electrical, an electrical-accessories company controlled by Arthur Levy. Arlen earned most of its money in the winter, because of the seasonal nature of its products, and had tried to diversify into television to provide a complementary stream of summer revenue. Transvideo began as an investment in a mobile video-editing suite for use at sports events, and then branched out into making pop promos and television programmes. At first the editing truck did not even have a formal home and was parked outside the Novotel Hotel in Hammersmith, 'plumbed' into the hotel's power system. Later, when the company leased a splendid nineteenth-century former Congregational church (complete with Corinthian columns) in St John's Wood, the truck was put on blocks and a hole was drilled in the wall of the former church to connect it to mains electricity.

One morning early in 1982 the Transvideo sales director, Barry Johnstone, was busy in his office when he was told by a member of his staff that a rather strange man was nosing around the building. 'Tell him to piss off,' said

Johnstone. But when it was pointed out that the intruder had got out of a
Bentley Johnstone went to investigate. Michael Green was taken on an
immediate tour of Transvideo.

Arthur Levy had bought Transvideo for around £150,000 but had added
facilities for shooting pop promos and television advertisements. The studios
and editing suites in the former church were let out mainly for making videos
to promote pop groups. The diversification had not gone well, and Levy,
facing difficult trading conditions in his main electrical-accessories market,
had decided to sell. He needed to get as much as he could for Transvideo as
quickly as he could, and Green quickly detected a sense of desperation.

'I met Michael at Tangent and we had several negotiating sessions, and he
did drive a very hard bargain. But my company was in very difficult
circumstances at that time, so I did do a deal with him,' recalls Levy, who
remembers Green padding around the office in his socks with his cigar and
continually interrupting his solicitors working on the final detail of the deal,
under which Levy got £174,000 in March 1982.

Mike Luckwell, founder of The Moving Picture Company – a dynamic
entrepreneur and a pioneer in introducing the latest computerized video-
editing techniques to the television industry – had taken a look at Transvideo
and the St John's Wood studios. He was running out of space in his Soho
heartland and was interested in acquiring the studios, but was prepared to
offer only around £50,000 for the business. He believed it would be difficult
to attract enough work to such an 'out-of-town' location to make Transvideo
profitable.

When Luckwell heard that someone called Michael Green had paid much
more than he considered sensible for Transvideo, he decided to meet Green
to find out how he could justify such a price. After a long conversation, he
formed the judgement that the purchase was, partly at least, designed to dress
up Tangent's image and that Green had bought Transvideo so that he would
have a noticeable presence in television before going for a Stock Exchange
flotation.

As a result of the Transvideo purchase Green was able to claim that in 1982
Tangent had been involved in a ten-part light-entertainment series for
Channel 4 and had edited thirteen out of the top twenty music video
promotions selected by *Music and Video Week*, the trade publication. A
promotional video for a national tour of Adam and the Ants made a particular
impact.

Green decided to rename the company Carlton Video – a choice that
horrified Johnstone. 'You cannot call yourself Carlton Video under any

circumstances. It has implications of wedding videos and all of that. We are a television company. It should be Carlton Television,' said Johnstone. Green sought a third opinion and, in front of Johnstone, dialled a number himself and without preliminaries just said, 'Carlton Television'? Green put the phone down and told Johnstone, 'You've got it. Carlton Television it is.' The call had been on the private line of Charles Saatchi.

Finding the right partner for a float remained a much more difficult problem than finding the best new name for Transvideo. It was becoming an increasing preoccupation for Green. On Sunday 24 October 1982 Green and his wife, Janet, were guests at the marriage of businessman Ronnie Fattal and Fiona Sosnow and at the reception afterwards at the Grosvenor House Hotel. At Green's table there was a former merchant banker, Peter Kleeman, who ran his own investment company, Allside Asset Management, which invested money for rich private clients. Green seemed bored and a little depressed.

'I asked, "What's the matter Michael?" He said, "I want to go public. I want to buy a company." Michael then described to me in complete detail the type of company he was interested in. It had to be leisure or publishing. It had to have a certain market capitalization. And the deal needed to be done pretty easily, which meant the shareholding had to be in one or two hands,' says Kleeman, who wondered briefly whether The Fleet Street Letter, the share-tipping publishers, would be the right company. It was run by Nigel Wray, a friend of Kleeman – they had once worked together at the merchant bank Singer & Friedlander – and Kleeman had put some of his investors into FSL.

The next morning he asked a friend at the stockbrokers de Zoete & Bevan to tap Green's specified characteristics into Datastream, the electronic financial-analysis service, to review possible options. Within five minutes the friend had come up with the names of six companies, one of which leaped off the page. It was The Fleet Street Letter.

Kleeman first telephoned Nigel Wray and then Michael Green. 'I said, "Michael, I've found you a company – debt-free, making around £500,000 to £600,000 a year,"' says Kleeman, who suggested Green and Wray should meet as soon as possible.

When Green and Wray met for the first time, one sunny afternoon in late October 1982, they hit it off straight away. 'We got on very well. He came to our office once, and I went to his place. Really it just made sense. We got on as individuals,' says Wray.

Wray, who is five months younger than Michael Green, is a tall, slim jogging and cricket enthusiast. His father ran a small printing company in the Angel, Islington, which printed everything from letterheads to the *Freethinker* magazine. Wray had worked in the company as a salesman during his holidays from Bristol University, where he studied economics. He learned a bit about the printing industry, but it was his experience of selling and trying to win orders in the summer vacations that was most character-forming. 'I used to go out repping for the printing business, and that is useful because you can get used to having the door slammed in your face and people not being interested in you and I was just delighted that I didn't evolve that as a career,' recalls Wray, who decided he did not want to work in the family firm.

Nigel Wray

Instead the young Wray chose merchant banking, although he had little idea of what was involved. Singer & Friedlander, a very traditional merchant bank, was preferred because it offered the young graduate trainee £35 a week – £10 a week more than a rival bank. Wray, whose office walls are covered with cricket and other sporting pictures rather than the modern art preferred by Green, says he was bored by merchant banking and left four years later to look for business opportunities of his own.

While at Singer & Friedlander he had already made a small fortune – £100,000 – in property deals using his own money, only to lose it all as a result of the 1973 secondary-banking crisis which in turn lead to a property crash. His first venture after the secondary-banking crash involved buying a 50 per cent stake in a share-tipping sheet called, ironically, *Foresight*. Wray's luck turned again when by chance in 1976 he was offered the opportunity to buy *The Fleet Street Letter*, an ailing publication specializing in coverage of current affairs, because the owner wanted to live in France. When the young entrepreneur acquired the weekly newsletter, for £7,500, its circulation was falling and it had an annual turnover of only £17,000. By the end of the year the business, which Wray turned into a share-tipping newsletter, most of which he wrote himself, was still going badly. He had only £98 in the bank and around 1,000 subscribers.

Wray gradually built up the business, mainly by doubling the price of a subscription while at the same time going for fortnightly rather than weekly publication, to cut costs.

The other half of *Foresight* was bought and merged with *The Fleet Street Letter* in 1977, and two years later another similar publication, *Equity Research*, was added.

By the time Wray took FSL to the Unlisted Securities Market in April 1981, by offering 3 million shares at 52p, it had a turnover of £581,000 and pre-tax profits for the year to the end of March 1981 of more than £300,000 – close to printing money. By then Wray had increased the circulation of the *FSL* to almost 14,000. He had tapped into the great strength of successful newsletters – readers pay their annual subscriptions in advance, and once costs are covered any further subscriptions are almost all profit. Mrs Thatcher's commitment to a share-owning democracy was also very good for business.

Green's purchase of Transvideo – or Carlton Television as it was now known – turned out to be extremely shrewd, whether or not Luckwell was right that it was overpriced. It certainly impressed Wray. 'The printing business didn't appeal to me, because it didn't seem special as a market flotation, but this was the time of Adam and the Ants, the pop promos, and Carlton Television did. That sort of visual message seemed to me to be very exciting, and the City went for it in a big way. I knew they would go for it in a big way, so obviously the Carlton bit of Tangent seemed to be very, very exciting. It was the Carlton bit one was interested in,' Wray recalls.

Negotiations between Wray and the Greens went well. Michael and David Green said they wanted control of the new enlarged company, and that is what they got. Control has never been an important issue for Wray, who says that maximizing value for both himself and his shareholders was always what mattered most to him.

That autumn Michael Green was invited to lunch at Hambros Bank and met Michael Sorkin, a rising corporate-finance banker. Sorkin was an unusual banker – amusing, unstuffy and iconoclastic. Green outlined his flotation plan and asked whether Hambros would be prepared to act for him. Sorkin was impressed by the way Green concentrated on basic issues and seemed to have a feel for the temperature and pulse of his business. The banker pointed out that, although he would like to keep in touch, acting for Green at that time would be impractical. The proposed deal was just too small for the fees he would have to charge. It was a job for a stockbroker to handle on its own.

Wray introduced Green to the stockbrokers L. Messel & Co., who had done a lot of work with Singer & Friedlander. Messel, which later became part of the US group Shearson Lehman, had a considerable reputation in the 1970s and early 1980s for bringing new growth companies to the market. Some of these proved to be more enduring than others: its clients had ranged from Trafalgar House and Ladbroke to Polly Peck.

Michael Green was invited to Messel's offices in Old Broad Street to meet Giles Coode-Adams, Messel's head of corporate finance, and Geoff Bowman, head of sales, both of whom were impressed by the Tangent executive. Coode-Adams, an old-Etonian in his mid-forties with a reputation for lateral thinking, was struck by two characteristics displayed by Green: he was a man of vision, yet there was also a financially conservative streak about him – he was someone who would always pay careful attention to his balance sheet. 'Even in those early days that came through. He was very impressive,' Coode-Adams remembers. Bowman, the thirty-eight-year-old top share salesman at Messel, who had been educated at a minor public school in Essex, was impressed by Green's forthright opinionated manner. 'We hit it off. He struck me as a person who had a destiny and knew really where he wanted to go.'

Yet, even as Messel started preparing the flotation documents, Green was unsure about whether or not to go ahead. At a dinner in the Kensington flat of Kleeman and his wife, Carola, in December 1982 Green was displaying doubt and indecision. Green kept insisting that he had got to have control of the new company, and Kleeman kept reminding him that that was exactly what he was going to have. Green said that evening over dinner that he didn't know what to do, even though the stockbrokers had already completed the due-diligence checks and the deal was virtually done. Exasperated by the uncertainty, Janet Green insisted that Michael go ahead, and the decision was taken there and then.

Messel created an imaginative corporate structure to take Tangent to the Stock Exchange in a reverse takeover of The Fleet Street Letter. The Tangent companies not involved in printing were to be sold to FSL in a reverse takeover. The newly enlarged company would then be simultaneously floated on the Stock Exchange and change its name to Carlton Communications. The modestly performing printing companies owned by the Green brothers would be left behind in Tangent, which would remain privately owned.

The three main companies being bought by FSL were Carlton Studios, one of the largest companies in Europe specializing in photography and design, Carlton Fox, the design and exhibition company, which had also become a major supplier of giant front-of-house pictures for theatres and cinemas, and Carlton Television. In the year to the end of September 1982 the companies had made a pre-tax profit of £506,00 on a turnover of £4.28 million, with the vast majority of the profits coming from Carlton Studios and Carlton Fox. There may have been an element of preparing the companies for flotation in this, because the 1982 profit figure represented a very considerable increase on the previous reporting period. In the eighteen months to the end of September 1981 the same companies, according to the offer document, had pre-tax profits of only £295,000 on a higher turnover of £4.58 million. A fourth company, Carlton Newsletter, was added to the Carlton side of the equation, although its earnings were not included.

Just before flotation Tangent paid £300,000 in cash for *The Penny Guide*, a monthly tip-sheet with more than 10,000 subscribers, of which Wray was a director, and the business was renamed and transferred to Carlton. The motive was almost certainly to buy out minority shareholders in *The Penny Guide* at the same time as making the Carlton side of the deal more substantial.

What was termed 'the old group' – which included all the assets of the Fleet Street Letter company – made profits of £412,000 on revenues of £871,000 in the year to the end of March 1982, the last full year's figures available. In the six months to September 1982 there had been an £188,000 pre-tax profit on turnover of £349,000.

The Fleet Street Letter, to be renamed Carlton Communications, would acquire from the Greens all the shares of the four Carlton companies – Carlton Fox, Carlton Studios, Carlton Television and Carlton Newsletter – for 4,623,000 new shares.

The plan was to sell nearly 25 per cent of the shares in the new Carlton Communications to create a proper market in the stock. A total of 1.77 million shares were offered at 115p out of a total of 7.623 million shares created. Out of their stake the Greens agreed to place 800,000 shares. In Carlton Communications the sellers of the Carlton companies together held a controlling 50.15 per cent of the 7.6 million issued shares, and Nigel Wray held 15.34 per cent. A further 970,000 shares were placed by two Fleet Street Letter directors, Peter Whitfield and Robert Tanner, who then resigned from the board.

Michael and David Green together had 3,061,200 ordinary shares, mostly held through Tangent, and Nigel Wray had 1,170,000. Two other directors – Paul Harding, company secretary, and June de Moller, now responsible for corporate strategy – each got 10,000 shares.

The flotation formally marked what had increasingly been the reality for a number of years: that the main driving force behind the business was Michael

David Green

Green. David Green, always the more artistic and less driven of the two, had accepted a secondary position, although the brothers held exactly the same number of shares. Michael Green became chairman of Carlton Communications and was also chairman of each of the Carlton companies, with overall responsibility for their financial control and strategy. David Green was director responsible for marketing and new business opportunities.

As Michael Green went through his second corporate metamorphosis, all the printing companies were left behind in Tangent, the private company still wholly owned by Michael and David Green. Tangent's results for the year to the end of September show the effects of all the corporate engineering and restructuring. The company had a turnover of £14.9 million but made a pre-

tax loss of £304,059 although there were still net assets of more than
£900,000. Tangent would at least benefit from the flotation in one other less
obvious way: it got the contract to print all the flotation documents.

The instincts of Green and Wray about the City reaction to Carlton
Television were right. The potential backers and analysts were brought in
minibuses to the old Congregational church in St John's Wood to see pop
videos being edited, and they liked what they saw. 'I would give them a whole
lot of spiel and they loved coming down here,' Barry Johnstone says.

It was clearly a case of Adam and the Ants and the pop-promo image
coming to the rescue as Green and Wray went to the Stock Exchange in
February 1983 in a confident mood. 'When it came to market, it was frankly
The Fleet Street Letter and not much else. All the Carlton businesses were
trumped up as the businesses that were going to grow rapidly. But one could
only be sceptical, in that they were the businesses with very little track record.
The flotation was, however, superbly packaged,' a close observer noted.

Carlton Television, for instance, had made only £21,000 profit in its first
year of Tangent ownership. The limited scale of the television business at that
time is underlined by a promise in the offer document that further expansion
was likely at Carlton Television as a result of 'the planned establishment of a
production company with the appointment of a director and a producer'.

Investors had been in a mood to be sold a stake in what was hoped would
turn out to be part of the 'information revolution' at a time when Kenneth
Baker, the information-technology minister at the Department of Trade and
Industry, was spreading what turned out to be wildly premature visions of
'wired cities' of the future and the cabling of Britain. Probably more
important for the investing community was the rumour that the new merged
company was talking to Mike Luckwell's Moving Picture Company about a
possible joint venture involving futuristic digital technology.

Messel did its job well, and the Carlton Communications float was
supported by some of the top institutional names in the City of London.
Bowman had taken Green to see Stephen Zimmerman at Mercury Asset
Management, one of the most influential institutional names, and MAM
decided to invest. 'I thought Michael Green had vision, drive and dynamism,'
recalls Zimmerman, who thought Carlton was a very exciting business and
quickly moved to a 5–6 per cent shareholding. Rothschild's and Friends
Provident were two other prominent institutions which decided to take a
stake in the small company.

When trading in the shares of Carlton Communications finally got under
way on the Stock Exchange, on 25 February 1983, it did not make headlines

even in the financial pages. The big City story of the day was a sharp drop in the share price of Polly Peck following a report in the *Financial Times* that the Cyprus government was drawing up exploitation and tax charges against the fruit and trading group. Wray, with his nose for a good share, had got into Polly Peck shares very early, and, although he got out well before they reached their peak, he was smart enough to miss their collapse.

On 25 February the nervousness about Polly Peck led to profit-taking among 'other recent speculative stocks'. But if Carlton Communications looked like another speculative stock it didn't show, and in what was described as 'a bright début' the shares moved between extremes of 190p and 220p before settling at 205p. When the shares of FSL had been suspended on the Stock Exchange in December, pending the reverse-takeover negotiations, they had stood at 100p.

'The float was extremely easy to get away. I think people recognized the quality of Michael Green. Those people who saw him and liked him wanted the stock very badly. That's unusual for a small company. They were prepared to pay up, and that I think was a function of the man,' Giles Coode-Adams suggests.

It was a particularly satisfying day for Nigel Wray, who watched as his 1.1 million shares increased in value. It was an even better day for the original shareholders of The Fleet Street Letter. The original flotation price had been 52p, but this had been reduced to the equivalent of around 10p through scrip issue of shares – first a one-for-one and then a one-for-three. At the share-placing price of 115p, Carlton Communications had a market capitalization of £8.77 million. By the end of the day the capitalization of the company was £15.6 million. At the age of thirty-five Michael Green had realized his ambition to be the chairman of a publicly quoted company. By then both he and his older brother were seriously wealthy and almost certainly worth more than £5 million each, including the printing companies still owned by Tangent.

Wray was grateful to Michael Green for more than increasing his wealth. He also felt that a huge weight had been taken off his mind. He had been concerned that The Fleet Street Letter was a bit stuck as a business, and he had not been sure where it was going. In the new corporate structure Wray was to concentrate on running the group's publishing interests and was happy to let Michael Green take primary responsible for driving the company forward. Peter Kleeman's clients did well as a result of the chance meeting at the wedding – through their shares in The Fleet Street Letter, they became significant shareholders in Carlton.

Mike Luckwell may have been sceptical about the wisdom of Michael Green's purchase of Transvideo, but he ran a connoisseur's eye over the flotation of Carlton Communications and was very impressed.

Compared with Michael Green, Luckwell almost qualified as an academic. He had gone to St Paul's School, London – very much a first-division public school – and obtained four A-levels: in English Literature, Geography, Geology and Economics. He had been accepted by the London School of Economics and intended to go straight to university, until the LSE advised him to take a year out to 'mature'.

Luckwell got a job as a 'blue button', or junior dealer, on the floor of the old Stock Exchange, and found he had a natural taste for such wheeler-dealing. After six months he was offered a more senior Stock Exchange job, but decided to take six weeks off before starting in his new post. During this period he worked as a junior in the production department of a feature-film company. Within a couple of weeks he was certain that he wanted to work in film and television and all thoughts of either the LSE or the Stock Exchange were abandoned.

Luckwell worked as an assistant director on a number of films in the early 1960s. He also worked with Ray Harryhausen, a leading special-effects expert. In the mid-1960s he learned about budgeting and cost control while working for World Wide Pictures, a documentary and commercials production company. In 1968 he became a partner in, and chairman and managing director of, HSFA, a production company that specialized in commercials and documentaries. Through a reorganization in 1970, HSFA turned into The Moving Picture Company (MPC).

Michael Green had turned to Luckwell for advice on how to solve the problem of making Carlton Television profitable. Green proposed that Luckwell should run the company for him in return for a share of the profits – an offer that was treated with disdain. After all, the privately owned Moving Picture Company was far more profitable than Carlton Communications. In the year to the end of May 1983 MPC had made pre-tax profits of £1.44 million on turnover of £5.94 million. Luckwell, who since 1980 had also had his own television production company, had been interested enough to look in detail at Tangent's old accounts and had not been impressed. But he was intrigued by Green, who kept on ringing up to seek advice and propose deals. Above all Luckwell was interested in Green's corporate construction skills, as he realized he needed to consider the future of MPC. Should he float, merge with a larger company or, as Green had done, go for a reverse takeover?

In business terms, a closer relationship between Green and Luckwell grew out of an approach to the Carlton chairman by a venture-capital group trying to sell IVC UK, the European arm of International Video Corporation of California, a digital-electronics company which was running into severe financial problems in the USA. The man who ran IVC in the UK, John Jeffrey, had started manufacturing rather than merely distributing picture-stabilizers for professional video equipment, and as a result IVC UK had begun to make money. The digital stabilizers allowed a signal from a video recorder to be broadcast by synchronizing it with the rest of the output of a television station.

When he heard about IVC and its digital picture-stabilizers Michael Green rang Mike Luckwell and asked, 'What are they? What do they do?' Luckwell remembers his heart beginning to race, because IVC was a company he already had his eye on. MPC often tested new equipment for television-electronics companies such as Quantel but Luckwell wanted to get into manufacturing so that he and technical director John Beedle could develop some of their own ideas. Beedle, an electronics engineer, had worked for a wide range of broadcasting companies before joining MPC as chief engineer in 1974, when the company set up a new video division aimed specifically at the television-commercials market. Luckwell told Green that if IVC was for sale he should buy it.

The £495,000 deal with Carlton Communications was announced on 6 April 1983, less than six weeks after the Carlton flotation – although the agreement was finalized on Tangent headed notepaper on 25 March. Carlton took a 51 per cent stake, and an unnamed 'private company with linked interests' took the rest. It was MPC. Luckwell surprised Green by simply writing out a cheque for his share of the purchase price.

Green had told Jeffrey that he was not buying the entire company only at the last moment. The reason for splitting the deal was that Green was worried that the purchase might be too risky for Carlton. But he need not have worried: in its first six months under new ownership IVC made £200,000 in profit, and by the end of the first year profits had leaped to around £1 million.

Apart from the shared profits, the joint venture played an important role in bringing Green and Luckwell together and suggesting the outline of a strategy in Green's mind. Luckwell knew about television, the area Carlton was supposed to be expanding into. Perhaps Luckwell could contribute his television expertise while making himself a lot of money by reversing MPC into Carlton Communications.

Luckwell rather liked Green and recognized a kindred spirit – they were perhaps not two of the most gentle people in the world, but each in his own way was a tough and effective businessman. But, despite warming to Green as a person, the MPC chairman was still sceptical, because his detailed investigation of the Carlton companies was worrying. There was no evidence that any of the companies was making real money – or, indeed, that Green was someone who actually knew how to run a business, though he had obvious talents. Green was an accomplished financial manipulator and deal-maker, and his negotiating skills were excellent. He also seemed to be a good financial manager of other people's management abilities.

Another concern of Luckwell was that many of Green's more important contacts seemed to be in the Wolfson circle. If Janet Green were to walk out the door, might those valuable contacts walk too? So there were carefully orchestrated getting-to-know-you dinners with wives, where Luckwell was eager to form a judgement on the stability of Green's marriage and how important, if at all, it was to the business. Green was, of course, charming and polite to his wife, Janet, but Luckwell felt the relationship didn't seem to go much beyond that. In fact by 1983 'stormy' would probably have been the first word friends would have used to describe the marriage.

The MPC chairman was not immediately convinced about the merits of a tie-up with Carlton Communications. He looked at other options, including a straight flotation for The Moving Picture Company, and held a 'beauty parade' of other potential suitors. The only attractive alternative to Carlton was a tie-up with the UEI subsidiary Quantel, a world-class manufacturer of digital television editing equipment – the sort of devices that makes objects appear to fly through the air. UEI provided a common roof for a wide range of high-technology companies, usually leaving the founding entrepreneur in charge. But Luckwell, who owned nearly 80 per cent of MPC, with Beedle owning the rest, did not consider the deal on offer from Peter Michael, the UEI chairman, to be very generous. Too much of the potential sale price was in the form of deferred payments. He also suspected that Peter Michael might be a very tough taskmaster.

For Luckwell, the prospect of becoming a large shareholder in Carlton Communications gradually began to look the most attractive option. Within four months of the flotation the market capitalization of Carlton Communications had more than doubled, to some £20 million, such was the positive sentiment surrounding Michael Green in the City. Those who had bought Carlton shares in February had already made a lot of money. Green – who was always a star performer at briefings for the financial institutions such as insurance companies and pension funds which hold most UK quoted shares – was developing a following. 'He always got the institutions on his side by quoting GUS's discipline. Every meeting in the early days he would say they controlled the business along the lines of a Gussie,' comments Geoff Bowman of Messel.

There was one small hurdle to overcome before Carlton bought MPC. Luckwell did not need or want any cash, and saw Carlton's accelerating share price as the best way of enhancing his own wealth. But an all-share deal would have given the former Stock Exchange blue button a very powerful position in the enlarged Carlton group. So, after lengthy debates, there was a compromise and Luckwell agreed to sell a tranche of his new shares worth about £4.7 million; but he would still become a large shareholder.

For David Jeffers, a director of MPC who had joined Luckwell in 1980, the first sign of the deal was when he and a colleague, Nigel Stafford-Clark, were invited to a private room above a restaurant in Soho. 'Who should be there but Michael Green, David Green and June de Moller? And we were introduced to them as the people from this company called Carlton. We were slightly taken aback,' says Jeffers, who was given the job of running MPC in the new organization.

The deal, structured by Michael Sorkin at Hambros, valued MPC at £12.95 million, and was to be financed by Carlton issuing just over 5 million new shares, representing 39.5 per cent of the enlarged group. Hambros was to place 1.87 million of the 5 million shares at 255p, compared with the 268p price when Carlton's shares were suspended on 22 June 1983 pending the MPC purchase. The placing was designed mainly to raise the money for Luckwell, but it also provided some extra working capital for the enlarged group.

Following the placing of shares, Mike Luckwell, then forty-one, had 20 per cent and John Beedle, aged thirty-seven, had 4.9 per cent of the new enlarged Carlton Communications, with the founders – the Greens and Wray – together owning 50.15 per cent. Institutional investors held the remaining shares. When the takeover was announced, on 15 July 1983, Carlton shares shot up to 338p, giving the enlarged company a market capitalization of £43.5 million. Luckwell's retained shares in Carlton were already worth more than £8 million.

Stephen Zimmerman of MAM was among the enthusiastic buyers of Carlton stock. 'I was prepared to stand there with a bucket [to get as many shares as possible] it was such an exciting company,' he recalls.

As soon as the deal was completed Luckwell became managing director of Carlton Communications, with special responsibility for developing the group's television and electronics activities. 'However, as chairman and chief executive of Carlton, I will continue to be responsible for the development of the enlarged group,' Michael Green told shareholders.

In his assessment of the prospects for the merged group, Green said
Carlton's videotape facilities would be the most comprehensive of any
independent production company in Europe. They would enable Carlton to
take advantages of the new opportunities arising in broadcasting, from the
launch of Channel 4 a few months earlier to satellite and cable television.

Green emphasized that the company would not be embarking on grandiose
high-cost media projects. 'We are in the nuts and bolts. We are not in the
venture capital side of those markets,' Green insisted.

It had been a remarkable six months since the flotation at the end of
February 1983. A company offering not much more than froth, future hopes
and the formidable will and marketing power of its chairman had been
transformed into an organization that looked, at least to some, as if it could
become a European leader in its emerging sector – the digital manipulation of
images of all kinds. And, while it would be a mistake to underestimate the
financial artistry of Green, it was the arrival of The Moving Picture Company
and Mike Luckwell that really made the difference in 1983 and began to give
substance to the original dream offered to the City. 'The thing that really got
Green going quickly was taking over The Moving Picture Company,' says
Bowman, who feared, however, that a clash of personalities between Green
and Luckwell would be difficult to avoid.

In a rapidly developing sector, MPC was a company with a considerable
track record. Soon after opening for business in Soho on 1 April 1970 it had
begun introducing simple technical changes to try to make film and television
production more efficient. Luckwell adapted for British use American film
lights that used lower voltages than the British versions. As a result the
company started winning competitive tenders for production shoots, partly
because its adapted lighting system ran off the mains, which reduced costs by
making it unnecessary to have a mobile generator and attendant electricians.

The whole business of television production – historically controlled by the
in-house unionized staffs of both the BBC and ITV – was just beginning to
open up to independents. In ITV one of the main new opportunities for
outsiders was producing and editing commercials. At the BBC the move to
colour also created film-editing opportunities, because the Corporation was
short of colour-editing capacity at the outset.

Luckwell noticed the arrival of computerized video-editing equipment in
North America and the development in Germany of new light and flexible
electronic video cameras. He did not think it likely that directors would
instantly begin shooting on video rather than film, but post-production – all
the editing processes once shooting is complete – might be a different matter.

With Beedle on board as chief engineer, the new video-facilities division of MPC opened up for business on April Fool's Day 1974. The premises MPC found for its three-machine editing suites, a small studio and lightweight cameras was the site of a Jewish restaurant that had closed some years before and lay empty. Setting up the business involved what seemed a massive investment of £300,000 in video-editing equipment, but within two years virtually all commercials were edited on video and MPC had more than 60 per cent of the market – although that was something it tried to keep as quiet as possible, for fear of attracting envy and growing competition.

The new technologies meant that a retailer could make a marketing decision on a Wednesday, shoot on film – which gave a quality look to the finished product – on a Thursday, and transfer from film to videotape on Friday for editing. Then on Saturday morning the result could be delivered all around the ITV network on the special video land-line which connected the commercial broadcasters. By Saturday evening the retailer could watch as a polished television commercial was broadcast to the nation. Such advertisements may not have won many awards, but they were effective, and some retailers were soon spending £500,000 or more a year in the obscure Soho world of the video post-production studio.

One other achievement of the MPC was also kept secret – but for a different reason. All the early Margaret Thatcher party political broadcasts were shot in the MPC studio, including the last one to go out before her first election victory, in 1979. The original version was unimpressive, so Mike Luckwell and Tim Bell of Saatchi & Saatchi worked with a team of editors late into the night to revamp the production, which then went out the next day. Credit was not given to MPC because, according to Luckwell, a key part of the deal was that only Saatchi & Saatchi was to be mentioned in the credits.

The bringing together of Carlton and MPC, of Green and Luckwell, linked not just two companies but also two men with complementary skills – the deal-maker joining up with the television technician. Even in dress the two men reflected their different roles. For a lunch at Hambros Michael Green would wear a conventional City suit; Luckwell was more likely to turn up in an open-necked shirt without a jacket. Their backgrounds were also complementary, and they very quickly perfected – quite deliberately – an effective double act to maximize their impact on any gathering of bankers, institutions or other investors. Green took on the job of charming the Jews in any gathering, and Luckwell, who resembles Liberal Democrat Paddy Ashdown and could pass for a former member of the SAS, would concentrate on sweet-talking the Gentiles.

'There was a real buzz about the place. There was really only Michael Green, June de Moller and Paul Harding. There were really only four offices. The company was so small that each deal involved a large amount of work,' recalls Mike Francis, a lawyer with Clifford Turner who represented Carlton on the MPC merger and stayed on with the aim of training for general management.

'It was a small company, but there was no doubt to us there then that one day it was going to be a very big company. Michael was so focused and made such great use of his talents,' Francis recalls. Francis eventually decided he preferred law to management, however, and he returned to what became Clifford Chance, where he continues to be the 'client partner' of Michael Green and Carlton Communications.

Despite all the work in creating the new corporate structure, Green also found time to restructure Tangent, which was still considered to be one of the largest printing businesses left in private hands in the UK – although mainly because there was not a lot of the British printing industry left in private hands.

Two weeks before the MPC takeover Tangent Industries sold its main printing company, the merged Metcalfe Caldwell, which now had only 135 employees, to a trio of experienced senior printing-industry executives. The price was £240,000, and did not include the New Roman House head-quarters. Green was emphatic that this did not mean that he and his brother were abandoning printing for the more lucrative world of television. With bare-faced cheek Green was quoted in *Printing World* as commenting, 'I would say that the management expertise which approached us to buy Metcalfe Caldwell promised to be far more successful than our own management set-up.'

It was a remark that would have made Christopher Bland at Joseph Causton smile. Earlier Green had turned up at Joseph Causton's headquarters in Hopton Street, Southwark, in his Bentley. Green admitted that Bland's original offer of £1 for Metcalfe Cooper had probably been right. Both men were keen to explore the possibility of selling their unpromising printing companies to each other. 'But neither of us was prepared to buy the other's dog,' Bland remembers.

Michael Green had also tried to sell Lund Humphries to Patrick Walker, chairman of Watmoughs, the successful Bradford-based printing company. Walker knew Lund Humphries well and had once admired it greatly, but he believed that by the time Green arrived on the scene its best days were already over. He remembers entertaining Michael Green to dinner at his home, Plumpton House, Thackley, near Bradford. That evening Green deployed all his charm and persuasion to try to offload the company on Walker. For a moment, Walker admits, he almost allowed himself to be convinced; then his better judgement reasserted itself and the spell of an expert salesman performing at the peak of his skills over a pleasant dinner was broken. Green was a model of politeness despite the rebuff, but, as Walker and his wife, Mavis, stood at the door to see him off, Green paused for a moment by the side of his car to admire the view across the valley and made what was in the circumstances an ungracious forecast to his host: 'I'm going to do a lot more exciting things than printing you know.'

Lund Humphries was finally bought in March 1984 by Richard Hanwell, then head of printers Norton Opax, which he built up in eight years from a market capitalization of £2 million to more than £400 million. The Greens got Norton Opax shares worth £600,000 for Lund Humphries, which Hanwell said had degenerated into a general jobbing print shop and was losing money at the time. Hanwell remembers being impressed by Michael Green during the negotiations and thinking that he was a very smart operator. 'He was very professional and got involved in the detail, which surprised me. When we got right to the end of the negotiations and into the details such as building walls, it was Michael himself who would pick up the phone and short-circuit the lawyers, and he and I had all sorts of discussions solving all sorts of problems on a commercial basis rather than a legal basis. I was very impressed with the guy, and it was a deal both parties were happy with,' says Hanwell.

The sale meant that Green was now out of printing, although it did not mean he yet knew a great deal about television. Around that time Barry Johnstone, by now the Carlton Television managing director, remembers Michael arriving unannounced, as he usually did, and wandering through the editing suites talking to customers. The director David Mallett was editing a long Tina Turner special, shot at the NEC in Birmingham. ' "Oh," says Michael, "were you there?" David said, "I directed it!" Michael didn't know about television. He came in and he innocently asked the director was he there when he made the shows – and that was in 1984,' says Johnstone, who was able to buy the St John's Wood company in a management buy-out.

The sale of the printing companies meant that Tangent's accounts were starting to look unusual to anyone unaware of what was going on. In the year to March 1984 there was a pre-tax profit of £331,249 on a turnover of only £3.1 million, yet there were investments of £10.5 million and net assets of £13 million. By 1985 the accounts were even more remarkable: turnover had dropped to £757,642, yet the pre-tax profits had leaped to £2.5 million. Investments were now worth £21.3 million and net assets more than £26 million. Tangent had become little more than a holding company for the shares in Carlton Communications owned by David and Michael Green.

Chapter 5

Takeover Trail

The agreement between Michael Green and Mike Luckwell was quite explicit: their policy would be rapid growth through acquisition. They would issue shares on the back of a rising share price to buy further companies in the high-technology back-room of the television industry and accept the inevitable dilution in their stakes in Carlton Communications.

Any deals had to satisfy two main criteria. First, the figures had to look right to Green – so that they could be presented in a favourable light to City institutions, which had to continue buying, or at least holding, Carlton shares. Second, the purchases should usually be in the television area – so that if there was a problem Luckwell could go in and sort it out.

To back their acquisition ambitions Green and Luckwell asked their shareholders for more money in advance. The first significant cash call came in December 1983, as Carlton announced a 45 per cent rise in pre-tax profit to £3.5 million on a turnover of £15.3 million in the year to the end of September. Shareholders were asked for £7.74 million in a rights issues – offering them the right to buy one new share for every five they already held, at 300p a share. Explaining the thinking behind the second share issue in less than six months – the first was to pay for MPC – Green said that the company had consolidated its position in the communications industry and was well placed to benefit from further developments within its existing markets in both the UK and the USA.

The directors of Carlton were not taking up their rights to subscribe for new shares, and as a result the directors' control of the company fell below 50 per cent for the first time. It was a symbolic moment: David and Michael Green had already given up control of the company, but now all the directors – including Nigel Wray and Mike Luckwell – could be outvoted by the institutional and private shareholders. But Michael Green has been consistent. He believes in cash and dislikes debt – a distaste underlined by both his father and the Wolfsons. However, he also wanted to expand rapidly to take advantage of the opportunities he saw before him, and that left only one option – to issue shares on the back of a strong share price.

'It took Michael a while to understand that control does not necessarily mean owning 51 per cent: control means doing a first-class job. When he did realize, he was willing to use paper [i.e. issue shares] and not debt,' Peter Kleeman argues. In complete contrast, Rupert Murdoch, chairman of The News Corporation, the international media group, has always been determined to keep a large percentage of shares under family control, to prevent any possibility that he could be ousted.

Carlton's growing appetite for issuing new shares was highlighted at the time by the *Financial Times*. In December 1983 companies reporter Dominic Lawson asked, rather sardonically, if it had really only been July when Carlton had issued 5 million shares to acquire The Moving Picture Company. Even though investors were being given a 23 per cent discount on the share price, the *FT* accused Carlton of 'opportunism', because no specific purpose was identified for the money. 'It might have gone down better with shareholders if Carlton had made at least a start in its programme of US expansion before making its cash call,' argued Lawson. He need not have worried: Green and Luckwell were about to embark on a Carlton takeover trail that over five years saw a new acquisition on average every five months – most of them in the television-facilities sector.

The first deal since the merger with the MPC came in March 1984, when Carlton paid £2.5 million in cash and shares for Video Time, a facilities company based in Greek Street, Soho. Video Time had been set up by Ray Brassington and Ray Hawkins in 1978 to offer a more utilitarian, less expensive service than that offered by MPC. The aim had been to create a 'factory' that would handle everything from adapting US television programmes from the incompatible American standard, so that they could be broadcast in Europe, to transferring programmes from film to videotape and editing corporate videos. Sometimes Video Time would complete as many as fifty jobs a day.

John Beedle of MPC knew Brassington and Hawkins to be two talented entrepreneurs, and he admired what they had achieved. He introduced them to Michael Green. Brassington, who had never met Green, before was immediately impressed. 'He was very sharp and obviously could work out a deal in his head almost instantaneously. Of all the meetings Ray and I had with him, we probably only won one of them. He got what he wanted, but we did all right too. We became instant millionaires – at least on paper,' says Ray Brassington. On the day the acquisition was announced the Carlton share price rose 5p, to 460p.

Ray Hawkins liked Michael Green and was impressed by the fact that he was at ease with numbers without being an accountant, understood people, and was entrepreneurial but never too embarrassed to ask naïve questions and learn from the answers. 'He relied very heavily on Beedle for his technical input, and also in the early days very much on Luckwell for his guidance on the television industry and where it was going,' says Hawkins.

By joining Carlton, Brassington and Hawkins were the latest recruits to what would be a growing band of executives who were millionaire employees, holding much of their wealth in Carlton shares, and who therefore had an obvious interest in trying to ensure that Carlton Communications continued to flourish.

Within a matter of weeks Carlton announced a 42 per cent rise in pre-tax profits, to £1.95 million, for the six months to March 1984. The company also unveiled the £6.2 million purchase of Superhire, a prop-hire company which did half its business with the ITV companies and the BBC, as well as supplying props to films such as *Alien* and *Death Wish III*. Superhire – paid for entirely by Carlton shares – just about fitted the overall strategy of expanding in the television sector but was hardly part of the digital television revolution that helped to keep the Carlton Communications share price high. Its founder, Roy Moore, had set up as a builder's merchant in 1954 after national service with £3,000 borrowed from his father. He was once asked for the loan of a tiled fireplace surround by Rank Film Services, and later the film-makers came back to borrow a sink unit and paid thirty shillings for the hire. Slowly Moore built up a business hiring out props. When he found out that film-makers had great difficulty in getting modern furniture for their productions, Moore bought a large quantity and stored it first in an old disused Odeon cinema and later in a warehouse in Acton. 'We had everything you might need in a film: from hospital beds to school rooms, china to lampstands to picture frames, carpets, cupboards, desks,' says Moore, who has become a multimillionaire out of the perfectly ordinary things – more than 250,000 of them – he has bought and hired out to film and television companies over the years.

One of Moore's regular customers was Carlton Studios, the photographic business run by David Green. And it was David Green who called Moore and, over lunch, asked him if he would like to become part of the Carlton group. After the £6.2 million share deal was completed, Moore's two partners – Chris Bailey and Brian Duffy – sold their Carlton shares, but Moore held on to his and stayed on as chairman and managing director of the Carlton-owned Superhire on a initial three-year contract. Moore says he was free to continue running what had been his own company with a minimum of interference, but got to know both David and Michael Green well. 'David is the elder brother, but I have heard Michael screaming at David and David just takes it. Michael is definitely the one with the ability,' says Moore, who adds that David Green is without question the nicer of the two brothers.

Superhire was not a high-technology company, but it was part of the Green-Luckwell strategy to invade the back-room of the television and film industries where serious money could be made by providing the industry's support services at very low risk. Even if a film or a television programme turned out to be a financial disaster, the provider of the technical services had always been paid up-front. 'It was quite simple to me. I saw the growth in television, media, screen-based entertainment, but I didn't have the courage to go into the software side, to go into the volatile areas where you could make a lot of money but where you could lose a lot of money. So we tried to cover every aspect of television on the back route – the nuts-and-bolts stuff that kept it [TV] going, where there was a lot of money to be made,' Michael Green explained.

Broadcasters trying to fill the huge expansion in the number of channels and the hours of programmes being produced were desperate to use any new technological 'nuts and bolts' to cut costs and make cheaply produced television look as professional as possible. The Carlton companies could help by offering slick editing and sophisticated special effects and title sequences.

Carlton's first acquisition in the USA, Abekas Video Systems, was a digital video-technology company based near Redwood City, California, that fitted the back-room strategy perfectly. Abekas was a company created by three young engineers – a Briton, a Pakistani and an Indian – who had become friends while working together at Ampex, one of the leading broadcasting-equipment manufacturers. Their aim was to create a company, build it up, and then sell it for as much as they could get. 'Abekas was for sale from day one,' says Phil Bennett, the Englishman and the technical brains behind the operation, who had worked at companies such as Link Scientific and Quantel in the UK before moving to California. Junaid Sheikh, who had studied at the University of California before working for Ampex, was the marketing specialist. Yaswant Kamath, the Indian, came closer to being a general manager than the other two.

Abekas was a high-technology company – and one that was about to display explosive growth. The company produced a sophisticated storage device that used a video disc to record up to two minutes of a programme. The digital pictures could then be played back in slow motion, one frame at a time, giving a new degree of editing flexibility. The editing could all be done without the loss of picture quality that happened with existing analogue technology. Abekas produced digital video special-effects equipment for $50,000 when rivals were offering more cumbersome versions for $200,000. It also took disc-recording technology forward with similar price reductions.

Luckwell and Beedle spotted the potential of Abekas because they were in the market for such equipment, and indeed Beedle had met the Abekas team at the National Association of Broadcasters exhibition in the USA just as they were about to launch their latest disc recording device. Later in 1984 the Abekas team were demonstrating their equipment at the International Broadcasting Convention in Brighton. The new Abekas products were displayed on the stand of GEC McMichael, the broadcasting-equipment division of GEC, which was just one of a number of companies thinking of buying Abekas. 'Two people came by and Michael said, "Hello I'm Michael Green and this is June de Moller," ' recalls Sheikh – a slim, elegantly dressed executive who could pass for a Pakistani squash champion. They talked over a cup of coffee, and very quickly the outline of a deal was put together that would give Carlton Communications 100 per cent of Abekas in return for an up-front payment combined with a five-year earn-out linked to future profits.

The Abekas deal was announced on 11 December 1984. Carlton was paying an initial $12.8 million (£10.7 million) and a further payment of up to $17.2 million over five years linked to the scale of profits. The structure of the deal was designed by Green to appeal to the entrepreneurs, to lock in their skills as well as phasing in Carlton's purchase price. It was also probably the only effective way of running a California-based high-technology company from London.

Once again Carlton paid for the deal by raising money from shareholders by issuing new shares. The announcement accompanied publication of Carlton's annual results, complete with a 58 per cent rise in pre-tax profits, to £5.5 million on turnover of £21.5 million. The one-share-for-six rights issue at 485p a share was designed to raise £13.25 million. Again the directors did not take up their rights, and as result their combined stake in the company fell to 45 per cent. Despite the raising of new money, which tends to depress the share price, Carlton's shares rose 60p on the day, to a new high of 625p.

Sheikh and his colleagues were very happy working under Carlton ownership. 'The deal was the deal, and everything was run well. We were left alone to do our thing, and we had excellent relationships. There wasn't much interaction. The primary form of interaction was the money being transferred to Carlton on a regular basis, because we were a highly profitable company – highly,' says Sheikh, who believes it was the Abekas purchase that made Carlton Communications as a company. Sheikh stayed for three years before moving on to found a new company, Accom.

'He made us a very attractive offer. I have nothing but admiration for Michael Green. He kept his side of the deal, and so did I,' says Kamath, who stayed for the full five years. He had been prepared to continue working for Carlton Communications, but negotiations on a new contract – carried out by de Moller rather than Green – were never satisfactorily concluded. Kamath finally left to set up a new company in the broadcasting-technology field, Kub Systems.

Green acknowledges that Abekas was important in the development of Carlton. The acquisition helped to make Carlton what many people already supposed it to be – an exciting high-technology company with high profit margins. Well before the end of the five-year agreement with the three entrepreneurs Abekas was making annual profits of $25 million on turnover of $70 million. The weakness of the pound against the dollar was also important. 'You've got to remember that the pound was almost at parity with the dollar at the time, and getting earnings from America was part of our strategy,' the Carlton chairman recalls.

The acquisition of Abekas impressed both analysts and journalists. In January 1985 the Tempus column in *The Times* said Carlton was emerging 'as a giant in an arena [television services] which has traditionally been a showplace for creative minnows'. Under the headline 'Carlton Towers Over TV's Service Sector', the *Investors Chronicle* suggested that 'if Britain has a future in communications electronics, it lies with companies such as this'.

The successful purchase of Abekas reminded Green about one that had got away two years earlier: Michael Cox Electronics – a small, profitable, British manufacturing company with a reputation for innovation. One day in late 1983 Michael Green had rung up and asked if he could come and visit the company, which employed about 100 people producing electronic devices for the television industry at premises on the Hanworth Trading Estate near Feltham in Middlesex. Cox Electronics was becoming quite well-known in television stations around the world for its devices. In particular, the Cox Box was a cheap way of putting programme titles and station logos on screen in colour.

Michael Cox had never heard of Green and had no idea what he wanted, but after a brief tour and a chat in Cox's office Green simply announced that he thought he would like to buy the company. Selling was not something that had ever occurred to Cox. But, even though he wasn't sure he wanted to sell his company, he decided to go to Carlton's headquarters at New Roman House for further talks. A dedicated reader of the *Guardian*, he turned up wearing his Campaign for Nuclear Disarmament badge.

Cox found Michael Green very personable, but as the conversation wore on he gradually felt himself getting cold feet. Green was unwilling to buy a minority stake, and Cox, who had worked for himself for fifteen years, was reluctant to cede control. The deal did not go ahead.

Two years later, in 1985, Green approached Cox again. This time Green had the perfect bait. Cox had always wanted to get into the huge American market, without really knowing how to do it. Green now suggested Abekas as the conduit for Cox products into the USA, and brought Phil Bennett of Abekas with him. Suddenly there was something to discuss.

Cox was surprised that, as the negotiations proceeded, all his conversations were with Michael Green and that Mike Luckwell, the one who knew most about television, was nowhere to be seen. 'Michael Green said first of all that the identity of the company will remain. "We buy a success. We want you running a successful company, and that's why we like it. We want you to stay and run it, as part of the Carlton family." It was all very good stuff, and I suppose I was sort of taken in by this. And maybe we should have asked to meet some of these guys who are in the Carlton family. But we didn't do that. That was a sad omission as it turned out,' says Cox.

Carlton paid £3.2 million, of which £1.3 million was in shares, for Michael Cox Electronics, a company with revenues of £3.8 million and profits of £300,000 a year. Cox, who was made another Carlton millionaire by the deal, formally announced the change of ownership to his staff in June 1985, at a company barn dance held in a spare building at Hanworth.

Right at the end of negotiations, when the final details of the deal were being hammered out, Cox found himself dealing with Luckwell and June de Moller for the first time. Then, almost from the moment the ink was dry on the agreement, Cox says, Luckwell began trying to change things. The first suggestion – and one Cox says was never mentioned during the takeover discussions – was that the company should be merged with Abekas UK at Reading. Luckwell also wanted to put in a new reception area in a building let by Cox Electronics to a small company called Wardgold, which carried out work for Cox under contract. Wardgold was to be given six weeks' notice, even though it was unlikely it could find new premises in such a short time. Cox made himself unpopular with his new bosses by giving Wardgold a longer notice period.

In August Cox was summoned to a Cox Electronics board meeting to be told that he had to get rid of his finance officer, Oliver Walker. He was horrified to find that a successor had been interviewed and appointed without any reference to himself or the board. Walker had not been with the company long enough to qualify for redundancy money. On his return to his office Cox got out Walker's contract and changed its terms to give him three months' severance pay – just before Luckwell arrived to inspect the document.

The next surprise for Cox – who still held the title of managing director – was that a new general manager was being brought in without his knowledge. 'I took the greatest delight in ringing him up and telling him a few home truths about what was going on, and it put him off,' says Cox, who at one stage was so exasperated that he asked Green if he could give him his money back and call the whole deal off.

Next came the ultimatum. Luckwell announced at a meeting that the merger with Abekas UK was going ahead and that if Cox did not agree to be chairman of the merged company it would go ahead anyway and new directors would be appointed from Abekas to run the merged group. After the unpleasant meeting, Luckwell asked the company's production director, Sam Cunningham, to stay behind and then dismissed him. When Cox heard what had happened he decided to go too. The last thing he did as he left that evening was to unscrew, and keep, the Michael Cox Electronics name-plate. Cox's formal relationship with Carlton came to an end when he was paid an extra £25,000 in compensation for breach of contract.

In November 1985 there was the opportunist purchase for £2.6 million in cash of the London facilities company TVi. The owners, the Rank Organisation, wanted to get out of the television-facilities business. TVi was at the low-cost end of the post-production market, working with programme-makers and broadcasters rather than the advertising industry. 'TVi wasn't a business we wanted to be in. We supply equipment like telecines to that market, but we don't want to run that kind of company,' Michael Gifford, the former chief executive of the Rank Organisation, explained. The deal showed Green's determination to have a presence across the range of price levels in the television-facilities industry, to maximize Carlton's share of the total market.

TVi also brought Michael Green into the business orbit of Rupert Murdoch for the first time. Since its launch, Murdoch's Sky Television had been broadcast from the central-London studios of TVi. 'Sky, the first year and a half, was broadcasting out of one of our buildings. TVi was Sky. All the first Sky employees worked in our building. We did every single transmission for them. We were their transmission. We edited every programme that they used to show. All the commercials were worked there,' says Green.

Unfortunately the acquisition of TVi coincided with a serious purge on costs at Sky. Murdoch told the Sky chief executive, Patrick Cox, that he had to cut £2 million a year from Sky's costs or the channel would have to close. The first target for cost-cutting had been British Telecom, which fed the channel's signal to the satellite; the second TVi. There was a clause in the Sky-TVi contract which gave Sky the right to pull out of the agreement if there was a change of ownership – a clause that was now used for a tough renegotiation. Green was asked for a 30 per cent cut in the price of the contract. The Carlton chairman took it personally and wanted to know why he was being treated like this. Patrick Cox replied that he needed the money. Murdoch, who at that time looked down on Green as 'a bit player' who wasn't very rich, got his price reduction from the facilities company.

There were two other deals which did not fit the Carlton image quite so well. In the first the company spent £900,000 on Integrated Holdings, which, through its Syma Systems trading arm, provided display units for exhibitions and the retail trade. It became a new subsidiary for Carlton Fox. The second, the acquisition of The Symmonds Drum & Percussion Company, featured the electronic products of percussionist Dave Symmonds. 'Loved the property,' was how Michael Green justified the purchase – which turned out to be a total turkey. The property had to be sold off to pay the company's debts.

During this period there were at least two detailed sets of discussions about merging Carlton Communications and Saatchi & Saatchi. Apart from the long-term friendships, there was a strong business connection – The Moving Picture Company was a major supplier to the Saatchi agencies, as to a lesser extent was Carlton Fox.

Martin Sorrell, then the Saatchi & Saatchi finance director, watched the conversations with interest, although they never got as far as discussing precise figures. 'These conversations used to go on. Saatchis were deemed strong and were probably a little bit disdainful of the relationship, and Carlton was feeling weak – it was a bit of a roller-coaster,' Sorrell recalls. 'It would never have worked, and it was doomed to failure because, although Charlie could, I think, genuinely have got on with Michael, I don't think Michael and Maurice could have got on. If it was ever going to work you would have had Charles as chairman, Michael as chief executive, and then the question would be, What would Maurice be? He certainly wouldn't be finance director. I think it must be galling for Maurice now – and maybe for Charles as well – that Michael has done so well. I remember we always used to say we should have bought The Moving Picture Company, not Michael.'

The spate of acquisitions enhanced growth, but it also made it difficult for the City to judge what was happening to the performance of the 'existing' parts of the Carlton empire. Analysts and other outsiders had to guess which companies in the group were making most profit and what the individual margins were, because for many years the group profit figure was not broken down to show the performance of individual businesses. Little was said in those days about the more mundane parts of the company such as the shop-fitting operations of Carlton Fox.

'There was a story that people believed in, and the story was perhaps more important than the underlying reality. The story was very much about a very sexy television-related company. There were very few companies in the group that were actually generating real organic profit,' according to one analyst who knew Carlton well in the 1980s. The City does not accept that all profits are equal. Profits produced by a mature company in a traditional sector of industry are fine, but profits in a new expanding sector such as television hold out the prospects of continuing growth. Shop-fitting companies, or even businesses like Superhire, were not rated by the City as being worth twenty, thirty or even forty times earnings – the sort of rating that a 'sexy' company such as Carlton attracted.

The flow of deals also meant that – entirely legitimately – Carlton had enormous scope to play with balance-sheet provisions by using acquisition accounting to provide two obvious and legitimate ways of boosting profits.

When a company is taken over, a conservative view can be taken of the value of the fixed assets and of the period over which they should be depreciated – something that sounds as if the purchaser is erring on the side of responsibility and extreme probity. If the value of the assets is heavily written down on acquisition, then in the following year there is a much smaller depreciation charge to come out of profits, which are correspondingly boosted compared with the previous year. The book value of the company's fixed assets may be lower, but if the City is looking at earnings per share as the key measure of performance, rather than asset value, then the company is judged to be doing extremely well and the shares are marked up in value. Carlton was always driven by the performance of earnings per share.

Profits can also be boosted by providing for reorganization and redundancy charges at the date of an acquisition. If the acquired business turns out to be in better shape than originally thought, some of the provisions can be released as profit. Again, an approach that appears to be ultra-cautious can help to boost profits in a future year, and the effect is difficult to see without detailed accounts of the subsidiaries involved. 'However carefully you look, you can't find it. Certainly there is no way of spotting it from group accounts,' says an accountant who knows Carlton well. Michael Green, however, has always said that Carlton Communications received no material benefit from such perfectly legitimate artifices.

A number of Carlton employees in those years of explosive growth in the 1980s point out that the company also benefited from taking stakes in other quoted companies. Profits from share deals may have helped to boost Carlton's performance in the early days, when an extra few hundred thousand pounds was capable of making a noticeable difference to the results. There was absolutely nothing wrong with such share deals, and at the time there were no rules to require companies to disclose such profits separately, as would be the case now. The danger, of course, is that such profits can prove more volatile than orthodox company earnings. 'The degree to which Carlton played the Stock Exchange was never fully appreciated,' one City figure close to Carlton said. It is a practice Green denies having followed, apart from building up stakes in companies Carlton was trying to take over. The market value of investments in quoted companies at the end of September 1985 was listed at just over £3 million, but no further details were given.

Less than three years after the 1983 flotation Carlton Communications had already emerged as a serious force in the back-room of the British television industry. In Europe, only the BBC was bigger than Carlton in video facilities. The company had grown dramatically, and now employed nearly 650 people. The financial progress was also impressive. In the year to September 1985 pre-tax profits reached £12 million on a turnover of £38.14 million. Abekas was one big factor in Carlton's growth in profitability: it was largely responsible for an increase in pre-tax profits in the USA from £6,000 in 1984 to £2.7 million in 1985.

By then Carlton was primarily a television company, with more than 70 per cent of revenues coming from television and related activities. Publishing, the stronger part of the business when the company floated in 1983, now accounted for only 8 per cent of revenues, with photographic studios and exhibitions making up the remainder.

Carlton still had an informal, small-company feel to it. Headquarters remained the unfashionable New Roman House in East Road. 'There were literally five rooms on one side of the corridor on the top floor of New Roman House and five rooms on the other side, and that was Carlton's head office. There was a bloody good working atmosphere, and a tremendous team spirit,' according to one of those who worked there then. It was also an exciting place to be, as propositions and potential deals came through the door all the time,

Power was largely in the hands of the Michael Green, still only thirty-seven, who as chairman and chief executive was little involved in the day-today running of the subsidiary companies. Carlton Communications was run in a very informal way. Legal requirements were met, but board meetings were called when Green decided it was time for a board meeting – which could be once every three months. The six-strong board was hardly Carlton's decision-making forum. Michael Green made the decisions, and if anything required a board resolution a board resolution was duly prepared.

When the small board was meeting to approve an acquisition there would be full and precise paperwork, although it was noticeable that Green's limited attention span meant he concentrated on the essentials. At other, more ad-hoc, board meetings there was rarely an agenda or formal papers – with one important exception: Michael Green always insisted on receiving detailed monthly management reports giving a full picture of trading conditions and the balance of cash in each Carlton subsidiary.

'Monthly management reports were very unusual at the time for our industry. But they turned out to be crucial,' David Jeffers of MPC recalls. Green later explained, 'I like the numbers. They mean something to me – they have relevance.'

Nigel Wray noted that, for all its informality, Carlton was run in a more formal way than The Fleet Street Letter had been. Yet Carlton was still a company driven more by entrepreneurial spirit than by bureaucratic procedures.

Although the forty-three-year-old Mike Luckwell was group managing director and had an office in New Roman House, he spent virtually all of his time either at MPC, on the road visiting the Carlton subsidiaries, or checking out new acquisition prospects.

June de Moller, at thirty-eight the longest-serving employee, was then company secretary. She was also the supreme loyalist, rarely disagreeing with Michael Green, either privately or publicly, and reading all the detailed documents for him.

David Ludlam, who was forty-four, had joined Carlton Fox as managing director in 1978 and had set up a colour-film-processing laboratory for the company a year later. The only other director was the thirty-nine-year-old David Green, who ran Carlton Studios, just one of seventeen operating subsidiaries of Carlton Communications.

That year Bernard Cragg, a talented thirty-one-year-old Price Waterhouse accountant who had been looking for a way into commerce for some time, was hired as financial controller to replace Paul Harding, who had been head of finance. Harding had been dismissed after a row with Luckwell, but Michael Green kept him on to look after Tangent's financial affairs. In June 1985

Cragg was joined by Charles Wigoder, a City analyst specializing in the media, who was hired as head of corporate finance and development. Wigoder's main task was to work on the acquisition programme with Green.

It was a small head-office team, but Carlton also had good advisers in Michael Sorkin at Hambros and considerable support from brokers such as Giles Coode-Adams and Geoff Bowman at Messel.

There was absolutely no doubt in Michael Green's mind where Carlton wanted to go next. He wrote in the 1985 Carlton annual report, 'It seems clear that with the current level of commitment by individuals, industrialists and Governments, a new era in broadcasting is on our doorstep. For those with the vision and foresight, these new opportunities will provide the background for significant and profitable growth over the coming decade.'

Chapter 6

The Audacious Bid for Thames

By 1985 it was clear that the old order in broadcasting was starting to break down. Digital technology had revolutionized television editing and enriched Carlton Communications. The same technology would invade the production and transmission process and make it easier to create new channels distributed by cable and satellite. Rupert Murdoch's Sky was already broadcasting seventeen hours a day to 5 million cable homes across Europe, and in the year to June 1985 it took £2.25 million in advertising revenue. And technology was already beginning to change the balance of power in ITV between unions and management.

When, in October 1984, the technical unions at Thames Television, the London weekday broadcaster, went on strike for the second time in two months in a dispute over film editors' pay and the introduction of new single-person portable cameras, it was assumed that ITV television screens throughout London would again go blank if the management did not give in. Instead Thames's managing director, Bryan Cowgill – nicknamed 'the Clitheroe kid', after his Lancashire home town – decided to make a fight of it. Thames management would transmit a service for the London area organized by Cowgill's right-hand man, production director Richard Dunn.

The dispute was important for two reasons – both of them signalling the possibility of change. Thames put out a service of old programmes and local news but, surprisingly, the company's share of the London audience and advertising revenues were hardly affected. Even more significantly, executives in the broadcaster's Euston Road headquarters found out how much easier it had become to transmit a television channel using the new electronic equipment produced by companies such as Carlton. One executive at Thames quickly mastered the computer-controlled machine which automatically inserts advertisements into the programme schedule and found the job 'very routine – very much like a production line in a car factory'. Yet the unions insisted that this particular job required six months' training and had to be staffed by a senior-grade engineer grossing around £20,000 a year.

If the 1984 strikes at Thames showed how commercial television in the UK was beginning to change, events at Thames in January 1985 suggested where the limits of change lay. Cowgill, a former controller of BBC1, exhilarated by his industrial-relations victory, was offered the chance to 'poach' *Dallas*. The popular American series featuring the oil-industry villain J. R. Ewing had been attracting audiences as high as 14 million for the BBC. Cowgill thought he would be congratulated by his colleagues for securing the rights to the popular series for ITV in a deal with Worldvision of the USA. Instead he ran into a storm of condemnation that eventually cost him his job.

Paul Fox, then managing director of Yorkshire Television and chairman of the ITV film-purchasing committee, and another former controller of BBC1, was vitriolic about the breach of the informal agreement that Britain's broadcasters did not drive up the price of Hollywood 'product' by bidding for shows or series already running on a British television channel. Only Hollywood would benefit, so the argument went, if there were auctions of the UK rights of the most popular American programmes. Thus, instead of being treated as an entrepreneurial hero, Cowgill was summoned like an errant schoolboy to the Independent Broadcasting Authority – the body that regulated commercial broadcasting and awarded ITV licences – and was told he would have to give *Dallas* back to ITV's main rival, the BBC.

This put Cowgill in an impossible position – particularly as he had done the *Dallas* deal without telling either the other ITV companies or even his own chairman, Hugh Dundas. Cowgill's resignation was accepted and, although there was a decent financial settlement, his career was effectively over at the early age of fifty-eight. He was never to work in mainstream television again.

After a dispute that ran for more than six months, an extraordinary agreement was reached between Lord Thomson, chairman of the IBA, and Stuart Young, chairman of the BBC. *Dallas* was indeed to be handed back to the BBC, but Thames also had to pay the Corporation around £300,000 in compensation for the increased price that Cowgill had agreed with Worldvision.

For Michael Green and Mike Luckwell the obvious tensions in ITV reinforced their view that the old, cosy, uncompetitive world of British television was starting to change. They decided to move. In early 1985 Carlton started buying shares in London Weekend Television, now chaired by Green's old printing-industry rival Christopher Bland, who had moved into television management by way of membership of the IBA, where he had been deputy chairman. Carlton gradually accumulated a stake in LWT totalling 4.9 per cent – just below the 5 per cent limit where, according to Stock Exchange rules at the time, a share holding has to be publicly declared.

In May, Green began to explore the possibility of going further. David Ludlam, the Carlton director who ran the company's photographic business, had mentioned to Green that he was a near-neighbour of David Glencross, the rather austere IBA director of television, and that the two had met at a number of local parties over the years. Ludlam was asked to telephone Glencross, a former BBC producer, and arrange a lunch with Michael Green. Lunch was fixed for Friday 14 June 1985.

Green was adamant that he would pick his guest up in his car and take him to lunch. The IBA director's protests that he would happily make his own way to the venue were swept aside. 'I will pick you up,' Green insisted. And so it was that, when Glencross walked through the revolving doors of the IBA's Brompton Road headquarters, there was Green in his chauffeur-driven Bentley waiting to whisk the IBA director of television and his acquaintance Ludlam round the corner to the Carlton Tower Hotel – a distance of about 500 yards.

Green wanted to know whether he could take over London Weekend Television. Glencross recalls telling his host carefully and unambiguously that he could not. The way broadcasting licences were allocated in those days, neither Carlton nor any other company could take over a broadcaster unless there were exceptional circumstances. The main exception was if there was the danger of an ITV company collapsing and going off the air. That had happened just once, in 1962, when Wales, West and North had nearly run out of money and had been replaced. But a healthy company like LWT could not be taken over in the middle of a franchise period. It was a matter of rules and of being fair to all those who had submitted applications for licences in 1980 but had been unsuccessful.

As lunch progressed, Glencross realized that Green was either not understanding his argument that television licences could not be bought and sold like any other business or was unwilling to accept the unpalatable information. Glencross got the impression that Green appeared to think the opposition to his plan was in some way personal, and the young entrepreneur went out of his way to establish his business credentials and demonstrate that he would be a perfectly respectable holder of an ITV licence.

The lack of mutual comprehension amounted to a clash between two distinct concepts of broadcasting. The traditional idea of public-service broadcasting represented by Glencross was still the dominant influence in ITV, even though the channel was funded by advertising. An alternative approach, represented by Green, viewed broadcasting as a wholly commercial enterprise which should be subject to minimum controls. The debate between these two viewpoints was only just getting under way in the UK in 1985.

Glencross found the animated thirty-seven-year-old across the table from him charming but determined. Green might smile and laugh, but Glencross formed the view that he was a man who didn't take no for an answer, who didn't like his ambition being frustrated by rules and who was used to getting his own way. When the lunch was over, Glencross, to his amusement, found himself walking back the 500 yards to the IBA.

Green had no intention of taking Glencross's view as definitive. There were other, more powerful, people in the IBA to approach – such as the director-general, John Whitney, the former boss of Capital Radio. A meeting with Whitney was quickly arranged which, because of an IRA bomb scare affecting the IBA headquarters, was conducted sitting in Whitney's Rolls-Royce Corniche in the Authority's basement garage. No target companies were mentioned by name, but Green believed he had been given the nod and that a takeover was possible – at least in principle.

On 25 June 1985 Green and Luckwell attended a meeting at LWT. Accompanying the LWT chairman, Christopher Bland, were Brian Tesler, the managing director, and John Birt, director of programmes. The Carlton executives made it clear that they were interested in taking a much larger stake in LWT. Birt in particular was 'flabbergasted' to hear that people from a facilities company appeared to think they could take over LWT. The two sides did not hit it off, quite apart from regulatory obstacles and the fact that LWT's articles of association specified that no single shareholder could hold more than 10 per cent of the company.

'Neither Brian nor I took a fancy to Mike Luckwell. Michael [Green] was fine. Mike Luckwell seemed chilly, tough and arrogant. My instinct was that if we let Michael and Mike Luckwell in the door then we might as well resign there and then and hand him over the business,' recalls Bland – a former Enniskillen Dragoon Guards officer with a reputation for toughness himself.

Green's plan was to take over LWT and become chairman, leaving Bland to run the ITV company. 'Bland asked me, "Michael, would you like to work for me?" I said, "No, Christopher." He said, "Well, now you know my answer to you." I have not forgotten it, and we have a business relationship and we get on very well,' Green explains. He also remembers the talks with Bland and LWT for an embarrassing *faux pas*. He had had the gall to tell Bland that he was an ex-printer who didn't really understand television – conveniently forgetting his own background.

Although there were further meetings between Green and Bland in August and September, it was hardly surprising that the talks with LWT went no

Richard Dunn

further. By then the Carlton team was beginning to focus on an even more audacious target.

Green and Luckwell returned to the IBA and met Lord Thomson of Monifieth, the IBA chairman, who was a former Labour Chancellor of the Duchy of Lancaster. Luckwell and Green were heard politely, and nothing was ruled out entirely by Thomson. Luckwell took the view that, while the IBA obviously did not like the idea of a takeover of an ITV company in mid-franchise, it was starting to come round to the idea. Perhaps, he thought, if there was an agreed takeover the Authority would not be overtly hostile.

For Richard Dunn, the Thames Television production director, that summer was proving to be traumatic. One evening in July the tall, handsome, half-Icelandic executive got the telephone call every parent dreads. His five-year-old son had been hit by a car in the road outside their home and had been rushed to hospital. A week after the incident, at the hospital where his son was in traction with extensive injuries, Dunn got a telephone call from Hugh Dundas the Thames chairman. Cowgill had resigned. Would Dunn please take over as managing director and chief executive of Thames. Dunn accepted.

Two weeks later, during a routine meeting between Dunn and Dundas – a tall, dignified man who had been a Battle of Britain fighter pilot and was chairman of the industrial conglomerate BET as well as of Thames – Dundas remarked almost casually that Hambros Bank had been in touch about a company called Carlton Communications. It was interested in acquiring shares in Thames. Apart from asking for a check at Companies House to see who or what was behind Carlton, Dunn thought little of it. The Thames chief executive paid more attention when Dundas, who was just about to leave on a long trip to the USA, revealed that he was meeting Michael Green, the Carlton chairman, on 6 September.

Dunn went on 'red alert' a week later, when he had lunch with Gary Dartnell, a director of both Thames and Thorn EMI, and was told that Thorn was considering selling its 48 per cent stake in Thames to Carlton. The Thames chief executive became even more concerned after another lunch, on 24 September, this time with Lord Brabourne, the film-maker, who was also a Thames and Thorn director. Brabourne said he believed BET, the other big Thames shareholder, was interested in selling too.

Dunn would have been even more alarmed if he had known just how close Carlton was to a deal with Thorn and BET, who between them owned more than 95 per cent of Thames. It had not been a difficult task persuading either of them to sell. Thorn was increasingly focusing on the development of its music business, while BET had decided its television and magazine interests were not substantial enough for the company to be a major player and planned instead to specialize in industrial services. Negotiations between Green, Luckwell, Colin Southgate, chairman of Thorn, and Nicholas Wills, chief executive of BET, were brief and almost painless. Carlton offered £50 million and the Thames shareholders asked for £100 million. The talks quickly started to focus on £80 million.

On 27 September 1985 Thorn and BET agreed to sell their shares in Thames Television to Carlton for £82.45 million, in a deal that included the valuable Thames programme library. Green and Luckwell had cleverly negotiated themselves an each-way deal: there was a clause in the sale agreement that said Carlton had the right to buy Thames whatever the attitude of the IBA, but if the Authority did indeed block the transfer of the broadcasting licence Carlton had the option of pulling out of the deal.

At Thames, Dunn felt left out in the cold and was unsure of what was going on. He had recently won board approval to float Thames on the Stock Exchange – something that was in line with an IBA requirement that the company should be floated before the end of its eight-year licence period. The Thames board had even agreed to appoint Barings, the merchant bank, to advise on the flotation. Yet Thames's two dominant shareholders were now planning a quick sale and Barings was advising BET on the sale of its stake.

Hambros and Morgan Grenfell were underwriting the Carlton offer, although
the two banks also acted for Thorn. Among this tangle of conflicting interests,
County Bank was quickly appointed to represent the Thames management
and staff.

The first call from Green to Dunn came at 8.30 a.m. on 30 September –
three days after the deal had been agreed. Could they meet the following
afternoon? Later that afternoon Dunn was summoned to the elegant
headquarters of BET, in Stratton House, Piccadilly, to be briefed by
Dundas, his chairman. Dunn was led to believe the briefing would be in
preparation for his first meeting with Green the following day, yet as soon
as the meeting started Dundas surprised Dunn by saying that Green was
waiting in an adjacent room. Dunn – a successful middle-heavyweight boxer
during his Cambridge days – refused to be bounced into an immediate
meeting with Green without knowing the full picture. He insisted on having
a detailed private briefing from Dundas covering every aspect of the
proposed acquisition while Green was left to pace up and down nearby.
During the briefing Dundas made it clear that neither Thorn nor BET had
been to the IBA to ask what its attitude was to the unprecedented takeover.
But that agreement had been reached for a sale subject only to IBA
approval.

When the Thames chief executive met Michael Green in the office of
Nicholas Wills, the BET chief executive, it was an awkward moment and
Dunn felt very much a 'piggy-in-the-middle'. His current chairman, Dundas,
who clearly wanted to sell the BET stake in the ITV company, had introduced
him to Green, the man who could be his new chairman. Dunn felt very
strongly that what was being proposed was not just a normal business
transaction between a willing seller and a willing buyer. It was important to
consider the impact on Thames Television's broadcasting contract – a
contract designed to ensure the continuity of a high-quality service for
viewers. What would be the effect of the deal on his programme service,
fellow executives and staff? How likely was it that the IBA might decide to
reject the takeover and readvertise the London weekday licence?

Green exuded confidence that in the end the IBA would not be a problem.
He believed he had been given hints from both Lord Thomson and Whitney,
and at the very least no one had ever actually said no. Dunn listened as the
warm, engaging, enthusiastic Carlton chairman talked virtually non-stop in
an hour-long charm offensive.

Green had a dramatic story to tell, even though Carlton was a much less
well-known company than Thames. Green described how in 1985 Carlton's

turnover had grown from £21.5 million to £38 million and how, more significantly, pre-tax profits had soared from £5.5 million to over £12 million and the company's capitalization – the value of the more than 26 million shares on issue – had reached more than £200 million. Green was able to hold out the prospects of a Carlton-Thames becoming the powerhouse of British commercial broadcasting – a combined company that would have a market capitalization of well over £300 million.

Green added how much he admired what Dunn had achieved during his years at Thames, and promised they would run the new enlarged company together and that nothing would change. The promises were not specific, but Dunn was left with the impression that he would become very rich in this new organization. 'For background', Green added that his wife, Janet, was Sir Isaac Wolfson's granddaughter, and that Stuart Young, the chairman of the BBC, was a cousin by marriage, as was David Young, the Secretary of State for Trade and Industry. It began to dawn on Dunn that, for all Green's charm, here was a man talking about money, relatives, contacts and power rather than broadcasting, programmes or editorial independence.

When he was formally asked if he would accompany Green to the IBA to present a united front on the merits of the 'merger', Dunn – the employee, who had been totally overlooked by the power-brokers until then – delivered an unambiguous answer. 'No. I totally reserve my position and that of my company until I have the Authority's decision on the principle of such an acquisition,' he said. Dunn was not playing the role expected of him either by his employers or by Green.

'I absolutely believed that the principle of the tradability of franchises in mid-term was a major issue – and it was an issue for George Thomson and the Authority members and not for me,' Dunn recalls. It was a line that Dunn was to stick to despite several attempts to make him change his mind and two further formal invitations from Green to come to the IBA to support the deal.

It has been widely assumed that Dunn was anti-Carlton and was, in a machiavellian way, orchestrating a campaign behind Green's back to ensure the IBA threw out the deal. In fact the Thames chief executive was more open-minded about the bid than that, although he certainly ensured that the IBA was kept fully informed.

On Tuesday 1 October Dunn asked for a secret meeting with Whitney. To protect confidentiality they met in a large bedroom at the Inn on the Park Hotel rather than at either the IBA or Thames. 'The tale he [Dunn] told me was startling. Carlton Communications was making a bid for the total shareholding in Thames, and both major shareholders were prepared to consider the offer. My first reaction was to say I'd be surprised if it got past first base,' Whitney wrote in his diary.

As the two drank tea in the plush hotel bedroom, Dunn suggested that for Thames the status quo was no longer an option. Both Thorn and BET were determined to sell, so Thames should be restructured. If Thames was going to be owned by Carlton, however, it was essential that it retain its own identity and have a separate board, and there should be satisfactory guarantees that the ITV company would honour its commitments as a commercial public-service broadcaster. There should also be an independent chairman of stature, and at least two independent directors. Dunn set out three possible options for the IBA. The Authority could simply refuse to countenance the sale. It could allow a sale but, in order to ensure a fair price, hold an auction for the licence. Or – and this was Dunn's preferred option – it could approve a sale subject to cast-iron guarantees.

That first week in October the pace and intensity of the meetings increased. There were meetings between Dunn, Green and Luckwell; between BET, Thorn and the IBA; and a breakfast meeting between Whitney, Green and Luckwell. One of the most crucial of the flurry of meetings was one at County Bank, Thames's advisers, where Green and Luckwell were interviewed about their intentions by David Reid, a senior merchant banker. One of those at the meeting recalls that Green was at his 'smarmiest and most annoying'. The Carlton chairman kept emphasizing that he was proposing a merger, not an acquisition, even though he wanted 100 per cent of the equity and conceded that there was no place for Dunn on the Carlton Communications board. County Bank later warned Dunn to be careful, because Carlton was a thoroughly commercial company with no record of public-service broadcasting. The bankers also emphasized the fact that Carlton was effectively run by Green and Luckwell and that there was neither a finance director nor an independent director on the board.

Michael Cox, of Michael Cox Electronics, also made his presence felt. He telephoned Dunn and warned him to 'beware of Greens bearing gifts'. Cox related how 'cast-iron' assurances he had been given by Carlton had virtually all been broken by Carlton, and warned Dunn to take great care. On the other side Green enlisted Johnny Goodman, a cousin of his mother and head of the Thames subsidiary Euston Films, to support his case with Dunn.

The Thames chief executive was becoming increasingly worried about the prospect of a Carlton takeover. Thames had recently decided to go ahead with a twelve-part serialization of John Mortimer's *Paradise Postponed* – a series that would cost far more to make than the ITV network would pay for the right to show it. Thames thought it would be a good series to make, even though, despite overseas sales, the programme might never entirely repay its production cost. Would Carlton be the sort of company to make a television series such as *Paradise Postponed*, Dunn wondered?

Dunn's attitude began to harden. He received at least qualified support from an influential non-executive Thames director, Mary Baker. She had been a Thames director since 1975 and is married to the Conservative politician Kenneth Baker. She would have supported Carlton having a minority stake but not control – although she says Green's 'different cultural position was not entirely alien to me'. In such circumstances Baker believes Thames would have benefited from the more entrepreneurial, hard-nosed approach that would have come from a Carlton minority stake, but that was not on offer.

As the meetings continued behind closed doors, the battle for the future ownership of the largest ITV company was about to become public. By Friday 4 October the *Sunday Times* had got wind of an £80 million-plus bid for Thames having been made and that Thorn and BET were willing to sell. But the paper had not been able to find out who the mystery bidder was. At the IBA, Whitney had called Thomson on Saturday evening to warn him there was likely to be a leak in the Sunday papers. The IBA director-general also warned his press-office staff that the line should be that, as no formal proposals of any kind had been submitted to the Authority, no statements would be made.

That weekend was also important for other, more personal, reasons.

Green's marriage had long been virtually over, and for some time he had been in full pursuit of an Irish actress, Jeananne Crowley – a vivacious, endlessly talkative woman who had been an *Irish Times* journalist before moving on to the stage. Green had spotted her when they were both in the audience at a poetry reading in London. At the dinner afterwards, Green held out the chair next to him and told Jeananne she was sitting beside him. The actress, who had appeared in *Tenko* and *Educating Rita*, had no idea who Green was and had torn up the business card he gave her. 'I thought I was too old and too wise to get involved,' she said. 'The next morning my phone rang at 10 a.m. and it was Michael saying, "Did you enjoy last night?"

'He didn't know who I was, really – except my name and that I was an actress – but he had got on to my agent and found out my number. Michael is like that. He moves very fast. If he wants something he goes for it, and he generally gets it,' Crowley explained in an interview with the *Daily Mail*.

Crowley, who as well as acting has written a play, *Goodnight Siobhan*, was cautious about starting a romance until Green's marriage was formally over.

Jeananne Crowley

But that weekend in early October Green flew to Sweden, where Jeananne was appearing in a play. It was there that he first heard the takeover story was about to leak in the *Sunday Times*.

The media correspondent of the *Financial Times* had spent most of Sunday trying to identify the bidder for Thames. After many calls, a Thorn EMI executive contacted at home said, 'It's a company called Carlton Communications.' A visit to the library produced a slim file containing articles about the reverse takeover of The Fleet Street Letter and the subsequent spate of acquisitions. A call to the security man at Carlton's headquarters was followed by a reply from Brian Basham, a member of the first division of City public-relations advisers who at the time also represented Saatchi & Saatchi. Basham in turn led to Green. An article identifying Carlton as the mystery bidder for Thames was carried on the front page of the *Financial Times* on Monday 7 October. That morning Carlton confirmed it was in bid talks and, at the company's request, the Stock Exchange suspended Carlton's share price at 820p.

As soon as the news became public Dunn started getting calls from other senior ITV executives urging him to stand firm against any takeover. All their companies would be vulnerable if the principle that ITV companies could not normally be taken over in the middle of a franchise period was relaxed.

The news that Carlton was bidding for Thames also caused consternation at the offices of Saatchi & Saatchi. 'It means Green will be bigger than us,' Charles Saatchi spluttered to his senior executives. The Saatchis had not known in advance what Green was planning, and Charles Saatchi, whose enduring friendship with Green had always been tinged with competitiveness, was apoplectic. Roy Warman, a senior Saatchi executive, was told to think of any way he could to stop the Carlton deal going through. He called Whitney at the IBA. Warman wanted to know the answer to an entirely hypothetical question: was there any reason why Saatchi & Saatchi could not make a counter-bid for Thames? After a long silence, Whitney said the IBA would frown on such a bid. The rules prevented advertising agencies owning television stations. But, Warman persisted, what if Saatchi & Saatchi, the public holding company, put together a financial consortium including other shareholders not in advertising? 'I think we would find ways of frowning on it,' replied Whitney after another long pause. Warman then inquired about Green's chances of getting Thames. The Saatchi executive was told he need not worry too much about that. When Charles Saatchi was told the news that the Thames deal was unlikely to happen he was delighted.

During the week following the identification of Carlton as a possible bidder for Thames, public attention began to focus on the IBA and what its decision would be. But what should the IBA do when the two major shareholders in the largest ITV company – which was also the largest programme-supplier to the ITV network – were obviously reluctant shareholders? In a sense the IBA had contributed to the problem by insisting that the ITV companies should get a wide range of shareholders by floating on the Stock Exchange just like any other public company. Yet the ITV companies were not like any other company, and until the Green-Luckwell challenge it had simply been assumed they could not be taken over. Inevitable tensions were set up by the process of turning privately owned companies with detailed regulatory obligations into publicly quoted ones.

The controversy over Thames was in part caused by the element of ambiguity in the IBA responses to Green and Luckwell's approach – compounded by the genial and polite personality of Lord Thomson, who is, for a former politician, unusually willing to listen. That very openness was misinterpreted by Green, deliberately or otherwise.

'When I first met Michael Green I rather liked him. It seemed to me at that stage that he might in fact be a rather stimulating element in the structure of Thames. He has got great charm. I rather like people and am reasonably good-natured with them, and I think he might have misread my degree of pleasantness and my telling him that he might be a useful younger element within ITV into a belief that he could take over Thames,' Thomson recalls. But the IBA chairman insists that at a second meeting with Green, in October, he spelled out in words of one syllable exactly what the Authority's legal obligations were and the unambiguous legal advice it had been given. A takeover of Thames by Carlton was simply not on.

Thomson says that if he had realized at his first meeting with Green that he was planning to go behind the back of the IBA, negotiate a deal with Thorn and BET, and then try to present the Authority with a *fait accompli*, Green 'might have not been misled by geniality'.

The IBA chairman was astonished when Green even managed to persuade his cousin by marriage Stuart Young, the chairman of the BBC, to ring up in support of the Carlton case. It was an unprecedented intervention by a BBC chairman in the affairs of the ITV system, and it only made those at the top of the IBA more irritated.

Whitney also insists that he did not give Green explicit encouragement, and is backed up by entries made in his diary. 'Michael Green is a very charming, presentable tycoon, certainly the next generation of media boss. His enthusiasm for the merger was infectious. But the more I looked at his proposal the more I became concerned it was not a merger but a takeover,' Whitney wrote.

Green certainly believes he was encouraged in his ambitions by Lord Thomson and John Whitney, although a businessman who knows him well suggests that 'When someone says "No" it's a "Maybe" for Michael. When they say "Maybe" it's a definite "Yes".'

That week Carlton sent a rather confused letter to the IBA. 'Notwithstanding press speculation to the contrary, Carlton has legally binding agreements enabling it to buy BET's and Thorn's interests in Thames. Carlton is committed to public service broadcasting and for that reason is attracted by the possibility of a merger with Thames but will not intend to proceed without the approval of the IBA,' the letter said.

On Thursday 10 October, over breakfast, Whitney advised Lord Thomson that the IBA should delay no longer. The legal advice from the IBA's solicitors, Allen & Overy, was clear – the Authority would be wrong to allow the deal to go ahead. They decided it was time to end the uncertainly rather than wait until the next IBA meeting, scheduled for 16 October.

In the course of the morning Thomson and Whitney telephoned as many IBA members as they could find, and the decision to reject Carlton, already effectively taken, was ratified. Whitney then rang Dundas with news of the decision, and afterwards contacted Michael Green to read out a brief statement. The five-line announcement said, 'The Authority has concluded that the Carlton Communications proposal, which would lead to a major change in the nature and characteristics of a viable ITV company, is not acceptable, having regard to the Authority's responsibilities under the Broadcasting Act.'

Green was taken aback that the decision had been taken so soon, and in advance of a full IBA meeting, and expressed astonishment and dismay. That evening Michael Cox was driving into London on the way to a Royal Television Society seminar and heard the news of the IBA decision on his car radio. 'I was laughing so much I nearly drove off the road. There was very nearly a awful accident on the Edgware Road,' Cox recalls.

Green's fury at the IBA decision was great. He was initially tempted to call the IBA's bluff, as Rupert Murdoch would undoubtedly have done, and push ahead with the takeover of Thames and dare the IBA to remove the licence and readvertise it. Readvertising such an important licence would have caused enormous disruption, and the IBA might have been reluctant to take such an extreme step. 'I've got my contract – now take it away from me. Go to the courts! Go to the courts! Take away my licence! That would have been the Murdoch way,' Green concedes.

At Hambros, Michael Sorkin advised caution. It was not just a question of upsetting the Establishment: there were practical financial considerations too. If Carlton had bought Thames and the IBA had taken away the broadcasting licence, there would have been great commercial uncertainty which could easily have led to a collapse in the Carlton share price.

The Carlton chairman could have provoked a political row over the issue through Lord Young at the Department of Trade and Industry, but it is clear from comments Green made at the time that Young advised that it would be better to avoid an immediate confrontation and public row. The broadcasting world was going to change anyway, Young suggested. Mrs Thatcher was going to have a close look at broadcasting soon. Green decided to wait and play a longer game.

The long-term strategy was also advocated by a powerful new friend in television. The approach had been made in the usual Green way – through an intermediary. Johnny Goodman of Euston Films had inquired if Michael Grade would like to have lunch with his relative, Michael Green. The men hit it off 'like a house on fire from day one', says Grade.

Grade, the controller of BBC1, believed it was important not to challenge the IBA's decision, because 'What that said was, "I accept the rules of the game. I am going to be a player in future. If I challenge these people, even if I win, I will lose in the long term because these people have the power to screw me. I'll go quietly, regroup, and wait for the next round." And that was a very important decision and absolutely the right decision,' Grade suggests.

So the prize for Carlton if it had won control of Thames can only be guessed at. In the year to March 1985 Thames, with 2,400 employees, had produced pre-tax profits of only £8.7 million on a turnover of £167.9 million. It had taken a £13.6 million contribution from overseas programme sales to offset a £4.8 million loss on its main UK television business. The Thames financial performance represented a poor 5 per cent profit margin for a company with a virtual monopoly of television advertising in the London area during the week, although profits had been dragged down by industrial action. However, even setting aside opportunities to increase profits, the Thames programme library alone was probably worth the negotiated £82.45 million purchase price.

'In the end he [Green] didn't have the balls to go for it,' said a former Carlton employee who believes there was a good chance that Carlton would have won but that Green had not done enough groundwork for such a daring move. He had not spent the previous six months getting to know the people in the IBA and understanding how they thought. The move on Thames was too much of a crude smash-and-grab raid to be successful. In retrospect, the Thames deal was bungled – and bungled in a way that would eventually cost Carlton several hundred million pounds.

Green now believes he was probably too cautious and should have ploughed ahead in the hope that it would have led to a compromise that would have been in Carlton's favour. 'I believe with hindsight that we backed off when we shouldn't have,' says the Carlton chairman, who still sometimes thinks of the large amount of money Carlton would have made if it could have bought Thames Television for £82.45 million and married Carlton's style of vigorous cost-cutting and tight cash management to the Thames talent for programme-making.

Yet the IBA determination to block takeovers of ITV companies in mid-term survived two subsequent assaults, as first Ladbroke, the gambling and leisure group, and then the Rank Organisation tried to take over Granada.

The barrier blocking takeovers of ITV companies had one unintended consequence: change was held back, and evolutionary reform of commercial television was therefore less likely. 'If television stations could have changed hands previously, Mrs Thatcher might have discovered a television industry that was better run and not the last bastion of restrictive practices, and then the Broadcasting Bill might not have been produced,' Green suggests in a reference to the Conservative Prime Minister's radical assault on the television industry a few years later.

However important the IBA ruling on Thames was for ITV and British broadcasting, the saga had an equally fundamental significance for Carlton and the relationship between its two strong-minded partners. Green's decision to accept the IBA verdict on Thames contributed to a rift with Luckwell, who advised that Carlton should call the IBA's bluff and pull the plug. The evening that London screens went blank the rules would have changed, he believed.

The Carlton managing director had also been becoming increasingly irritated that the company was usually referred to in the press as 'Michael Green's Carlton Communications' – a description he felt Green had done nothing to discourage, even though Luckwell was a major shareholder and, he believed, had contributed many of the ideas behind Carlton's growth.

Until the move against Thames, however, the two partners had few difficulties in their working relationship beyond the normal give and take of two powerful and ambitious people who would occasionally disagree. The fact that the relationship had worked tolerably well probably owed a lot to there being an implicit understanding on the division of responsibilities which covered what they did separately and what they did together. Green had specialized in dealing with the City and the financial affairs of Carlton, while Luckwell had handled the business side of the operations – in particular the business of television, where his expertise lay. But during the Thames negotiations Green had attended meetings at IBA without Luckwell's knowledge – the first time this had happened. 'Suddenly he was dealing with the television people, on his own. He crossed an invisible line of demarcation, and we had a real bitter row about that. And within a few days of that row Thames hit the papers,' says Luckwell.

Green had not handled the IBA very well, Luckwell believed, and it had turned out to be counter-productive to ignore Dunn until it was virtually too late. Could the whole thing have been handled better? What if Green had been willing to accept a sizeable minority stake in Thames – something that might have been on offer? Then there could have been the chance before too long that BET and Thorn would have sold another tranche of shares, allowing Carlton to reach its desired destination by stealth over a year or two.

A number of issues eventually came together to persuade Luckwell it was time to go. They included the row with Green over their respective roles, the increasing size of the business, and the long hours he had to work. He wanted to be able to spend more time with his wife, Mary, and their young children, Adam and Victoria. He was also unwilling to wait patiently until the next ITV franchise round, in 1991, when Carlton could apply for the Thames licence. And he didn't expect the Carlton share price to increase much in the interim years. 'Certainly I did hold the view that we should have rattled the bars [over Thames], that is true. But that wasn't the cause of the row, or indeed the cause of my leaving. I think the cause of my leaving was when that deal fell through I certainly didn't want to sit and wait in Carlton for five or six years until the new round of franchises,' says Luckwell.

Those around at the time say Green 'went green' at the prospect of Luckwell's departure, and there were repeated attempts to persuade him to stay – particularly from Hambros Bank. When it was clear that Luckwell was determined to leave, a secret meeting was called one Sunday evening in February 1986 at the Inn on the Park to decide how the announcement should be handled to avoid destabilizing the company's share price. John Beedle, Luckwell's technical partner, had gone down to the south coast that day but was summoned back to attend the meeting with Green and Luckwell, together with a number of advisers.

It was agreed that Beedle would become a Carlton main-board director and that he would stay for a minimum of two years, to provide an element of continuity and a sense of stability. Before he went, Luckwell agreed to tour the institutions to explain that Carlton could manage perfectly well without him and that Green was a wonderful manager who could definitely cope on his own.

On 25 February 1986 it was announced that Luckwell had sold his 11 per cent stake in Carlton Communications for about £25.5 million and was resigning as managing director. Messel had placed the shares with institutional investors at 740p, compared with the market price the previous night of 820p. That day the Carlton share price initially fell 55p but rallied to close at 780p. The sale meant that Luckwell had earned more than £30 million from his stakes in first The Moving Picture Company and then Carlton. Green – chairman and chief executive of Carlton – told newspapers the parting with Luckwell was 'definitely amicable'.

After leaving Carlton, Luckwell took the first six-week holiday of his life, in the USA with his family, followed not long after by a six-month vacation. In 1986 he set up Parallel Media Group, a company specializing in sports sponsorship, and sold his stake four years later for a profit of £2.1 million. He made a further £2.1 million on a 5 per cent stake in TV-am, the commercial breakfast-television company bought from Jonathan and Timothy Aitken after the IBA required the Aitkens to sell their shares following a breach of the ownership rules.

Chapter 7

Satellite Adventures

The failure to win Thames and the departure of Luckwell were serious blows to Michael Green's broadcasting ambitions. But there was an exciting new opportunity – satellite television. Satellite offered the chance to get into a new venture at the beginning, and Green had been studying its potential for years. Instead of owning a small part of a complex and highly regulated channel like ITV, satellite television meant the latest technology could be used to launch a wholly commercial service – the sort of popular television that people would want to watch.

In 1982 the then Home Secretary, William Whitelaw, had offered the BBC the exclusive use of two of the five high-power DBS (direct broadcasting by satellite) channels awarded to every country in western Europe by the World Administrative Radio Conference, the international body that allocates broadcasting frequencies. The old low-power satellite system needed a large dish to receive the signal and so was often used to feed a cable network rather than broadcasting direct to homes; the new system worked with a much smaller dish, so it was hoped that the new technology would be more attractive to potential viewers. But the offer came with strings and enormous risks attached. The supposedly free-market Thatcher government wanted to provide a boost for British satellite technology and the consumer-electronics industry, so the BBC was to use a satellite system provided by United Satellites (Unisat), an all-British consortium which brought together GEC Marconi, British Aerospace and British Telecom. For good measure, the Home Office made it clear that it would like British DBS to use a system for transmitting pictures that was a variant of the MAC (Multiplexed Analogue Component) system developed largely by IBA engineers.

In January 1984 Alasdair Milne, the BBC director-general, and Stuart Young, the BBC chairman, decided that the risk the Corporation faced in launching a direct-broadcasting service on its own was too great. The cost would be at least £300 million over seven years, and there were no guarantees that the service would work. The project could have bankrupted the BBC.

The government's next move was to try to put together a consortium linking all of Britain's broadcasters with a group of private-sector companies.

The Club of 21 brought together the BBC, the fifteen ITV companies, Thorn EMI, Pearson, Virgin, Granada and Consolidated Satellite Broadcasting, a small independent producer. The odds were always against such an unwieldy group succeeding, in part because the ground rules had not changed: it still had to buy a British-made satellite system and use the sophisticated MAC technology. To no one's surprise, in June 1985 the Club of 21 members decided they could see no way of making the project financially viable. It looked like the end of DBS in Britain.

In 1985 Rupert Murdoch took control of a service using an existing experimental satellite to broadcast Sky to a small number of cabled homes in Scandinavia and Germany before later expanding into the UK. Partly to counter this threat, the ITV companies – or most of them – had another satellite venture in mind. All but Thames were planning the launch of Super Channel, a 'best of British' channel, aimed at the cable networks of continental Europe and designed to blow what they saw as Murdoch's cheap and tacky Sky channel out of the market.

One of the few who persevered with the apparent lost cause of DBS was John Jackson, chairman of Celltech, the British biotechnology company, and a director of the consumer-electronics company Philips UK. In 1985 Jackson persuaded the government that it was worth another attempt to launch DBS in the UK, and the IBA was asked to seek expressions of interest to see whether there was any point in formally advertising a franchise for three channels.

One of the most enthusiastic of a dozen expressions of interest came from Michael Green and Carlton Communications. The Carlton chairman told the IBA he could put together a consortium of 'significant companies', but he emphasized he was prepared to go ahead only if the government allowed the operator to use the satellite of its choice and have the freedom to broadcast whatever programmes it wanted to – subject to the normal rules on taste, decency and impartiality.

In Carlton's 1985 annual report Green noted that DBS would provide the company with new opportunities for the provision of both services and products. 'The Company has held discussions with the IBA and other interested parties and it is hoped that minimal Government regulations and an "open skies" policy will provide the catalyst for this new industry to become established,' Green wrote. The 'open skies' policy he was referring to was the right to buy the best and most economical satellites from American companies such as Hughes Aircraft or RCA.

On 2 April 1986 the IBA advertised three DBS channels, and Green began putting together a powerful consortium to apply for the new franchise. The deadline for applications was 29 August 1986.

By then Green had put a toe into a market that scarcely existed in the UK – providing satellite equipment for the domestic viewer. Carlton had bought a company called Skyscan Systems, set up to import motorized satellite receivers from Canada. Skyscan was the idea of Terry Goldberg, an entrepreneur who had worked as a logistics consultant for companies such as Honda and Unilever. While travelling in the USA he had visited a cable and satellite show in Tulsa and saw the 'backyard' satellite systems that Americans were starting to use to watch television channels broadcast by what were essentially telecommunications satellites. On his return to England, Goldberg saw an article in the *Daily Telegraph* reporting that the Department of Trade and Industry had decided to allow individuals to own satellite receivers for a one-off licence fee of £10, although planning permission was still required. But when Goldberg tried to buy a satellite receiver in the UK he found that the price was £3,000.

Goldberg tracked down a number of North American manufacturers and put together a motorized satellite receiver adapted for the European market at a much lower cost than anything available at the time. 'Ten months to the day after I visited the Tulsa exhibition we had all the bits together, but we needed to raise funding. If we could place orders with various manufacturers for a minimum of 10,000 systems I thought I could get them made for £700 a system,' says Goldberg. When he hawked his concept around the City of London looking for money no one was interested.

But then Goldberg's wife, Maggie, spotted a *Financial Times* article about Carlton's interest in satellite television. She telephoned Michael Green and was given two minutes to make her case. The Carlton chairman was immediately interested, and Luckwell was dispatched to Goldberg's house in Camberley to see his system in operation. The report was positive, and tough negotiations got under way at once between Green and Goldberg, who had already spent £100,000 on the project. 'I got stripped. He paid £35,000 for my outstanding bills, a twelve-month contract at £35,000, and a guarantee to spend £4.5 million [on the project] – plus a percentage of profits on sales for me,' says Goldberg.

The deal was rushed through at 2 a.m. on 5 March 1986, so that Goldberg could make an announcement that day in a speech given at the *Financial Times* Cable and Satellite Conference. He told delegates he had signed a preliminary contract with a 'major British PLC, who have seen the development potential in this new market and are providing us with the funding and facilities for Skyscan Systems to play a major part in establishing this new industry'. Carlton was not mentioned. But before long 10,000 dishes 1.2 metres in diameter and capable of receiving up to twenty-four channels started arriving at a warehouse near Maidenhead found by the man Carlton appointed to run the venture, Ray Brassington of Video Time.

Not long afterwards, following a dispute over arrangements to make payments to a Canadian supplier through a Swiss bank account, Goldberg left abruptly with £18,500 compensation. A £400,000 launch and marketing plan was drawn up, but Skyscan quickly turned out to be a financial disaster. At a retail price of £1,500 the systems were too expensive, the dishes were too large, and the programme choice available was still too poor.

John Jeffrey of IVC, who was increasingly taking on the role of sorting out problems and burying bodies at Carlton, was sent to Maidenhead to do something about the warehouse stuffed with thousands of satellite receivers. The equipment was sold off for about one-third of what it had cost, and Carlton wrote off several million pounds.

But the DBS venture would be different from Skyscan. Three national channels would be aimed specifically at the UK and, because of the high power of the satellites, the dishes needed to receive them would be little bigger than dinner plates. Direct broadcasting by satellite, Green forecast, would be the main broadcasting opportunity of the 1990s.

Green drew on his friends and business contacts to put together a powerful consortium to bid for the satellite franchise under the name DBS UK. Saatchi & Saatchi were in the group, as were LWT and Hambros Bank. Also attracted by the concept and Green's growing business reputation were Columbia Pictures International Television, consumer-electronics retailers Dixons, and Robert Fleming, the merchant bank. The founder shareholders in DBS UK agreed to put up £70 million. A further £90 million was to be raised from institutions. One channel would have news, business and sport; a second would concentrate on entertainment; and the third would be offered to the ITV Super Channel to make it available to a wider audience in the UK. DBS UK was proposing that £25 million should be spent on original programmes in the first year, with a gradual rise to £450 million a year by the year 2004. All three channels were to be financed by advertising, and the consortium was forecasting profits of more than £100 million a year by the end of the 1990s.

However, the Carlton-led consortium was just one of five plausible groupings to apply for the franchise, all attracted by the fact that the official mood had clearly changed and a greater degree of commercial freedom was being conceded to the operator. The front runner, British Satellite Broadcasting (BSB), was made up of five British companies with a combined turnover of more than £2 billion – Amstrad Consumer Electronics, Anglia Television, Granada, Pearson and Virgin. BSB was planning four distinct programme services – one of them a film channel to be funded by subscription; the rest to be paid for by advertising.

The other player who could not be ruled out was John Jackson, because of his feel for what was technically possible and his widespread corporate contacts. His consortium Direct Broadcasting Ltd (DBL) brought together British and Commonwealth Shipping, Cambridge Electronic Industries, Electronic Rentals, Ferranti, Sears, and Rupert Murdoch's News International and planned to use subscription to fund the service. Jackson says he had the greatest difficulty in persuading Murdoch to join the consortium. Murdoch was wary of the IBA because in 1971 its predecessor had blocked changes he believed were essential to turn round LWT in its troubled early days when the Australian newspaperman had saved the ITV company from near collapse. Even though his stake in LWT had long been sold, Murdoch was very sceptical about whether he would get a fair hearing.

There had been weeks of manoeuvring between members of the various groupings to try to put together an unbeatable consortium, with Sir Denis Forman, the distinguished Granada Television executive, trying to persuade Jackson of the importance of protecting British public-service broadcasting from the influence of Murdoch. Jackson went to see Green to discuss whether there was any possibility of their two consortia getting together. 'We came to the conclusion that we were on completely different tracks. He believed that the correct way to finance satellite television was advertising income, and I didn't believe it could be got off the ground on that basis and that subscription would have to feature largely in it. We decided to remain good friends and go our separate ways,' says Jackson, who was nonetheless impressed by Green's intelligence and forthright manner.

Michael Green was keen to win the satellite franchise, and an enormous amount of work was put into the DBS UK application. The bid was largely put together by Charles Wigoder of Carlton, Rod Allen, head of new developments at LWT, and Alex Kenny, media director of Saatchi & Saatchi. Wigoder constructed a basic plan. He and Allen then spent months of detailed work on the application, with Kenny supplying the advertising expertise. The programme plans were relatively cheap and populist – exactly what was required to make a viable business out of DBS but probably not what the IBA wanted to hear. Everyone knew the best plan when submitting franchise applications to broadcasting regulators was to include lots of high-quality current-affairs and arts programmes to win the licence. Then, if there was not enough money to offer such an expensive programme choice, financial imperatives could always be blamed for being forced to make the schedule changes necessary to survive. BSB, for instance, was promising that Independent Television News would be tied into the project to provide a high-quality news service on one of the satellite channels.

Despite his experience over the failed Thames takeover, Green had not yet learned the gentle art of doffing his cap to the regulator. In DBS UK's formal interview with the IBA director-general, John Whitney asked what was probably the killer question: 'Are there any circumstances in which you would consider adding a subscription movie channel?' For better or worse the answer from Allen, who represented the consortium at the hearing and was committed to a service funded by advertising, was an emphatic 'No.' 'That stuffed it for us. No question. But I thought we needed to become a dominant broadcaster rather than a niche player, which Sky still is,' said Allen.

Jackson was not at all optimistic about DBL's chances. At his interview at the IBA he had been alarmed to notice that Lord Thomson, whom he had known for years, was avoiding his gaze. And right at the end, after more than an hour of inconsequential questions, it was Thomson who said the director-general had one final question and passed the knife to Whitney to wield. 'If we gave you the franchise, would it be correct to say we would be offering it as a mother ship for Sky?' asked Whitney. Jackson absolutely denied that Murdoch's presence in the DBL consortium meant any such thing. 'But I felt six inches of cold steel between my ribs,' he says, and he believed then that the Murdoch factor was going to be his undoing. Later, when Murdoch's Sky was making all sorts of trouble for the UK's official DBS project, Jackson told Lord Thomson that it would surely have been far better 'to have had Murdoch in the tent pissing out rather than outside the tent pissing in'.

On the afternoon of 11 December all the applicants were summoned to the IBA headquarters and were placed in separate rooms to receive the envelopes spelling out the fate of their applications. Green drove Rod Allen and Christopher Bland of LWT there in his Bentley, and they were shown into the bleak ante-room of the IBA's personnel department, where they waited in creaky old armchairs. 'David Glencross came in wearing a slightly outdated suit – it had flared trousers. He produced this envelope and handed it to Christopher and said, "The director-general has asked me to give you this." And then he fled,' Allen remembers. It was the thanks-for-applying-but-no-thanks letter.

The winner was BSB – a consortium which Lord Thomson said 'contains the reality of the present with the vision of the future'. The former IBA chairman admits that behind closed doors there had been an almost theological debate about the merits of particular funding methods. Was Green's advertising route best, or was Jackson's subscription method the more powerful? To the IBA the hybrid option – BSB's mixture of advertising and subscription – seemed the right compromise, and that is why the consortium was chosen. In fact subsequent events have proved Jackson to have been closest to a workable solution. Satellite television, whether direct to the home or relayed through cable networks, has turned out to be primarily a subscription business, and channels based entirely on advertising have found it very difficult to make a profit even on a pan-European basis.

The DBS UK approach was fundamentally flawed, and the consortium members could each have lost many millions if it had won the licence. Green was lucky he was merely a runner-up. Bland says the advertising error was largely his, although it was an approach fully supported by Green. Bland thought that the release of films on video for purchase and rental would be totally dominant and that few people would be interested in paying to see a film subscription channel at a later date. 'And that was just totally wrong – totally, totally, totally,' says Bland, who accepts that the economics of an advertising-financed satellite service would not have been good.

After the DBS UK representatives had had time to absorb the bleak news in their letter, Glencross, then IBA director of television, came back to see whether they wanted to attend the press conference where the winners were about to be announced. They did not. On the drive back along Knightsbridge and down Piccadilly, Green and Bland were shocked to have lost. It was Green's second failure at the hands of the regulators of commercial broadcasting.

But Green at least had the Carlton Communications year-end financial results, which came out four days later, on 15 December, to cheer him up. Carlton was doing very well indeed. In the year to September 1986 Carlton had increased pre-tax profits by 57 per cent, to £18.8 million on a turnover of £58.3 million – boosted by the continued success in the USA of Abekas, which helped Carlton's North American profits to more than double to £5.17 million. In November 1985 Carlton had sold The Fleet Street Letter and the other Carlton Publishing businesses to Barham, the media-services group, for £12.3 million in cash – a sum that was treated as an extraordinary item and not included in Carlton's pre-tax profit figure. Despite the sale, Nigel Wray agreed to remain as a Carlton non-executive director. Carlton now had nearly

900 employees. Its investments in shares were growing rapidly too – the market value of its quoted investments at the end of the year had risen from £3 million to £12.9 million. By then Carlton was worth a total of £367 million.

David Green, however, began spending more and more time at Colefax & Fowler, the upmarket wallpaper, home-furnishings and interior-decoration company founded in 1934 by John Fowler and Lady Sibyl Colefax. Jacob Rothschild became a director in 1985 and in 1986 brought in David Green as 40 per cent shareholder for £3.2 million – a deal financed by a sale of 500,000 Carlton shares. At that time Michael Green also took control over all the shares in Carlton owned by the two brothers. For the first time the 2.665 million shares were held by a subsidiary of Tangent controlled by Michael Green; in 1985 the shares had been held in Tangent Industries Group, owned by David and Michael Green. It marked a symbolic change – David Green had been withdrawing from Carlton for some time. Increasingly he found the stress of working full-time for such a company to be uncongenial. He was far more interested in working in an artistic business, and in a much smaller business such as Colefax & Fowler. When the interior-decorating group floated on the Stock Exchange in 1988 David Green became chief executive.

The discussions over the DBS satellite venture helped to find a new managing director for Carlton. The choice – if not an exactly an entrepreneur with killer instincts like Luckwell – was to be a credible managing director for a growing public company and an ideal man to lead the Carlton campaign to win an ITV franchise when the licences were next advertised. Green had first met Bob Phillis, then the managing director of Sun Printers in Watford, in 1977, when Green had poached his finance director, Paul Harding, for Tangent Industries. The two had met again at a private dinner organized by Messel, the stockbrokers which organized the Carlton reverse takeover flotation and which had also placed shares in Central Independent Television with institutional investors after Phillis became managing director in 1981. The dinner led Green and Phillis to indulge in a minor corporate courtesy one level higher than sending each other Christmas cards: the exchange of annual reports.

Phillis, a cheerful, stocky man, is not an entrepreneur – he has never started a company of his own – but is an experienced and talented executive. Brought up on a council estate in Croydon, he left school to become an apprentice in the printing trade and became a member of SLADE, the Society of Lithographic Artists, Designers, Engravers and Process Workers. The young apprentice printer continued studying in the evenings, and then

Bob Phillis (right) with John Birt

went to Nottingham University to read industrial economics as a twenty-year-old 'mature student', supported by his wife, Jean, and weekly collections from his SLADE union branch. After stints at Thomson Regional Newspapers and the British Printing Corporation, he became a lecturer at both Edinburgh University and the Scottish Business School before becoming personnel manager and then managing director of Sun Printers.

His move into television came by accident. Phillis tendered for the printing contract for *TV Times*, published by Independent Television Publications, a subsidiary of the ITV companies, and instead was offered the managing director's job in 1979. Two years later he became managing director of Central Independent Television, the second largest ITV company, and virtually a new company. The IBA had insisted that a new dual region based on both Birmingham and Nottingham should be carved out of Lord Grade's ATV empire, with the additional specification that 49 per cent of the shares held by Grade's holding company ACC had to be sold. 'The franchise had been awarded to a company that didn't have a name, that wasn't financed, didn't have a chief executive, didn't have a site for its second studio [Nottingham] and which had to get rid of 49 per cent of its shares. I am absolutely certain three or four industry figures were approached before me,' is how Phillis described the task he faced.

Given the enormous difficulties posed by the reorganization, the Central managing director had been pleased at what had been achieved. It wasn't just that the restructuring had been successfully financed and new shareholders – Sears, Ladbroke, BPC and D. C. Thomson – had been found. Equally important, Central had quickly found a programme-making voice with productions such as *Auf Wiedersehen, Pet* and *Spitting Image*.

Green had come into contact with Phillis again in the early stages of the DBS venture in 1986. The Carlton chairman had driven to Nottingham for a private lunch with Phillis to see whether Central could be persuaded to join the DBS consortium. The Midlands television group had already been deep in talks with Granada, but in the end the Central board, and Ladbroke in particular, rejected Phillis's recommendation that the company join BSB, deciding that the project was too risky. Phillis had accepted the verdict but was disappointed and irritated that the board had rejected his recommendation on such a fundamental issue. He had hoped that Central could expand beyond ITV and establish a broader base in the television industry.

It did not take Green long to learn that Phillis's satellite proposal had been blocked by the Central board and invite him to another lunch. Was Phillis frustrated enough to be amenable to a move? Green came for further confidential chats at Phillis's home, a former vicarage in the Berkshire village of Wargrave, and made him a beguiling offer. To Phillis it was not just a question of money, although Green was offering to almost double what Central was paying – a salary of £150,000 a year compared with the £75–80,000 he was getting at Central. The real issue was the future. Central had, symbolically at least, turned its back on new opportunities. In contrast, with customary plausibility and charm, Green was selling his vision of the future. Carlton would be going for all the media opportunities available and was determined to become a major international media player. Phillis could become a key part of that adventure.

For Phillis, who places a considerable premium on loyalty, the opportunity posed an enormous dilemma. Although Green's offer was attractive, Phillis had built up Central from scratch and was proud of the team he had assembled. It included talented television executives such as Charles Denton, Margaret Matheson and Andy Allan.

In the end Green set a deadline. The Carlton chairman was in Ireland on holiday with Jeananne Crowley but said he would call on a particular day for his answer. Phillis said yes, and on 11 November 1986 it was announced that Carlton was to get a new group managing director from 1 February 1987.

The appointment was generally seen as a coup for Michael Green. He had managed to entice one of the new generation of top managers away from the glamorous world of network television. Phillis would join the tiny Carlton head-office staff still based in the bleak, uninspiring New Roman House headquarters of a supplier of technical services to the television industry. Richard Dunn, the Thames chief executive, described the Phillis move as 'a great loss for ITV. I think Michael Green has made a shrewd acquisition. I think the board of Central must be crazy to let him [Phillis] go.'

At the same time as Green was pursuing Phillis, the Carlton chairman was in turn being sounded out for his first public role – and a remarkable opportunity for someone with just three O-levels.

For years professionals in the world of further and continuing education had been interested in exploiting television more creatively as an educational tool. The Open University (OU), which used both radio and television to back up its texts, had been a great success, but little was being done to improve the skills and knowledge of adults who had left school early but who were not academic enough to study for a university degree. It was a problem that had interested Naomi Sargant for years. Her career had begun in market research before moving into education through the OU, where she became pro-vice-chancellor for student affairs. In 1981 she joined Channel 4 as Jeremy Isaac's first senior commissioning editor for educational programming.

An opportunity had opened up when the IBA had asked Channel 4 to devote around 15 per cent of its broadcasting time to educational material. Yet Channel 4 failed in its attempts to develop a partnership with the Manpower Services Commission, the government training agency, along the lines of the BBC's partnership with the OU – mainly because the MSC insisted on editorial control in return for putting up money for programming. But by 1985 there was a chance to try again, partly because schools programmes were moving from ITV to Channel 4. This meant that Channel 4 transmitters would have to open up early, and it would be easy to add extra educational programmes for the unemployed or anyone in need of further vocational training.

This time what Geoffrey Holland of the MSC had in mind was a College of the Air using transmitter 'down time' – the time when transmitters are not being used for conventional broadcasts. The concept was fleshed out at a series of informal dinners attended by people such as Sargant and Sheila Innes, the BBC's head of educational broadcasting, although the intention was that Channel 4 should be the lead broadcaster. Sargant thought the College should be able to build up to 50,000 students among the employed and unemployed over five years. The then chief executive of ICI, John Harvey-Jones, was mentioned as a possible chairman.

When Holland approached Lord Young, then Employment Secretary, with the College of the Air proposal, Young thought it was a tremendous idea. But when Young was presented with the usual list of notables he had other ideas about who the chairman should be. He wanted someone young, enthusiastic and less obvious. The new college was going to use television, and Young knew a man obsessed by television – his cousin by marriage, Michael Green. 'One day I rang him up and said, "Come and have breakfast, Michael. Come on – you can't spend all your time making money. I've got a job for you that doesn't pay anything, and you should do it,"' Young says. Over breakfast Green was offered the chairmanship of what was to become the Open College. He leaped at the opportunity.

Lord Young has expressed incomprehension that he could be accused by the press of nepotism for offering a relative a job that carried no salary – although this ignores intangible benefits such as positive publicity, fame, an enhanced reputation, and some day perhaps a knighthood or even a peerage. For Young it was enough that Green was 'a fully paid-up member of the band of enthusiasts. If enthusiasm and drive could make this work I knew we were in good hands.'

Sargant heard just after Easter that Green was going to be the chairman of the College, and her heart sank. She feared it was a political appointment. But, despite her reservations, she rang Green to ask if she could help to bring him up to speed. Green turned up that very evening.

Sargant was struck by Green's sense of life and enthusiasm and she was favourably impressed until he started to ask jarring questions. 'This was the very first time I had ever met him. He came to my office. We talked a bit about the idea, where it had got to, how he felt about it all. And then in this very first, completely informal conversation, in the evening after work, he asked me about my age and politics,' she says. She got over her surprise quickly enough to describe herself as an old-fashioned democratic socialist who had once been a Labour local councillor. She left Green to deduce that she was in her early fifties.

The press release confirming that the thirty-eight-year-old Green was to be the first chairman of the Open College went out on 10 September 1986. 'The College is about making it easier for people to learn, at their own pace, more about the practical things that interest them and about the skills that they use at work,' Green's official quote read. He explained that he had a long-standing interest in psychology – in particular the psychology of abnormality and its relationship to creativity. He even revealed an ill-starred attempt to take up the study of psychology. The bid had been abandoned, he claimed, because he could not grasp the importance of devoting time to the study of rats rather than people. The Carlton chairman also said he was interested in the relationships between human motivation and industry, especially in the field of industrial relations. And the press release mentioned that he had two daughters – Rebecca, aged twelve, and Catherine, aged ten – but there was no mention of a wife. Following their separation, Janet Wolfson Green was being airbrushed out of the story.

The *Jewish Chronicle* also covered Green's appointment, and he added some ethnic colour for this report. 'As the opening is adjacent to Rosh Hashanah [the Jewish New Year] I would like my wish granted for 50,000 students in our first year, which should give my mother even more *nachas* [combined pride and pleasure].'

The perception that the Open College was at least partly aimed at the needs of the unemployed – encouraged by an early leak in the *Sunday Times* headlined 'College for the Jobless' – appealed to both Holland and Sargant. Trying to improve the lives of the unemployed and perhaps offer them a way back to the labour market had been one of the points of planning to broadcast vocational programmes at lunchtime on Channel 4. Yet Green berated Sargant on the issue. The Open College wasn't meant to deal with the unemployed, he insisted. The argument erupted again that week at a launch reception in the offices of the Open College. 'He [Green] was absolutely incandescent with me and said that he had never agreed that he would be chairman of a "College for the Jobless",' said Sargant. Green's main worry was that a college for the unemployed could not be financed. Indeed the Treasury opposed the inclusion of the unemployed on the grounds of cost – additional public money would have to be found for what could, in theory, be large numbers of unemployed students. But the decision not to include the growing army of the unemployed in its target audience meant that from the outset the College stood little chance of meeting its target for student numbers.

Setting up the College was made even more complex when the BBC decided it did not want to be left out of the venture. Lord Young went with Green to see his brother Stuart, the BBC chairman. As a result, all sectors of British broadcasting were going to be involved in the Open College – thereby confusing the audience, weakening the College's identity, and greatly irritating Channel 4.

The politics of broadcasting – not to mention straight party politics – also bedevilled the vital choice of who should be the first chief executive of the college. Sargant decided not to apply, because she did not believe she would get the job and she had no intention of making up the numbers on the short list. However, a senior Department of Employment civil servant called to urge her to reconsider, and in the next post there was a copy of the job advertisement with a personal compliments slip from Green.

After a detailed interrogation by the head-hunters, Sargant was put at the top of the short list. But just before the interview Jeremy Isaacs, the chief executive of Channel 4, told her he had heard on the grapevine that Sheila Innes was in the frame for the job. Innes said later she had been approached personally by Green.

Apart from Green, the interviewing panel was made up of Holland of the MSC, John Whitney of the IBA, and Lord Dartington, the noted educationalist. Sargant says Green once again asked her directly about her politics. By an unfortunate coincidence her husband, Lord McIntosh, had just been appointed Labour's front-bench spokesman on education in the Lords.

Green insisted the job should go to the BBC's education director, Innes – a perfectly plausible candidate, though not one with as wide a range of experience as Sargant. 'When one knows that Geoffrey, Michael [Lord Dartington] and John Whitney all sat there wanting me to do the job – I know this – I'm absolutely certain it's politics,' says Sargant, who still quivers with rage when recounting how she was treated by Green.

The chances that the Open College would fulfil the hopes of its more optimistic supporters were finally blighted when, after a review, the Treasury decided that the Open College would receive funding for only three years and then would have to be self-financing.

During those months when Green was trying to win a satellite television licence from the IBA and was becoming a member of the 'great and the good' he never forgot the Carlton imperative – to expand, acquire, and drive earnings per share upwards. The stream of acquisitions strengthening Carlton's presence in the British television market, while at the same time adding to its presence in the USA, never stopped.

It was Green himself who was responsible for the first American purchase since Abekas. Green and John Beedle had been visiting the National Association of Broadcasters convention in Las Vegas, where all the latest television technology is on display, and were about to head for home when Green heard that the Complete Post-Production Center – one of the leading Hollywood post-production facilities companies, whose customers ranged from the US television networks to film studios – was available for sale. Green asked Beedle to go to Los Angeles immediately and check the company out.

Beedle liked the company – whereas MPC had six editing suites, Complete Post had twenty – and he was impressed by the men who ran it, Ed Migliore and Neal Rydall. Complete Post was one of the top ten television-facilities companies in the USA and was renowned for the quality of its work. Like MPC in the UK, it was able to charge premium prices. The company was non-union, and editors, motivated by profit incentives, worked whatever hours were required. Beedle produced a glowing report.

A deal was structured and finalized in time to be announced on 23 May 1986 in conjunction with Carlton's results for the six months to the end of March. Carlton's half-year results showed pre-tax profits of £8.2 million on turnover of £27.23 million. Carlton sold 2.3 million new shares to finance the £20.8 million purchase of Complete Post, and both Migliore and Rydall stayed on to run the business. The City liked the combined acquisition and financial news, and Carlton shares were marked up 40p on the day, to 920p.

The next American deal was only seven months away. This time it was Beedle who spotted the potential. A prospectus came in from a bank offering Gordon Enterprises for sale. When Beedle investigated he found a larger-than-life character called Herb Gordon who had cornered the market in radio commercials in New York City and also specialized in recording the soundtracks for television advertisements. As with Complete Post, the prices charged by Gordon Enterprises were at the upper end of the range. Carlton bought the company, run by Herb Gordon and Donna Levis, in December 1986 for £14.7 million in cash, and used the acquisition for a rapid expansion in New York City. More than $12 million was invested in creating a sister company, Post Perfect, to capitalize on Gordon's reputation and expand into the complementary video side of the television-commercial market.

That December, as Green unveiled his 50 per cent increase in pre-tax profit to £18.81 million for the year to the end of September 1986, the Carlton chairman also had an important announcement for the City that reflected the recent activity in Los Angeles and New York. 'In view of the importance of the United States to the company, Carlton intends to make an offering of its ordinary shares, in ADR form, which it is intended will be admitted for quotation through the NASDAQ exchange,' Green said.

ADRs – American depository receipts – offer a convenient way for Americans to invest in British companies. The dollar-denominated ADRs are backed by normal sterling shares in a company held in trust by an American bank. The plan to get a quotation on NASDAQ, the second-largest stock market in the USA, was an important statement of the scale of Carlton's ambition and its determination to tap the American capital markets as well as the City of London. Companies such as Saatchi & Saatchi had made the journey to New York before Carlton, but it was still unusual then and a sign of Green's continuing ambition.

In January, Green, Wigoder and Giles Coode-Adams of Messel toured the US financial community in a thirteen-day 'dog and pony show' to tell the Carlton story. Although Phillis had not yet formally joined Carlton, Central had agreed to a request from Green that he be released early to join the US tour.

Normally Green is not the easiest person to travel with. He has to be everywhere in good time, and everything has got to be just right. This time, apart from business, there was the distraction of his new love, Jeananne. Calls of some intimacy were placed with almost embarrassing frequency by Green from the car phones of stretched limousines in front of his financial team.

The trip took in New York, Chicago, San Francisco, Houston and Boston. Carlton was seen as a company that had achieved a lot very quickly, and there was a great deal of curiosity. The meetings with analysts in each city were well attended. 'It went reasonably well. It wasn't the blow-out which the UK one [the float] was, but people liked the style of Michael and Bob Phillis. The combination was a very good one,' Coode-Adams believes.

On 30 January 1987 Carlton made its Wall Street début, underwritten by the US investment house Shearson Lehman, by offering 4.6 million shares in the form of ADRs at $16.50. This raised £49 million for the UK company.

Despite the new emphasis on America, acquisitions also continued in the UK. They ranged from small add-ons to existing businesses – some more central to the Carlton strategy than others – to much more significant departures. In February 1987 Carlton paid £5.48 million in cash for Comelin, a Bedfordshire-based manufacturer of specialist printed circuit boards which had been a subsidiary of Matra, the large French electronics and defence group. And, of much greater importance, the first steps towards finally getting a significant stake in ITV were taken on Concorde that month when Green found himself on the same flight to the UK from New York as Cyril Stein, chairman of Ladbroke.

Green passed a note to Stein asking if he would sell Ladbroke's 20 per cent stake in Central, suggesting a price of more than £5 a share. Stein was not particularly anxious to sell, but he talked it over with John Jackson, a Ladbroke director, and Keith Edelman, a senior Ladbroke executive who, like Green, was a former pupil of Haberdashers' Aske's School. They decided that, at the right price, everything was for sale. Jackson mentioned that he had a gut instinct that they should not sell. 'You may be right,' said Stein, 'but I

think we had better accept.' The price agreed was 578p a share, or a total of
£29.5 million. Carlton paid for the Central shares with £18.2 million in cash
and the issuing of 1 million new shares. The Carlton share price had
continued to rise and stood at more than £11 when the Central stake was
bought.

The deal, announced on 15 March 1987, which finally brought Green into
the ITV system represented a remarkable return on Ladbroke's original
investment. Ladbroke had paid 120p a share, or £6.1 million, for its Central
shares in 1983. Yet Jackson's gut instinct had been right – Ladbroke could
have made much more if it had held on.

The purchase meant that Phillis hardly ever left Central. His last Central
board meeting as managing director had been in January 1987. He missed the
February board meeting for diplomatic reasons while the talks were under
way between Green and Stein, but by March he was back on the Central
board representing Carlton as a non-executive director.

In June, in the middle of the continuing acquisition programme, Wigoder
left Carlton, determined to become an entrepreneur in his own right. The
departure of Wigoder, who ran the successful People's Phone company until a
boardroom row in January 1996, caused bitterness, because Green likes to tell
people when they are leaving, not the other way around. There were also
important personal consequences for Green. The previous year there had
been an addition to the small Carlton head-office staff – an ambitious young
woman called Tessa Buckmaster. Buckmaster, who had been orphaned during
her first year at Oxford, had written to the chairmen of a number of public
companies looking for a job as a personal assistant. She had been hired by
Wigoder as his PA.

For a while it was not clear whether Buckmaster would make it at Carlton.
She was not a 'yes girl', and Green warned her on a number of occasions that
if she wasn't careful she would be out. However, Wigoder was not replaced
and Buckmaster began to work much more closely with Green as she
gradually took on Wigoder's former role in planning acquisitions.

On 25 September 1987 Green added an acquisition that was of far greater
strategic significance than the price tag implied. Central felt forced to sell
Zenith, its programme-production subsidiary, because of government
insistence that independent producers should have access to 25 per cent of
the UK's four national television channels. As a wholly owned subsidiary of
an ITV company, Zenith would not qualify as an independent for the
purposes of the 25 per cent quota and might find it more difficult to get
commissions from ITV companies. Carlton's new close relationship with

Central helped to clinch the acquisition of Zenith for £6.3 million. It turned Carlton into the largest independent production company in the UK, with £30 million worth of programmes in production.

With Zenith, which gave Carlton its greatest presence so far in programme production, came the former Central executives who ran the company, Charles Denton and Margaret Matheson. Zenith had made films such as *Wish You Were Here* and *Personal Services*, as well as one of the most popular series on ITV – *Inspector Morse*, featuring the opera-loving Oxford detective played by John Thaw. Carlton could now effortlessly attach its name to a stream of classy drama and films produced by someone else.

A few questions were raised about the possibility that the Zenith sale had been a 'sweetheart deal'. Carlton, after all, had a stake in Central, and Phillis had even been chairman of Zenith. Could the new Central managing director, Leslie Hill, have got more than the £6.3 million purchase price by holding an auction for the production company? In reply to that question, Central said that bankers S. G. Warburg had been brought in specially to ensure the selling price was fair. Besides, Central would not have sold to Carlton unless Denton and Matheson had agreed. Without their experience, skills and contacts there would have been little to sell other than a small catalogue of programmes.

At their first meeting Denton had been struck by the 'huge charm' of his new potential owner. 'When Michael wants something, his charm knows no bounds. He was intelligent, civilized, witty – all-round an attractive potential owner. So we succumbed,' he says. There were also attractive incentives if profit targets were met. 'He [Green] had no interest whatever in what was being proposed editorially, except in the financial context – a risk. This was an ideal stance really, and only became soured when it was quite clear the company wasn't making financial advances at the rate that he wanted,' says Denton, who has a reputation in the television industry for being both straight and determined. Zenith found it very difficult to meet its profit forecasts because uncertainty in ITV over future government broadcasting policy greatly reduced programme commissioning.

Green, Denton believes, persevered with the company because there was a larger purpose for Zenith than adding immediately to Carlton's earnings per share. 'Michael wanted for strategic reasons to demonstrate that he was interested in and sympathetic to production and had a quality production company in being. One of the things he was quite clearly missing at the time of the Thames disaster, when he failed to buy Thames, was any kind of track record in that area,' he says.

Indeed, despite the indifferent profit performance of Zenith, Green soon added another independent production company to his roster. Jeremy Fox, the television-producer son of Sir Paul Fox, the former controller of BBC1, had built up his own company, Action Time, by buying the UK rights to American game shows. He then either produced them in the UK or packaged the concept for other producers, such as the ITV companies. Jeremy Fox wanted to sell a majority stake in Action Time to concentrate on developing a joint Hollywood venture with Scottish Television.

Under the understanding reached with Jeremy Fox, Carlton was to buy 75 per cent of Action Time for a small up-front sum and further payments linked to turnover and profit over five years. Fox would keep the remaining 25 per cent. On the day the deal was due to be formalized Fox was told Green wanted 100 per cent or nothing. Fox was unhappy but decided he had no option. He was on his way to Los Angeles, and a successor, Steve Leahy, had already resigned from his job at Granada to run the company. Yet, as the months passed, Fox received hardly any money. Many excuses and explanations were given, but payments came only in dribs and drabs and Fox found it difficult to get detailed information on how Action Time – now part of Zenith – was performing financially. It was to take three and a half years of complaints, solicitors' letters and finally a threat to sue Carlton before Fox got a cheque in settlement. Fox has never worked with Green again.

The next US acquisition was very important in a different way. It took Carlton into the videocassette-duplication market for the first time. The purchase was of Modern Video, an innovative Philadelphia-based video-duplication business which had also just opened a plant at Helmond in the Netherlands. One of the Carlton Video Time executives had brought a tape about the company to show Beedle. It was not long before the Carlton technical specialist flew off to Philadelphia to investigate.

Modern Video, founded by an entrepreneur called Gene Mason, was using the latest technology to take on the giants of the duplication industry, Technicolor of the USA and the Rank Organisation of the UK. To turn out copies of the latest video, Technicolor and Rank simply lined up dozens and dozens of 'slave' video recorders linked together to copy from a master tape in 'real time'. To get a copy of a two-hour feature film took two hours. Mason had speeded up the process, and Modern Video machines could copy a two-hour tape every eighty seconds, although, at $150,000 each, the machines used were much more expensive than using ordinary video recorders. The company had set up the first high-speed mass-duplication plant in Philadelphia, giving Modern Video the capacity to copy 20 million videocassettes a year. But the video-duplication business was not revolutionized by high-speed video overnight. The Hollywood studios were more familiar with 'real-time' duplication, and, as a result, Modern Video was largely confined to the unglamorous corporate and industrial end of the video market.

The deal followed the normal Carlton pattern. There was an initial payment of $45 million financed by the sale of 3.6 million new Carlton shares at 725p – a 4 per cent discount to the existing share price. Then, to tie Mason in, there was to be a further maximum payment of $35 million depending on profits over the next five years, making a potential total purchase price of $80 million or £45 million. When the acquisition was announced, on 25 March 1988, Carlton's stock price scarcely blinked.

In the year to September 1983 the newly floated Carlton had pre-tax profits of £3.5 million on a turnover of £15.3 million. By 1988 the pre-tax profits for the year to September were £49.1 million on turnover of £217.4 million and Carlton was now capitalized at no less than £927 million. The formula, whether or not it amounted to a well-thought-out strategy, was clearly working, and Michael Green was determined to go on expanding in both the UK and the USA.

The American acquisitions and the NASDAQ ADRs led to increasing attention – and admiration – from the Wall Street investment community. Jessica Reif, then entertainment analyst at Crédit Lyonnais Global Partners, made the following judgement on the company in August 1988:

We believe Carlton is strategically positioned to benefit from the enormous growth of the European television market. We admire Carlton's foresight in acquiring companies involved in every major broadcast area, keeping it abreast of industry trends. The 1990's should be years of continued excellent growth for the company as all macro-trends, deregulation, technological innovation and pan-Europeanization, combine to drive the overall market demand even higher.

Chapter 8

Technicolor Dreams

There are a number of controversial corporate raiders in the USA – the sort of people who appear to be able almost effortlessly to shake millions, and sometimes billions, of dollars out of the capitalist system. They were in their prime in the 1980s amid a mania for takeovers, often financed by 'junk bonds' – securities whose high rate of interest usually reflected the high degree of risk in the projects they financed. One of the banks that made most money in the 1980s from junk bonds, and at once stage controlled 70 per cent of the total junk-bond market, was Drexel Burnham Lambert. Michael Milken, the notorious head of its junk-bond department, was earning $550 million a year at his peak, before he ended up in jail.

Supporters of junk bonds argued that the unconventional method of funding shook up corporate America and helped to power a new generation of businessmen who increased efficiency and rejuvenated industry. However, many jobs were lost in the corporate restructurings or 'downsizings' that inevitably followed as the new owners squeezed out the extra profits needed to pay the high interest rates on the bonds. Drexel Burnham Lambert funded the ambitions of such noted corporate raiders as T. Boone Pickens, Carl Icahn, Marvin Davis and Ronald Perelman.

Among the ranks of the corporate raiders Perelman was definitely in the first division, although he was never primarily a predator who bought and broke up companies for a quick profit: he insisted he only stalked companies he wanted to own. Born in 1943 in Greenboro, North Carolina, Perelman was attending board meetings of his father's company RPG Holdings by the age of eleven, and as a teenager he was happily reading company accounts and annual reports. He earned his MBA at the University of Pennsylvania's Wharton Business School and then went to work in his father's metal-fabricating company, Belmont Industries in Philadelphia. Perelman first went on the takeover trail in 1978, when he raised nearly $2 million to purchase 40 per cent of a small Philadelphia jewellery retailer, Cohen-Hatfield Industries. A year later the company bought MacAndrews Forbes, which made liquorice extracts and chocolate. It became Perelman's corporate vehicle, and he expanded it fivefold during his period of control.

In 1983 Perelman bought Technicolor, a company founded in 1915 which had gone on to create the colour-film-processing industry. Technicolor's main business was processing film for the major Hollywood studios – providing everything from the daily rush prints for the production teams to thousands of prints of completed films for cinemas around the world. In 1981 it opened its first purpose-built plant in California to duplicate videocassettes in a natural extension of its relationship with the studios. Perelman paid $23 a share or $105 million for Technicolor – a price that led to a thirteen-year legal battle by minority shareholders who thought he had been able to buy the company too cheaply.

Perelman put a lot of effort into building up Technicolor and regularly commuted from New York to Los Angeles to develop the business. The new owner ended a disastrous move into one-stop photo-processing centres and sold off a number of assets, but he also added two new film-processing laboratories and acquired a state-of-the-art video-duplication plant in Michigan. He was proud of Technicolor's progress and its universally known brand name.

In 1985 Perelman acquired Pantry Pride, a Florida-based supermarket chain, and, with money raised by Drexel, used this as a corporate vehicle with which to buy the Revlon cosmetics group for $1.8 billion in one of Wall Street's most hotly contested takeover battles. A year later he launched a daring hostile $4 billion takeover bid for another famous name, Gillette, the personal-care products group; although he failed to get control, by 1986 Perelman was a billionaire.

On his office sofa at the Revlon headquarters high up in the General Motors Building, overlooking New York's Central Park, were two green embroidered cushions. One said, 'Love me, love my cigar', and Perelman did indeed like to pad around his office in socks wearing an old cardigan and smoking cigars. The other cushion was more in tune with his business reputation. It carried the message 'No guts, no glory'.

Perelman has always insisted he is a private person who likes to go to bed early, and in contrast to his reputation as a consummate corporate raider the *New York Daily News* gossip columnist Liz Smith once wrote, 'He's really a small, unprepossessing person.' He did, however, hit the social columns in 1985 when he married a television entertainment reporter, Claudia Cohen.

In 1987 Michael Gifford, chief executive of the Rank Organisation, tried to buy Technicolor from Perelman after Rank had realized it had to have a laboratory in Hollywood if it was going to be taken seriously as a world-class player in the feature-film-processing business. The conversations between

Gifford and Perelman continued over six months, although each man was wary of the other. Perelman, in particular, was reluctant to give too much information away to Rank, Technicolor's main rival, until there was a commitment to buy. Gifford, in turn, was not prepared to offer anything like the $750 million asking price as Perelman tried to raise money to help fund his continuing ambitions to own Gillette.

The talks came to an abrupt end in Perelman's Manhattan office at noon on Monday 19 October 1987 – Black Monday. Gifford and Perelman watched in disbelief as the Dow Jones Industrial Share Index fell and fell on its way to 1,738 – a 22.6 per cent drop on the day, and a larger percentage decline than that recorded on 29 October 1929. There was nothing more to talk about.

Less than a year later Michael Green decided to take on Ronald Perelman in face-to-face negotiations to try to buy Technicolor. Through the purchase of Modern Video, Green had gained an insight into the US video-duplication market. Overall, the growth of the videocassette had been spectacular – particularly the 'sell-through' market: videos for sale rather than for rent. The total US market had grown from 5 million cassettes in 1982 to more than 150 million in 1988, but within that total the sell-through market grew from 5 million cassettes in 1985 to 88 million in 1988.

Gifford's next move made Green realize that if he wanted to expand in the video-duplication market then time might be short. In April 1988 Rank spent $120 million for a video-duplication business owned jointly by Columbia, Paramount and Bell Howell. But Green had a stronger motive for targeting Technicolor than merely wanting to get into a particular market before it was locked up by rivals, or even copying the strategies of his contemporaries' companies such as Saatchi & Saatchi and Martin Sorrell's WPP, which were expanding into the USA on the back of a weak dollar. By 1988 he needed to pull off a big deal to buy the turnover and cash flow necessary to keep Carlton moving forward at the speed that the City had become accustomed to.

Carlton, as a company well-known for its interest in takeovers, was usually bombarded by confidential dossiers from merchant banks about companies for sale. But there is a limit to the number of attractive small start-up companies to buy, and, anyway, with an annual turnover of more than £200 million Carlton was now getting so big that just adding another £20–30 million acquisition would no longer be sufficient to provide a big enough boost to turnover and profits to maintain its historic rate of growth. Carlton was beginning to look like the victim of its own success and the expectations it had quite deliberately created that it was a company where profits just continued to grow. 'I think he needed a big play,' says a former Carlton employee.

The pursuit of the biggest Carlton deal so far began because Green picked up the rumour that Perelman, although not actively looking for a buyer for Technicolor, might be willing to sell at the right price. In late May 1988 a formal approach to Perelman was made through Felix Rohatyn, head of acquisitions and mergers at Lazard Freres in New York, which that year had joined the growing list of Carlton's financial advisers. 'Perelman said Technicolor was not for sale but to come over and talk,' recalled Green.

The new target surprised even senior Carlton executives. The corporate strategy was supposed to involve expanding in the broadcasting market in continental Europe. Yet Green was preparing to stake Carlton's reputation, and ability to issue new shares, on an American company that processed copies of feature films for distribution to cinemas and linked hundreds of ordinary $400 video recorders to produce duplicate videocassettes. Technicolor provided services to the media industry, but it was neither a high-technology company nor offered the long-sought breakthrough into broadcasting.

There were long debates with close advisers such as Michael Sorkin of Hambros about whether this was the right business to buy. If successful, it would mean that Carlton would virtually double in size, while the likely sums of money involved would be too large to be covered entirely by issuing new shares: Carlton would have to take on a higher level of debt than it ever had before. Apart from the sheer scale of the funding that would be needed, the business was based in California. Would the management be able to cope with that? Sorkin had always been impressed by the way that Green tackled his difficult questions head-on, rather than trying to duck them or wishing them away. 'By the time you have finished a review of a business with Michael, I feel I understand why he wants to do it and I am convinced that it should be done,' he says. In the case of Technicolor, the decision to try to buy the company was based on Green's vision that the sell-through videocassette market was going to continue to show dramatic growth and that the efficiency of the business could be improved.

The first meeting between Green and Perelman, who has a reputation for brusqueness and lack of humour, was in June at Revlon's headquarters. When the day-long meeting was over, Green was convinced that he would be able to persuade Perelman to sell.

There were three months of detailed negotiations, with most of the crucial sessions being conducted between the two Jewish cigar-smokers, Green and

Perelman, on their own. Perelman had put a lot of effort into building up Technicolor – now a very different company from the one he had bought in 1983 for $105 million. In 1983 Technicolor had pre-tax profits of $24.2 million on a turnover of $161 million. By 1987 profits had almost doubled to $47.7 million on a turnover of $289 million. Even stronger profits were expected for the first half of 1988 – an estimated $34 million. As the talks with Carlton continued, in July the US company expanded further with the acquisition of CBS Fox in west London for £5.6 million, and a month later it added the videocassette operations of TapeTech, another UK company, for £15 million.

The negotiations were remarkably sensible and even-tempered according to one of those involved. Perelman is undoubtedly tough, but the Carlton team found him straight, and when he said something would be done it was. But deep into the negotiations the issue of whether or not Perelman would sell at all became more important than the haggling over price. Sorkin, who had previously known Perelman only by his formidable reputation, quickly became convinced that he was far more than a 'Wall Street hooligan' who would buy and sell anything if the price was right. Perelman was carefully assessing Green to see whether he wanted to do business with him at all.

'The key to it was that Technicolor was one of the two foundations of Perelman's wealth and empire, and he had a very real attachment to it,' Sorkin believes. 'Technicolor was not a piece of meat to him. He may have had other businesses that were for trading, but Technicolor wasn't one of them. Obviously he realized he had bought it for X and was being offered Y and it was a very acceptable return on his investment, but there was always something pulling him back. And the key to it was that Michael worked on him for a long time, and at the end of the day, in my view, Perelman was convinced that, if someone else was to own it, Michael was ideal.'

As the negotiations between Green and Perelman continued, Bob Phillis and June de Moller travelled around the Technicolor businesses from New York to Chicago and on to Hollywood in an enormous corporate jet, accompanied by a senior Technicolor executive, Art Ryan.

Although Green would always consult his senior colleagues on the overall progress of the talks, the actual negotiations were driven by him personally. Green admits to walking out of the talks a few times, but never for more than three minutes, and thought throughout the process that Perelman 'had to be a logical seller and we had to be the obvious buyer'.

It still was not going to be an easy decision. Usually after all the checking had been done things were clear-cut and the only thing left to do was perhaps to try to shave a bit more off the price. This time – and unusually for Carlton – the top four executives were split on the deal. Two thought the price was too high. The doubters were almost certainly Phillis and Bernard Cragg. Even de Moller, who is utterly loyal to Green and usually sees things his way, is believed to have had some reservations. But, although Green does listen to senior colleagues, the votes hardly carried equal weight at Carlton. Yet, even though Green dearly wanted Technicolor, the Carlton chairman was still concerned about spending nearly $800 million on one deal which could bring Carlton to its knees if it were to go disastrously wrong.

The man who played an important role as an intermediary – and perhaps even the midwife who enabled the deal to go ahead – was Jarvis Astaire, a man best known in the UK as a boxing promoter but who has made a fortune estimated at more than £80 million in property. He is also a director of many companies, including Mappin & Webb, Wembley Stadium and, at that time, Technicolor (UK). He had been a friend of Perelman for some years and had been asked to become a director of Technicolor (UK) to keep an eye on Perelman's business in the UK. Astaire was also close to the Wolfsons and had met Green socially. He now lives with Lady Wolfson, Green's former mother-in-law, who is divorced from Lord Wolfson.

Surprisingly, Green, with Perelman's knowledge, went to see Astaire in his role as a director of Technicolor (UK) almost to seek reassurance about the wisdom of what he was planning to do. 'One of the things he [Green] complained about was the high price Perelman was asking. But Perelman was not a totally willing seller. He liked the idea of owning what was a great trade mark,' says Astaire, who advised Green not to be mesmerized by the apparently high price. Buying Technicolor would turn Carlton into a serious international player, and as a result the value of all its existing assets would be enhanced. But how, asked Green, could he be sure he would be able to hold on to the relatively small number of customers – the big Hollywood studios – who accounted for a disproportionate amount of the business? What if they went somewhere else when their exclusive contracts were up, or at the very least used the threat of taking their business elsewhere to drive down Technicolor's profit margins? Astaire told him he had to make sure that Technicolor became so much an integral part of their businesses – as close as the relationship between Marks & Spencer and its suppliers – that they wouldn't dream of taking their contracts to rivals.

Astaire was also able to soothe Perelman's worries about the deal, and about Green in particular. 'He was not totally happy in dealing with Green. He doubted whether Green could raise the money. As it happens I was able to convince him. Michael Green thought I was helpful, and evidently Ronald Perelman thought so too,' says Astaire.

Apart from the growing need for a big play, two main factors influenced Green in his decision to go ahead with the Technicolor deal: there was growth in both film processing and video duplication. Single- or double-screen cinemas were beginning to give way to entertainment complexes with up to ten screens, to give the audience greater choice. Every extra screen meant an additional print to be processed by companies such as Technicolor. Against the odds – and despite the increasing competition from the growing number of television channels – cinema was making a comeback, helped greatly by higher standards in the new multiplexes. However, Green knew there was more than a theoretical possibly that satellite distribution of films would one day replace the cumbersome task of delivering prints of a new film to several thousand cinemas across a continent. If all cinemas had a satellite dish, a copy of each new film, in encrypted form, could be sent to them all simultaneously. But there are problems with such a high-technology route – problems of cost, of picture quality and of exposing the signal transmitting a new film to the dangers of piracy, however sophisticated the scrambling. Carlton's experience with the high-speed Modern Video duplicators also suggested that the Hollywood studios did not rush to embrace the latest technology. Green took the view that, at the very least, the processing of films and their physical distribution to cinemas would continue for the foreseeable future.

Anyway, it was the video-duplication business he was primarily interested in. Carlton might even sell the film-processing division to Rank, to help pay for the deal. With video duplication Green was backing his judgement that the video would become almost like a book for a new more visually conscious generation. Increasingly, Green argued, consumers would want to own videos – not just do-it-yourself videos or collections of cartoons or the best goals of Manchester United, but their own properly packaged copy of the latest Hollywood blockbuster. To back up his judgement, the Carlton chairman naturally had a sheaf of numbers to justify the price he would undoubtedly have to pay Perelman. There were 23,000 cinema screens and 77,500 video stores in the USA. And Technicolor was expected to produce 60 million videos in 1988 and 75 million in 1989.

Green admits that he almost drove Perelman crazy in trying to persuade him to sell. But, although there were the usual last-minute frantic transatlantic telephone calls and late-night sessions involving lawyers, in September 1988 he had reached agreement to pay Perelman $780 million, or £458.8 million, for Technicolor.

Before Green finally signed the deal, which would involve the largest issue of new shares in the UK since the 1987 stock-market crash, he tested out the proposal in a series of confidential presentations to Carlton's twenty largest institutional shareholders. Green concedes that the institutions' initial reaction was that the market was not at the ideal stage for such a dramatic deal so soon after the crash. They were persuaded, however, that it was a logical next step for Carlton, and gave it their backing. To a very real extent they were supporting Green's track record and judgement.

Giles Coode-Adams, who had been presenting the Carlton story to institutional shareholders since 1983, was a member of the team that accompanied Green to sell both the concept and the terms of the share issue. He had no doubts about the Technicolor acquisition. He saw it as a serious business, and thought that buying Technicolor would make Green a player in 'industrial America'. But persuading the institutions of the wisdom, scale and timing of such a move was not easy. 'It was purely a question of time. It went quite well after a few days. It took longer to get the story out, but then it performed reasonably well,' he recalls.

The purchase of Technicolor was to be paid for by a £364 million rights issue underwritten by Hambros and Barclays de Zoete Wedd (BZW), combined with Carlton's existing cash reserves and £117 million of debt raised through a five-year loan. Shareholders would be asked to subscribe for seventeen new shares for every twenty already held, at a price of 555p.

During the evening of Thursday 8 September, as the lawyers were working on the final details of the deal in New York, the lead underwriters of the share issue – Hambros, Shearson Lehman and BZW – had managed to sub-underwrite the deal to other banks, thereby spreading the risk. It was a very positive sign.

When Perelman finally signed the $780 million agreement and the deal was announced, on 9 September 1988, it inevitably received a great deal of attention from both journalists and analysts. The American news agency Dow Jones said the purchase 'catapults a British upstart into an eagerly sought Hollywood role', and noted that Carlton's market capitalization would now rival that of Saatchi & Saatchi, the group that had blazed the global-expansion trail for British service companies. It added, however, that the acquisition promised 'to test Carlton's steadiness'. *Business Week* noted that Carlton was paying fourteen times net earnings for Technicolor – higher than analysts would have expected. In response, Green told the US magazine, 'I'm happier paying a full price for a business that's doing well. Cheap can be expensive in the long run.' *Forbes Magazine* was later to note approvingly of Perelman –

who later went into the television business in the USA – that he had 'bought Technicolor in 1983 for $125 [*sic*] million, sold assets, cutting his cost practically to nil, and then sold it in 1988 for $780 million – virtually clear profit'.

At one stage on 9 September the markets knocked 106p off the Carlton share price, taking it down to 578p, although it recovered later in the day to close at 585p compared with the previous night's price of 654p. The City was divided on the wisdom, or at least the timing, of the deal. 'This is just not the market for doing a big rights issue,' Mark Shepperd of stockbrokers Phillips & Drew commented. Other analysts, such as Jason Crisp of County NatWest WoodMac, thought the acquisition was right up Green's street and shared the Carlton chairman's belief in the future of the video-duplication market.

At the press briefing at Hambros, Green said that 'Technicolor is a quantum leap for us in terms of the industry we are in. Although it may not be the right deal for the market, it is for Carlton.' After the briefing, as he posed in front of Technicolor logos, Green was beaming from ear to ear. One close observer that day also remembers that, as Green later gave a one-to-one interview, Tessa Buckmaster, the young investor-relations executive, was sitting on the floor looking up at her chairman in an adoring way.

In a single deal Green was paying nearly three times the total cost of all the acquisitions since The Moving Picture Company and taking on, by Carlton standards, a huge amount of debt. For Green and Carlton it was a momentous single roll of the dice that took the company's market capitalization above £1 billion but which, almost for the first time in its short history, had the potential to destroy the company. City sceptics wondered how it was that a company that had been bought for $105 million in 1983 could be worth $780 million only five years later. Had Michael Green, in his determination to land a big deal, overpaid – and to such an extent that the future of Carlton could be threatened if things went awry? There were, however, considerable tax advantages for Carlton.

The audacity and size of the deal nevertheless impressed most City journalists, although usually with reservations. The Lex column in the *Financial Times* conceded that it was difficult to spot the flaws in a deal that gave Carlton half of the duopoly operating in the growing video-duplication market. But the column also added, 'Rapid profits growth, a flurry of acquisitions, involvement in the media, a chief executive who has been voted young businessman of the year – Carlton has all the elements of a company which is going to come a mighty cropper some day.'

In the *Sunday Times*, Ivan Fallon also sounded a note of warning. 'As so many others have found recently, you only have to slip once. For Green's sake I hope Perelman is not as good a seller as he is a buyer.' The Tempus column in *The Times* was more enthusiastic. It suggested that having a name like Technicolor under its control would be the equivalent for Carlton of hanging out flypaper – corporate deals and opportunities would simply flock to the door and stick.

Michael Gifford of Rank was happy to confirm that the business Green had bought might be a sound one but he had paid 'over top dollar' for it. Tongue firmly in cheek, the Rank chief executive added, 'I think he [Green] has more capacity to lose market share than gain it. We will be working to help him to do that over the next few years.'

The Carlton chairman emphatically denies that Technicolor was a risky deal. The price was always backed by assets such as exclusive film-processing and video-duplication deals with many of the leading Hollywood studios. Carlton's assets now included 22,000 Technicolor video 'slaves' which could turn out videocassettes twenty-four hours a day, 365 days a year.

The purchase of Technicolor meant that Carlton would now have videocassette-duplication plants in California, Michigan, Pennsylvania, the UK and the Netherlands, and film-processing plants in Hollywood, New York, London and Rome. Technicolor had had more than 40 per cent of the world video-duplication market; including Modern Video, Carlton now had nearly 50 per cent. The deal also more than doubled the number of Carlton employees – from 1,200 to over 3,000.

By instinct, luck or judgement, Green got his timing right on the expansion of the sell-through video market. The Walt Disney Company's strategy of launching a classic such as *Snow White* on video each year was just one factor that helped to boost the video sell-through market around the world. However, a careful look at Carlton's 1989 accounts suggests that making the Technicolor deal pay its way was more difficult and tense than most people realized.

The consolidated profit-and-loss account shows nothing untoward. Under 'exceptional items' there is only the tiny net sum of £38,000, compared to nearly £3 million the previous year. Yet note 7 to the accounts, dealing with exceptional items, tells a more revealing story involving two much larger amounts. A gain of £41.326 million, mainly coming from the disposal of a subsidiary, almost exactly cancels out a cost of £41.288 million, which is described as 'costs of non-recurring intangibles purchased following the acquisition of Technicolor (net of taxation)'. No further explanation is given, but the mysterious extra intangible cost – not included in the already generous purchase price for Technicolor – almost certainly relates to payments made to Hollywood studios to ensure the absolutely vital renewal of long-term contracts.

Gifford believes the 'non-recurring intangibles' represent 'up-front' payments to Disney and Warner. The purpose was to help ensure that there was no sharp fall in the actual unit rate of processing film and duplicating videocassettes. The effect was to disguise, to some extent, the pressure the big Hollywood studios were able to apply to get the keenest prices. Even former Carlton executives decline to give details of the precise mechanisms, but nothing improper was involved. 'I think arrangements were put in place to keep the contract price more stable [than it would otherwise have been],' said one analyst.

Gifford believes that Carlton was particularly lucky in keeping Disney as a video-duplication customer. The late Frank Wells, president of Disney, came to see Gifford in London to see why Rank apparently did not want to bid for a large exclusive contract for all Disney video- and film-processing work. The Rank chief executive explained that he did not want the contract because of penal clauses attached to such things as service and delivery. 'That is not the way we do business. But I know a man who will sign up for them. If you go from here to his office, which I know you will, and if you walk in the door and say "Mike Gifford sends his regards", I'm sure he will sign up for them. And he did,' says Gifford of his competitor the Carlton chairman.

At the time of the Technicolor purchase Green played down the risk and emphasized, quite correctly, that most Technicolor customers were committed to long-term contracts. It was not, however, a foregone conclusion that Carlton would keep all the contracts, and indeed one film-processing contract, with Paramount, was later lost to Rank when the contract ran out.

Paramount executives were staggered by the price Green paid for Technicolor and inevitably compared it with what Perelman had paid five years earlier. 'Were we overpaying them for our processing. Too fucking right we were,' was one executive's conclusion. Paramount was tied by contract for a further three years, but when it was free to do so it called for a bid from Rank, which offered lower prices than Technicolor. Paramount was surprised when June de Moller, who was handling the negotiations, did not come back with a counter-offer. As a result, Paramount's worldwide film-processing business went to Rank, although Technicolor retains its European video-duplication business.

Paramount was the only major contract that Carlton lost, but there have been a number of other outward signs of just how rough a game it is to win and keep Hollywood film-processing and video-duplication contracts.

In 1991 Technicolor paid $14 million for 1 million shares in Carolco Pictures, the independent producer of box-office hits such as the *Rambo* series. As a result Technicolor, and ultimately Carlton, owned 3 per cent of the film company – hardly a proportion of much significance. The deal made no business sense at all other than as a down-payment for a film-processing and video deal. It is thus not surprising that at the same time as the share purchase it was announced that Technicolor had won a seven-year exclusive agreement to process all Carolco's film in the USA and most other parts of the world. There was a similar deal with Republic Pictures, where Technicolor acquired 200,000 newly issued shares for $3 million and an exclusive video-duplication contract.

Green did not manage to sell the Technicolor film-processing business to Rank, although news of a Carlton approach leaked into the newspapers – complete with a rumoured price tag of $300 million. 'We never got anywhere near a deal. There were just early discussions about it,' Gifford confirms. One of the reasons the Rank executive hesitated was that part of the Technicolor premises in Hollywood were on land leased from the music, film and theme-park business MCA. Gifford did not relish the prospect of having to move the laboratories some day if agreement could not be reached with MCA, because a lot of fine-tuning is involved in setting up a film-processing lab. It can take up to two years to get an equipped lab fully up to speed technically. Instead Rank bought two other film labs: Film House, in Canada, and Deluxe, on its own freehold site in Hollywood.

The US Justice Department in 1990 challenged the Deluxe deal on the grounds that it would give Rank too dominant a position in film-processing worldwide, but many studios supported Rank on the grounds that they wanted it to be a more effective competitor to Technicolor. The Carlton subsidiary went to court to argue that Rank ownership of Deluxe would indeed lead to a reduction in competition. Gifford was happy to win against both the Justice Department and Technicolor, although he says he likes Green personally and has always found him straightforward.

The Technicolor acquisition immediately fattened Carlton's accounts. In the company's annual report for the year to September 1989, boosted by the first contribution from Technicolor, Green was able to report a a 129 per cent rise in pre-tax profits, to £112.4 million, on a 165 per cent increase in turnover to £576.6 million. Technicolor also enhanced growth in earnings per share, which in the year to September 1989 grew to 53.2p a share, compared with 40.9p the previous year and 2.6p in 1982. Carlton was now capitalized at £1.5 billion.

It was not long before it became clear that the Technicolor acquisition would consistently throw off cash and profits for Carlton and enhance the company's international image and importance. Fears that either film or the videocassette is about to become obsolescent because of the speed of development of digital technology have proved unfounded – or at least very premature. In the first year of Carlton's ownership of Technicolor, total industry sales of videocassettes in the USA exceeded 200 million – an increase of 50 per cent on the previous year. The Technicolor acquisition did precisely what Green hoped – it continued to fuel growth and helped to finance further adventures.

'Technicolor was always described as a deal too far, not a very good deal, but it has performed fabulously year after year. It was said Carlton paid a high price, but five years on it didn't look a high price,' says Nigel Wray.

Martin Sorrell assesses the risk Michael Green ran in buying Technicolor in a slightly different way, suggesting that buying a business from Ronald Perelman and surviving was quite an achievement, because Perelman drives hard bargains.

Chapter 9

Dancing Cows

At first glance there are many similarities between Peter Michael, the chairman of United Engineering Industries (UEI), and Michael Green, the chairman of Carlton Communications. Both have fathers who were business-men, and both lived and breathed business from an early age. Both are utterly determined to win and have been successful at creating and building companies. And both have amassed enormous personal wealth.

In 1982 Peter Michael – now Sir Peter – was chosen as *Guardian* Young Businessman of the Year. It is often a dangerous accolade to win: in recent years the award has become notorious for coinciding with the collapse of reputations and share prices. In April 1989, at a lunch in the Mansion House, Michael Green matched Peter Michael by becoming a *Guardian* Young Businessman of the Year and was told by Sir John Hoskyns, of the Institute of Directors, that he was an 'outstanding example of skilful business manage-ment and technical and market innovation'.

There are, however, significant differences between Michael Green and Peter Michael, who is ten years older. The short, pugnacious UEI chairman is more blunt than charming and also has three more university degrees than Green. After a degree in electronics, Peter Michael worked for Plessey, Smiths Industries and Rolls-Royce before adding postgraduate studies in aeronautical engineering and nuclear physics. Then, after realizing he would never be a brilliant mathematician, he studied for a master's degrees in business administration and turned at the age of thirty to the management of technology companies.

In 1981 Peter Michael reversed a group of independent electronics companies, based largely on image processing, into a group of electronic-engineering companies, UEI. At the heart of the enlarged UEI were businesses such as Quantel, which was at the forefront of digital image manipulation. Quantel is famous in the media world for its Paintbox, the £500,000 digital-effects machine that had enabled The Moving Picture Company to make the cows dance in the famous television advertisement for Anchor butter. Other UEI companies included Link Scientific, a world leader in industrial X-ray analysis machines, and Solid State Logic (SSL) a leading producer of professional audio systems for the music, broadcasting and film industries. But perhaps UEI's best-known division was Cosworth Engineering, which concentrated on developing grand-prix racing engines as well as high-performance engines for production cars such as the Ford Sierra Cosworth and the Ford Sierra Sapphire Cosworth and also for Mercedes.

Even at the best of times UEI was a difficult business to manage. There were many different fiefdoms, run by scientists and engineers with enormous talent and expertise. And because they had equity stakes in the organization their views could not be disregarded, even though they did not always have a precise feel for business realities. 'We had people like Keith Duckworth [founder of Cosworth] on the board who was an absolute near-genius as an engineer but should never be let near business,' Peter Michael says.

The UEI board members were individually wealthy and had achieved a measure of distinction in an individualistic way – usually by ignoring or bypassing conventional wisdom. They had been proved right in their chosen fields, so they were not always responsive to the opinions of their fellow board members. It had not even proved possible to contain all the engineers and visionaries within the rather flexible UEI structure. Phil Bennett, for instance, had left Quantel to join Ampex, the US broadcasting-electronics group, before going off on his own to found Abekas, Green's first US acquisition.

Over the years Peter Michael and Michael Green had meet each other

Sir Peter Michael (left) with Michael Green

many times, including several dinners for two. The Green approach took the form of an invitation to dinner in Scotts Restaurant, Mayfair, to 'talk things over', even though Peter Michael did little to disguise his lack of enthusiasm for the invitation and thought there was nothing to talk about. Then, Peter Michael remembers, as soon as he was safely settled down over dinner, and with minimum preliminaries, came the inevitable proposition from Green – 'I'd like to make you an offer for your company.'

Green would ooze charm and drop names, inevitably including his links with the Wolfson circle, which were maintained despite the separation from his wife. Even though Green knew nothing about the businesses involved, according to Peter Michael, the conversation would continue, 'Obviously I want to run the business completely. It needs just sorting out, between you and me, and that's what we are going to do together. And I will give you a good price for it. On paper it's worth a lot . . .' Peter Michael says he used to switch off. According to the UEI chairman, Green raised the issue of a sale about half a dozen times, even though the answer never changed.

Peter Michael had, however, noted the Carlton purchase of Abekas, which he thought an excellent business. He was also aware that Carlton was being seen as a much more serious player internationally following the acquisition of Technicolor. UEI had Quantel, the 'Rolls-Royce' of the industry, producing the most sophisticated digital editing equipment at the top end of the market, while Carlton with Abekas had bought the 'Ford'. Peter Michael would have liked also to own a 'Ford', to increase his coverage of the overall market for editing and post-production.

By 1988 UEI was making pre-tax profits of £25 million a year on turnover of £142 million. It was a very decent business, but one in danger of approaching a plateau. There was uncertainty about what the future strategy should be, and, even if a clear strategy was identified, doubt as to whether sufficient board agreement could be reached to implement it. 'It was steadily becoming clear that what the board wanted to do was do nothing,' says Peter Michael. He would have liked to sell Cosworth to fund further expansion through acquisition – to extend the range of UEI products beyond the 'Rolls-Royce' end of its markets – but suspected that the board would never agree.

Colin Sanders, another of the UEI 'near-geniuses', who had spent eighteen years building up Solid State Logic, accepted there was a pressing need for change at the top of UEI. Around the boardroom table healthy discussion was starting to degenerate into personal conflict. Other UEI directors were convinced the company was facing 'a crisis of management' caused by what they saw as Peter Michael's determination to run the company as if he owned it rather than merely being a significant shareholder. A number of directors wanted to persuade him to give up the executive chairmanship and take on a non-executive role, although the potential rebellion did not get as far as a formal board resolution. The UEI chairman responded to the ferment by calling in an intermediary to try to settle the series of personal and business conflicts – to no avail.

Faced with such a complex series of structural and personal issues, Peter Michael began to believe that the problem could not be resolved internally and thought of a radical solution – merging UEI with Carlton Communications. After all, Green had been pursuing him for years. For shareholders who wanted to leave it would be a good way of realizing maximum value for their shares; for those who wanted to stay, there would be a combined company large enough to compete effectively in world markets in its chosen sectors.

The idea of selling to Carlton originated with Peter Michael rather than the UEI board, in the early summer of 1988. For the UEI chairman it brought the irony of ringing up and asking to see Michael Green, the man he had always fobbed off. Peter Michael went to see the Carlton chairman in his new, much more stylish, all-white offices in St George Street. Green, as usual, had his feet up on the tidy desk, with a glass of water already poured. Apart from paintings, there were old Technicolor posters featuring Mickey Mouse on the walls, in honour of the recent acquisition.

Peter Michael announced that he thought he had got to the stage where he could see real potential in putting the two businesses together. Green, who had been rebuffed so many times by UEI, was absolutely stunned. Peter Michael told him, 'Here is the way I see it. It could be a fantastically good deal for you, and I think it could be a very good deal for our shareholders. I laid out the way I saw it, which was essentially to put these companies together, to sell Cosworth and use the money to build electronic businesses. And my proposal was that he was chief executive and I was the chairman.'

There was inevitable tension between Green's interest in owning UEI businesses such as Quantel and his equally strong desire to remain unambiguously in control. But the necessary compromises were made on both sides and a price was agreed with a link to future profits. A formula was also found for the trickiest part of all – the corporate structure and who should be in charge. The plan was that Peter Michael and Michael Green would be joint chairman of Carlton until the enlarged company's next annual meeting; then Peter Michael would become Carlton deputy chairman on a twelve-month rolling contract worth £100,000 a year.

Peter Michael still had to convince his board that a sale to Carlton was the right thing to do. The proposed deal came as a complete shock to the UEI directors. 'We were summoned to a meeting, an extraordinary board meeting, at a hotel – some God-awful place between Newbury [where UEI had its headquarters] and London – whereupon Peter Michael sat down and said he had been to see Michael Green. There was an offer on the table. He intended to sell his shares, and that was that,' an UEI director says.

Colin Sanders, of SSL, was as surprised as the rest. 'In my view the move to sell came from him [Peter Michael]. I was the second major shareholder, and I judged it was in the best interest of all the shareholders [to sell]. It didn't come from the board, and as far as I know the deal was virtually done before I knew about it,' he recalls. The other directors also felt they had little choice. Green would agree to a deal only if he had the unanimous support of the UEI board. In the end he got just that.

But a group of directors on the nine-strong board – including two of the most powerful: Richard Taylor, chairman of Quantel, and Keith Duckworth, chairman of Cosworth – accepted the takeover only on condition that Peter Michael would not be running the enlarged company. They believed undertakings were given that the UEI chairman's role would be non-executive.

On Wednesday 24 May 1989 the City was startled to be told that Carlton was offering shares worth £513 million for UEI just eight months after paying £459 million for Technicolor. That morning, to prevent the possibility of a counter-bidder emerging, Michael Sorkin of Hambros sent brokers into the market to buy UEI shares on behalf of Carlton. In a well-organized operation the brokers bought 12 per cent of UEI to add to the 39.3 per cent already committed by UEI shareholders. Carlton had control.

Because the deal came so soon after the Technicolor acquisition, the finances had to be carefully structured. Carlton could hardly ask its shareholders for more money after the £364 million Technicolor rights issue, even though its shares had performed well in the interim. At the time of the UEI deal Carlton shares stood at 849p, compared with the Technicolor rights-issue price of 555p. Instead, UEI was paid for by an enormous issue of new shares – although that had the immediate effect of diluting the value of the existing equity. Carlton offered 56 new ordinary shares and 229 new convertible preference shares for every 100 UEI shares. The deal, generally welcomed by City journalists and analysts, turned Carlton into a company capitalized at £1.7 billion.

On the new joint chairmanship, Michael Green commented, 'We have got to live with this, and let's hope it works.' Inside the new Carlton headquarters those who remembered the departure of Mike Luckwell shook their heads sceptically and wondered whether there was room for two such large egos in the company, even if it was only for nine months.

Peter Michael said that once he gave up the joint chairmanship he intended to take 'a less active role', although what that would involve was not specified. The joint chairmanship, and the fact that a total of three UEI directors were joining the Carlton board, made it all sound a bit like a merger and that harmony and continuity were being preserved.

'From my point of view, I felt if I joined the company the profits of the company would be higher,' said Peter Michael, who was going to be a large minority shareholder in the merged organization. He would have 6.16 million shares and in addition he would have rights over 25.2 million convertible preference shares.

At the press conference at Hambros, just across the road from the Tower of London, Michael Green and Peter Michael beamed in unison. There was nothing to disturb the idea that here was a merger of minds and that for nine months at least the joint chairmen of Carlton would cooperate amicably to get the very best out of integrating the two companies.

Green told journalists there were no plans for radical reorganization, redundancies or disposals. 'We are complementary to one another now, but would probably soon be competitors in most areas were we to remain separate. In the industry it is largely agreed that UEI is better at research and development, while we are better at getting products out on to the market,' he added. The one thing Green was adamant about – much to the scorn and disbelief of journalists – was that there would be no disposals. 'No companies are for sale,' Green insisted at the press conference.

Nevertheless, that afternoon Dr Peter Williams of the metrology company Oxford Instruments, another successful *Guardian* Young Businessman of the Year, was on the telephone trying to buy UEI's Link Scientific business. Another call that came that evening impressed Green even more. It was from the legendary Italian industrialist Giovanni Agnelli, head of Fiat, inquiring about Cosworth.

At that particular moment it was true there was nothing for sale – particularly not Cosworth. There would be a large bill for capital-gains tax if Cosworth, which UEI had bought years before for £5 million, was sold immediately. However, an accountancy technique called value-shifting might reduce the tax bill if the disposal was postponed until the following financial year.

The *Financial Times*'s Lex column commented that it was worth asking whether Carlton was overreaching itself, as many 'go-go' stocks had done during the Thatcher years. 'So far, the answer is no. It is not asking its shareholders for more money, its balance sheet is strong, its businesses throw off cash, and its management seems up to the task.'

Green was in such a good mood that week that he even agreed to a rare on-the-record interview for the weekly Man in the News column in the *FT*. As he characteristically slipped off his shoes and fiddled with a plastic clown's red nose from the Comic Relief charity, he was principally pleased that the day after the deal Carlton's share price had bounced back 30p from the 41p drop which occurred as soon as the UEI deal was announced, and it was still rising. UEI, Green said, was going to be vital for the future of Carlton. 'There is so much in that company to get extraordinary growth from, and there is no need to think of any acquisitions for the foreseeable future,' he predicted.

Soon after the merger with Carlton, Peter Michael departed for a long trip to the USA which was to be a mixture of business and pleasure. While he was away, Green and other senior Carlton executives such as Bob Phillis talked to the members of the old UEI board and asked what they thought of their chairman and of the new structure being put in place. The results of the conversations caused surprise and alarm. Over dinner, Richard Taylor, the Quantel chairman, was astonished to be told by Phillis that Carlton believed that he [Taylor] had agreed to the takeover only as long as Peter Michael was still centrally involved in the running of Carlton. The dinner led to a meeting between Taylor and Michael Green at which Taylor told Green that if Peter Michael started playing an executive role there was no question of the other UEI directors continuing with the company. Green was told bluntly that Carlton had a clear choice: it could have the board of Quantel or Peter Michael, but not both.

Within a matter of weeks a number of UEI directors became concerned at how Peter Michael might interpret his new role. The story spread around the company that when one UEI manager telephoned Peter Michael's Newbury office the secretary answered, 'The office of the chairman of Carlton.' Other UEI board members had worries about the future and were concerned that inevitable rows between the two joint chairman would damage the company and their investments. Colin Sanders insists the directors were not motivated by personal spite: 'They felt that the interests of the combined shareholders would best be served by a straightforward chain of command at Carlton. It was not a thing directed at Peter. It was very much if you had these two characters together I genuinely don't believe it could have worked. I wouldn't knock either of them, but they are very similar – talented and single-minded. Two would have been a disaster.'

Michael Green faced a difficult dilemma. The value of the company would be seriously diminished if the Quantel directors, and perhaps others in UEI, carried out their threat to resign. If such a dispute became public, the Carlton share price could be badly affected. He agonized over what to do. He felt uncomfortable about taking action against Peter Michael and in effect going back on his word. 'It was very tricky, but we came to the conclusion that as a pure business decision we didn't have any choice in the matter,' Michael Sorkin recalls. The risk of losing key people from UEI was just too great.

Not long after his return from the USA, Peter Michael was rung by Michael Green, who wanted to come and see him at his home. In Peter Michael's living-room, Green explained that Carlton directors had met at the weekend and decided that they could not have the former UEI chairman on the Carlton board.

Green went on to tell the man he had pursued vigorously for five years that in his left-hand pocket he had a press release saying that Peter Michael had agreed to go. In his right-hand pocket there was a press release saying Peter Michael had been fired. Green was warned that if he pulled either press release out of his pockets he would immediately face a High Court lawsuit for breach of contract. The press releases stayed where they were. But Michael Green and Peter Michael negotiated a parting agreement, and after the initial shock the former UEI chairman eventually regarded it all as just another business deal. Financially Peter Michael did very well out of the deal with Carlton. It valued his UEI stake at £76 million.

Peter Michael believes that Michael Green regarded the joint chairman-ship as little more than 'an interesting cosmetic arrangement, because the very first thing he did, as soon as the deal was signed, was to renege on it'. In fact, faced with a defection of vital UEI directors, Green had gone to the City Takeover Panel to get formal permission to change the board structure announced as part of the takeover terms. The permission was granted. 'I didn't want to be accused of reneging on anything,' says Green, who believes he had no choice but to act as he did.

On 3 August 1989 Carlton issued a press release announcing that the three UEI directors named at the time of the deal would not after all be joining the Carlton board. The trio, who made up the executive committee that ran the day-to-day operations of UEI – the recently knighted Sir Peter Michael, finance director Jeffrey Harrison, and operations director Jon Richards – had all decided to pursue other interests. The three had been paid their contractual obligations, which Carlton said amounted to £100,000 for Sir Peter and £150,000 each for Harrison and Richards. In addition, Sir Peter was allowed to buy UEI's headquarter offices, a beautiful medieval building at West Mills, near Newbury in Berkshire, at a fair independent valuation. A Carlton spokesman said, 'The integration of the two companies has gone rather well, and we really do not need two head offices. They have gone to do their own thing.'

Sir Peter's anger at his treatment, and his conviction that some board members may have taken the opportunity of his absence in the USA to wield the dagger to settle old scores, remains, although it was not the straightforward act of betrayal that he imagines. 'I think one must see Michael Green as a very clever and ruthless businessman. He has built up a very large company through dealing. He is an excellent dealer, and one now knows his dealing techniques are at the point where one has to ignore anything that is written on a piece of paper, because it is probably fairly useless,' Sir Peter claims.

Sanders regrets the way the affair turned out: 'I think it is to many people's eternal regret that it wasn't handled in a straightforward way in a conversation along the lines of "Really it wouldn't work with both of you."' But Michael Green was probably not all that unhappy with the outcome. Even if the original agreement had stayed in place, there is little doubt that within a year Sir Peter would not have had much executive involvement with Carlton.

Most of the other directors, such as Taylor of Quantel and Sanders of SSL, were happy to remain at the enlarged Carlton. Indeed Sanders, who spent a total of twenty-one years at SSL, says he found Green very straightforward and a man who had never let him down. 'I have a lot of respect for Michael Green. His is a no-hidden-agenda style of management,' he says. Taylor, who still runs Quantel, goes as far as to say, 'I could think of few people that would be more careful, caring and a responsible owner than Michael Green.'

The UEI deal, mainly because of Quantel, markedly strengthened Carlton's presence in digital electronics for both television and publishing. At the high end of the market the Harry video-editing system was establishing itself with broadcasters all over the world, and the Graphic Paintbox was winning large orders in publishing, particularly in Japan.

Even though Carlton had not yet realized its ambition to be a broadcaster – apart from the 20 per cent stake in Central – the company continued the process of transformation, of regularly turning its back on its own history. In July, two months after the UEI deal, it sold a majority stake in its oldest businesses – Carlton Fox and Carlton Studios – to the Stanco Exhibition Group, a company that builds and hires out exhibition and display stands, for a total of £16.2 million. David Ludlam joined Stanco as its group managing director. In a statement of the obvious, Carlton said the businesses no longer fitted with the company's core business, although Carlton would retain a 23.2 per cent stake in Stanco.

On 11 September 1989, less than four months after Green had said none of the UEI businesses was for sale, Link Scientific Group was sold to Oxford Instruments for a maximum sum of £57.5 million. Of the total, £47.5 million came in cash, with up to a further £10 million in Oxford shares, depending on performance over the next year. A Carlton spokesman dealt quite happily with the apparent contradiction that nothing had been for sale: 'It was not our original intention to sell the business, and we were under no pressure to sell.'

Not all the difficult decisions Green faced in 1989 were business ones. He was in the middle of choosing between two women – Jeananne Crowley, the actress who had introduced Green to a wide range of people and ideas in the arts but who was not exactly overawed by business tycoons, and the new love in his life, his young employee Tessa Buckmaster. Tessa was an intelligent and determined, if more conventional, woman than Jeananne, and loved business and could slip comfortably into Green's world and values. She was only twenty-four years old – a good ten years younger than Jeananne, and sixteen years younger than Michael Green.

The relationship with Jeananne had been intense and serious, and was recognized as such by Green's family. His mother, Irene, had even travelled to Dublin to see her perform in the theatre. Friends say Green proposed to Jeananne but that she turned him down, although it is far from clear whether that was ever intended to be her last word on the matter. Green had been greatly influenced by Jeananne and her circle of friends – which included actors, writers, journalists and television executives – and adapted himself chameleon-like to that environment. She was a friend of Tony O'Reilly – the former Irish rugby player, chairman of H. J. Heinz, and rising newspaper baron. O'Reilly, one of Ireland's most distinguished and richest businessman, remembers meeting Green for the first time with Jeananne at a pre-rugby-international lunch at the Savoy – and jumping entirely to the wrong conclusion. 'My first impression was of someone who was in theatre, in films, and who would be creative and not very businesslike,' says O'Reilly, who found Green immensely charming.

To an outsider it would have seemed a very unequal struggle – the attractive, sophisticated actress versus the unknown businesswoman. Jeananne had sometimes felt sorry for Tessa, and even once lent her a suitcase to take on holiday. She saw no possible threat coming from the rather gauche investor-relations executive. Yet whereas Jeananne mocked many of the things that were most important to Green – such as business, money and success –

Tessa could offer unconditional admiration and support. And, despite being a tough-minded, capable woman, Tessa was also much more predictable and less threatening to someone like Green than the spirited and sometimes wild Irish actress. In a reference to the fact that Tessa was taller than Green, the joke in Carlton's headquarters was that staff finally knew that the relationship between the two had become serious when Buckmaster started wearing flat shoes.

When Michael Green made his choice it was with the finality and ruthlessness of a boardroom decision to sack a senior executive. Green's decision came as a bitter blow to Jeananne, who clearly continues to love Green to some extent and is outraged by how she was treated.

Jeananne has expressed herself publicly with some bitterness about the end of the affair and how Green handled it. 'As he said when he turfed me out of his Bentley Turbo, "If you ever write a word about me I'll break every bone in your body," ' she told the *Daily Mail*. He was probably joking, but Jeananne added that there are only two things Michael fears in life – 'poverty and personal publicity'. Being 'turfed out' of the Bentley Turbo is actually only a dramatic metaphor for what happened. Jeananne was given two days to vacate Green's Mayfair mansion. She even left behind on the wall one of his personal gifts to her – a valuable painting by one of Ireland's most famous painters, Jack Yeats, brother of the poet William Butler Yeats.

Although Tessa offered convenience and comfort, there was passion too – sometimes displayed overtly. Green and Tessa were among a group of around fifty invited to a concert at the Barbican by Sir Colin Southgate of Thorn EMI. 'They were like a pair of cobras snogging away as if they were at the back row of a cinema on a Saturday night. It was a bit off. The light's weren't even very low,' said a banker who was a distracted guest at the concert.

In one dramatic year Green had bought Technicolor and UEI and sorted out his love life, yet he still had failed to consummate his desire to own a broadcasting company. However, the flirtations with Thames and its shareholders BET and Thorn EMI who remained willing to sell continued unabated. On 19 January 1988 Richard Dunn, the Thames chief executive, had rather mischievously invited Green and Bob Phillis to a dinner of the Thirty Club, a black-tie, men-only dining-club for the media élite. The speaker was Lord Young. Over dinner, Green assured Dunn that he would not bid against Thames for the London weekday licence when the ITV licences next came up for renewal. 'You're impregnable,' said Green – although the Thames chief executive regarded it as more a friendly remark than a binding promise.

In May Nicholas Wills and Colin Southgate met Lord Thomson at the IBA with Sir Ian Trethowan, the Thames chairman, present. The chief executive of BET and Thorn EMI sought IBA approval for the sale of their combined 17% holding in Thames. The answer was 'yes' in principle, but not to one buyer. The IBA insisted that Thames should be broadly owned.

One afternoon later in May, when Dunn and Phillis had tea together at the RAC Club in London's Pall Mall, Phillis said that Green still wanted to control Thames. But now 50 per cent would do, and he also wanted the support of management. Dunn pointed to the IBA's attitude as a major hurdle.

On 6 June, Green went to see John Whitney, director-general of the IBA, and gave him the impression that Dunn would really rather like Carlton to take control of Thames. But it was the old story: Green the deal-maker was talking up his hand. When Dunn met Whitney the next day the Thames executive said his mind was open but he was still feeling his way towards the right structure to give Thames the best chance of retaining its broadcasting licence when it next came up for renewal, in 1991.

Later in June, Dunn and the then Thames chairman, Sir Ian Trethowan, a former director-general of the BBC, dined with Colin Southgate of Thorn and Nicholas Wills of BET. Wills enlivened the proceedings by saying the reason he wanted to sell was that he thought Thames was going to lose its licence. Both Thames owners were looking for around 500p a share, but the TV company's share price stood at only 320p. With such a gap between their hopes and the market valuation an early sale was unlikely, especially if they could only sell small parcels of 10%.

By September 1988, after the purchase of Technicolor, Carlton seemed to have lost interest again. Green had other things on his mind. But an unexpected meeting prompted him to start thinking about ITV once more. Green had spent the 1988 Christmas holiday on a yacht in the Caribbean with the film producer David Puttnam, the BBC2 controller Alan Yentob, and other television-industry friends. Much to their amusement, they found themselves moored beside Robert Maxwell's yacht *Lady Ghislane*. Green sent over a note to 'Cap'n' Bob Maxwell. It said, 'Why don't you put Central in my Christmas stocking?' Maxwell had acquired a 20 per cent stake in the company after his takeover of the British Printing Corporation. The media gamesmanship continued when Maxwell issued an invitation for drinks on his yacht and Green, accompanied by Tessa and Yentob's wife, Phillipa, accepted. Maxwell, as befitted a tycoon, told Green, 'I'll take Central. You take Thames!'

A few weeks later at another Thirty Club dinner Green hurried towards

Dunn across the bar when he saw him and said that, after looking at othe
possible takeover targets, he was once again very keen to get control c
Thames. By March 1989 Dunn's views had evolved further, and he tol
Green and Phillis at a meeting in Carlton's St George Street headquarter
that he had decided he would prefer to have Carlton rather than Thorn as
controlling shareholder. And on 11 May, at an Ulster Television function a
the Tate Gallery, Dunn bumped into Phillis and told him formally that th
Thames executives would support a Carlton bid.

A number of things stood in the way of a full takeover but a steppe
approach seemed possible. George Russell, the new IBA chairman, said h
would prefer to see what the government's planned Broadcasting Bill woul
say before he allowed any wholesale restructuring of ITV. The economi
climate was also hardly conducive to BET and Thorn getting 500p for thei
shares. In May 1989 intense market pressure on sterling forced the tent
interest-rate rise in a year, to 14 per cent.

Then on 5 July 1989 the *Financial Times* carried a modest single-colum
story saying that Thames had opened exploratory talks with Carlton about th
possibility of Carlton making a takeover bid for what was now a publicl
quoted television company. The effect was immediate. Green, who is an avi
reader of the pink newspaper, called the reporter responsible at home befor
breakfast. He was very angry. 'What are you trying to do to me?' he screamed
Despite taking some pride in his media-handling skills, Green has never quit
grasped that what a journalist does is try to find things out and put them int
his newspaper. Dunn, in a quieter way, was equally horrified. He was worrie
that the leak would undermine his hopes of strengthening Thames b
replacing his two reluctant shareholders with one committed one in advanc
of the campaign to win the renewal of its broadcasting licence when it cam
up for renewal. The Thames share price rose 30p on the news.

By 16 November 1989 there was a significant disposal by Carlton – a sal
which could also legitimately be described as an important strategi
opportunity. Charles Denton of Zenith had spotted the potential of linkin
the Carlton subsidiary with a major US studio in the hope of learning mor
about the all-important American production market. Carlton sold 49 pe
cent of Zenith to Paramount Television of the USA for $7.5 million. Ami
growing fears of media protectionism – particularly in France – the America
company wanted a respectable European joint venture and a productio
foothold in the European industry. 'Paramount Television truly wanted to b
associated with European television-makers,' a Paramount executive com
mented. Zenith wanted financial backing from both Paramount and Carlto

to make programmes for world markets and to gain access to Paramount's distribution system in the USA. Following the deal, Zenith could describe itself as a Carlton/Paramount production company.

When the deal was announced, both sides said explicitly that they would jointly fund an expansion of production, with a strong emphasis on television programmes for the international market. 'It looked very good, and should have been very good had Paramount decided that it wished to develop a European strategy along the lines it outlined at the time it bought into the company,' Denton comments. But it turned out to be one of those nightmare deals where the parties have completely different expectations and each side was convinced that it was the other that intended to put up the money. Paramount, in particular, didn't wish to invest in new productions outside the USA. Zenith thought it would be tapping into the resources of a huge American media organization and that enormous production opportunities would result.

'We didn't have control. Carlton still retained control, but we paid $7,500,000 for it, for this privilege. We paid that money, but we have never seen a penny piece out of that investment,' a Paramount executive recalls. The deal was dead almost from the outset.

At the time of the Paramount deal – which eventually unravelled completely, amid considerable acrimony – Carlton was already hawking around a prospectus for the sale of Cosworth Engineering, and some fevered City dealers began to gossip that the company could raise £200 million or even £250 million from the sale. Everyone from Fiat and Ford to General Motors was said to be knocking on Michael Green's door.

Chapter 10

Edge of a Cliff

As Christmas 1989 approached, the outlook was good for Michael Green and for Carlton Communications. The once tiny company now employed about 5,500 people and had a market capitalization of more than £1.7 billion. The Technicolor purchase was beginning to transform Carlton's financial performance. Christmas orders for videos had broken all industry records, and titles such as *Bambi* and *Batman* were expected to boost sales of videos to more than 30 million copies worldwide. Thus it was a confident and relaxed Green who on 11 December announced that Carlton's pre-tax profits had more than doubled, from £49 million to £112.39 million, in the year to the end of September. Turnover, boosted by almost a year's contribution from Technicolor and the first few months from UEI, had leaped from £217.4 million to £577.6 million, and earnings per share had risen by 30 per cent to 53.2p.

The only minor irritation was that, despite the doubling of profits, Carlton's share price actually fell on the day of the announcement – by 17p, to 852p. Such a fall is not unusual in the City if actual profits are not as large as expected or uncertainties are seen on the horizon. One of the uncertainties had already been picked up by Stephen Zimmerman of Mercury Asset Management. Earlier that year, although no one noticed at the time, MAM had gradually reduced its stake. From holding 74 million shares, or 12 per cent of Carlton, in 1987 – by far the largest institutional stake – by April 1989 MAM had begun to sell its shares and eventually unloaded more than half its stake. Zimmerman, an enthusiastic supporter of Carlton in the past, had growing doubts about whether Green could sustain the Carlton growth rate.

On 12 December, the day after the results announcement, Carlton issued a single-paragraph statement. Michael Green had sold about 20 per cent of his stake in Carlton – or 1.3 million shares – at 820p, to raise a total of £10.5 million. The shares had been placed with institutions by Geoff Bowman at Messel. The reason given for the sale by Carlton staff was that Green was reorganizing family trusts. Before he had sold the shares, Green had sought the advice of Michael Sorkin at Hambros, who saw nothing unusual about the plan. The Hambros banker was also an adviser to Selim Zilkha, the founder of Mothercare, who every year or two would 'lighten' his stake by selling some of his shares but remained equally committed to his company. Sorkin's judgement was that a sale of 15–20 per cent of Green's stake would probably be understood by the markets. Green sold his 1.3 million shares at the first legally permissible moment – the day after Carlton's results were announced and the end of the 'close period' when directors cannot sell shares.

That same day, 12 December 1989, Green attended the annual BBC Christmas drinks party organized by John Birt, who had become the Corporation's deputy director-general two years earlier. For his Christmas party Birt manages to assemble a cross-section of the British Establishment: Cabinet ministers, bishops, industrialists and top media executives mingle shoulder to shoulder in the crowded BBC Council Chamber – a room lined with portraits of former BBC chairman and director-generals. A number of the media journalists who cover the affairs of the BBC are usually invited too. That evening the journalists could not resist teasing Green. When the chairman sells it is obviously time for everyone to get out, they suggested. Green explained that he needed the money to fund the divorce settlement with his ex-wife, Janet Wolfson Green.

Green's divorce from Janet – no co-respondent is listed in the divorce decree – had been declared absolute on 28 February 1989. It was the last rites for a relationship that had long been dead, although Green has maintained a good relationship with both Janet and the Wolfson family and is close to his two daughters.

'She [Janet] is a very rich young lady, very rich family, and she did not want to play the role of the wife of a successful businessman. It's as simple as that,' a family member said. 'She is very strong-minded and she was very keen on her modern art and she just wanted her independence. And to the best of my knowledge there was no other person for either of them [at the time]. Just people drifting apart – different interests – and she wanted to go and live her own life. And she spent a lot of her time going round the world. Michael wanted a wife who would be at home, whom he could go home to at night. If he'd bring business people round at night, they'd be entertained. In other words, a wife with no other interests – and she wasn't that at all,' the family member added. A close friend of many years says the two 'just drove each other nuts. Janet and he were too alike. They were like two lions in a cage.' Michael Green admits that the very similarity which brought them together in the first place – both were intensely ambitious – also pushed them apart.

Green's share sale made a paragraph or two on news-agency wires and in the broadsheets. However, it was more carefully noted in the City. Some analysts routinely monitor the sale and purchase of shares by directors – transactions which have to be declared – as one of the most reliable guides to what is really going on behind the public façade of companies.

The following week, on 18 December, Bronwen Maddox, media analyst at stockbrokers Kleinwort Benson, published a detailed assessment of Carlton under the title 'What Price The Picture Palace?' It advised investors to take their profits in Carlton by selling in February 1990. The reason for her precise timing was that Green was going on an investor 'roadshow' in the USA and Japan in early February, and, Maddox had noticed, he was so good at charming investor groups that the Carlton share price usually rose after such trips.

At the beginning of Maddox's assessment there was a polite paragraph praising Carlton for its astonishing and impressive track record and its achievement in building a business with annual revenues of more than £800 million a year (including a full year from UEI) out of the notoriously difficult television services and facilities industry. But then she went for the jugular: 'However, we have concerns about the future. We believe the challenge of marketing the manufacturing [products] is considerable and beyond are competitive threats. The facilities benefit from growth in independent production, but that can be overstated. Parts of Technicolor are slower and less cash generative than we expected.' She went on to express concern that Carlton still did not publish a detailed profits breakdown of its individual businesses and added that, because of the rate and size of Carlton's acquisitions, it was hard to work out what the underlying profitability was, or the company's true rate of growth.

After weeks of work, which included ferreting around in Companies House, she was able to publish her own estimates of the profits earned by individual Carlton subsidiaries for 1989 – estimates that Green grudgingly admitted were 'in the right ballpark'. It was the first time anyone had got so close. They ranged from trading profits of £54.5 million for Technicolor and £27.4 million for Abekas to £16 million for The Moving Picture Company and the other facilities companies and £3.5 million for Quantel.

Maddox then added, in a paragraph that infuriated Green, that one measure of the performance of Carlton acquisitions was the return on capital invested – adding back to the capital employed the £900 million of goodwill written off over the company's history. The calculation based on the capital invested in the company gave a return of 14 per cent for 1989 – perfectly decent, but hardly spectacular for a company whose share price had risen relative to the market for five years. Maddox also estimated that the company was going to have earnings growth of only 10 per cent in the current year. 'It is hard to argue that the added stability of a larger group compensates for the inevitable slowing down of growth, given the market risks and the inadequate divisional information. While Carlton is exceptionally positioned to exploit the changes in European television, the share price rating may overstate the rewards and understate the risks,' she argued in the careful language typical of analysts' reports.

Green was not used to carefully argued 'sell' notes, and he took it personally. 'Why does she hate me?' he later asked a journalist – obviously not understanding that the analyst was merely doing her job.

The Kleinwort analysis did not help the Carlton share price, which continued to slide. However, the limpness of the share price did not adversely affect the closeness of Green's relationship with his young investor-relations executive, Tessa Buckmaster. The engagement of Michael Green and Tessa Buckmaster was announced on 15 January 1990. Yet life was about to get very much more difficult for both of them.

The turning-point was Carlton's 1990 annual general meeting, held, as usual, surrounded by ancient suits of armour in the Armourers' Hall in the City of London. It is a relaxed, almost family, occasion, and a seat is always reserved in the front row for Irene. The proceedings are usually brief, bland and uncontentious, although Green traditionally makes a brief statement about the trading performance of the company in the months since the company's year end. The AGM held on Tuesday 27 March 1990 was different. That morning, before Green spoke at the AGM, two stockbrokers, James Capel and Barclays de Zoete Wedd – one of Carlton's brokers – downgraded their profit forecasts for the company.

At the AGM Green finally announced that Cosworth had been sold to Vickers, the defence and engineering group that owned Rolls-Royce cars, for £163.5 million – very much at the lower end of City expectations. Less than half the total was in cash. Vickers was to pay Carlton £80.5 million immediately and the rest in loan notes, most payable in January 1991, but the final £18 million was not to be paid until January 1992. The sale price just about reached the middle range of Carlton's internal estimates. Hambros, which handled the sale, had hoped there would be enough bidders to create an auction, but, despite the telephone calls from international tycoons such as Giovanni Agnelli of Fiat, there was little serious interest.

The disappointment of the Cosworth sale price was compounded by Green describing Carlton's sales in the first four months of its new financial year as 'respectable'. Green had in the past always described his progress as, at the very least, 'healthy'. The linguistic nuance was leaped on immediately by analysts. Combined with the disappointing Cosworth price, the remark knocked 81p off Carlton shares, which closed at 590p. As stockbrokers rushed to cut their profit projections for the current financial year, one big question was being asked: Was the last genuine go-go stock of the Thatcher years about to go the way of most of the others? During March Carlton was the worst performer in the *FT*-SE 100 share index – down 25 per cent, reducing the value of the company to £1.25 billion.

Michael Green's engagement probably did not help his case. 'You don't put your mistress-turned-fiancée on the phone to tell the world your shares are all right. That is absolutely incomprehensible, and it did not go down well – particularly with the Scots,' according to one analyst on the receiving end of the calls. 'What you got was Michael without the charm and without the knowledge,' the analyst says.

In April, to try to reassure investors, Green travelled to Glasgow and Edinburgh to make presentations to a number of Scottish financial institutions which held significant stakes in Carlton. Some felt that Carlton had paid too little attention to its Scottish shareholders. Robert Nugent, the senior investment manager at the Edinburgh-based Standard Life Assurance, which held 2 per cent of Carlton, later commented, 'They revealed disappointing news, and we heard they were in talks with Thames. Having had the assistance of shareholders in two major deals, that's not an acceptable situation.'

The Carlton team flew to Scotland in the executive jet which came with the UEI acquisition. However, they were warned that if anyone inquired they were to say they had travelled by a scheduled flight as usual – corporate jets were not the right image for a company with a collapsing share price.

In Edinburgh one of the most important sessions was at the fund-management group Scottish Widows, which was a significant Carlton shareholder and was considering its position. Green faced determined questioning from a number of bright and very serious young women. He misjudged the situation, the charm turned oily, and Green gave the impression of being patronizing.

The Scottish Widows executives were concerned about the effects of competition in the video market and whether Green would allow his ambitions to become a broadcaster to overcome his prudence and lead him to pay too much for Thames. 'He was given a tough time – tough but fair,' according to Robin Garrow, an investment director at the fund-management group. As he got into the car after his grilling on the Thames issue, Green said, 'I hate fucking Richard Dunn!'

Later that month the pressure and the tension led Green to dump Messel, the brokers now owned by Shearson Lehman, which had looked after Carlton's interests since the reverse takeover and flotation in 1983. It looked very much like a case of shooting the messenger. 'Anyone who was young, upstart, a bit flash was getting branded. And Carlton – particularly when you saw WPP sinking [the international advertising and marketing group had been almost overwhelmed by a high level of debt] – was a relatively easy target and I think the City lost confidence. Should Messel's have done more? Well, if the tide is going against you, you can only do so much. So I think we were probably unfairly dumped. But Michael felt he had to vent his frustration on somebody, and we were a fairly easy target,' says a Shearson Lehman executive.

There was another factor working against Shearson: it had been running down its sales force, and Green felt exposed – there were not enough salesmen at the brokers to sell new Carlton share issues effectively, and by then Carlton had a desperate need to improve its credibility in the City. Green, who had casually mentioned his decision while in Edinburgh before writing the formal letters, did, however, make it absolutely clear that the move was not a reflection on Geoff Bowman – a salesman with a following of his own – or on Chris Alexander, the Shearson media analyst. This was more important than mere politeness: in the cut-throat world of the City, Bowman and Alexander could have been clearing their desks if they had been held responsible for the loss of such an important corporate client as Carlton.

To increase City confidence in Carlton, Green traded up to the blue-blooded stockbroking firm Cazenove. Persuading Cazenove to become Carlton's joint broker with Barclays de Zoete Wedd was a considerable coup for Green. There are few firms in the City more respectable than Cazenove, and not just anyone gets to be represented by it. Cazenove is the Queen's stockbroker, and it is not a firm that would take on a company that is about to collapse, or where there are doubts about probity or respectability. 'They vetted him very carefully. It was not a snap decision by Cazenove to take Carlton on – they thought about it hard and long. And I think that Michael realized that if they took him on that was going to be a sign of confidence and credibility. So Cazenove coming on as the broker was a huge success, and I would say certainly trading up from Messel's, or Shearson Lehman, was seen to be a real step up for him by the City,' said a merchant banker who knows Cazenove well.

On 29 April 1990 Green got another opportunity to fight back – at an editor's lunch at the *Financial Times*.

Most weeks there is a private, off-the-record lunch for leading industrialists, politicians or foreign statesmen in the *FT*'s sixth-floor dining-room overlooking the Thames. The lunches are informal, and the guests usually come on their own to face questions from as many as eight senior *FT* journalists. Apart from the editor and possibly the paper's chief executive, the visitor might be interrogated by the likes of Sir Samuel Brittan, the *FT*'s formidable chief economic commentator, the head of the Lex column, a senior leader-writer, the foreign editor, and always the specialist journalist who covers the guest's field. Usually the conversation ranges widely and is frank and informative, because the guest can rely on not being quoted. Even if nothing can be reported directly, however, such sessions are invaluable to the *FT* in gaining an insight into how the chairman of ICI, the Chancellor of the Exchequer or even occasionally the Prime Minister is thinking.

The Green visit was particularly interesting because of its timing – right in the midst of the remorseless decline in the Carlton share price. So, as the Portuguese butler unobtrusively served the dry white wine accompanying the salmon, it was forcefully pointed out to Green that the steep decline of his share price matched the pattern of a company about to go over the edge of a cliff.

Green put on a virtuoso performance, emphasizing Carlton's £112 million profit in the previous year and its strong balance sheet, with £250 million in capital and reserves. Carlton, he was able to argue with considerable justice, was a sound company. He admitted, however, that he had learned a cruel lesson – that markets were not as rational as he had imagined, nor as simple in their operations. Not everyone was rushing to sell Carlton shares. The institutions, such as the insurance companies, had largely stayed loyal despite obvious concern about the fall in value of the company's shares. It was the market-makers – the brokers who set that day's and often minute's price, and who react to the latest news and sometimes rumours – who had done much of the damage.

Over lunch, Green explained that when he had called for an internal investigation of what had actually happened on a particularly bad day for Carlton shares he eventually found out that only 700,000 shares out of the company's 184.38 million shares in issue had actually changed hands permanently. The 700,000 shares had been bought and sold several times during the day, so it appeared that a total of 3 million shares had been traded. It was like antique dealers buying and selling between themselves, he argued.

As the then *FT* editor, Sir Geoffrey Owen, showed Green to his car after lunch, there was general agreement among the journalists that the young tycoon had mounted a spirited defence – although not all were convinced that the worst was over for Carlton. After all, in less than six months nearly 350p had been wiped off its share price, reducing the value of the company by around 36 per cent. By then the stock market capitalisation of the company had dropped to £831 million.

The concern over Carlton's share price did nothing to dampen the style or the extravagance at the party following the forty-two-year-old Michael Green's second wedding, at Droxford Register Office in Hampshire on 19 June 1990 to Tessa Buckmaster – or, as the wedding certificate quaintly puts, it to Theresa Mary Buckmaster, formerly known as Teresa Mary Buckmaster, twenty-five-year-old spinster. The party, for several hundred guests, was held the following evening at Green's splendid country house, Tyle Mill, near Reading. Some called it 'the wedding of the decade'. It had a New York or Hollywood scale and grandeur to it. While some found it vulgar, ostentatious and over-the-top, others thought it was simply a splendid, memorable evening. 'It was a big Jewish wedding – there was no other word for it – with a hell of a lot of money having been spent,' said a senior television executive who is Jewish. Security men in dinner-jackets with mobile radios were everywhere. There was even an ambulance on standby in case a guest had a heart attack.

The guest list was a *Who's Who* of British broadcasting, with Green and his new bride sharing the top table with his friends Michael Grade, Alan Yentob and Paul Fox. Grade, an accomplished and amusing speaker, had been asked to give the main speech. Green's instructions had been 'Anything you like. But we don't want anything embarrassing. Just say something nice, decent and praiseworthy. And don't go talking to Gerald Ratner.'

The Channel 4 chief executive took his responsibilities seriously and even carried out some research on Green – questioning his mother, Ratner and Charles Saatchi. A Jewish wedding, Grade explained, was just like a Greek wedding – except that you don't pin the money on the bride: you pin it on the caterers. Grade looked around theatrically. 'Seeing the lilies and the Krug champagne, you say to yourself, "Who needs money?"' Grade – who went on to describe himself as 'probably the only person here I have never heard of' – added that before Green met Tessa he liked to delegate everything – 'to himself basically'. The problem was that Tessa didn't delegate either. So how were disputes ever going to be resolved, Grade had asked Green's mother? 'Easy,' smiled Irene. 'She is stronger than he is. She can hit him.'

Michael Grade

Alan Yentob

During Grade's research Charles Saatchi had commented that if anyone could get Green's nose out of the *Financial Times* it would be Tessa. But then the advertising man had added a more serious note: 'It has been a testing six months or so for Michael. I really doubt that he could have handled it so well if he hadn't had the continued love, support and companionship of Tessa.'

After a few words of thanks, Michael Green danced with his new bride to a band that had come from France. In the grounds, which reminded guests of Glyndebourne, the great and powerful of the television industry drank champagne, gossiped, and wondered why they had been invited. Sarah Morrison, a GEC director, was heard telling Paul Fox how she had helped to furnish Tyle Mill, because Green was not very knowledgeable about buying furniture or giving the house a style. Green's cousin Johnny Goodman was heard bringing David Elstein of Thames up to date with Green family scandal. Irene and her husband were there, of course, and Elstein talked to both of them. 'They were not classy in any way, but without any pretensions to class either – thoroughly nice people actually. The mother warm-hearted, very proud of the son,' Elstein says.

The wedding was a happy interval amid the problems of Carlton. Despite the collapsing share price and the extra stress he was under, Green never lost his sense of style or his commitment to outward appearances. Staff at Carlton's St George Street headquarters were surprised to be given stylish new desks each costing around £6,000 – desks personally chosen by Green. At the same time a splendid new boardroom table arrived, and the flow of modern art to adorn the office walls never ceased. 'One used to sit there in dread of what piece of bloody art was going to be stuck in your office. You didn't have any choice – someone would just come round and something new would appear. I am no judge of art, but I thought that everything in the building was complete crap – though he made money out of it,' a former employee said.

That summer Green faced continuing assaults from the 'short sellers' – those who gamble that a share will continue to fall and therefore have a vested interest in doing what they can to ensure that that is actually what happens. They sell shares they do not yet own, in the knowledge that if the price falls before they have to hand over the share certificates they can buy more cheaply and make a profit. Carlton, where there appeared to be plausible cause for concern, was a delight for the short sellers. A series of damaging rumours were spread in the City – usually involving Green himself, but there was also a false story that Technicolor had just lost an important film-processing contract. In the first week of August Green popped out of his office for a haircut. By the time he came back rumours were already sweeping the Stock Exchange that he had resigned and, as a result, the Carlton share price was falling again. According to one extravagant story, Michael Green had not only resigned but had fled the country.

It was partly perception and partly herd instinct. Even though most thoughtful analysts agreed that there was no 'black hole' of debt at the centre of Carlton, as there had been at the heart of other corporate disasters such as Coloroll or British & Commonwealth's Atlantic Computers, it was much easier to trot out 'no-smoke-without-fire' theories than to carry out detailed valuations of a company that had always sought to control the information it released and which, crucially, refused to provide profit figures for individual businesses.

And so the decline in the share price continued. There were brief rallies, but by the middle of September the price stood at 320p and by the end of the month the stock-market value of the company had fallen to £555 million. This exposed the company to possible takeover if anyone thought the break-up value of the company was more than the price a hostile bidder would have to pay to buy 51 per cent of the shares. The share collapse also limited Carlton's ability to acquire new companies. It was difficult, if not impossible, to issue more shares when the price was so low, and the much-reduced capitalization of the company also cut the amount that could be borrowed to finance a takeover. The acquisition programme was stopped in its tracks, and any growth in profits at Carlton would now have to be generated from inside the company.

Bronwen Maddox was not alone in her assessment that Carlton was no longer a growth company, or in expressing reasoned concern about Carlton. The 'ex-growth' argument was one of no less than eight negatives listed against the company in November 1990 by Robert Fleming Securities, the stockbroking arm of the Robert Fleming merchant bank. The others ranged from competitive pressure in video-duplication markets and patent disputes over Quantel's Paintbox and Harry with imitators of the products, to Carlton's determination to become a broadcaster and its removal from the FT-SE 100 share index caused by the sharp fall in share price and its reduced market capitalization.

Inside Carlton there was a sense more of bewilderment than of panic. As there was no significant corporate debt, everyone knew the company was not about to collapse. Yet there was no doubt that it was facing difficult trading conditions because of the deepening recession. Financial returns from individual divisions were dropping, and Green couldn't believe just how bad some of the monthly sales figures were – particularly from subsidiaries such as Quantel and Abekas. Broadcasting companies had simply stopped buying expensive editing equipment. But, despite the genuine difficulties, Green remained convinced the reaction of the markets to Carlton was greatly overdone.

'The article that upset Michael most was a piece in the Saturday *FT* which was talking about preference shares, and he was compared with Saatchi, Next and British & Commonwealth. He erupted, and for once he was right,' a former senior employee recalls. However, what Green did have was a serious credibility problem, and the negative perceptions which began with the £10.5 million share sale could have cost him control of Carlton.

'Michael had no concept at all about the reaction he was going to unleash – none at all. And what he didn't understand was how fantastically unpopular he was and that the number of people over the years he had been arrogant with and had treated like shit were . . . You know it's the classic thing: no one had any sympathy for him,' the senior employee added.

By the end of September 1990 the share price was at 301p. Michael Sorkin warned that there was nothing Green could do about the reaction to his share sale and he should just ignore it. 'As far as your share price is concerned, it's a question of time,' Sorkin said. 'You just concentrate on building the business and continuing to run it and expand it and forget about acquisitions for the next period, however long that may be, because it is not practical. Concentrate on business. And when your results improve that's the best way of answering the critics,' he advised.

The concern voiced earlier in the year at Scottish Widows about Green's interest in acquiring a broadcaster before the next round of awarding ITV licences was, of course, well-founded. Green was still looking at Thames and talking to its reluctant owners. There were also detailed conversations with James Gatward, chief executive of TVS, the south-of-England broadcaster, which was considered a favourite to lose its licence because of the continuing problems with its expensively acquired MTM subsidiary in Hollywood. There was also a third possibility – Central Independent Television, where Carlton already had a 20 per cent stake. All Green had to do was buy Robert Maxwell's 20 per cent to get effective control, and Maxwell was prepared to sell as soon as he realized that the government was determined to ensure that national newspaper owners could not own more than 20 per cent stakes in ITV companies. But for a number of years Green had been dreaming even grander visions – a 'merger' with Granada.

Green saw himself as an outsider and Granada as the insiders of the television industry. Green first put the proposal to Alex Bernstein, the Granada chairman, at a private lunch at Granada's headquarters in Golden

Square, just off Piccadilly Circus. He told Bernstein that he would love to merge Carlton with Granada, but would do so only with Granada's agreement and approval. Bernstein was too wily a bird to be caught by such a soft sell. He politely explained to Green that he didn't believe in mergers, because in reality they were always takeovers with winners and losers – and he knew which he would be in a Michael Green 'merger'. That appeared to be the end of the matter, except that much later Bernstein heard that Green had been very much in earnest and perhaps only the collapse in the Carlton share price had saved Granada from a much more forceful approach.

The corporate-finance department at Kleinwort Benson, looking for extra business, had earlier suggested to Green a more limited approach to Granada – that he might try to buy Granada Television from the Granada group. There were signs at the time that Granada might be moving away from television, and the two top Granada television executives, David Plowright and Andrew Quinn, were looking over their shoulders to see how the future of Granada Television might be safeguarded – perhaps through a management buy-out. Green reacted with initial ridicule to the idea, but after twenty minutes of cross-examining the corporate bankers he decided it was one of the best ideas brought to him in years. But the plan came to nothing, because Granada decided to keep, and indeed expand, its television interests.

The disquiet of Carlton's institutional shareholders in autumn 1990 was also fed by Green's joint interest with Conrad Black, the powerful Canadian owner of the Telegraph group, in buying into the BSB satellite consortium. Alan Bond, the west-London-born sign-painter who had become a multi-millionaire in Australia before overstretching himself financially, had put his 28 per cent stake in BSB up for sale. (The distress sale was not, ultimately, enough to save Bond – winner of the Americas Cup and all-Australian hero – from bankruptcy.)

Green and Black met representatives of the main BSB shareholders in the office of the Pearson chairman, Lord Blakenham. After giving an entertaining account of his meeting with the outspoken Bond, the Carlton chairman warned that Anthony Simmonds-Gooding, the BSB chief executive, was getting into serious trouble with the project. Green made it absolutely clear that he and Black would take on the Bond stake only if Carlton was given full managerial control of the venture. If that happened, merger talks with Rupert Murdoch and Sky would probably not have been far behind.

Lord Blakenham, Alex Bernstein, and Peter Davis, chairman and chief executive of the media and information group Reed International, which had bought a stake in BSB, were not yet worried enough about the prospects of

BSB to listen to ultimatums from a rather brash young man whose share price was on the slide. 'I don't think there is much doubt that Michael was right. But if you want to do a deal with those people you don't insult the management in quite that way,' says Black. The talks went no further, and Green lost the chance to have a significant stake in what turned out, in the longer run, following the merger of BSB and Sky, to be a successful £8 billion venture.

Among those watching Carlton's falling share price with keen interest was Sir Peter Michael. After his departure from Carlton, Sir Peter and his small team in the old UEI offices in Newbury had started looking for interesting business challenges. They were not long in coming. Within three months they were asked by bankers to step in to run Cray Electronics. The UK company was losing £5 million a year, and had debts of nearly £50 million and assets of less than £20 million. As an incentive, Sir Peter and his team were given a large share-option package. For Sir Peter it was to be the foundation of another huge fortune as the old management was removed, subsidiaries were rationalized, and a new data-communications division was created through the acquisition of Case Communications from the Dowty group. The recession made progress tough, but by the third year Cray was back to profit.

Looking at Carlton, Sir Peter was struck by what he saw as the very disappointing price obtained for Cosworth, the failure to merge Quantel and Abekas, and doubts about the future level of Carlton profits. 'It seemed to me that it [Carlton] was a company which was ripe for a new management. So I guess at the back end of 1990 I mounted a takeover bid which never became public but it came as close as anything had to unseating him,' he recalls with considerable relish.

Sir Peter and Cray were being advised by the merchant bank Robert Fleming, and together they went to a number of institutions and argued that Green was not going to make his profit forecasts and that a number of key executives were planning to leave. 'We said we think it's time to change the board, the chief executive, and it [Carlton] should become part of Cray's. And we got a lot of people on side for that – a lot of people on side.'

The former UEI chairman believes Green did not know about the potentially hostile bid until very late in the day. Then his reaction, according to Sir Peter, was one of 'absolute horror to find out he was being seriously threatened'.

Sir Peter Michael had gone secretly to Carlton's main institutional shareholders to put his case for removing Green. His campaign had included a visit to Scotland to address the four main institutions holding significant stakes in Carlton – Scottish Widows, Standard Life, Scottish Amicable and

Bailey Gifford. In late October 1990 this important group of shareholders was concerned enough about the future of Carlton and the doubts sowed by Sir Peter to meet at Standard Life's offices in St George Street, Edinburgh, to discuss the situation. The four senior investment managers – Ernie McKnight of Scottish Amicable, Robin Garrow of Scottish Widows, Max Ward of Bailey Gifford and John Thomson of Standard Life – to a very real extent held Michael Green's future in their hands. If they had collectively decided to sell or to back Sir Peter, Green's position as chairman of Carlton could have become very precarious.

At the meeting the four decided on an unusual course of action. They would 'request' that Michael Green come to Scotland to explain himself, and an official invitation was issued by McKnight.

On 1 November 1990 Green, June de Moller and Bernard Cragg (who had joined the board as finance director three years earlier) travelled north for a 3 p.m. make-or-break meeting with the four institutions in the modern black-glass headquarters of Scottish Amicable at 150 St Vincent's Street, Glasgow. Half an hour before the meeting the four investment managers got together to discuss the issues they wanted to raise – rumours in the market, disaffection within the management team, and the suggestion that Green was *persona non grata* at some of the Carlton subsidiaries. 'I'm not sure the meeting would have taken place but for Sir Peter indirectly pointing us at various things that were going wrong within Carlton,' one of the fund managers recalls. 'We were determined to be firm with him,' Thomson remembers of the mood as the two sides sat down to face each other across a meeting-room table.

Thomson of Standard Life made it clear that he was unhappy that there were no independent heavyweight non-executive directors on the Carlton board, and Green gave an assurance that he would bring in non-executives. Bernard Cragg was asked directly whether he was planning to leave Carlton. 'Bernard looked very uncomfortable and swallowed a few times and gave a fairly lame reply that left me in no doubt that he was thinking of leaving,' Thomson remembers.

For another investment manager the main issue was whether Green's acquisitive instincts had taken him too far off his established track and whether the business 'was just careering out of control'. There was real concern about Green's ambitions to become a broadcaster. Nevertheless, Green made no attempt to disguise his ambitions. 'He was quite open about it. He said, "I really do want to run a television contracting business." I am absolutely certain you could not look back on that meeting and say he was in any sense misleading,' Ward of Bailey Gifford says.

Halfway through Green played a carefully prepared card thrown up by research in preparation for the meeting. 'How can you possibly speak with one voice as united shareholders prepared to support me when one of you is already selling their shares in Carlton?' Green asked. Scottish Amicable had been selling a large part of its Carlton stake. 'After Green left, we gave Ernie McKnight an absolute bollocking. He hadn't told us, and it did undermine our position as responsible shareholders,' Thomson concedes.

The disarray among the four investment managers helped Green to survive, but the four were already suspicious of Sir Peter Michael and would probably have supported him only if Green had been completely intransigent. They had mainly been interested in using Sir Peter as a threat to persuade Green of the need for reform, and the consensus view following the meeting was that there was not enough hard evidence to justify trying to take away Carlton's independence or to remove its chairman. 'We decided to hold firm on the basis of that meeting,' Garrow explains.

The managers heard later from London stockbrokers that Green felt that he had been 'read the Riot Act' on his visit to Glasgow. Thomson believes the outcome was very positive. 'Michael Green was given quite a shock from the share-price performance, from shareholders complaining openly, the pressure of a possible takeover by Sir Peter Michael, and then being confronted by us. I think it was quite a maturing experience for him. But I would give him really good marks for listening.'

Sir Peter believes the outcome was finely balanced, but after Green's rearguard action in Glasgow the attempted coup fizzled out. Fatal flaws, Sir Peter believes, undermined his effort. The timing was not quite right. The deal on offer would have involved a straight share swap, with Carlton shareholders getting Cray shares, and the old UEI team would then have gone in to give Carlton a new direction. But Cray had not yet been fully turned around, and it looked a bit as if the computer company was trying to save itself through a merger with Carlton. Another flaw, Sir Peter believes with hindsight, was that he should have topped up the proposed share swap with cash, which could have been easily raised.

The attempted coup failed, but 'I think it became very, very close,' said Sir Peter, who would have enjoyed enormously arriving in Carlton headquarters with a press release already in his pocket announcing that Green had decided to stand down as chairman and chief executive of Carlton to pursue other interests. In 1993 Sir Peter left Cray, which has never quite got totally out of trouble, and sold his 9 million shares for around £12.6 million.

In the same month as the Glasgow meeting an echo of the disquiet among institutional shareholders started to reach the public domain. A story by Margaret Park in the *Sunday Times* on 11 November 1990 set the ball rolling. The headline read, 'Carlton's Green Faces Rebellion.' 'Institutional investors in Carlton Communications, the television services group, are believed to have discussed the possibility of forcing Michael Green to step down as chairman and chief executive,' the first paragraph said. It quoted one unnamed investment manager as saying that people had been trying to stir the pot with a view to replacing Green. The article also carried a comment from 'sources close to Green' denying that the institutions had made any such feelings known.

Green, who had got an early Saturday-evening edition of the *Sunday Times*, was incandescent. That Saturday evening he called a *Financial Times* journalist at home, spluttering with rage and denouncing the story as a wild piece of journalism that peddled damaging rumours without a single attributed quote. In fact it would be virtually impossible to get investment managers to go on the record with such sensitive views, but Park had correctly picked up the mood of disillusionment with Green and the share-price fall in a number of institutions. If there was a flaw in the story it was that it understated the seriousness of the situation.

It was not Green, or Cragg, who left but Bob Phillis, the Carlton managing director. In November he announced that he would be leaving, of his own free will, to become chief executive of Independent Television News, the organization that supplies news for ITV and Channel 4.

Phillis was happy to tell anyone who asked that there had been no dispute with Green and that he was simply leaving for a more interesting job running one of the UK's most influential news organizations. And of course that was true. But it was not the complete story. Phillis was desperate to leave. The frustrations of being group managing director of Carlton were considerable. Obviously it was Green who ran Carlton, and Phillis was never more than a part-time member of the small inner circle at the company. But it was worse than that. For it was not only Green whose judgement could overrule internal executives such as Phillis: Green's vast external network of highly placed contacts had that ability too.

When Phillis recommended buying Maxwell's 20 per cent stake in Central to give Carlton 40 per cent – which in retrospect would have been an absolutely brilliant deal – he was told, 'Look, Central is shit.' When Phillis – who had set up Central and had been on its board for ten years – inquired why Central was 'shit', he found out that this was the view of some members of the external network – which included friends such as Bland, Grade and Yentob.

The Carlton managing director, who had been hired to help prepare the company's bid for an ITV licence, was also frustrated that Green seemed unable to make up his mind about which ITV company to go for. The balls were all in the air at once – Thames, TVS, BSB and even sometimes Central, despite it being 'shit' – and Phillis could never get an answer from Green on what the target or the strategy was supposed to be. Green in turn believed Phillis was too uncommercial for Carlton and too interested in his unpaid role as chairman of the Royal Television Society.

Phillis also did not care much for being shouted at in front of visitors to the company. On one occasion the Carlton managing director was asked on the telephone for some figures. Green was told repeatedly that they were on the way up to him. Five minutes later Green appeared in Phillis's office screaming at the Carlton managing director as a guest cringed in embarrassment. On another occasion Phillis was conducting an RTS committee meeting in his Carlton office – the meetings were usually held in the office of whoever was chairman. Green rang in the middle of the meeting, and those there could hear Green's raised voice down the telephone line. In the end Phillis had to leave the meeting he was supposed to be chairing.

But, as Phillis left, new expertise was added to the Carlton board in the form of a very talented old-age pensioner. Lord Young, who had that year been appointed executive chairman of the international telecommunications group Cable & Wireless, had introduced Green to Lord Sharp of Grimsdyke, Young's predecessor at C&W. The arrival of Lord Sharp in November 1990 as Carlton's first completely independent non-executive director – the others, David Green and Nigel Wray, were still significant shareholders in the company – was the first sign that Michael Green realized, or had been persuaded by institutions in Scotland and the City, that the one-man-band days were over. It was clear that, if the company was going to regain its reputation among investors, the Carlton board would need some weighty non-executives of the calibre of Lord Sharp.

'Eric Sharp was a most marvellous, enormously able, eternally young man. Michael never stopped thanking me for that introduction,' says Lord Young. 'And Eric was also chairman of Stanhope Properties' – a connection that was to turn out to be important.

Chapter 11

Competition, Choice and Quality

Michael Green has always seen himself as an outsider struggling against the forces of the broadcasting Establishment – the man who was rejected twice by the IBA. But as Mrs Thatcher's new Broadcasting Bill made its way through Parliament during 1990, promising the biggest revolution in UK commercial television since its launch in 1956, Green, if not yet an insider, was everyone's favourite to become a broadcaster at last.

In fact Green's credentials as an outsider had been suspect for some time. He was a great admirer of Mrs Thatcher and had received a personal invitation to what many now see as a defining moment in the recent history of British broadcasting – the Prime Minister's Downing Street seminar on Monday 21 September 1987. It was there that she revealed her near-contempt for Britain's broadcasting élite and denounced ITV as 'the last bastion of restrictive practices'.

As the likes of John Birt, Michael Grade and Jeremy Isaacs filed into a reception room in the Chief Whip's house at 12 Downing Street, they found Michael Green chatting to Lord Young, the Trade and Industry Secretary. Young believed the IBA's decision to reject Green's takeover of Thames in 1985 had been 'silly' and a sign that the broadcasting ambitions of entrepreneurial businessmen were being blocked by a well-entrenched Establishment. 'It could have been anybody. Deciding that he [Green] couldn't take over the company, that actually said to me, "You have got to change the system that's protecting insiders,"' Young says.

At the seminar there were forty-nine men, including senior civil servants, and one woman, with a handbag. Three semicircles of chairs faced a heavy desk behind which sat Mrs Thatcher, Nigel Lawson, the Chancellor of the Exchequer, Douglas Hurd, the Home Secretary, and Lord Young.

The first presentation was given by Professor Alan Peacock, the idiosyncratic Scottish economist who fourteen months earlier had submitted the report of his committee examining the financing of the BBC. In the report, Peacock elaborated a twenty-year vision of the future of broadcasting that envisaged a gradual transition to true consumer sovereignty when broadcasters offered their wares just like newspapers and magazines and consumers would be able to buy the individual programmes of their choice.

Although the Peacock report had irritated Mrs Thatcher by rejecting advertising on the BBC and supporting a licence fee indexed to retail prices, the Prime Minister was more taken with two other Peacock ideas – opening up the airwaves of 'the comfortable duopoly' of BBC and ITV to the programmes of independent producers and auctioning off ITV licences to the highest bidder. That morning an unrepentant Peacock also repeated his view that public funds should be available for all channels and not just the BBC.

However, it was Richard Hooper, joint managing director of Super Channel, who most attracted the Prime Minister's attention. He had brought along a bag of tricks, and as he outlined the new technological possibilities he fished out of his bag bits of coaxial cable capable of carrying thirty television channels or optical fibres with virtually limitless capacity. It was just the sort of thing to appeal to the scientist in Mrs Thatcher. Here was the broadcasting revolution before her very eyes – clear evidence that the old order would inevitably change. The civil-service mandarins had even prompted Hooper to mention that, if two frequencies – 35 and 37 – then being used for astronomy and video recorders were reallocated for broadcasting use, Britain could have a fifth and possibly even a sixth television channel.

As the morning wore on it became more and more obvious that the 'insiders' were not going to be protected any longer and that anyone who tried to argue for the merits of the old system risked provoking the wrath of the Prime Minister. When John Whitney of the IBA tried to defend current programme standards and regulations he received a handbagging. He took on the uphill task of persuading Mrs Thatcher that there was no need to end broadcaster's exemption from obscenity legislation because broadcasters already observed stricter standards than the law required. He then added that regular public-opinion polls showed that only a very small proportion of people – 5 per cent – thought there was too much violence on ITV. These were not the sort of facts the Prime Minister wanted to hear. Green and the others watched as the she inquired peremptorily, 'Is that all, Mr Whitney?' Instead of taking the cue, Whitney continued to argue his case, annoying the Iron Lady even more.

Shortly after, David McCall, chief executive of Anglia Television, tried to argue that to preserve programme quality standards ITV needed to be protected from too much competition. He was was struck down in full stride with the words 'I think we have had enough grinding axes. Next!'

Green was wise enough to say very little and allow the broadcasting Establishment to get on with the task of condemning itself, but in a brief intervention he did say he had spent twenty years building up a business worth £600 million yet his takeover of Thames had been blocked and he had been turned down for DBS. What did he have to do to become an 'insider', he asked?

The meeting was of enormous symbolic significance. It brought to a head a debate on the future of broadcasting that had been simmering. It was a debate between the free-marketers and deregulators, who believed that the extra choice that cable and satellite had to offer would make the old protected world of the traditional broadcasters an anachronism, and those who thought that, despite the extra choice becoming available, there would always be a need for properly funded public-service broadcasters such as the BBC and ITV.

The old Establishment of broadcasting and the would-be pretenders to their thrones continued the discussion informally over lunch around an enormous rectangular table in 10 Downing Street. On one side of Green sat Bernard Ingham, the Prime Minister's notorious press secretary, who would later explain to the press in an unattributable briefing just how determined the Prime Minister was to see radical change in broadcasting. Ingham tried to convince Green that Mrs Thatcher was a lot more gentle and that he was a lot less powerful than everybody thought. On the other side of Green sat Graham Grist, the finance director of BSB. Grist thought the morning had moved to an orchestrated agenda and that Mrs Thatcher had already decided to open up the club to competition. Even BSB, though not yet on air, seemed to be lumped in with the Establishment because it had won a licence. 'Green looked pretty pleased with himself. I said to him, by way of a joke, would he now be considering an investment in BSB? He had always been considering an investment to get the facilities work, but Virgin had always blocked that,' recalls Grist. Green took the joke as a serious comment, looked stony-faced at Grist, and said, 'Not a chance!'

Mrs Thatcher was very interested in broadcasting, and nothing she had heard that September morning changed her view that here was a cosy, inefficient duopoly long overdue for shaking up. The minutes of the seminar produced by the Civil Service do not record Mrs Thatcher's colourful and central 'last bastion of restrictive practices' remark – although she said it twice. Even so, the bland summary still manages to convey the lady's resolve:

The Prime Minister said that she was concerned that the monopoly powers of the broadcasters and what were effectively subsidies from public funds, led to excessive pay demands and restrictive practices on the part of the unions. This held back new developments and operated against the interests of the consumer. These appeared to be central reasons for seeking to increase competition within the industry.

As she often did, Mrs Thatcher set up a small Cabinet committee to decide on the outlines of policy. It was her way of keeping control of the process that would produce new broadcasting legislation. She personally chaired Miscellaneous Committee 128 – or Misc 128 as it was known. Other members included Nigel Lawson, Education Secretary Kenneth Baker, Douglas Hurd and Lord Young, with Chief Whip Lord Wakeham attending occasionally. To boost the position of the Home Office – the department then responsible for broadcasting – Hurd had requested, unsuccessfully, a second place on the committee for Tim Renton, the broadcasting minister.

Apart from the Prime Minister, two Cabinet ministers exerted the strongest influence. One was Lawson, who, partly for ideological reasons and partly to raise the maximum amount for the Treasury, argued strongly that the licences should go to the highest bidders with no quibbles. The other was Lord Young, whose most inventive suggestion was that the way to boost satellite television in the UK was to transfer BBC2 and Channel 4 to satellite so that viewers would have to buy dishes to watch. The vacated terrestrial frequencies could then be used to launch new commercial channels. It was a 'courageous' idea that was looked at briefly before being rejected as impractical.

One of the problems facing Britain's broadcasters was that the Misc 128 members hardly ever watched television – except sometimes on Saturday nights. 'I used to ring up all my friends in television and say, "For God's sake, change the programmes for Saturday night and make them better!" And when they asked why, I said, "Because the only time Margaret and all the others ever watch television is Saturday night, and of course that's the worst night of the week and she thinks all television is like that," ' Lord Young explains.

To outsiders, the evolving debate looked like a battle between the Prime Minister, the Home Office and the DTI, with the Home Office often caught in the middle. 'Douglas had a very difficult row to hoe,' says Renton, the suave former City merchant banker who was broadcasting minister from June 1987 to November 1989. Another government minister says that what emerged was 'what three of them [Thatcher, Lawson and Young] wanted and what Douglas Hurd was prepared to accept'. Yet Lord Young insists it wasn't quite like that. He says he had enormous rows with Hurd because 'Douglas would tend towards changing more and I would tend towards changing a lot less.'

The White Paper, *Broadcasting in the '90s: Competition, Choice and Quality*, published on 7 November 1988, was a radical document proposing a considerable measure of deregulation for commercial broadcasting. After an initial quality test, licences were to go to the highest bidder. It promised a transparent and open process and an end to franchise winners being chosen behind closed doors on largely subjective criteria with no explanations ever given. A new television commission which would regulate with 'a lighter touch' would replace the IBA. Channel 4 would retain its remit to be innovative, but full privatization was one of the options set out in the White Paper.

One month after the publication of the document, the first sixteen-channel Astra television satellite was successfully launched from French Guiana. Rupert Murdoch had options on six of the channels and was planning to launch the Sky Television network – a vast expansion of his existing single channel, which was mainly carried by cable television networks – in February 1989. However, the White Paper had virtually nothing relevant to say about Rupert Murdoch or what to do about anyone broadcasting to the UK from outside British jurisdiction.

There was still concern in the government about the auctioning off of ITV. 'I was not in favour of the auction, but I could never find another way of tackling the problem,' says Renton. 'Time and time again I said to Richard Dunn of Thames or Leslie Hill of Central, "OK, you don't like it, but you haven't got a freehold. It is only a leasehold. Other people deserve a chance to come in. So what else do you suggest?" And that's where it really failed.' Renton points out that nobody did come up with a workable alternative – something the broadcasters deny.

On holiday in the summer of 1989 at a fishing village near Corunna in Spain, Renton wondered for a minute or two if he had not found the answer. He watched the operation of a local fish market where they started trying to sell fish at a high price – say 500 pesetas a kilo – then gradually reduced the price until there was a bid. 'I thought should we do the ITV auctions that way round. Would that be appropriate? We were desperately looking for alternatives,' says the former broadcasting minister, who at least took one decision during his Spanish holiday. 'I took the view during the summer holidays that I really could not go along with the privatization of Channel 4. To me Channel 4 would have been the resigning issue. And then, rather surprisingly, she gave way,' Renton recalls.

Part of the explanation as to why Mrs Thatcher changed her mind on Channel 4 – apart from the intensive lobbying of Michael Grade, the channel's new chief executive – is that Lord Young says he opposed privatization because he feared the channel would inevitably be forced down market.

At the Independent Broadcasting Authority – soon to become the Independent Television Commission – the man who would have the difficult task of implementing the government's plans took over as chairman one week after the government published its White Paper. George Russell was a businessman born in Gateshead in the north-east of England. He might have become a professional footballer, as he was good enough to get a trial for Sunderland, one of his local clubs, and had attracted attention as he played the game of his life. Russell, however, feared the game flattered his skills and might be the best he would ever play. He decided to stick to his studies.

After working for multinational companies such as Alcan, the aluminium group, Russell ran Marley, the building-products group. He became a member of the IBA in 1979 and was involved in the decision to block Carlton's original takeover of Thames. The issue then could not have been clearer to Russell: under the existing rules you could not take over an ITV in mid-franchise, although he believes now that if Green had been successful it would have been beneficial for the ITV system.

Russell, who was also chairman of Independent Television News, was an obvious candidate for the chairmanship of the IBA because he combined a growing knowledge of broadcasting and the arts with the practical mind of a man used to taking pragmatic business decisions. The telephone call from the Home Secretary came when Russell was chairing a board meeting at ITN. Could he come to the Home Office as soon as possible? He handed over the chair to ITN chief executive David Nicholas and went directly to see Hurd in his enormous office at Queen Anne's Gate. There was no discussion about the White Paper, his attitude to auctions for ITV licences or anything else: Hurd simply asked if he would become chairman of the IBA – a post Russell accepted after a brief consultation with the retiring chairman, Lord Thomson.

Russell was under no illusion about the complexity of the task he was taking on. Increasing competition was obviously on the way from cable and satellite television, while the commercial broadcasters themselves had increased their broadcasting hours by more than 200 per cent in the previous eight years – largely because of the launch of Channel 4 and commercial breakfast television. In such a competitive environment, he believed, it would be a real achievement if 80 per cent of the quality and diversity traditionally provided by ITV could be preserved.

When the IBA under Russell produced its response to the government's

White Paper it accepted some of the government's approach but offered an alternative system of competitive tendering. Under the IBA scheme, the Authority would, with City advice, set a minimum lease price for each franchise, to be paid in annual instalments. This would give a guaranteed return to the Treasury. The balance of the bid would then be paid in the form of specific percentages of an applicant's net advertising revenue. The assessment of both business plans and programmes with respect to the quality requirements would be 'united parts of a single process'.

The IBA had been forced a long way down the government's road. Lord Thomson would have preferred something much simpler – allow ITV companies to be taken over on the Stock Exchange, like any other public company, as long as they fulfilled their licence obligations. That way efficient companies would be able to defend themselves by keeping their share price high, and those who were inefficient would get new owners. But, although he had accepted the principle of a competitive tender, Russell was determined that the quality of programmes should be as important in deciding who won broadcasting licences as the size of the financial bid.

At a press conference held on 21 March 1989 to outline the IBA's proposals, Russell showed just how determined he was. The *Financial Times* asked Russell what he would do if, in the end, licences had to be awarded to the highest bidder, with only rudimentary protection for quality and no discretion for the IBA. Russell parried the question. It was too early to say. There was a long way to go in negotiating with the government, he replied. The question was put again. But what if in the end there was no real discretion for the IBA? What would he do then? Russell paused, and there was silence for a second or two as he pondered whether or not to answer. 'If I am faced with a straight envelope tender, which I cannot believe in, if that actually happens, I do not think I could continue the job.' Russell's honest answer made the headlines in the broadsheet papers the next morning and posed a serious threat to the government's emerging broadcasting policy.

But the impact was even more immediate. That afternoon an alarmed Renton called the *FT* journalist and suggested that it had been grossly unfair to trap Russell into such an answer. After all, said Renton, the IBA chairman was 'a civilian' rather than a politician – implying that a politician would not have been naïve enough to give such an honest answer and would instead have trotted out the stock reply about never answering hypothetical questions.

Russell views the moment differently. He regarded the issue of discretion on matters of quality as absolutely vital and, although he had not intended to be so frank quite so soon, he had decided that when faced with a direct question he would make his position clear. 'That was the moment that turned the Broadcasting Bill. The government did look to see why I should think that this issue was so critical – everyone was on to me – but that doesn't matter. It was a logical next step from the kind of arguments we were putting out, which did indicate that there should be some checks and balances on quality,' he says.

At the press conference Russell also made it clear that he might be prepared to consider friendly takeovers of ITV companies in 1990, but that after the award of the new licences he would like to see a two- or three-year moratorium on takeovers, to allow the new system to settle down.

When Douglas Hurd announced the details of the government's Broadcasting Bill on 13 June 1989 there were signs of compromise. The sixteen licences would still go to the highest bidder, but the Home Secretary indicated that a lower bid might be acceptable in some exceptional circumstances. If the highest bid was not accepted, the IBA would have to give its reasons and the decision would be subject to judicial review.

The final rules of the game and the obligations expected in terms of programme quality were greatly influenced by yet another of Mrs Thatcher's Cabinet reshuffles, on Thursday 30 October 1989. Hurd became Foreign Secretary, John Major moved from the Foreign Office to the Treasury, and David Waddington went to the Home Office.

The following day David Mellor, the health minister, was sitting in his office working on a speech to be given later in the day when the new Home Secretary, a former judge, telephoned and said he wanted to see Mellor immediately. Waddington was worried about the Broadcasting Bill which would soon be introduced into the House of Commons. He knew nothing about broadcasting. When he was being offered the job by Mrs Thatcher he had asked for Mellor to come and see the bill through Parliament.

Waddington explained that he knew how much of a sacrifice it would be for Mellor to return to a job he had already done for several years. At the very least it would appear that Mellor was being kicked sideways. In return he promised that the Broadcasting Bill would be Mellor's baby and that if there were any rows with Mrs Thatcher he would go and argue on Mellor's behalf. It was a promise that Waddington kept. There was a brief tussle over the body of Mellor at a meeting in 10 Downing Street before Health Secretary Kenneth Clarke conceded that Waddington's need was greater than his, and the broadcasting industry heaved a large sigh of relief that Mellor rather than the bone-dry Waddington was to be in day-to-day charge of the legislation.

Michael Green monitored every step of the political debate over the

Broadcasting Bill, but there was still great uncertainty in his mind over the best way to become a broadcaster. Should he buy an ITV company? And, if so, which one? Or should he be a green-field bidder when the new licences were advertised?

In mid-February 1990 Bob Phillis made it clear to Richard Dunn, yet again, that Carlton was still very keen to buy Thames. But a number of barriers stood in the way. Russell at the IBA had not yet made it completely clear whether or not Carlton would be allowed to mount a takeover before the pending legislation was passed. Green also blamed Thames's purchase of Reeves, the US independent television production company, for his uncertainty about going ahead with a bid, although the disappointing price gained for Cosworth and the falling Carlton share price soon became more important. At the same time BET and Thorn EMI were very aware that if they were going to sell their Thames stakes before the franchise auction got under way they would have to move quickly.

Despite the vacillations, Green never totally lost his interest in Thames, although Phillis was growing increasingly exasperated by Green's indecision and what he described to friends as 'the petulant, truculent, whining' behaviour of his boss. At a meeting at Carlton's headquarters on 28 March 1990 Green tried everything he could to find out unpublished information about the state of Thames's profits. The next day BET and Thorn formally announced that their shareholdings in Thames were for sale. Their long series of confidential on-off talks with Green appeared to be at an end.

That summer James Gatward, chief executive of TVS Entertainment, made Green's decision on future strategy even more complex by approaching Carlton with a proposal. Gatward realized he had to do something quickly. There was a danger that financial problems at the US-based MTM, bought for $320 million, would drag down TVS and prevent it winning back its ITV franchise. Gatward knew he couldn't sell MTM then without a large loss, so instead he suggested demerging TVS Television, the profitable south-of-England broadcaster, and selling it separately. The parent company could then bid for a licence in another part of the country. Gatward, who had started his working life as a scene-shifter at the BBC before becoming a television director in Canada, offered Green 80 per cent of TVS Television for £80 million.

The discussions, conducted in a room in the St Ermin's Hotel in St James's, were characteristically tough. Green's team beat the price for TVS Television down to £65 million, and it began to look as if a deal was likely. TVS was clearly seen as a problem, and there was a good chance that the

IBA would have approved a reconstruction as the deal could have been portrayed as increasing the stability of ITV in advance of the round of competitive tenders for new licences. But there was a problem – the French.

Canal Plus, the successful French subscription television company, and Générale de l'Image, part of the French utility group Compagnie Générale des Eaux, had both bought into TVS Entertainment, the group holding company, at the time of the MTM deal and were not keen to sell. The French insisted on meeting Green. After the meeting they decided they liked the Carlton chairman but then sat on the fence for several nerve-racking weeks neither rejecting nor accepting the Carlton offer. Finally they told Gatward the answer was 'Non.' When Hambros, on behalf of Carlton, sent a letter setting out the final terms of the deal on a 'take-it-or-leave-it' basis, Gatward had to reject the offer because he could not deliver his French shareholders. It was to prove an expensive mistake by the French.

The failure of the TVS deal meant that Green now began to look once again at the possibility of buying Thames. It was an ironic situation for some of those involved. As deputy chairman of ITN, Dunn was given the task by the board of finding a new chief executive for the television news organization. It was widely believed that David Nicholas, who had spent thirty years as a journalist and manager at ITN and was both chairman and chief executive, should in future concentrate on being chairman. Nicholas's choice for his replacement as chief executive was Bob Phillis. So, at the same time that Phillis was talking to Dunn about a possible takeover of Thames, Dunn was talking in great detail to Phillis about the terms under which he would become chief executive of ITN – and in particular about the worsening financial position he would find there.

In December 1990 Green suddenly moved again on Thames, with another offer. On 5 December he met Sir Colin Southgate of Thorn EMI and offered 225p a share plus a further 50p a share if the television company retained its licence.

The offer was lower than Thorn's assessment of how much Thames was worth even without its broadcasting licence. Apart from the programme library, Thames also owned Teddington Studios and a 10 per cent stake in the Astra satellite company SES, as well as the loss-making Reeves. Even if the company were to lose its broadcasting licence there was the option of becoming a leading independent producer – an attractive proposition now that the government was proposing in its new legislation that 25 per cent of air time should be set aside for independents. The Carlton offer was rejected.

The Thames shareholdings were publicly put up for sale, and attracted

media companies from all over to world – including Time Warner of the USA
and Silvio Berlusconi's Fininvest. All the potential overseas buyers were
thrilled at the possibility of buying control of Thames, until they got round to
asking the question at the heart of the matter: how does this franchise auction
work? Dunn, as he followed the evolving state of government thinking, could
only explain 'It's like this. The highest bidder will win – unlss he doesn't.'
Thus executives in the boardrooms of New York, Paris and Milan decided
they didn't understand what was going on in the UK and that buying Thames
would just be too risky.

By 19 December 1990 Thorn and BET were trying to place their shares
with UK financial institutions, but still no one was willing to take the risk. In
the circumstances, Green really was the ideal buyer. He knew the company,
was aware of its many 'hidden' assets, and understood better than most what
the government's system of competitive tenders for ITV licences really
meant. A combined Carlton-Thames would have been firm favourite to retain
the London weekday commercial-broadcasting licence. Rivals might even
judge it to be too strong to compete against and choose other targets.

Green knew there were obvious advantages in taking control of Thames
and never quite let go of the idea. But time was running out and, as the
Thames share price fell below 300p and the prospects of a sale seemed to
recede, Southgate decided the best solution might be to buy out BET and
either sell the entire stake or hold on and battle through the franchise round.

On 23 January 1991 Green telephoned Dunn and asked him to call round
for talks to try to break the impasse – just the two of them. After checking
with Southgate, the Thames chief executive went that afternoon to Green's
St George Street office. Green wanted to be sure he had Dunn's support, and
that was immediately given. Since at least May 1989 the Thames chief
executive had realized that it would be far easier to go into the battle to retain
his licence with the backing of Carlton rather than being linked with reluctant
shareholders, there only because they had failed to find suitable buyers for
their stakes.

During the meeting it quickly became apparent that the only issue
separating the two sides was price. Green was unwilling to pay an amount
acceptable to the Thames shareholders, even though Carlton's share price
had shown some signs of recovery since the worst days of 1990 and on the
day of the meeting stood at 354p. The Thames price stood at 269p but
Green would not go beyond 225p plus the 50p success fee. So Thorn EMI
decided to offer BET 268p plus a warrant linked to future performance, and
on 31 January BET finally sold its 27 per cent stake in Thames to Thorn

EMI for 250p a share plus bonuses linked to profitability and success in the franchise round.

Dunn believes that Carlton could and should have clinched the deal. If the merged group had retained the London licence – and the odds would have been good – he estimated that the difference between Green's offer and what BET actually obtained was 25p a share. It would have been considerably cheaper than having to bid against Thames in the highly competitive tenders for the London weekday licence. But Green's principal worry, with the 1990 Carlton share-price collapse fresh in his mind, was that the City would react negatively to any bid that was seen as overpaying for a company widely believed to be overmanned and unreformed, although Thames staff levels had fallen from 2,500 in 1985 to 1,450 in 1990. He was also concerned about whether Thames could be changed in time to submit a winning bid.

On 7 February 1991, in response to Thorn's purchase of BET's stake in Thames, Carlton said it had decided to go for a 'green-field site' in the upcoming franchise auction and that it had hired the managing director of Capital Radio, Nigel Walmsley, to be in charge of its bid. Walmsley, a former Post Office civil servant who has successfully made the transition to the private sector, was also familiar with the IBA, which at that time was the regulator for commercial radio as well as television.

Walmsley was not Green's first choice. The candidate he had always wanted – and the one everyone had assumed he would get – was Michael Grade, the chief executive of Channel 4. It was widely assumed that Grade, whose wealth is modest compared with that of his show-business uncles Lords Grade and Delfont, would leap at the chance of adding serious share options to his already considerable reputation in the television industry. Grade surprised most people by turning down a Carlton offer that would have been worth around £2 million, including share options and a success fee for winning a franchise.

'Money doesn't motivate me, otherwise I'd be doing all kinds of different things. I would still be in America. People forget I went to the BBC [as controller of BBC1] for £40,000 a year. Forty thousand! I was earning half a million dollars a year in the States. I got more for my Christmas bonus,' Grade emphasizes. He did not, however, end up completely empty-handed. He negotiated with his chairman, Sir Richard Attenborough, 'golden handcuffs' of £250,000 for taking himself 'off the market'.

Grade also believed it would be wrong to leave Channel 4 as it faced the threat of privatization, and he was influenced by his brother-in-law Brook Land, a lawyer, who advised him against the Carlton job on the grounds that two such large egos would inevitably clash and it would all 'end in tears'. It is a view Grade disagrees with. 'In the end the deciding factor was not "Oh, I couldn't work for Michael Green!" I could work for Michael Green; I could handle him. I don't think I would have had any problem with him at all. The problem was the timing was wrong. I couldn't leave this place,' Grade recalls.

When he got the bad news, Green immediately asked Grade who he should go for instead. 'Go and look at Nigel Walmsley,' had been Grade's advice. He knew Walmsley through Attenborough, who was chairman of Capital as well as Channel 4, and had been impressed by Walmsley's performance at the commercial-radio group.

Green took Grade's advice on Walmsley, but he rejected another tip.

When Carlton bought Zenith, Green had told Grade he was thinking of changing its name to Carlton. Grade spelled out the implications for him. The company has made a movie. There is a première. The City analysts, the bankers, the board, all the big media players in town are there. 'And up it comes – "Carlton Presents" – and the picture's a dog – and your name's over the door.' 'Oh, Christ!' Green said. 'How awful!' Zenith remained Zenith.

When it came to naming the television company that would apply for a licence, Grade repeated his advice – but this time Green wanted his company name on the licence application. 'Granada is called Granada,' he pointed out. 'Yes, that's true,' replied Grade, 'and I don't know how to argue against that. But instinctively I think it's a big mistake to call it Carlton. It will put you too much in the frame.'

At the same time, in March 1991, Green found a replacement for Bob Phillis as group managing director. The head-hunters had come up with Keith Edelman, who was responsible for strategic and business planning at the Ladbroke Group as well as running its Texas Homecare subsidiary. Not only was Edelman, a cheerful forty-one-year-old with a mop of greying curly hair, an old pupil of Haberdashers' Aske's School, but Green remembered him from the time he had been involved in the negotiations for the sale of Ladbroke's 20 per cent in Central to Carlton.

Edelman, the son of a north-London accountant who died when Edelman was eight, has a business degree from the University of Manchester Institute of Science and Technology, where he studied marketing under Professor Roland Smith, later a hard-hitting chairman of British Aerospace. After university he embarked on a business odyssey which took in Fiat, IBM, Rank Xerox, Bank of America, Grand Metropolitan and Express Dairies before he joined Cyril Stein's Ladbroke.

At Carlton, Edelman took over day-to-day charge of all the existing usinesses, including being responsible for the complex and vitally important negotiations on new Technicolor contracts in the USA. He also looked at everything from strategy to general management.

The return of David Mellor to the broadcasting portfolio at the Home Office in the October 1989 reshuffle had increased uncertainty for the Carlton chairman. Green wanted clear and unambiguous tender rules – as uncluttered as possible by subjective concepts such as quality. If regulators were given too much discretion they might exercise it in favour of established companies such as Thames. According to Professor Brian Griffiths, now Lord Griffiths, then head of the policy unit at 10 Downing Street, Green had little direct impact on the initial formulation of policy. 'Everyone knew, of course, that he was related to Lord Young. But in terms of an impact on policy he just wasn't there. He was simply considered a very good, young, entrepreneurial businessman,' Griffiths says.

Later, during the passage of the Broadcasting Bill in 1991, Mellor felt Green's presence even though he never actually met the Carlton chairman. Mellor believes he saw Green's influence in the form of memos coming down the line from Downing Street. In what was almost certainly a misjudgement of the subtlety of the situation, Green, as usual, was conducting his lobbying at the top and was concentrating his fire directly on Mrs Thatcher. The Green-inspired objections that filtered down from Downing Street, Mellor believes, all had the common theme of trying to stop the insertion of the growing number of checks and balances designed to protect programme quality and diversity.

To Mellor, who saw a clear need to improve a dogmatic Thatcherite bill, it seemed ironic that Green seemed to be almost alone among people in the television industry in apparently believing that the original thinking of the bill scarcely needed improvement. Green was lobbying in his own and Carlton's financial self-interest. But in government circles there were powerful voices, such as that of Griffiths, also arguing that the free-market line should not be diluted – that the details of a contract should be spelled out and then the licence should go to the highest bidder.

Mellor was just as determined to improve the Broadcasting Bill and provide greater safeguards for quality programming. He was able to do so within well-defined limits, and with the exercise of a degree of political courage. Whenever he wanted to change things, Waddington would go on his behalf to Mrs Thatcher. She would hit the roof, and Waddington would explain patiently that as a former Chief Whip it was his view that the changes being proposed were absolutely vital if the controversial measures were to get

through the House. 'There would be fuming and spitting, and then it woul
finally be agreed,' said one of those involved in the process of persuading th
Prime Minister.

On a small number of areas she could not be persuaded, and there was n
point in trying. Sir Alastair Burnet, a former editor of both the *Daily Expres*
and *The Economist*, persuaded Mrs Thatcher it was wrong that Independen
Television News should be a wholly owned subsidiary of the ITV companies
Burnet saw ITV ownership as the chains shackling ITN and preventing it
expansion, and wanted to see new capital coming into the organization. Mr
Thatcher agreed, and the Broadcasting Bill specified that in future at least 5
per cent of ITN should be owned by organizations which were not holders o
commercial-broadcasting licences. Mellor thought such a thing very odd, an
made a half-hearted attempt to change it. The word came back that there wa
no question of the Prime Minister changing her mind on the issue.

There was equally no point in trying to dissuade her from the concept o
awarding new ITV licences by competitive tender, even if Mellor wanted to tr
– which he didn't. The broadcasting minister was never opposed to th
principle of an auction to allocate such scarce and valuable resources as th
airwaves and to ensure that the public got a decent clawback from what th
newspaper baron Lord Thompson of Fleet once famously described as
'licence to print money'. But he was adamant that there should be rigorous pre
qualifying tests to ensure that established television companies could not b
simply outbid by any multimillionaire who wanted to become a media mogu
So, during the committee stage of the Broadcasting Bill, Mellor accepte
amendments that began to turn the qualifying threshold into what Russel
wanted: a 'Becher's Brook' of a threshold – a reference to the most difficul
fence in the Grand National. In particular, programme obligations were spelle
out. In addition to providing news and current affairs, broadcasters would b
required to offer both children's and religious programming.

But the most important change was Mellor's willingness to give the new
Independent Television Commission much greater discretion to turn dow
the highest bid in favour of the highest quality. Mellor came close t
promising the change during the committee stage of the bill, but he then ha
to persuade Waddington, who in turn managed to get the agreement of Mr
Thatcher. Earlier Mellor announced to a meeting of the Campaign for Quality
Television – an apparently independent lobbying group which in fact ha
been initiated at Granada and funded by the ITV Association – that ITV
franchises could be awarded on the basis of 'substantially higher quality
rather than to the highest bidder.

Mellor-inspired amendments – and there were many others designed to soften the free-market thrust of the legislation – terminally damaged his relationship with Mrs Thatcher. It was all too obvious that his rearguard action to soften the free -market thrust of the bill meant he was definitely seen as not 'one of us' – something that contributed to keeping him out of the Cabinet until John Major became Prime Minister. 'I do feel that, although one is sometimes attacked for one's political activities, I honestly do feel that if one had ever had a finest hour then this was it. Because the easiest thing in the world would have been to have said "Yes, sir. No, sir. Three bags full, sir" to Mrs Thatcher and got on with it,' says Mellor, whose political reputation has subsequently suffered because of his affair with the actress Antonia de Sanchas and revelations that he accepted a family holiday from Mona Bauwens, daughter of a Palestine Liberation Organization official.

Chapter 12

Blind Poker

The enormous scale of the challenge facing all bidders, including Michael Green if he was to become a broadcaster, became fully apparent on 15 February 1991 – the day the Independent Television Commission published its invitation to apply for the new regional Channel 3 licences. The invitation was 101 pages long and made it clear that deciding how much to bid was only one of a long list of tricky choices to be made. Applications had to be submitted by noon on 15 May, some three months away.

The financial information required was particularly daunting. Applicants for commercial-broadcasting licences had to provide detailed profit-and-loss projections for ten years from 1 January 1993 to 31 December 2002, along with forecasts for the annual rate of growth of overall television advertising revenue and ITV's share of it. The ITC also wanted interest-rate projections, estimates of exchange rates, corporate tax rates, dividend policies, details of contingent liabilities – all on top of a detailed exposition of programme plans for the appropriate region. To mount a serious bid for a large ITV region was likely to cost between £2 million and £4 million, without any guarantee of success.

Green's task was not made any simpler by the fact that he was planning to bid as a publisher-broadcaster – working with a programme-commissioning team rather than an in-house production staff. To reduce overheads to a minimum, the vast majority of Carlton's programmes, apart from regional news, would be made by independent production companies. Unless Carlton had production deals with independents, or agreements to develop programme ideas, the ITC could legitimately ask where Carlton's programmes were going to come from. Without a roster of independent producers, Green would have nothing.

By 15 February, when Green was finally able to read the invitation to apply, his plans were not in good shape. He had been indecisive. He had considered buying both TVS and Central, and it was only earlier that month that his on-off attempts to buy Thames had finally come to nothing. Now he knew he would have to bid against Thames and try to dislodge one of the best-established programme-makers in the ITV system.

Green had not even got the people he wanted to front his bid. Not only had his friend Grade turned him down, another friend, Alan Yentob, controller of BBC2, had also rebuffed initial soundings, as had John Birt, the BBC deputy director-general. Over breakfast at the Connaught, Green offered Paul Fox the chairmanship of Carlton Television, but even that did not run smoothly. When Fox realized there was no question of a seat on the main Carlton Communications board the old campaigner, who was just about to retire after a stint back at the BBC as managing director of BBC Television, said he would think about it. There were other offers around, and he had not forgotten how his son Jeremy had been treated by Carlton.

Now that Bob Phillis had gone, there were very few Carlton executives who knew how to prepare such a complex application. Given the size of the prize involved, surprisingly little progress had been made. It was Charles Denton of Zenith who looked after the early stages of the application, although he was emphatic he did not want to get involved in running a franchise – he'd done all that at Central a decade before. Instead he wanted the opportunity, if Carlton won a broadcasting licence, to arrange a management buy-out of Zenith. 'He [Green] said, "What do you want? £50,000 each? What do you want?" I said, "No. What we want is the opportunity to buy out the company at the original price,"' says Denton. He insists that Green promised a management buy-out of Zenith as the reward if Carlton won, although nothing was ever put on paper.

Dorothy Berwin, a senior producer at Zenith, remembers that Denton came back from a meeting with Green and told Zenith staff that the Carlton chairman had promised the right to mount a management buy-out of the programme-making subsidiary as the reward for franchise victory. 'Charles has always been totally consistent that that is what Michael said to him from very, very early on in the franchise right the way through – that Michael did promise this,' she says. Green now denies promising Denton a management buy-out – although he concedes that other members of his staff may have encouraged that impression.

It was Denton who came up with the approach designed to give Carlton the best chance of getting over the programme quality threshold. The Carlton team would look at everything that Thames did on the programme side and 'mirror the whole damn thing'. The aim was to try to prove to the ITC that the network would not come to a juddering halt if Carlton replaced Thames. Consequently many of Carlton's programme offers were simply Thames look-alikes with a different name. *This Is Your Life*, for instance, was to become *This Is Your Life Mark 2*. Denton was also vital in signing up – for relatively small sums of money – leading independent producers, many of whom were initially suspicious of Carlton's slender programming credentials. He called on his twenty-five years' experience and contacts in the British television industry to persuade independents that working for Carlton would lead to a revival of independent production in the important London television market.

One of those excited by the prospect of having a publisher-broadcaster within the ITV system was Denise O'Donoghue, managing director of Hat Trick Productions, creators of hit comedies such as *Drop The Dead Donkey* and *Have I Got News For You*. It was Denton who persuaded Hat Trick to join the Carlton bid. 'Charles was inspiring. He was the most important thing for us. He grasped some of the more experimental things we wanted to do, such as comedy drama,' O'Donoghue recalls. Denton also impressed Linda James, managing director of Red Rooster Films, an experienced independent producer of drama, which signed up with Carlton.

Green had also needed to appoint consultants who would play a central role in crunching numbers and producing the crucial advertising-revenue forecasts that would underpin any cash bid. Janice Hughes at Booz Allen & Hamilton, who had already done some work for Carlton, had hoped she would get the contract, which could be worth more than £1 million in fees. But Green had been advised by Hambros Bank that he should put the contract out to tender, and he had called in rival consultants McKinsey & Co. to make a formal presentation. Then he asked Hughes to come to see him on her own and explain, without papers or charts, why she should have the contract. It was the first time in her career that such a thing had happened. The conversation lasted two hours and ranged widely enough to include the latest books she had read. However, Green was really interested only in what she could do to ensure a Carlton victory. It was obvious that he was desperate to win – indeed that he knew, for the future of Carlton Communications, it would be very damaging to lose.

At the end of the meeting, without any formal presentation, Green told Hughes she had got the contract, and from the beginning of January a seven-strong team from Booz Allen had been at work.

At around this time Green also had to deal with an irritating issue involving Roy Moore, chairman of Superhire, the Carlton props company, and a controversial payment made to a member of the Thames staff. One evening in December 1990 three Superhire managers had gone to the Surrey home of Moore, who by then only went into the office one day a week. They said they were concerned about some of the Superhire invoices. Moore went into the office the next day and took away three months' worth of invoices to study at home. He says he found around six 'bad' ones, where things didn't quite add up. In particular, he found a cash voucher for £100 made out to a buyer who worked for Thames Television. A Superhire employee who had offered Thames £700 for some old hospital furniture left over from a series said he had been asked by a Thames employee, 'Anything in it for me?'

Moore's policy on such issues has always been emphatic: 'Never ever cheat your clients – ever. You never ever give backhanders.' The Superhire chairman says he confirmed that G. 'Mutch' Mulchandani, who had been recently been sent from Carlton headquarters to become managing director of Superhire, had authorized the payment of £100 to the Thames employee.

On 19 February 1991 Moore wrote to Green 'with great concern and in the positive belief that you have no knowledge of the problem that has arisen within Superhire'. Moore explained in his letter how he had shown his evidence to the head of design at Thames – the departmental head responsible for props – and had been given assurances that the matter would be taken up with Carlton. Moore related how he had then had a meeting with Geoff Rampton, a Carlton executive, on 6 February and had provided him with copies of the documents. 'He promised me he would investigate further and report back to me,' the letter read. 'He failed to do so, and when I telephoned him on 13 February, he told me he had indeed questioned Mr Mulchandani, who had admitted his part in the defrauding of Thames TV and that he had been reprimanded. As Mr Mulchandani had claimed that this was an isolated case, the matter should be considered closed.'

Moore believed the police should have been called in, and urged Michael Green to give his personal attention to the affair. The next day, 20 February, Moore received a letter, signed by Rampton, notifying him of his immediate dismissal as chairman of Superhire. Moore believes such a letter of dismissal was not something that could have been sent without Michael Green's knowledge. 'He [Green] had sanctioned my immediate dismissal. Not for anything I had done. Not for anything I had ever done. They have never said to me I had done something wrong. The reason for dismissing me was that I no longer had confidence in Mulchandani,' says Moore, who never returned to the offices of the company he founded.

Moore's letter to Green and Rampton's dismissal letter to Moore had crossed in the post. On 20 February, when Green received Moore's letter, the Carlton chairman called and accused Moore of putting him in an intolerable position. According to Moore, Green offered to honour his contract until the end of the year and throw a big party for him. 'He [Green] wanted to keep it quiet, without any question at all. He was absolutely desperate to keep it quiet – desperate,' says Moore, who also got the impression that Green believed that as only £100 was involved it really wasn't such a big deal. Moore, who was worried that people would believe he was being dismissed for wrongdoing, asked Green, 'How much can you cheat out of £600? You can't cheat £500 out of £600.' To the Superhire chairman it was the principle of never paying backhanders that was important.

Moore went to see Green and talked about the issue for an hour or so. Green was adamant – the matter had been investigated and was now closed. After consulting with his solicitors, Moore started an action against Carlton for wrongful dismissal and added on a lawsuit for damages. There was every chance that it would all come out in public just as the ITC was considering the ITV bids.

It must have seemed a minor issue to Green compared with the formidable task of trying to put together a winning franchise bid on such a tight schedule. Nigel Walmsley arrived formally as chief executive of Carlton Television only in February, but still had to double up with his job at Capital while he worked out three months' notice. The second on board was Peter Ibbotson, former editor of *Panorama* and a deputy director of programmes at BBC Television. Ibbotson would actually write much of the application. Ibbotson suggested that Jonathan Powell, controller of BBC1, was unhappy at the Corporation and would make an excellent director of programmes. But on 24 February Powell turned Walmsley down, and conversations then began with the second choice, Paul Jackson, who ran Noel Gay Television, the independent programme-maker. In early March Jackson agreed to take the job. Brian Wenham, a former director of programmes at BBC Television, also joined the team, as did John Egan, a Price Waterhouse consultant, who produced comprehensive flow charts to make sure every aspect of the bid was proceeding on time.

The practical difficulties of producing a first-class application were compounded by Green's decision to bid for the TVS franchise as well as Thames – more as an insurance policy than from any real desire to win the licence. The Carlton chairman was still worried that the ITC might decide to save Thames, and he wanted to give himself the chance of winning at least a consolation prize. The main bid against Thames was code-named Hawk, the TVS bid was dubbed Eagle, and Dawn was the name for the bid, as a member of a consortium, for the commercial breakfast franchise held by TV-am.

As Denton continued to work on the programme plans, the team from Booz Allen painstakingly built up every cost and revenue factor that had to be

ncluded in the business plan. Hughes even managed – with difficulty – to
persuade Green to accept a Italian minority shareholder, Giovanni Agnelli's
Rizzoli Corriere della Serra (RCS) group. It was not an easy task. Green did
not see why he needed other investors or why he should not simply have 100
per cent. Would this not let a powerful tycoon like Agnelli through the door?
Green finally saw the logic of making his application look a little more
international and more broadly based to impress the ITC, even if RCS would
have only 5 per cent of the consortium plus a matching 5 per cent of the costs.

The Carlton chairman also let Conrad Black, chairman of the Telegraph
group, in for another 5 per cent. 'He agreed just as a goodwill gesture to allow
us into his Thames bid, but he would only give us 5 per cent. I had occasion
to recall Mussolini saying "I am not a collector of deserts." I was not much
interested in 5 per cent participation, but on this occasion I said, "Michael, I
am happy to take the crumbs from the rich man's table," ' says Black.

The first big meeting that brought all sides of the bid team together was on
Friday 15 March at the headquarters of Booz Allen, 100 Piccadilly. By that
stage a large amount of financial work had been done, and the eyes of the
programme-makers glazed over as the accountants and consultants talked of
cash flows, profit-and-loss accounts and internal rates of return. 'Green
arrived and pulled his usual trick of taking exaggerated exception to a small
detail in the financial forecasts, implying that such sloppiness simply would
not do. It was his way of making sure everyone knew he was the boss, after
which he subsided and was quite well-mannered. Obviously he wasn't going
to allow Walmsley to be seen to be running the meeting,' observed one of
those present.

There was no doubt that Green was determined to win – but not at any cost.
We were very determined not to overbid, and Michael – unlike TVS or some
of the others – was not prepared to go after the numbers. He really wasn't, and
we were very mindful of that – all of us,' according to a bid member.

Although the work was beginning to accelerate, it was not until 22 March
that the team took over the top-floor offices of Zenith's headquarters in
Dorset Street. Later a suite at the Montcalm Hotel, near Marble Arch, was
also used for application-drafting sessions that often ran on into the middle of
the night.

From the very beginning, Booz Allen also had a team dedicated to
modelling the likely application from Thames, based on every scrap of
published information they could find. They wanted to try to work out what
the ITV company could realistically afford to bid.

Over at Thames the top management had no doubt that they were

Carlton's main target, and had a team collating every scrap of information about the company, but they were much less certain about what would be the most effective strategy to beat Green off. Thames argued that its skilled production teams making programmes such as *This Is Your Life*, *Wish You Were Here* and *The Bill* were vital to the ITV national network schedule. The current-affairs series *This Week* added a dash of serious purpose, although one particular edition may have added to Thames's problems. The programme 'Death on the Rock', dealing with the killing of three IRA terrorists in Gibraltar, screened in April 1988 despite government protests, was widely credited with stiffening Mrs Thatcher's determination that broadcasting was greatly in need of 'reform'.

David Elstein, the Thames director of programmes, who had been a leading independent producer himself, realized the enormity of the challenge Thames faced. From the day he arrived at the company as director of programmes in 1986 he says he argued for the closing of the Thames studios. They were expensive, underused and overmanned. Not only did they lose a great deal of money, they were even not separately accounted for. Elstein had taken the Thames non-executive directors out to lunch one by one to make his case that there was absolutely no in-house service that he could not get more cheaply on the open market. 'It was just impossible to sell that concept to the non-executives. They were all too squeamish. And Richard [Dunn] just didn't want it. He didn't think it was right and he didn't think it was necessary. And, as the shareholders supported him and they owned the company, in the end you just get on with it,' says Elstein.

The Thames programme director believes that, if action to drive down costs had been taken early enough, Thames could have matched any Carlton bid. Redundancies would have been inevitable, but the cost could have been partly offset against the special Treasury tax on excess ITV profits that all ITV companies had to pay.

In the absence of a radical cost-cutting programme, Thames faced a difficult dilemma. There were clear limits to how much Thames could bid. Equally, it would not be in shareholders' interests to bid a sum so large that the profits of Thames as an ITV broadcaster would be lower than the company could make as an independent producer without a broadcasting licence, selling its programmes on the open market.

Thames could alternatively bid deliberately very low, in the hope that it would be the only bidder to get over the quality threshold. That strategy was dismissed as too high-risk, because Thames executives believed that Carlton had a good chance of passing the quality test.

Perhaps the best strategy would be to make it easy for the ITC to invoke exceptional circumstances by trying to ensure that the gap between the Thames and Carlton bids was small – perhaps no more than a few million pounds. A narrow financial gap might show off to advantage the difference in quality between Carlton and Thames and the contrast between existing performance and future promises. Over the year, as much as 40 per cent of the prime-time weekday ITV schedule came from Thames. Surely it would be difficult for the ITC to turn its back on such a company. The decision was taken to emphasise that Thames was a 'centre of excellence.'

But a further serious problem for Thames was the fact that the legislation insisted that the ITC could not take an incumbent's track record into account. The purpose was to ensure that newcomers would have a chance to compete for the scarce right to broadcast, but it meant that, unlike in most competitive tenders, here only the future was being judged.

Thames had its own equivalent of Hughes and the Booz Allen team – Kip Meek, a former McKinsey consultant who had become the media specialist at Coopers & Lybrand, the accountancy and consultancy firm. With the help of a seventy-strong group, Meek took on no less than seven applications – the defence of six ITV companies, apart from Thames most of them small, and one new bidder, Meridian, another challenger for the TVS franchise in the south of England. For Meek, the issues at Thames were the most complex.

Dunn increasingly believed that Thames could win on exceptional circumstances. At a board meeting, the Thames chief executive said he felt he could see into the ITC chairman's mind. A number of executives shuffled nervously at the thought that the strategy for the survival of Thames as a broadcaster was dependent on something so flimsy.

During the passage of the Broadcasting Bill, Dunn had been chairman of the ITV Association, the industry trade organization, and had been unselfish in pursuing, on behalf of the industry, the ITV campaign to modify what it saw as deeply flawed legislation. In the process he had worked closely with the ITC chairman, George Russell.

Dunn produced an elaborate metaphor to describe the importance of Thames's contribution to the ITV system. Think of the timpani in the orchestra, he suggested. The timpani, the orchestral kettledrum, is not vital for every piece of music, but when its thunder is needed for a particular piece it becomes important for the overall effect. Thames was not just offering violins and oboes but the whole orchestra – including the timpani. Some came close to telling Dunn his theory was nonsense – that as a result of Mrs Thatcher's Broadcasting Act it would be fortunate if there were many string quartets left at the end of the process, never mind full orchestras complete with timpani. Some in the team could not make up their mind whether Dunn was being brave or foolish. 'I like people who are passionate about lost causes, and he was definitely passionate about this particular lost cause. We used to laugh at the timpani thing, but nevertheless here was a sort of noble figure, thoroughly decent, saying "No, I will not budge", and those sort of things are heroic about him,' said one of the Thames bid team.

Dunn suspected that, to be absolutely sure of winning, Thames would probably have to bid above £50 million – a figure the board thought would be ludicrous. Even if the board had been prepared to go so far, Thames might still be rejected for overbidding. 'So overbidding was execution. Under-bidding was execution. We had to step back and say, "There are two ways of doing this. One is we make the highest bid we can possibly think up which we are pretty sure that no one else will bid, and hope we don't get excluded for overbidding. Or we place the maximum value on the retention of the broadcasting part of our business that we can possibly justify, and hope that it will be either a winning bid or that the ITC will decide on exceptional circumstances to award it to the underbidder." We took the latter route without any hesitation,' the Thames chief executive says.

Over the river at London Weekend Television, Christopher Bland and his chief executive, Greg Dyke, were facing a rather different dilemma. They

Christopher Bland (right) with Greg Dyke

knew they were going to face a rival bid – but from a group of independent producers backed up by the financial muscle of PolyGram, the music and film division of Philips, the multinational consumer-electronics company. The group, London Independent Broadcasting, was clearly serious, but equally it was no Carlton.

On the surface, Bland also faced a serious choice. At a strategy weekend at Hever Castle all the top LWT executives had suggested bids ranging from £18 million to £25 million. But LWT calculated that a green-field rival could bid between £30 million to £36 million a year against it. LWT had already reduced staff numbers and costs and taken further drastic action in preparation for the bids. To prevent itself overbidding, it had financially reconstructed the company. No less than £135 million was given out in special dividends to shareholders, paid for by raising £100 million in debt. To increase the incentive to win, 15 per cent of the company was reserved for a top-management share scheme. Fifty managers were able to subscribe for shares at 83.2p a share. If the franchise was retained and the LWT share price averaged at least 278p in the twenty business days following the announce-ment of the half-year results to the end of June 1993, many would become multimillionaires. Few imagined the share-price target could be met, but the whole package – including the debt – was put together to try to ensure that the company's hard-earned wealth would not be given to the government through a high bid, rather than to shareholders.

During a walk with his dog at his country home near Winchester one weekend, Bland thought through the implications of bidding anything like £25 million and came up with a radical approach. 'Suppose you do get it [the bid] up to £25 million. You would be absolutely stretched for ever, and who is going to have any fun? It would be better to lose than to spend the next ten to fifteen years really struggling with a bid at the outer level. So it was then only zero or 5 or 6 million,' says Bland. The rational choice seemed to be between bidding the minimum £1,000 a year or something small but respectable like £5 million, in case a tiny bid would anger the government and the Treasury.

But before committing LWT to such a daring course Bland needed to be sure that Thames would not bid against LWT for the weekend franchise as an insurance policy. The rules did not preclude an existing ITV company from bidding for any of the other licences. A £45 million LWT bid for the Thames franchise had already been prepared, but the company wanted to retain its own licence rather than win someone else's. Dyke, a tenacious former local-newspaper journalist, set out to take Thames out of the frame. 'When we decided to bid low we had to get rid of Thames. We had to stop Thames

bidding for us,' says Dyke, who met Dunn in a London hotel to try to
negotiate a deal. 'Richard and I discussed it and we said, "It doesn't make
sense. Let's not bid against each other,"' says Dyke, who was delighted to
knock out a large potential rival at no cost. Dunn, who had considered the
possibility of backing London Independent Broadcasting, and had his own
team working on a bid for the London Weekend licence, was equally pleased
to get the informal deal. Preparing such bids seemed a diversion and total
waste of time.

The two sides also agreed not to help any of their opponents. Earlier,
however, while Carlton had still been interested in acquiring Thames, the
LWT team had provided Michael Green with a great deal of information
about the weekday company – in particular, how its costs could be cut. In
return Bland had shown considerable foresight and asked for and received a
written agreement from Green promising that he would not bid against LWT.

The third bidder for the London weekday franchise was Richard Branson's
Virgin Group. Although the main battle was always seen as being between
Carlton and Thames, Virgin could not be ruled out. Branson himself, whose
main obsession was Virgin Atlantic airlines, was unenthusiastic. The driving
forces behind the bid were his brother-in-law, Robert Devereux, chairman of
Virgin Communications, and Charles Levison, an entertainment lawyer who
had once represented the Beatles and who had considerable media experience
running music satellite channels.

Levison had produced a paper for the Virgin board as early as November
1989, setting out the possible options. As Virgin had no real presence in the
north of England or feel for broadcasting there, the target would be the south-
east of England – Thames or TVS. Levison thought Thames was the really
big opportunity. He believed the company had not changed and the
management appeared to lack focus, with Dunn deeply involved in the
politics of ITV and buying Reeves the US production company. 'They were
not setting themselves out as the London station – more providers of
programmes to the network. They didn't serve their market,' Levison
thought.

Throughout the autumn of 1990 Virgin went unsuccessfully through a
similar list of candidates as Carlton for its top jobs, including Grade and
Phillis, Andrew Quinn of Granada, and Julian Mounter, the former Thames
journalist then running TV New Zealand. There were even conversations
between Green and Devereux to see whether Virgin could get together with
Carlton, but the talks never got far: Devereux wanted at least 50 per cent of
any joint venture, while Green was equally insistent on having control.

Devereux also had had a number of breakfasts with David Frost, the celebrity interviewer and media entrepreneur, who not only knew everyone but had been a founder of LWT in 1968 and of TV-am in 1980. Frost was extremely interested in what Virgin was planning, but nothing was consummated. Branson then added to the difficulties of Virgin's plans by personally blowing apart the emerging financial structure of the bid.

Sensitive conversations had been under way throughout 1990 with Westinghouse, the large US energy and communications group. It was known that Virgin had a possible overseas partner, but the name had not leaked. In December the founder of the Virgin group agreed to be interviewed for Mary Goldring's *Answering Back* programme on Channel 4. Staff warned Branson that he could talk about anything he liked but should under no circumstances mention the Westinghouse talks. Asked by Goldring who his foreign partner was likely to be, Branson blurted out the name Westinghouse. No agreement had been signed, and Branson compounded his error by appearing to suggest that whatever happened it would not be Virgin which would be taking the main financial risk. The Americans took fright and the Westinghouse deal fell apart.

The Virgin bid appeared to be in trouble. Qualified top executives had not been hired, and there was a shortage of weighty financial backers. Virgin could not, however, be ruled out. The Virgin 'brand' had an aura of youth and excitement, and, as with Carlton, the approach was to be a publisher-contractor, commissioning programmes from independent producers. This low-cost structure would enable Virgin to make a high bid.

The Virgin bid began to take more promising shape in January 1991, when independent producers Noel Gay suggested there was another secret bidder for the Thames licence. If Branson joined the consortium, together they could beat Carlton. Was Virgin interested? Half an hour later Branson's telephone rang and it was David Frost. The famous interviewer had the backing of Charterhouse Bank and Herb Siegal of BHC, a large American broadcaster. Frost had already signed up John Gau, an extremely experienced broadcaster, to run his bid. Gau was a former chairman of the Royal Television Society and had been deputy chief executive of British Satellite Broadcasting. The outlines of a deal were thrashed out by the two sides over a dinner in the Carlton Tower Hotel, and the Branson-Frost consortium – CPV-TV – was created.

Frost's arrival changed everything. He thought it would be a good idea to go for three franchises – Thames, TVS and Anglia. 'The instigator for going for three was David. His argument was that this is a lottery – there is no way you can really tell – and we have a team that can pass the quality threshold,' says Levison.

There had then been talks with Central about the possibility of its taking a stake in a CPV-TV bid, but Central's chief executive, Leslie Hill, after looking at the Virgin bids, doubted whether they would get over the quality threshold. Instead Central planned to get involved in Meridian's bid for the South and South-East franchise in opposition to its 20 per cent shareholder, Carlton. The issue came before the board on the same day that Green waited, none too patiently, to be elected to the Central board. Because of the obvious conflict of interest, he then had to withdraw from the meeting again as the board discussed involvement in the bid for TVS. It was an awkward position for Hill. He had to make sure the ever-inquisitive Green did not receive commercially sensitive information he was not entitled to. 'I think Leslie Hill plays it absolutely straight – straight down the middle – and there was never any suspicion of information being passed across,' says a member of the Meridian team.

The Meridian team – led by Clive Hollick, chief executive of the financial services and media group MAI – always saw Green as being principally interested in the London franchise. Hollick, who became a Labour peer in the run-up to the bidding, believed that Carlton's lack of serious interest and Virgin's lack of focus meant he was in a two-horse race with TVS for the south-of-England franchise.

Lord Hollick

But it was in the contest for the commercial breakfast licence that most of he competing interests, suspicions and clashing egos of the ITV system came ogether.

The breakfast station looked extremely vulnerable to everyone but the executives of TV-am, led by the pink-shirted Australian Bruce Gyngell – the irst man to appear on television in Australia on the day it launched in 1956. n the final years of its franchise TV-am's comfortable mix of news, views and sofa-bound chat had pulled in large audiences, and the result was a pile of cash. Two strong consortia, attracted by this success, were already starting to circle. One of the determined potential bidders was Patrick Cox, head of the European activities of NBC, the US network company. Cox had been in Phillis's office at Carlton, trying to persuade the then Carlton chief executive to join NBC's Daybreak bid against TV-am, when Green had walked in unexpectedly and asked what he was doing there.

When he heard the outline of the Daybreak bid, Green was instantly attracted and then startled Cox with the surprising news that Phillis was on his way to becoming chief executive of ITN. 'Now I tell you what to do, Bob. You go to ITN. You bring ITN in [to Daybreak], and Carlton will come in oo. All right?' Green asked.

When Phillis arrived at ITN he took on the task of coordinating the Daybreak bid, and Carlton, the *Daily Telegraph*, MAI and the construction group Taylor Woodrow joined. There was a lot of tension in the group – not eased by the fact that Paul Fox, the man who had turned Green down, was chairman of Daybreak.

Things got worse in April, when, to mark his imminent retirement from the BBC, Fox gave a farewell interview to Russell Twisk for the *Observer*. In it the former paratrooper expressed robust views about the quality of TV-am, which he denounced as 'garbage' and 'cheap couch television'. TV-am, said Fox, offered an absolutely terrible service, and had proved it during the Gulf War. When the breakfast station had finished its morning programme, ITN had had to come on with a bulletin of its own to provide 'the real facts'. Asked whether he would be watching breakfast television from now on, Fox replied, 'I'll be quite honest. I listen to Radio 4 in the mornings. I'm going to chair the thing. I'll leave that [watching] to other people.'

In the same issue of the *Observer* there was also a story saying that Fox planned to join the board of Thames – a company where he felt he would be among friends.

Later that Sunday morning, 28 April, Green stormed into the Carlton suite at the Montcalm Hotel where a number of the bid team were already at work.

'Fuck fucking Fox!' said Green, who was soon on the phone ranting at one of
the most distinguished representatives of the British public-service-broad-
casting tradition. He was infuriated that Fox, the chairman of Daybreak, was
to join the board of Thames and had, without consulting consortium
members, expressed indiscreet views on the nature of breakfast television –
views that might irritate the ITC. If TV-am was garbage, it was the ITC and
its predecessor that had let it get away with it for years.

In fact Fox's views, although expressed in an extreme manner, were
consistent with the thrust of Daybreak's programme proposals. Daybreak
planned to take news more seriously and to produce something much closer
to a television equivalent of Radio 4's *Today* programme. Next morning, at a
specially convened board meeting, Green was 'unbelievably rude' to Fox,
according to one of those there. But after a shareholder session with the
chairman out of the room it was decided that Fox would stay – although he
was told to curb his press interviews.

The tension over Fox was only one disruptive element. Another was
Michael Green's hyperactive approach. Conrad Black thought Green was
sometimes so jumpy as he discussed the Daybreak bid that he needed to be
hosed down. 'He would present these fantastic suggestions that we should
throw out one or other party and bring in others. My general view was
"Michael, these are our partners. You have a deal with them. You can't keep
rewriting the deal. You can't build an aeroplane in the air. We're in the air
now. We have to stick with what we've got," ' says Black.

But the greatest tensions of all arose over deciding how much to bid.
Green's position was consistent throughout: he didn't want to bid high, and
the number he had in mind was lower than that of most of his colleagues. Ten
days before the bids went in there was little agreement. Phillis, who was
convinced the consortium could bid up to £40 million and still make a profit,
was arguing for a bid of between £34.5 million and £35 million. Cox and
Black would go as far as £33.5 million. But Green's preferred figure was
£32.5 million. One of those advising him not to overbid for the breakfast-
television licence was Leslie Hill of Central. Indeed Green had turned up
instead of his usual representative, Piers Inscape, at a meeting in Phillis's
office and announced that he was 'here to stop you guys going crazy on the
bid' and that he was not budging from his figure. When it was suggested that,
to protect security and increase flexibility, Phillis should be given the right to
add to the size of the bid – within limits – Green looked 'as if someone had
pissed on the table'.

There was a feeling of unease and lack of harmony as the shareholders convened at a meeting at Price Waterhouse the day before the bids were due in. Black and Hollick would go to £33.5 million, but Green was still arguing that that was more than the licence was worth. 'Michael held it down. If he hadn't done it would have gone up,' said one of the partners.

To complete the incestuous nature of the bidding, Michael Green's old friend Christopher Bland was one of the leading influences behind the third bid for the breakfast licence, Sunrise. Its backers included the Walt Disney Company, Scottish Television and the group that owned the *Guardian* and the *Manchester Evening News*.

Green also played an important role in the decision by Central, the second largest ITV company, to bid low to retain its existing licence, even though Carlton was only a 20 per cent shareholder. In fact Green was everywhere during this period – talking to everyone, sucking in intelligence, and making sure he knew as much as he could about the progress of the bid process, even in areas where he had no direct interest.

Central approached the bid deadline with growing confidence that the company was not going to be opposed. A number of potential bidders were put off – just as they were intended to be – by Central's decision to increase the complexity of its television operations by splitting itself into three regions, each with its own dedicated news service. Many looked at Central and decided it was just too complicated to match what was already being offered to local viewers. To make sure the company would not be ambushed at the last minute by a serious rival, a sophisticated intelligence-gathering operation was organized by Marshall Stewart, the company's strategic adviser and a former editor of the *Today* programme. Every local-authority area was trawled in search of any sign of planning applications for studios or anything relating to broadcasting. There was a momentary scare when a story was picked up that a company was looking for new studios in Birmingham. There was just such a company, but it turned out to be Central itself.

Four alternative bids, complete with business plans, had been prepared, but Leslie Hill became more and more confident that Central would not be opposed and decided that a low bid would be the most rational. Although some board members wanted to bid many millions of pounds, the Central chief executive gradually formed the view that £2,000 was a real option – £2,000 rather than £1,000, just in case £1,000 did not meet the ITC's stipulation that bids should be in multiples of £1,000. But the Central board had to be convinced to take the risk of bidding low. Until noon on 15 May no one could be absolutely sure that a secret rival would not suddenly emerge. Green was one of those advocating that Central should make a very low bid.

The emotions generated by the battle for the breakfast franchise and the fixing of the Central bid were skirmishes by comparison with the contest for the London weekday licence. In London, because it was so important to him, Green wavered, changed his mind several times, and even came close to panic. The Carlton chairman did not contribute much on the programme side, but the bid numbers were his province.

Three weeks before the bids were due there was a dummy 'brown-envelope' session in a meeting-room on the first floor of Carlton's headquarters when all the members of the team were asked to write down their bid figure on pieces of paper. Green went round the table picking up the pieces of paper and quickly took in that they ranged from £35 million to £46 million. For two hours he paced round the room discussing the logic of everyone's position. Although a figure of £42–43 million was emerging as the likely Carlton bid, Green could be swayed by which of his powerful contacts and confidants he had been speaking to most recently.

In the final run-up to the deadline he had a telephone chat with his friend Lord Weinstock of GEC and then went round for lunch. At the lunch, Weinstock – hardly an expert on the economics of commercial television – warned Green about the dangers of overbidding and told him not to throw his money away. Green came back and put enormous pressure on his franchise team to reduce the bid. The numbers and paperwork were adjusted accordingly.

On the programme side the application was looking more substantial. Paul Jackson had brought in a whole raft of comedy, light entertainment and drama to add to Charles Denton's initial offerings. Twenty new sitcom, variety and other entertainment shows, including *Comedy Premiere* and *Comedy Playhouse*, were detailed in the application. The bid appeared less strong on the factual side, however. Peter Ibbotson, who had spent most of his broadcasting career in current affairs, late in the day spotted a significant flaw. There was no equivalent of *This Week*, the award-winning Thames current-affairs programme. He promptly invented a programme called *Seven Days*. Ibbotson also spent three days rewriting Carlton's regional programming plans and strengthened them by inventing a number of new programmes.

The bid against TVS, which was put together by Brian Wenham, relied on the same programmes but separate regional programmes were also devised.

The team at Zenith's Dorset Street headquarters had been toiling away on version after version of the application, combined with review meetings that could sometimes last as long as seven hours. Michael Green popped in occasionally on morale-raising visits, and Michael Grade of Channel 4 came round to see how his friend's franchise application was progressing. Green, Nigel Walmsley and Grade had already discussed the bid a number of times over dinner at Tyle Mill, Green's country house.

On 2 May, Grade came to Dorset Street to comment on the programme draft. His view was that it lacked passion and was as dull as ditch-water. Hasty efforts were made to liven the application up a bit, although Walmsley seemed most concerned with layout and graphs and making sure that paragraphs were properly indented.

Then, early on the morning of Sunday 12 May, shortly before the bid documents were to be printed, Michael Green really began to panic. He had obviously been talking to someone with completely different views from those of Lord Weinstock. Members of the team were already at work on the final tidying up of the documents when he called to say he had changed his mind. The bid amount was going up again. Carlton finance staff were summoned from their beds to get to work on the changes. 'He really flipped at that point,' says one of the team.

The Carlton team got there in the end, despite the last-minute alarms, and it was in an optimistic mood that Nigel Walmsley and Paul Jackson – Michael Green was nowhere to be seen – arrived just after 8 a.m. on Wednesday 15 May to deliver Carlton's applications for the London-weekday and the south-of-England licences in two separate vans to the ITC's underground garage where bids were received. The application for the London licence alone ran to more than 500 pages, and there was a total of 54 copies. Apart from copies needed by the ITC, publicly available sections such as programme plans had to be provided for the main public libraries throughout the region concerned.

In its application, Carlton said £2 million had already been invested in developing seventy new programme ideas from thirty of the UK's most creative production companies. 'This is just the beginning. From 1993 we expect to spend around £80 million a year on new high quality and original programmes to add to the best of the current schedule.'

There was much less optimism at Thames as Richard Dunn delivered its application soon after Carlton. The bid team had modelled the Carlton bid and they were convinced that Thames was going to be outbid. Whether it was stated explicitly or not, the company that made *Minder* and *Anglo-Saxon Attitudes* was relying on exceptional circumstances to survive, or acceptance of the argument that its role as the linchpin of the ITV network was too vital to be discarded. After all the agonizing, the level of the Thames bid was simply set by placing the maximum valuation on retaining the broadcasting –

as opposed to independent-production – side of its business. The company felt it was not in a position to do anything else.

In public and to his staff Dunn put on a brave and confident face, but he knew there was a strong likelihood that Carlton would have bid more. Dunn was not totally resigned to losing, but, unlike all the other ITV companies, as soon as the bids were in Thames began work on planning its future without a broadcasting licence – just in case.

The Branson-Frost team got tangled up in the traffic surrounding the changing of the guard at Buckingham Palace and arrived only half an hour before the noon deadline. CPV-TV had put together a strong roster of independent producers and was proposing to offer Londoners more comedy, more drama and a one-hour news-magazine programme – *The Capital Hour*. It was only in the two weeks before the deadline that it had become really apparent to Levison just how much work was involved in fighting for three franchises, but he had at least been able to make what he thought was a very competitive bid for London.

After the noon deadline had passed and all the hundreds of boxes of applications and millions of pieces of paper had been stored away, a small ritual took place. George Russell, the ITC deputy chairman Jocelyn Stevens, chief executive David Glencross and the Commission secretary Ken Blyth opened the envelopes to make sure that each contained the right documents. They were then signed and locked away in the ITC safe.

Russell had arrived only after lunch, and he came carrying two trout. When the future of sixteen ITV companies was being carried into the ITC, the man who would ultimately have a considerable degree of influence over their fate had been fishing in Hampshire – partly to stay out of the way of his staff.

The colourful Stevens, who had been editor of *Queen* magazine through most of the 1960s and was a former managing director of Express Newspapers, described opening the envelopes as 'the sweatiest-palm moment of my career'. Russell's first thought was one of alarm at the number of established ITV companies which had been outbid and therefore could lose their broadcasting franchises.

But most of all the envelope-openers were absolutely astonished by the enormous range of bids thrown up by Mrs Thatcher's game of blind poker.

Chapter 13

Winners and Losers

Two weeks after submitting the ITV bids it was back to reality for Carlton Communications with the announcement of less than sparkling results. For the six months to March 1991 pre-tax profits had fallen by nearly 30 per cent, to £46.3 million. Michael Green spoke of 'demanding trading conditions', but insisted it was still a 'very creditable result'. He was also keen to reassure analysts that he had not succumbed to the temptation to overbid for a television franchise – something that could have led to a run on the share price when combined with the decline in profits. Green promised shareholders there would be a good financial return if Carlton, whose capital value had by then recovered to more than £840 million, won an ITV franchise. To hedge his bets, he also emphasized to the City that, even if Carlton failed in its bid, under the new rules it could launch a takeover of an ITV company from 1994. Carlton would be a broadcaster one way or another.

Apart from demanding trading conditions, the spring and summer of 1991 was a trying time for Green. A man whose normal attention span can be measured in minutes rather than hours now had to wait six months to find out whether Carlton had won a broadcasting franchise – six months of endless speculation and little hard information. The ITC had asked those who submitted a total of forty bids for sixteen licences to keep all the financial information confidential until the winners were announced. Many aspects of the applications, such as programme proposals, were in the public domain, but the ITC was worried about the effect publication of financial details would have on share prices, and also wanted to be able to take its decisions quietly and calmly away from the public gaze.

ITC officials quickly got to work sifting through the mountain of paperwork generated by the forty applications. One team, under David Glencross, began assessing the programme plans to see whether they passed the quality threshold. Another team, under Peter Rogers, the ITC finance director and deputy chief executive, checked the numbers and ran sensitivity checks to ensure that applicants would have enough money to sustain a high-quality service throughout the ten years of the licence. In addition, each of the ten ITC members – apart from George Russell and Jocelyn Stevens – was assigned to oversee two licences, so that when the final decisions were taken there would be an ITC member familiar with the contest in every region. The officials were to make recommendations on which companies had passed and which had failed the quality thresholds – recommendations that would have to be ratified by the members. Only then would the applicants which had passed the quality thresholds be ranked according to the size of their financial bids.

In the final stage the ITC members would judge whether any qualified underbidders deserved to win a licence because they offered exceptional quality. Every step the ITC took was carefully scrutinized by the ITC's legal advisers, Allen & Overy, in case decisions had to be justified later in the High Court.

In June, however, Green was able to get away from the tension for a holiday – in Israel. He had been there before – to attend the funeral of Sir Isaac Wolfson – but he wanted to take Tessa. They decided to go with Michael Grade, who had always been reluctant to go to Israel to face the Holocaust Museum and the suffering it represented.

Once there, they hired guides and academics to explain the history and culture of the country. One of the highlights was the trip to Masada, the hilltop fort where, in AD 73, besieged Jewish zealots committed mass suicide rather than surrender to the Romans. A guide asked Grade whether he would prefer the two-mile hike up the Snake Path or the 438-yard ride up by cable-car. 'I don't want to climb Masada,' Grade replied. 'I want to land on it.' Permission for the two Michaels and Tessa to land on Masada by helicopter was refused, although they did manage a helicopter ride to the sea of Galilee. They did also go to the Holocaust Museum.

But even in Israel the group could not totally get away from the ITV franchise bids. That week in Jerusalem they were celebrating the eightieth birthday of the city's legendary mayor, Teddy Kollek, and a number of distinguished visitors from London were staying at the King David Hotel. They included Jocelyn Stevens of the ITC – one of only four people who knew the size of all the bids. 'All anybody wanted to talk about was the ITV franchises. Yet there we were in Jerusalem. It was hilarious,' says Grade.

In London the franchise affair continued to generate enormous publicity. There was the drama of the secret bids, the possibility that ITV companies which were household names could lose their right to be broadcasters, and the fact that no one knew who the winners and losers would be – apart from Central and Scottish, both of which had been unopposed. However, that summer the relative size of most of the bids came tumbling out – to the irritation of both the ITC and the Stock Exchange.

On 9 July the media correspondent of the *Financial Times* was having lunch with an independent producer in the cavernous City Brasserie in Plantation House, near the Tower of London. The main topic of conversation was the franchise auctions. A remark made by the producer over the last glass of wine startled the journalist. 'Did you know Scottish has bid less than £1 million,' said the producer, who had been told by a member of Scottish Television's staff.

If true, the implications were enormous for Scottish, its share price and its future. It meant that chief executive Gus Macdonald had guessed correctly that the company would be unopposed and had bid really low. Both Macdonald and the Scottish chairman, Bill Brown, became instantly unavailable', and the press office said it could not comment on such price-sensitive information. A call to another extremely well-informed television executive produced the answer 'You're absolutely right.' The headline in the next day's *Financial Times* read, 'Scottish TV bids less than £1 million to renew franchise', and the Scottish share price began to shoot up.

A senior television executive then confirmed that, contrary to top industry rumour, Central too had bid under £1 million – and that company's share price also began to rise rapidly.

But in London it was particularly difficult to persuade anyone to talk, because so much was at stake. Green was eager for every snippet of information, but was giving absolutely nothing away. He was also getting very nervous. He was sure he had outbid Thames, but was convinced that he had been outbid by Branson's Virgin consortium. He was so worried that he even attended a private lunch with David Frost at Charterhouse Bank to explore whether the two consortia might merge. The plan was quietly dropped, because Green was unwilling to give up enough of his shareholding.

The first leak of information in London came from the Branson camp. An executive involved with the bid suggested the figure was between £45 million and £46 million – a high but not unrealistic bid for the lucrative London market. Rumours were already widespread, but unconfirmed, that Carlton had probably bid around £48 million. A call to Thorn EMI with what turned out to be only partially accurate information produced shock and the clear admission that Thames had bid considerably less than £40 million. Green took in the information about Branson without giving anything in return, despite several telephone calls to his office and later his car. Nothing would persuade him to divulge anything about the size of his bid – he was insistent that he was saying nothing at all. But he also knew that the *FT* was going to report that Carlton was believed to be the highest bidder. The story that appeared on 14 August also said that Thames had been outbid by both its rivals and was therefore in serious jeopardy.

By then Carlton's lawyers were taking the first steps to try to get Roy Moore of Superhire's case for wrongful dismissal thrown out. They argued that, as Moore was working less than eight hours a week for Superhire, the industrial tribunal was not competent to hear the case. In August the Carlton argument was rejected – Moore worked longer than eight hours, although some of it was from home – and permission was granted for a full hearing. It was, however, likely to be a long-drawn-out affair, and the former Superhire chairman decided he wanted to settle. Carlton also wanted an agreement, and Moore says he received an informal offer from David Green outside the tribunal. 'David Green offered me £50,000 to drop the case. I said, "I don't want any money at all. All you have got to do is pay me the money you owe me. I don't want anything else at all. But what I do want is a letter of apology from Michael Green – that's what I want." And he said, "Right. I will see what I can do."' Moore claims that David Green came back after making a telephone call and said that Moore would get his letter of apology from the chairman of Carlton. On that understanding Moore dropped both the industrial-tribunal case and the lawsuit for damages.

That summer the battle between Thames and Carlton was fought in a variety of ways. Some encounters were public, at a debate organized by the *Guardian* where both sides set out their plans and attacked those of their rivals. There were also background briefings for journalists, casting the opposition in the worst possible light. In August, for example, Green asked staff for information on Thames weaknesses to feed to the *Sunday Times*, while David Elstein at Thames prepared detailed analyses of the programme plans of its rival bidders – assessments that were sent to the ITC.

Elstein was particularly scathing about the Carlton application, denouncing it as 'highly conservative'. Where it offered change, such as in the promise to have a London news hour in the early evening, 'virtually all its proposals are impractical or uncommercial to an alarming degree'. But mostly, Elstein argued, Carlton had proceeded 'by slavish imitation'. He had correctly identified the Carlton strategy. *The Bill*, the successful Thames twice-weekly police series, was going to be replaced by *Routes*, a new twice-weekly saga set in the trucking industry. In place of the *Wish You Were Here* holiday programme, ITV's longest-running factual series, Carlton proposed two programmes – *The Good Getaways* and *Away From It All*.

The Thames executive went on to suggest that the true cost of the Carlton slate of network programmes was closer to £120 million than the £80 million estimated. And, in his final barb, Elstein pointed out that Carlton programmes would still be available to the ITV network if Thames lost, but it would not necessarily work the other way around. 'All their independent producers will continue to offer their wares – and, indeed, will continue to qualify as independents. No such certainty applies to Thames programmes, currently so crucial to ITV's success, which might, post-1992, for the first time become available to rival broadcasters.'

Elstein was equally dismissive of Virgin's programme plans, although he conceded that its network programme ideas were 'on the whole more interesting than Carlton's'. The Thames executive's fiercest attack was on Virgin's regional plans, under which everything from current affairs to lifestyle, fashion, history and investigations was to be carried in one daily programme, *The Capital Hour*, which he argued was under-resourced and something the audience did not want.

In October, not long before the ITC was due to announce its verdicts, the issue of Moore and the £100 Superhire 'bung' surfaced unexpectedly in the *Sunday Telegraph*. Journalist Ray Mgadzah wrote, 'With less than two weeks to go before the Independent Television Commission announces the winners of the franchise auction, the mud-slinging has sunk to new depths.' The *Sunday Telegraph* said it and other newspapers had seen documents concerning a £100 payment authorized by Superhire's managing director Mutch Mulchandani to a Thames employee.

More interesting than the timing – the fact that the story had found its way into the public domain just as the franchise auction entered its final stages – was Carlton's official response to the allegation. It was a masterpiece of damage-limitation. Carlton told the *Sunday Telegraph*, 'Almost a year ago, an employee of Superhire, a Carlton Communications prop hire business, paid £100 to an employee of Thames Television as part of a transaction to buy some props from Thames.' The money had been a tip, but the statement conceded that Moore had approached both Carlton and Thames saying that disciplinary action should be taken against those involved, although in fact the Thames employee had already left the company as a part of a redundancy programme. The statement went on, 'Following a thorough investigation, Carlton concluded that the matter did not warrant such action – a view confirmed in a discussion between Michael Green and Richard Dunn of Thames Television.' The spokesman said Mulchandani was still managing director and retained Carlton's 'full confidence'.

Two days later Russell, the ITC chairman, received a detailed report on the Superhire affair from Thames, including copies of correspondence between

Carlton and Moore. The main purpose of the Thames report was to repudiate
the statement made by Carlton and reported in the *Sunday Telegraph* that
Dunn had in any way confirmed the Carlton view that no disciplinary action
should be taken. In fact Dunn and Green had met by chance at the Garrick
Club on 21 February, at a party to celebrate Paul Fox's recent knighthood. On
that occasion Dunn told Green no disciplinary action could be taken against
the Thames property-buyer because he had already left the company. Green
said he wanted to keep his managing director and was trying to calm the
Superhire chairman, who was demanding dismissal. Several months later
Dunn found out that, far from Green trying to calm Moore, the Superhire
chairman's immediate dismissal had been ordered on 19 February, two days
before the Garrick conversation. But if the ITC paid any attention to the issue
of the £100, and who said what to whom and when at the Garrick, it did not
show.

It was only a week until the final verdicts were to be announced. By then
the Commission's task had largely been done. Those who had got over the
quality thresholds were ranked according to the size of their bids. It was time
for the possible exercise of the ITC's discretion – the right that most of the
television industry had fought hard for. Were there any exceptional
circumstances to justify setting aside the highest cash bid – in particular the
idea supported by David Mellor that a truly exceptional bid in terms of
quality could, and indeed should, win whether it was the highest bid or not?
For Carlton this could be the most dangerous phase of all. If the conspiracy
theorists were right and the ITC would try to massage the results to get the
ITV system it wanted, this was when it could happen, behind closed doors
with no one watching. This was where Green could become a loser again.

During that last week before the announcement, Green was growing
increasingly confident that Carlton would win. More staff were being hired,
and on 7 October Carlton Television had an all-day meeting at the Langham
Hilton during which very detailed issues about how the company should be
run – everything from budgetary control and petrol for company cars to
pension rights – were discussed. Green arrived for lunch in an excited mood.
Charles Saatchi has just told him that a Cabinet minister believed that Carlton
had won.

Two days later, on Thursday 10 October, the ITC began the final stage of
the licensing process – discussions that continued over dinner in the ITC
headquarters, accompanied, as always, by lawyers from Allen & Overy. That
same day Green invited the key Carlton Television executives to lunch at
Claridges. He told Nigel Walmsley, Paul Jackson, Peter Ibbotson and Chris

Hibbert, who was in charge of engineering, that if there was a bad result the following week he wanted to keep the team together. A friendly acquisition of an ITV company might be permitted by the ITC before 1994. Bidding for Channel 5 or setting up a satellite television channel were all possibilities.

When the ITC resumed its deliberations next morning the most important remaining task was to look for exceptional circumstances in the bids for the London licence. Virgin's CPV-TV was out of the running by that stage. At £45.32 million, its bid was the highest – with Carlton in second place on £43.1 million and Thames a long way behind with a bid of £32.79 million – but the ITC had formed a unanimous view that none of the three CPV-TV bids for Thames, TVS and Anglia was good enough to get over the quality thresholds. The applications were judged to be insufficiently focused and sloppy, but they were not completely hopeless and there was a clear view at the top of the ITC that, if Virgin had concentrated on London and, as a result, put in a more polished application, it could easily have won. In contrast Carlton had sailed through all the quality thresholds and was judged to have put in a very good application which appeared to demonstrate that Carlton could step into the shoes of Thames with the ITV system, or the viewer, hardly noticing.

With Virgin out of the reckoning, and Carlton outbid by Meridian in the south of England, Green's chance of becoming a broadcaster now depended entirely on whether Russell, Stevens and the other ITC members found that there was an exceptional case to save Thames.

Before they dealt with Thames and Carlton, the ITC had looked for exceptional circumstances that might save TV-am, which had been heavily outbid by both its rivals, Daybreak and Sunrise. TV-am had bid just £14.13 million, compared to £33.26 million by Daybreak, the Carlton-backed consortium, and £34.61 million by the LWT-led Sunrise consortium.

From the chair, Russell led the discussion that might have saved Bruce Gyngell, Mrs Thatcher's favourite television executive. TV-am had not only helped to straighten out the labour practices of the entire television industry but had built up a 75 per cent audience share at breakfast and was the most successful broadcaster in its time slot anywhere in the world. But the legislation made it clear that, to give new applicants a fair chance, history should not be the determining factor. The other two bids looked just as good and had equally eminent broadcasters on board. Where, Russell wondered, was the exceptional quality that could save the breakfast company? The other ITC members couldn't see it either. The fate of TV-am was sealed when the lawyers were consulted. Their advice was stark: they did not see how the ITC could legally sustain an exceptional-circumstances argument to award TV-am the licence.

Thames was a different matter, and Russell felt there was a substantial case to be considered. Thames represented no risk. It had a tremendous programme record – *This Week* was one of many programmes singled out for praise by ITC members – and all its best programmes were in the application. They could be sold to a rival channel if Thames failed to keep its ITV licence. It was an emotional occasion, and if each of the ITC members had been asked individually if they wanted Thames to win the answer around the table would probably have been an unanimous yes. One serious doubt was raised about Thames that counted against the company, however. It was obvious that Thorn EMI, the company's dominant shareholder, was not committed to its future. If Thames regained its licence there was a good chance that Thorn EMI might sell, and then there would be no guarantee that the current high programme standards would be maintained.

The discussion ranged back and forth for nearly two hours, but, without anyone needing to articulate it, the ITC was heading towards an inevitable conclusion. Carlton had provided an exceptionally well-written application and appeared to have the backing of the independent programme-making industry. Awarding the licence to Carlton would not be a complete shot in the dark. It had a record of making programmes. The ITC members were impressed by the fact that, through its Zenith subsidiary, it had produced programmes of the quality of *Inspector Morse* for ITV. Slowly but inevitably a consensus emerged that in the end didn't even require a vote. Nobody around the table believed that under the exceptional-circumstances clause they had before them Thames was exceptionally better than Carlton.

Perhaps if Thames had submitted a much lower bid and devoted the money saved to a roster of additional impressive programmes and special series it might have given the ITC members a serious argument to consider. 'I have always felt that money thrown at programmes, once we'd got the quality threshold in, was a far better way of winning than money thrown elsewhere. But that is history,' said Russell. As it was, the ITC chairman felt as if he was running an execution service rather than a broadcasting service when he gathered in the views of his members that sealed the fate of Thames.

As the ITC members trooped out, the Archbishop of Canterbury, who had by coincidence been invited to lunch nine months earlier, was waiting. Russell informed His Grace that the franchising task had been completed, and added jokingly that they had thought of calling him in for a bit of divine guidance at the end.

That weekend, although no one admitted it at the time, Thames virtually knew it was going to lose. The ITC had made it clear that, if it was planning to use the exceptional-circumstances rule, those companies affected would be informed and called for interview. There was no telephone call from the ITC offering a last-minute reprieve for Thames.

Wednesday 16 October – the day of the announcement – was inevitably traumatic, but many thought that it was made more nerve-racking by an attempt by Russell to modernize the process. In December 1980, when the last franchise winners had been announced, all the applicants had had to turn up at the IBA just after Christmas to be told of their fate. Winners and losers ended up milling around in the middle of a media circus. Russell thought there had been a lack of dignity about the proceedings and no chance for those who had just lost their livelihoods to compose themselves. This time Russell decided to use a bank of fax machines in the ITC headquarters to send out the good and the bad news simultaneously, so that the losers could absorb the verdict in relative privacy before deciding how to tell their staff. The faxes were to be sent out at 9.50 a.m. The Stock Exchange and journalists were to be informed at 10 a.m.

At Carlton the fax machine was located in a small basement room big enough to hold only six people. Over at Thames the fax that would decide the company's future came to a machine in Dunn's large mahogany-panelled outer office. In the Carlton basement Paul Jackson, wearing a trade-mark multicolour waistcoat and a garish tie with a pig on it, almost ripped the tray off the fax machine in his impatience – only to find a page that said, 'Two more pages to follow.' As he finally picked up the good news, Jackson said, there were 'cheers, huge relief and euphoria. But that was very quickly replaced by the realization that we had a very big mountain to climb.' At Thames, soon after the confirmation of the worst, Dunn went to Studio 5 to address his staff and promise them that Thames would bounce back as the UK's largest independent producer. Staff hardly needed to be told that if the company did indeed bounce back it would be without most of them. Dunn said it was 'a tragic loss for 1,000 people who have done nothing but make programmes of quality'.

As the packed press conference at the ITC waited for George Russell to begin his televised speech, the word began to spread that four ITV companies had indeed lost their franchises – Thames, TVS, TV-am and TSW. The ten-minute time gap between the two announcements meant that Press Association reporters stationed at the offices of the main applicants had already picked up the news and it spread by mobile telephones to journalists at the press conference.

At the ITC, Russell made journalists and the live television audience wait for the news – rather like a Chancellor of the Exchequer who saves the key tax changes until the end of a long speech. First he wanted to pay tribute to an industry that had continued to win awards abroad and the ratings war against the BBC at home, 'at the same time as living with this undoubted turmoil'. He also pointed out that eight of the sixteen licences had not gone to the highest bidder and that, as a result, compared with special tax payments under the old system, the Treasury would in total be getting only around £45 million a year extra from ITV as a result of the competitive tenders, although this turned out to be an underestimate. Then he laconically went through the winners one by one. When he got to the London-weekday contest he simply said, 'Two applicants, Carlton and Thames, passed the programme quality threshold. The higher of the two cash bids was from Carlton Television and they are awarded the licence.' The losers noted, with some bitterness, that there was no word of thanks or commiseration for them.

For Green it was the end of a long race, but for him there was no champagne-spraying vulgarity of the sort favoured by racing drivers, and there were certainly no television interviews. He did stand briefly outside Carlton headquarters just long enough to be photographed holding a Carlton Television sign, but that was it.

During a long telephone conversation, the ITC chairman told Michael Green that Carlton's London application had been the best of the entire forty. Later that day Green called the *FT* to apologize for not having helped with the story on his bid amount. He simply could not admit that Carlton had been outbid, because he feared that, had he done so, Virgin would then have mounted a major public propaganda campaign to try to influence the ITC.

It had been a very good day for Michael Green and Carlton Communications. His breakfast-television consortium, Daybreak, had lost by the narrowest of margins, but Central had been reawarded its licence for a bid of just £2,000 a year. That evening at Annabel's nightclub in Mayfair, in a private dining-room lined from floor to ceiling with racks of wine bottles, Green celebrated the victory in style with June de Moller, Bernard Cragg, the directors of Carlton Television and their partners, and later with very energetic dancing.

As Carlton Television began the task of building its executive team, a controversy emerged to haunt Green – over the closeness of the Daybreak and Sunrise bids for the breakfast franchise. There was a widespread rumour that there had been a leak of information from Daybreak and that, as a result, Sunrise had increased its bid at the last moment by enough to win. Suspicion

ointed to Green. He had been the one arguing vociferously to keep the
Daybreak bid low, and he was a friend of Christopher Bland in the Sunrise
onsortium. 'I find it hard to believe that Christopher Bland's group did not
et some notice of our bid, and the Carlton area is the most likely conduit –
lthough I wouldn't go as far as to say it was Michael,' says Conrad Black of
he Telegraph group, a member of the losing Daybreak consortium. 'Unlike
Dickensian characters, Mr Green and Mr Bland are not at all what their
urnames would indicate,' notes Black. The rumours became so widespread
hat Green had to warn a number of journalists he would sue if the allegation
vere ever printed.

There had indeed been a leak of information that helped Sunrise to win.
However, neither Green nor Carlton had anything to do with it. It was Greg
Dyke of LWT who was told by a television-industry source he will not name
hat the Daybreak bid was over £30 million but not by all that much. Green
nd Carlton, Dyke insists, are 100 per cent innocent. His source, he says, had
o connection with Carlton. 'I was just talking to someone – someone who
vas not actually involved in their bid. The security of the Daybreak bid was
ot very good. Quite a lot of people knew,' Dyke claims. At the last minute he
ersuaded his partners to add more than £1 million to their bid and go to the
op of their planned range, thereby submitting what turned out to be the
vinning amount of £34.61 million, compared to Daybreak's £33.26 million.

When, in November, Carlton bought a 20 per cent stake in Sunrise, which
ater changed its name to GMTV, conspiracy theorists were able to suggest it
ad all been prearranged. In fact it is difficult to see what advantage Green
vould have obtained by deliberately torpedoing his own bid in order to take
p a prearranged stake in a consortium offering more money to the Treasury.

The rumour, which had little logic to commend it, turned out to have no
asis in fact either. Sunrise did indeed keep 20 per cent of its equity open, but
he intention was to offer it to financial institutions. The City plan was
hwarted after Bruce Gyngell made well-publicized predictions that Sunrise
vould be bankrupt within eighteen months of going on air, because of the size
f its bid. It was only when the company failed to attract City investment that
he stake was offered to trade investors, and Carlton was one of three
ossibilities. The others were Emap, the local-newspaper and magazine
roup, and the Telegraph. Green rang Conrad Black to explain that Carlton
ad been offered the stake because Sunrise preferred to bring in another
elevision company. He asked the Telegraph chairman if he minded. 'I said,
You're not shouldering me aside again! Is this some kind of a bloodless
arlour game you're playing – every few weeks or every few months you're

going to give Black a shaft again? I don't mind an initiation procedure, but
when do I get accepted to the fraternity?" ' says Black.

Nigel Walmsley explained in newspaper interviews that Carlton had been
approached by Sunrise only a week before the deal was agreed. 'The new
factors which made it attractive were that we were paying the same price as
the founding shareholders and we got a close look at their business plan,' he
said. For Green, the purchase of the Sunrise stake for £5.4 million
announced on 22 November, gave him another stake in the UK commercial
television market.

Among the small team primarily responsible for the franchise victory -
Walmsley, Paul Jackson, Charles Denton, Peter Ibbotson and Brian Wenham
- it became clear almost immediately who would be the real winners. The
main beneficiary was Walmsley. Apart from a large salary, he had also
negotiated a £250,000 bonus to be paid the day Carlton went on air, plus
according to the 1992 accounts, 136,551 share options. The shares would
make the former civil servant a paper millionaire. Walmsley was also moving
towards the inner Carlton sanctum in a way that no one had really managed
for many years. He was gradually earning the right to join the small group
who actually ran Carlton Communications - Green, de Moller and Cragg. By
comparison the others felt they were simply hired help receiving modest
success fees - Jackson got £50,000 and Ibbotson £25,000 - and equally
modest share options.

In the months ahead, despite being one of the UK's most experienced
broadcasters, Wenham's advice was rarely sought - something that led to a
number of missed opportunities for Carlton. It was almost as if Wenham, who
had once edited a book on the future of television, was there as an intellectual
ornament - more important for winning licences than for actually getting
involved in running an expanding television company.

The most bitter and disappointed of the group was Denton, who believed
that Green reneged on an agreement to allow him to mount a management
buy-out for Zenith in the event of a successful franchise application. 'I fear
that was withdrawn after he'd got the franchise,' says Denton, who claims that
at a meeting after the ITC decision Green said that was then, this was now.
Green concedes that there was a very acrimonious meeting at which he made
clear a management buy-out was not on.

Following the franchise victory, Green had either to sell Zenith or to
greatly reduce Carlton's stake in it. As a broadcaster, under the 1990 act he
was allowed to own no more than 15 per cent of an independent producer. 'I
made a proposal to Michael about buying it [Zenith], and he said he was no

nterested in a management buy-out under any circumstances. I suspect he
hought he would get more money than he did do,' says Denton, who was told
o stop thinking about the possibility of a management buy-out and get on
vith the job of selling the company.

It is Denton's view – backed up by others involved in the Carlton bid – that
Green could have lost if Zenith had not been part of the franchise application
n the critical early months. 'I don't think he would have got it. I think it was
ouch and go at the time and it wasn't a guaranteed conclusion he was going
o overturn Thames,' says Denton.

Michael Green with Nigel Walmsley (left) and Paul Jackson (right)

The two most important people in developing Carlton Television and
getting it on air were the flamboyant Paul Jackson and the more formal and
estrained Nigel Walmsley.

Jackson was steeped in the show-business ethos. His father, T. Lesley
ackson, had produced programmes such as *This Is Your Life* and *What's My
Line?* for the BBC. After an English degree at Exeter University, Paul Jackson
aad worked on programmes such as *Basil Brush* and *The Two Ronnies*, before
ecoming either producer or director on a series of light-entertainment
rogrammes including *The Young Ones*.

While Jackson was the main influence on developing programme ideas and
teering them towards the screen, it was Walmsley who was responsible for

the overall progress of the company and for making sure that everything happened when it was supposed to. His achievement – born of eighteen-hour days and obsession with the minutiae – cannot be overestimated. His love of detail, command of numbers, taste for work and natural dislike of waste of any kind was to commend itself to Green, who has been heard to say, 'Give me three Nigel Walmsleys and I can conquer the world.'

Yet the things that endeared Walmsley to Green had precisely the opposite effect on a number of his colleagues. 'He is a crazed workaholic and a bottom-line man who goes around asking whether that plant in the corner is really worth its space. He's known in the company as a nickel-and-dime merchant – though actually more dime than nickel,' said one of his team. It is a standing joke in Carlton that, if there is any entertaining to be done, Walmsley, who has little interest in wine, has got to be prevented from ordering. He always chooses the second cheapest on the list. Another colleague, while recognizing the scale of his achievement, adds that Walmsley does not understand the television business, and never will. 'He is completely unaware of what a television company is about, because he has no concept of risk in this context. He has a mathematical concept – a financial concept of risk. He has no concept of creative risk.'

But Walmsley did understand the importance of the details, and he immediately asked for John Egan, the Price Waterhouse consultant who had helped with the bid, to come to work at Carlton Television as controller of commercial development. The thirty-one-year-old Egan created more elaborate flow charts and set 'milestones' marking every step of the way to transmission on 1 January 1993, complete with deadlines.

It also took Walmsley less than three months from winning the franchise to solve the vital issue of who was going to be responsible for selling Carlton's advertising air time. He appointed Martin Bowley as sales director of Carlton Television in January 1992. The thirty-seven-year-old Bowley had been head of sales at Television South West, the smallest ITV company to lose its licence. He had begun his career as a management trainee at Cadbury's before moving on to selling advertising first in commercial radio and then in television. After becoming head of sales at TSW in 1987, he pushed up the small broadcaster's share of ITV advertising each year, and many of the talented young sales team built up at TSW followed him to Carlton.

The aim was to have the department heads in place early in 1992, and they in turn would hire their own staff closer to switch-on date, when they were actually needed. The plan was that by June 1992 a team of twelve would have expanded to fifty, with the complete staff of 360 in place by October, three months before the launch. Staff numbers were always going to be small compared with a traditional broadcaster, because Carlton was making none of its own programmes, apart from regional news and current affairs.

The first clear indication of how Carlton Television would be run had come on 28 November 1991, at the first board meeting following the franchise victory. The meeting was dominated entirely by Green, and was run like a finance subcommittee of Carlton Communications. As Walmsley ploughed through his report he was questioned frequently about financial controls, and Cragg was almost gleeful as he described the 'meanness' of the group's employee benefit package.

A long exchange between Green and Jackson revealed that wherever possible the aim should be to ensure that Carlton retained all the rights to programmes commissioned from independent producers – the opposite of what most independents were hoping for. Independent producers were ambitious to build up intellectual property rights in the programmes they made, rather than just handing them over for a fee to a company like Carlton. The policy led to a parting of the ways between Carlton and Denise O'Donoghue of Hat Trick Productions. 'They wanted too much for too little,' the Hat Trick managing director recalls, and the company decided not to make programmes for Carlton.

Amid growing tensions between the privileged and those who were made to feel like mere employees, new programme ideas were developed and key staff were hired. Carlton went to another of the smaller ITV companies, tiny Border Television, for its head of regional and factual programmes. Paul Corley, the forty-one-year-old director of programmes at Border, had been the producer of *The Tube*, the mould-breaking pop-music programme from Tyne Tees, and had been the planned programme director for North East Television, the Granada–Border joint venture that had bid unsuccessfully for the north-east licence against Tyne Tees.

Corley enjoyed enormously the challenge and excitement of starting with a blank sheet of paper. 'It was one of the most creative times I had in TV.' As he looked for gaps in the ITV schedule where Carlton might make a mark, he almost invented a new genre – popular peak-time factual programmes. Many of Corley's ideas for regional programmes were later to be shown nationally – programmes such as *Blues and Twos* and *The Day I Nearly Died*.

The drama-controller's job went to thirty-one-year-old Tracy Hofman, who had ten years' experience in films and television and had worked at the BBC, Central and Channel 4 on popular dramas such as *Boon*, *Inspector Morse* and *The Manageress*. But her most recent job was running a tiny independent production company in a two-room garret above the Fulham Road. 'She has an extraordinarily big reputation with writers and producers, and I wanted someone unexpected,' explained Jackson.

Comedy was put in the capable hands of John Bishop, who came to Carlton as controller of entertainment after twenty years at the BBC, where he had been assistant head of variety.

Carlton Television was mainly choosing people in their thirties who had made their mark outside the large ITV companies. It was very noticeable that, as the posts were filled, only one person from Thames got a job at Carlton: Tim Riordan, who had been in charge of scheduling at Thames, became Carlton's director of broadcasting. At the same time Peter Ibbotson started building the press and information team who would promote Carlton programmes to newspapers all over the UK.

At the Carlton Television board meeting on 29 January 1992 an emerging pattern became even more apparent. There was only a brief discussion about programmes. Green dominated the proceedings and time and again queried figures and challenged Walmsley on issues such as interest charges and cash-flow projections. He also gave an appearance of outrage when told that the company would need twenty-five more staff than the number forecast in the licence application. Was Jackson going native and behaving like other profligate ITV companies, Green inquired?

As a result, budgets were tight and very strong management systems were put in place to control the relations between Carlton Television and all the independent producers who make its programmes. Carlton went to Channel 4 for its expertise in the management of independents, and Maureen Semple-Piggot was appointed head of programme finance and Morag Naylor was put in charge of legal systems.

Important strategic decisions were also being taken which would influence how Carlton's in-house regional news programmes were to be made and transmitted – decisions that represented a break with ITV's past. In January Carlton set aside the traditional jealousy between the two London ITV companies and created a fifty-fifty joint venture company with London Weekend. It was to be called the London News Network (LNN), and the aim was to provide news and sports coverage for both London ITV companies seven days a week. LNN would also produce Carlton's planned one-hour weekday news and magazine programme. The idea had originally been developed by Thames and LWT.

When Dyke at LWT suggested the idea – which could save Carlton £4 million a year – Green and Walmsley had wanted to base the venture in

Canary Wharf, in London's Docklands. They were eventually persuaded that Canary Wharf was hardly an ideal place to base television crews whose task was to cover breaking news stories in the capital, and the company was based in a new purpose-built studio overlooking the Thames in LWT's head-quarters on the South Bank.

LNN involved a total investment of £40 million and was to be run by the very experienced Clive Jones, former deputy managing director of TVS. It would also be the joint transmission point for all the programmes of both companies – again avoiding unnecessary duplication and saving yet more money. It was the first time that such a close level of cooperation had been agreed between London's rival ITV companies, which competed ferociously for advertising revenue. It was just one sign of how much commercial television was changing.

Another change had been imposed by the government legislation. It had been decreed that the ITV companies should create a new Network Centre which would have its own budget of more than £500 million a year – provided by the companies – to commission the national, as opposed to local, programmes, shown on the ITV network. In the past the big five ITV companies had carved up the schedule between them and made all the important programmes, and the smaller ITV companies received few commissions. The Network Centre would be free to judge all programme ideas on their merit, whether they came from large or small ITV companies or from independent producers. To ensure that the Network Centre really would deal even-handedly with everyone, its performance was to be monitored by the Office of Fair Trading. It was yet another anomaly of the 1990 Broadcasting Act that companies bidding for franchises were being judged on their programme offerings, yet that same act gave a Network Centre total power over commissioning. Carlton, for example, could not guarantee to broadcast the programmes it had proposed in its licence application: it could only put forward ideas for consideration by the Network Centre. If the ideas were rejected there was little Carlton could do.

Green was very aware that whoever ran the Network Centre would be not only one of the most powerful figures in ITV but also a vital figure in the commercial success of the channel. In February the Carlton chairman once again tried to lure Michael Grade away from Channel 4 – this time to run the Network Centre. Once again Grade turned down the Carlton approach, even though Green's final offer was for £3 million spread over a four-year contract. The offer was so high that Green might not have been able to guarantee that the rest of ITV would support it.

Nevertheless Green was in an ebullient mood at Carlton Television's March board meeting. Discussion concentrated again on budgets, programme rights and stationery, and little was said about programmes.

Paul Jackson had the exciting task of developing a wide range of programmes with some of the best of Britain's independent producers. He made no attempt to hide the fact that Carlton was concentrating its energies on popular entertainment – game shows, comedy, music and light entertainment – and shocked the television Establishment when, to make his point about the need for a more commercial approach and less investigative journalism, he said that it was 'not ITV's job to get people out of jail'.

Tracy Hofman was looking for mainstream drama that would attract audiences of 12 million people, and her department was at the time being sent forty scripts a week.

In factual programmes Paul Corley was developing *Seven Days*, which later changed its name to *The Big Story*, as a current-affairs replacement for Thames's *This Week*. He complained, however, that a lot of the ideas he was getting for factual programmes were not focused on ITV. 'They're not popular enough. They don't fit into a slot on ITV. A good single documentary that would pull 3 to 4 million on Channel 4 or BBC2 is not big enough to get on to ITV,' he commented. He did not, however, find his relationship with independent producers remote once a programme was commissioned. He says that, compared to practice in a traditional ITV company, he was able to get closer to the production process and to the series of rough cuts and fine cuts that have to be made before a programme is ready to be broadcast.

The fact that the Network Centre had not been set up yet and there was no programme commissioner did not help a new broadcaster like Carlton, but an interim committee of the ITV companies gave the go-ahead for a total of 100 hours of Carlton programmes for the first half of 1993. *Comedy Playhouse* – six pilots comedy shows, any one of which might become a successful series – was commissioned from Carlton.

The commissions also included *Body and Soul* from Red Rooster Productions, a six-part adaptation of Marcel Bernstein's novel about a nun 'learning what it is to be a woman'. Red Rooster's managing director, Linda James, had several rows with Carlton over the more than £500,000 an hour drama as minor budget items were queried. There was a crisis meeting with Jackson before she agreed a fixed-price contract. Another star drama series ordered from Carlton, *Head Over Heels*, was set in the 1950s world of rock 'n' roll. Planning was also already under way for *A Woman's Guide to Adultery*.

In an interview at the time, Jackson noted two unusual things about his work at Carlton: the close links he was forging with advertisers and the level of financial information that Green required. During more than twenty years as a programme-maker and television executive Jackson had rarely had much contact with advertisers. Now, as director of programmes at Carlton Television, he was meeting 'client' groups for lunch or dinner once or twice a month. And within Carlton the financial disciplines were the most rigid and infinitesimally detailed he had ever come across. Often Carlton Television's monthly accounts ran to sixty-five or even eight-five pages. 'Everything is there. We all see each other's accounts. We all take direct line-by-line responsibility for our own budgets, and we are expected to know what we are talking about and to monitor them very carefully. No overspends. You are told and then expected to be responsible,' Jackson said as he prepared Carlton for switch-on.

By April the core staff had moved into Carlton Television's elegant new headquarters in the heart of the West End – 101 St Martin's Lane, close to leading advertising agencies and restaurants and almost opposite the London Coliseum. Green had not gone for the cheapest option in housing his new television company. At the 16 June board meeting he did, however, overrule both Walmsley and Cragg and insist that the rent of 101 St Martin's Lane should be averaged over the five-year life of the lease. Carlton had managed to get the first two years rent free but didn't want to be showing exaggerated profitability in those years. The possibility of a profit-sharing scheme was also raised for the first time at the meeting. But, again, programmes were hardly mentioned.

On 24 June Green attended a Carlton Television executive committee meeting and ended up squatting on the floor looking at mock-ups of possible Carlton television logos. At the end of the meeting Green invited everyone to come outside to see his new toy – a £250,000 Aston Martin. 'We all had to stand on the pavement looking at his fucking car!' recalls one of the Carlton executives in disbelief.

By September's board meeting the main theme was on-screen presentation. Everyone had ideas and opinions about how Carlton should look. The main theme – getting Londoners from many walks of life to say, 'This is Carlton – television for London' – was both innovative and distinctive. The on-screen idents and the Carlton Television logo were unveiled at a press conference at the London Palladium on 12 October. At great expense the designers had come up with the idea that the 'T' in Carlton should be tiny and nestle inside the arms of the 'L'.

On 12 October more details were also given about Carlton's schedule – a

schedule that emphasized continuity for the ITV audience. Dave Allen would
return with his own comedy show, Nicholas Parsons would host a television
version of BBC Radio's *Just A Minute*, there would be a regional *Frost
Programme*, and Desmond Wilcox's *A Day In The Life* would look at all
aspects of London. Green skipped around during the event, half-timid, half-
proud of what had been achieved so far, but behind the scenes worrying that
too much money was being spent on overheads such as taxis.

As the big switch-on of the new franchisees approached, Carlton
Communications was also making gradual but real progress against the
background of a difficult economic climate. For the year to September 1992
the pre-tax profits rose by 15 per cent to £102.3 million, and turnover
increased by 17 per cent to £701.6 million – although the performance
represented only a return to the pre-recession level of 1990. By December the
capitalization had risen to £1.5 billion.

The results included the first contribution from the Pickwick Group, the
video publisher and distributor bought in February for £60 million. The
largest shareholder had been Pearson, which had held a 20 per cent stake.
The strategic point for Carlton was obvious – the company was in video
publishing and, increasingly, programme production. Pickwick would
complete the chain and provide a video label and a distribution outlet for
Carlton programmes. Despite a flurry of profits from sex-education videos
the purchase was not an instant success, with the video group's French
operation in particular losing money and needing considerable management
attention.

When Carlton's annual report was published, however, the press, with its
untiring interest in the salaries of top businessmen, honed in on the small
print where directors' pay is recorded. A remuneration committee of the
board, supported by outside consultants, had decided that 'the Chairman's
salary failed to recognize the significant contribution that he makes to the
company, the progress the company has made in the last year and the market
level of remuneration of a person of his status within the company'. As a
result, Green's payment package rose from £287,807 in 1991 to £530,020
only a year later – including a performance-related £120,000 bonus. The
committee that obliged the Carlton chairman to take such a large pay rise had
been made up of Lord Sharp, Nigel Wray and Green himself.

On 23 December Green inspected Carlton Television's headquarters to
ensure that everything was ready for the big day. He greeted everyone with an
initial criticism. Don Christopher, the Carlton Television lawyer, was asked
why he had chosen a particular outside law firm to represent the company.

Maraid Curtin, a junior in the press office whose job was to cut all relevant articles from the newspapers, was given Green's view on the subject. The Carlton chairman told Peter Ibbotson he preferred the analysis of the ITV ownership issue developed by Leslie Hill of Central to his. It was Green's way of keeping staff on their toes in the hours before the launch.

Richard Dunn made his last appearance on Thames Television on New Year's Eve, just before midnight. It followed the final programme to be transmitted by the company – an hour-long special which looked almost like a history of ITV, with clips from programmes broadcast over the previous twenty-five years. It was a curtain-call for *Callan* and *The Bill*, *The Sweeney* and *Minder*, *George and Mildred*, *Bless This House*, *Sooty*, *The World at War*, *Jack The Ripper*, *The Naked Civil Servant*, *A Voyage Round My Father*, *Rumpole* and *Mr Bean*. It ended with a black-and-white Morecambe and Wise Christmas show which also starred Leonard Rossiter. Then Dunn simply thanked the artists, the viewers, and the talented men and women behind the cameras who had worked so hard and creatively 'to bring you the best television we could'. Rather pointedly, he finished without a mention of Carlton or any good wishes for Thames's successor by saying, 'And for now from all of us at Thames we wish all of you a happy new year.'

Not all viewers would have known what was going on, but an ITN news bulletin that followed just before midnight reminded everyone about the lost franchises and the new broadcasters that were about to take over. And after the chimes of Big Ben faded on the start of 1993 Maurice James, town crier, came on to ring his handbell and announce, 'This is Carlton – television for London.' Radio disc jockey Chris Tarrant, standing in front of the crowds in Trafalgar Square, introduced *A Carlton New Year* – a ninety-minute variety show shown nationally. The programme featured the pop group Take That, a Canadian comedian called Marty, who ran around saying 'Cool', the hypnotist Paul McKenna, who persuaded people on stage they were riding racehorses when they were only sitting on chairs, and the Chippendales, showing off their well-oiled, shiny, shaved bodies. It was a graceless, unimaginative production that even senior Carlton programme executives conceded afterwards had not quite worked. The contrast with the last hour of Thames was very great.

But nothing could dampen the spirit of celebration at the Carlton Television headquarters. A large screen had been set up in the basement, and as the new year dawned and Carlton Television went on air the moment was accompanied by the popping of champagne corks.

As Green glided around, it was obvious to everyone that for him this was

very much a dream come true. Yet his first complaint as an owner of an ITV
company that was actually on the air came at 12.01 a.m. 'Why did we fade Big
Ben after only two bongs?' he wanted to know. But by 12.04 he was saying, 'It
feels wonderful – absolutely great. I am delighted.' Then his concentration
moved back to the big screen. He did not want to miss Carlton's first
commercial – a special arranged for the first night. It was an advertisement for
the Vauxhall Carlton executive car.

Chapter 14

Now over to the Studios of ITN

Owning one ITV company was never going to be enough for Michael Green. But to get control of more of the commercial-broadcasting system the ownership rules would have to be overturned. Takeovers of any kind were forbidden until 1994, and none of the largest ten ITV companies could take each over at all.

An intensive lobbying campaign was under way long before Carlton Television went on air. In October 1992 Green concentrated his efforts on the Conservative Party Conference at Brighton. On 8 October he hosted a dinner at the Grand Hotel whose guest list included two former Home Secretaries, Douglas Hurd and Kenneth Baker, as well as other senior politicians such as Judith Chaplin, Tony Newton and Robert Key, the broadcasting minister.

Green, sitting next to Hurd, immediately launched into his theme – the need for radical change in the structure of ITV. The Carlton chairman cited the weakness of HTV, the ITV company for Wales and the West, which had been forced to bid high to retain its licence. Surely it would be in the public interest for such a company to be taken over by a well-funded operator. 'Green and Walmsley were just relentless from the beginning. I mean, Douglas Hurd's jaw dropped. There was no foreplay. No charming the wives. No hellos. It was just straight in – tap the glass and off you go,' recalled one of those there.

The dinner was also remarkable for another reason: it was the first time that another Green scheme began to emerge. After dinner, Green explained to the politicians plans for his latest takeover. Carlton, LWT, Central and Reuters were planning to buy control of Independent Television News (ITN), the supplier of national and international news to both ITV and Channel 4.

As the politicians left, Green complimented his staff on the successful dinner but asked why Hayden Phillips, the permanent secretary at the National Heritage Department, had not been there. It had to be explained to the Carlton chairman that civil servants like Phillips never attend partisan events like party political conferences.

The move on ITN came the following week. The proposal was to acquire the existing 400,000 shares in ITN at £1 a share and a promise to commit £30 million to the news organization. For some time ITN's editorial skills had not been matched by the quality of its financial management. In October 1990 ITN had reported a £10 million loss because of higher than expected spending in the previous year. The overspend coincided with the move to new headquarters in London's Gray's Inn Road. The ITN board had decided to take on a thirty-five-year lease at around £5.5 million a year from the owners of the building, Stuart Lipton's Stanhope Properties. The aim was to make money by letting out spare floors in the elegant building designed by the world-famous architects Norman Foster Associates. Apart from the value of the site the reconstruction cost more than £40 million and a further £45 million had then been spent on the latest television technology. Unfortunately, ITN's decision to move from its previous cramped headquarters in Wells Street coincided with the collapse of the London property market, and the news organization was saddled with an expensive lease and a near-empty building.

Bob Phillis had faced a financial crisis as soon as he took over at ITN in February 1991. The new chief executive admitted there had been 'a serious breakdown in the financial and management accounting processes'. Expenditure had not been properly accounted for, and the hole in ITN finances was £9.8 million deeper than previously thought. The cost of covering the Gulf War in early 1991 was aggravating the situation. Over the next eighteen months Phillis steered the news organization towards break-even mainly through ruthless cost-cutting that included the loss of more than 400 jobs. But fundamental problems remained – the lease and the shareholding structure.

ITN was owned by all fifteen regional ITV companies. It was an unwieldy number, but when costs had overrun in the past the shareholders had grumbled but had always paid up. Now three shareholders – Thames, TVS and TSW – were about to lose their licences and had little interest in funding the consequences of unfortunate property decisions, even though all had been involved. Richard Dunn of Thames was even the ITN chairman. Also, the companies which had retained their licences were divided between the haves and the have-nots – those who had bid low in the franchise auction and those who had bid high. Several of the ITV companies would be fighting for survival, because of the size of their bids and the deepening recession in the television-advertising market. With such conflicting and tangled interests it was not at all clear how agreement could be reached on a future strategy.

On 30 September 1992 Andrew Quinn, the former managing director of

Granada Television, who had been appointed chief executive of the Network Centre, memorably described the value of the shares in ITN as possibly nil. There was no money to pay the £5.5 million annual rent, and, unless something was done, the accumulated ITN deficit could rise to more than £25 million over the next five years.

Greg Dyke of LWT had always taken a hard-nosed attitude to ITN. He couldn't believe that so much money could have been lost in such a simple business. In the ITN boardroom he had not tried to disguise his contempt for the way the place was run. His aggressive approach had been considered so unacceptable in what had always been a federal, cooperative system that he had even been rung at home by a senior ITN executive and denounced as 'an enemy of ITN'. Dyke finally resigned from the board when ITN decided to mount a separate bid for the national teletext licence, even though the incumbent, Oracle, was a subsidiary of the ITV companies. Dyke thought it was crazy to have one ITV subsidiary competing against another for the teletext licence. He also believed that ITN was in such a serious financial position that it really could go into liquidation.

Because of the structural problems it was difficult to do anything about ITN's fundamental problems, and Christopher Bland and Greg Dyke toyed with the idea of selling LWT's stake in the news organization. But if the receivers were called in at ITN it would affect all of ITV and be very embarrassing. Most viewers wouldn't realize there was any difference between ITN and ITV. 'It was Greg who said, "Look, I've been thinking. I've got an idea. Let's turn it round. Why don't we become serious,"' says Bland. 'And he did some interesting back-of-the-envelope numbers, and I said to Michael [Green], "Look, Greg has had this idea. What do you think?" So Michael then took it up and ran hard with it – particularly on the property side, which was the key to sorting it out,' Bland recalls.

Dyke concedes that Green may already have been thinking of something similar, and indeed other big media players such as Ted Turner's Cable News Network and Reuters had already been approached by Phillis, who had his own plans for reconstruction, with a view to taking a stake. Under the 1990 Act at least 50 per cent of ITN had to be owned by non-broadcasters by the end of 1994, so a new structure was needed anyway. It was unlikely, however, that new shareholders could be attracted until something was done about the growing property deficit.

Before a consortium could be put together to take over ITN, it had to have a chairman. According to Bland, Green's first thought was to bring in someone from outside. 'I said to him, "Listen, Michael, there are only two people who should be chairman of ITN – either you or me. And I think it should be you." Faced with the alternative, he agreed.'

A deal began to take shape very quickly – largely because of Green's contacts, directorships and shareholdings. Carlton, LWT and Central each agreed to take a 20 per cent stake in the restructured ITN, as did Reuters.

The news organization was an obvious candidate to join the consortium, and it helped that Green had recently been brought into Reuters as a non-executive director by its chairman, Sir Christopher Hogg, who saw him as a very talented businessman. Green had been delighted by the invitation to get experience of how such a large and successful company was run. 'Part of the reason I took on a non-executive position with Reuters was to learn about a bigger business. It is a fascinating business, but it is also a business which is well run, with very able managers, which is not necessarily entrepreneurial but it is one hell of a business. You've got to learn that Carlton has now got to develop the skills and a strategy of where will we be in five and ten years,' says Green.

The Reuters involvement in the ITN deal made particular sense because Reuters Television – the old Visnews, the international television news agency – would also make an ideal tenant for the near-empty ITN building and help to ease the ease the property problem. The remaining 20 per cent of ITN would be offered to the other ITV companies.

'ITN is very important to the ITV network. There appeared to be a log-jam. This is a solution,' said Green on 13 October 1992, the day the plan was announced.

Even before Carlton had become a broadcaster, Green was emerging as a power-broker in ITV. He had always been a news addict, and on holiday would travel miles to get a newspaper. He was equally fascinated by how the news is put together – whether in newspapers or television – and his interest in restructuring ITN had been immediate. It was equally obvious that being chairman of the television news organization would confer status and political access far beyond that of merely being chairman of Carlton Communications. Green was prepared to devote time and money to rebuilding ITN even though it would have little direct impact on Carlton's bottom line, however great a success he made of it.

On 31 December – the day before Carlton Television went on air – another piece of the ITN puzzle fell into place for Green. Agreement was finally reached in principle on ITV's contract with ITN – worth more than £50 million a year for five years. Lord Hollick, chairman of Meridian, had delayed signing to the last possible moment, as he continued to quibble about the price. If Meridian had gone on air without an ITN agreement and therefore without an ITN news supply, the new broadcaster could have created a record by being in breach of its licence, which included the obligation to broadcast high-quality national and international news, from day one. Green was scathing about Hollick and predicted that he would have to sign before the day was out. Roger Laughton, the Meridian managing director, eventually signed at 4 p.m., but also wrote on the licence, 'We are signing this under duress.' There would have to be further negotiations on the details, but the ITV companies were obliged by the ITC to use the ITN service for at least the first three years of the new franchise period.

Green was in a better position than anyone else to do something about the property lease that had turned out to be a millstone around ITN's neck. Not only had he known Stuart Lipton, the Stanhope chief executive, for twenty-five years, from the early days in Conduit Street, but the Stanhope chairman was none other than Lord Sharp, a Carlton non-executive director. Lipton has confirmed that he was sounded out and that there was the possibility of a deal on the Gray's Inn Road building before the ITN restructuring went ahead. However, persuading Stanhope to cancel the lease and sell the building to ITN still involved prolonged negotiations. Convincing all the ITV companies that the restructuring was in their best interests was equally difficult.

At the same time as the ITN negotiations continued, Green never wavered in his single-minded determination to persuade the government to change the ITV ownership rules. On 28 January 1993 the guests at the lunch following a Carlton Television board meeting were Peter Brooke, the new National Heritage Secretary, and Paul Wright, the senior National Heritage Department civil servant responsible for broadcasting, who had been in charge of the 1990 Broadcasting Act. Brooke, a former management consultant who happily hides a very sharp brain behind cricketing jokes and an old-buffer image, was already starting to think about where UK commercial television should go next, and, apart from wanting to hear the views of such a powerful player in the broadcasting industry, Green was a constituent – Brooke represented the safe Conservative seat of Westminster, which included Green's Mayfair home.

Years earlier, when Brooke had been chairman of the Conservative Party, he had sat next to Green at a parliamentary dinner and had been struck by the young man's prediction that in five years 30 per cent of the stock of bookshops would be videos and people would collect videos in the way they have always collected books.

Also among those around the large oval table at lunch that day was Lord

Armstrong, the former head of the Civil Service, who had joined the Carlton Television board as a non-executive director.

Brooke, who sat opposite the Carlton chairman, made it clear he was getting exasperated at being lobbied by a stream of ITV companies all wanting different things and with widely differing views on ITV ownership. Would Green organize a meeting with all the ITV companies – perhaps over dinner?

Just as there were conflicting views on ITV ownership, Green's plan for the future of ITN split the companies. Not all were prepared to roll over, give up their shareholdings, and become mere customers of ITN. There was inevitable suspicion about Green's motives. Were they missing a trick, they wondered? Why did Green want these supposedly worthless shares? Yorkshire Television in particular was determined, at the very least, to have a review of the news contract after two years. Yorkshire wanted to ensure that, if Green managed to turn the organization round, ITV companies which were no longer ITN shareholders would also benefit.

Granada was even more certain it did not want to be left out. 'We were not

Gerry Robinson

part of the original deal. We really had to kick the door down,' says Gerry Robinson, the softly spoken and utterly determined accountant who had transformed the profitability of the Granada group as chief executive. 'When everyone else was saying "This [ITN] is a good thing to get out of", when someone like Michael was saying, "Actually we are going to take this thing off your hands and help you sort it out", that's the first sign we are in this for the kill. There is no way we are going to miss this,' adds Robinson, who was born in Donegal and was originally destined for the Catholic priesthood. Two other ITV companies, Scottish and Anglia, also wanted to retain a stake.

To get the necessary agreement of 75 per cent of the shareholders, the share structure was shuffled so that Granada joined the original four consortium members – Carlton, LWT, Central and Reuters – each with 18 per cent of the equity, leaving 5 per cent each for Anglia and Scottish.

Apart from agreeing a new shareholding structure, a better financial deal had to be offered to the three ITV companies which had lost their franchises. Each was eventually offered £14 a share, compared with the original £1. The improved offer – achieved after intensive lobbying by Dunn – meant that Thames netted £1.12 million for its 22 per cent stake. Yorkshire got the review it wanted at the end of two years, and, although the other ITV companies only received the original £1 a share, the news-supply contract was structured so that their payments were lower in the difficult first year of the new franchises. The final ITN news contract averaged around £53 million a year. 'Green pushed and screamed and smoked a cigar and got what he wanted,' said one of those involved in the negotiations.

For Bob Phillis, Green's sudden interest in ITN had been a nightmare. Having escaped Green once, he was now likely to have him as his chairman once again. By then the two men clearly had a strained and competitive relationship. Green had the money, but Phillis was accumulating more conventional prestige from his growing reputation in the television industry. Close to the finalization of the ITN deal, Green was in his Carlton office with more than a dozen of the bankers and advisers involved. In the middle of the meeting Green took a call from Phillis, who on occasion can add a new dimension to the word 'loquacious'. After a while Green set the phone down on his desk and walked out of the room, leaving Phillis talking to no one. Green obviously thought this a huge joke, although the startled bankers and advisers had never seen such behaviour before. It surprised no one in the television industry when Phillis, who had, with the exception of the property problem, straightened out the finances of ITN, quickly accepted an invitation from John Birt, the BBC director-general, to become his deputy.

Green could scarcely contain his pleasure at the prospect of becoming chairman of ITN, and took Michael Grade to see 'his' ITN – even though it would hardly have been a novel sight for the chief executive of Channel 4, as

ITN had provided *Channel 4 News* under contract ever since the channel was launched. Green was offered a place in the gallery from where the producer and his staff control the programme, but that was not close enough. Instead he squatted on the studio floor, just out of range of the cameras, with headphones on his ears to listen to the gallery conversation as Jon Snow presented the programme.

Yet in February 1993, even before the ITN deal was finalized, Green was reminded of the sensitivities involved in controlling one of the UK's most important television news organizations. Nick Gilbert of the *Independent on Sunday* unearthed from Companies House the fact that sometime between 1 April 1991 and 30 March 1992 – the period during which Carlton had applied for, and won, the London television licence – Green, an ardent admirer of Margaret Thatcher, at least in the early years, had donated £15,000 to the Conservative Party from the Tangent Charitable Trust, which he had set up in 1985. The *Independent on Sunday* reported that, oddly, it seemed to be the only time Tangent had made such a donation – leaving the clear impression that the donation had been related to the franchise process.

The story caused a political row. Peter Mandelson, the Labour MP for Hartlepool and the party's former communications director, commented, 'It is totally unacceptable for the person heading up one of the main five TV franchises in Britain, and who may shortly be taking control of ITN, to align himself with the Conservative Party.' Mandelson put down an early day motion in the House of Commons, which was signed by more than seventy Labour and Liberal Democrat MPs, describing Green's possible appointment as unacceptable given ITN's statutory requirement 'to maintain strict political independence and impartiality'. For good measure Mandelson appealed to Sir George Russell, the recently knighted ITC chairman, to rule Green out as chairman of ITN.

Green responded to the original story with an amusing riposte to the *Independent on Sunday*. 'If only Nick Gilbert were right that a major television licence might be secured by a private donation of £15,000 to Tory Party funds made five months after the licence had been awarded: As reported in the *Independent* on 17 October Carlton's successful application was accompanied by a cash bid of £43 million a year. If the figures and dates had been the other way round, Mr Gilbert might have had a story.' The letter missed the point. Even if the donation had been made five months *after* winning a licence to broadcast to all the people of London, whatever their political views, it was hardly wise to be making donations to the Conservative Party whether they came from Tangent or from Carlton Communications.

Privately Green was far more rattled than the bravado of his letter implied, and in particular by the Mandelson attack. Green took Mandelson's remark as a personal affront, although he was too reticent to speak to the MP directly. Again an intermediary was deployed. A mutual friend, film producer David Puttnam, was used to ask Mandelson whether he would have lunch with Green at Claridges. Green wanted to know why the Labour MP appeared to hate him so. The Carlton chairman failed to understand that early day motions are merely the small change of politics – ritual acts of no more than symbolic significance, changing nothing. Mandelson came away from lunch thinking it was all very surprising behaviour.

Green moved quickly on the ITN property front, and by the end of March 1993 he had achieved a deal, at least in principle. With a mixture of blandishments and threats, he managed to persuade Stanhope that its best interests lay in giving up the lucrative but probably unsustainable lease and selling the freehold of Gray's Inn Road to ITN for around £74 million. It was not easy. As the negotiations came to a head, Lipton called a journalist and said, 'Green has gone too far this time. He is threatening to walk away from ITN unless I agree.' Lipton concedes that the negotiations were tough, but he believes that negotiating is a sport that Green enjoys. 'I think in the circumstances it was a reasonable deal for both sides. He was paying a rent that was over the market rate,' says Lipton, who adds that he never really believed that Green would push ITN into receivership. He saw the threat as just a negotiating ploy. But it was still remarkable for Green even to suggest that he might walk away from the ITN deal, creating at least the possibility of liquidation.

By March, Green had also found the chief executive he wanted for ITN – David Gordon, for many years chief executive of *The Economist*, where he had overseen the successful move into the international market and the resulting rise in circulation. The two men had got to know each other around the lunch table at *The Economist*, where Green had been an occasional guest. The two also shared an interest in art and films.

Green marked the confirmation by the ITN board of his chairmanship and the appointment of Gordon as chief executive by making a rare press-conference appearance on 5 April 1993. At the conference, Gordon made a bit of a gaffe by joking that he knew nothing about television but that he 'knew a man who did' – referring to the television ad at the time for the Automobile Association. Green said that ITN must move from being 'cost-driven to profits-driven' and had to seek new sources of revenue from home and abroad. He also somewhat unnecessarily warned staff, who had seen their numbers fall from 1,100 to 650 in two years, that 'There are no jobs for life.'

The new ITN chairman was questioned about the £15,000 political donation, and seemed completely unrepentant. 'I've made it quite clear that Carlton makes no political donations whatsoever. To the best of my knowledge ITN makes no political donations whatsoever. As long as that continues, I don't see I have any problem [chairing ITN] whatsoever. What Michael Green does as a private individual is entirely up to him,' said Green, still not accepting that he was taking on a role where it did matter very much what he did as a private individual.

Despite the increased public attention, Green loved being chairman of ITN. Indeed he sometimes introduced himself as chairman of ITN rather than Carlton. He used his new status as the head of a news organization to get passes into the Press Gallery in the House of Commons. On another occasion he went out with an ITN camera crew filming around London and spent a day at *Channel 4 News* watching how the programme was put together. And naturally he was in attendance when the Prime Minister or the Chancellor of the Exchequer came to lunch at ITN. In the evening he would sometimes bring in guests to see *News at Ten* going out.

'Michael Green identified himself totally with ITN, and the chairmanship of ITN became the defining thing about his life. He suddenly was listened to. He was important. People would come to lunch. He wasn't just a business-man, he wasn't a wheeler-dealer any more but a man of consequence,' said an ITN shareholder.

But there was always the potential for controversy in such a role, and the next political row was not long in coming. Once again it was provoked by a journalist digging out a story – this time Nicholas Hellen, of the London *Evening Standard*. The first edition of the paper on 20 June 1993 splashed with the news that 'the power brokers of ITV' were to demand that *News at Ten* give up its fixed time slot, so that Hollywood films and extended dramas would no longer be interrupted. 'LWT and Carlton TV's chief executives Greg Dyke and Nigel Walmsley are supporting demands for the bulletin to go out at 7 p.m. or 8 p.m. They believe the 10 p.m. news splits up adult dramas, forcing them to finish too late for most viewers,' the story read.

The plan was to be discussed at ITV's annual strategy conference being held that day at the Moor Hall Hotel, Sutton Coldfield. At the meeting, Gus Macdonald of Scottish, chairman of ITV's Broadcasting Board, which supervised the activities of the Network Centre, went round the table sounding out views. No formal vote was taken, but senior executives from all fifteen regional ITV companies – among them Paul Jackson and Nigel Walmsley from Carlton – wanted to explore moving *News at Ten* by autumn

1993 and, although further detailed research was envisaged, 6.30 p.m. was the preferred option for its new time.

In the light of the *Evening Standard* leak Andrew Quinn, the Network Centre chief executive, was detailed to call David Gordon at ITN to tell him what had happened. Quinn, who assumed the content of his call would be confidential, was blunt: ITV was planning to move *News at Ten*, and the only doubt was over the new time. The content of the call did not stay confidential for long. Gordon called a meeting of the ITN executive committee, which decided to give further thought to the issue rather than immediately oppose it. Gordon believed, however, that the staff, who had suffered a series of blows to morale, ought to be told what was happening, as most national newspapers were already following up the *Standard* story. And, as further leaks would then be inevitable, a press release was issued. Stuart Purvis, the ITN editor-in-chief, decided the issue should be covered in that night's programme as a legitimate news story. Gordon, as chief executive, took the decision to go public, and Green, his chairman, who was on holiday in Portugal, was not consulted.

When Green found out, that afternoon, he went ballistic, and according to a colleague Gordon was treated to 'the full range of obscenities' down the telephone line from a Portuguese hotel. Green was now in a very tricky position. He was chairman of Carlton Television, which had clearly been seen to support a move of the news programme, and chairman of ITN, whose staff – not to mention leading politicians – were horrified at the prospect.

Green could reasonably argue that on such a sensitive issue he should have been consulted before a press release was issued, and Gordon's relationship with Green was never to recover. Yet it was the decision to go public that almost certainly saved *News at Ten*. The story quickly began to build into a peculiarly British *cause célèbre* which attracted political attention at the highest level. After all, crucial divisions in the House of Commons usually come around 10.15 p.m. – right in the middle of *News at Ten*. The vote that brought down James Callaghan's Labour government in 1979 had been covered live on the programme. Politicians loved *News at Ten* for the national showcase it gave for some of the most dramatic moments in their trade. The extra hour following the BBC's *Nine O'Clock News* also meant that important breaking stories from Washington could be covered in *News at Ten*.

Sir Alastair Burnet, a former *News at Ten* newscaster, argued that if the main news programme was moved to early evening 'some pathetic, patched-up, late-night news epilogue for insomniacs would earn only scorn'. Sir Alastair also warned that, apart from Sir George Russell, 'the man who must look to his reputation and even his ambition, is Michael Green'. His accountants and fellow directors would not tell him that the backbone of a national television network depended more on the authority of its news than on its entertainment revenues or the pursuit of quick profit.

Although it seemed positively eccentric to argue that transmitting a news programme at a particular time was vital to the defence of public-service broadcasting, there was the serious point that if ITN was to move to early evening the BBC would have no effective competition later in the evening, when most people were watching. The issue, which seemed to symbolize the newly rampant commercialism of ITV unleashed by Mrs Thatcher, struck a raw nerve among the articulate classes who probably watched few other programmes on ITV. Buckingham Palace called to inquire if the story was really true.

The day of the leak ITN's political editor, Michael Brunson, met Labour's communication director, David Hill, and the two went off immediately to see the Labour leader, the late John Smith. A letter to the ITC chairman was drafted on the spot, and even the Archbishop of Canterbury wrote to Sir George Russell to express concern.

By coincidence Sue Tinson, associate editor of ITN, was having lunch that day with Gus O'Donnell, the Prime Minister's press secretary. The inside story of what might happen to *News at Ten* was carried straight back to Downing Street. John Major was concerned because he wanted to ensure there was effective competition between the BBC and ITN. In a letter to Russell, pointedly copied to Green, the Prime Minister wrote, 'I am particularly concerned that one of the strengths of the ITV network, the provision of authoritative news programming, may be seriously impaired if the main evening news is not part of the schedule.'

Strictly speaking the ITC had no power to dictate when the ITV companies showed their main evening news, as long as it was in prime time – defined as between 6.30 p.m. and 10.30 p.m. But Russell decided that as most of the ITV companies had specified *News at Ten* in their applications for new licences they would be held to that undertaking. The ITC decision stretched the rules, and could have been challenged in court, but, faced with the opposition of the ITC, the Prime Minister and leader of the Labour Party, the ITV companies caved in and it rapidly became very difficult to find anyone who had ever been in favour of moving *News at Ten*.

In his 1994 James MacTaggart Lecture – the set-piece lecture that launches the annual Edinburgh International Television Festival – Greg Dyke recounted that the ITN change had been proposed by Granada at the ITV onference, after a great deal of lobbying by Carlton. 'I know that because I was lobbied,' he said. He went on, 'In the furore that followed, both Granada, under their chief executive Gerry Robinson, and Carlton, under chairman Michael Green, disappeared without trace from the public debate. Both had PR men out there telling journalists and politicians that it wasn't their company's idea. Michael Green even went around telling all and sundry that he decision had been taken by low-level executives, which was an odd way of describing his managing director and director of programmes.'

Dyke's version of events was rejected by Green. But Dyke was also arguing a more general case: that commercial television was in danger of compromising its editorial freedom by becoming too dependent on government, because the ITV companies were always asking to have the rules changed for their financial advantage. There was no doubt the Carlton chairman was a prime example of someone who wanted something from government – most of all a relaxation of the rules that prevented any one company from owning two large TV licences. Green's position, which had a measure of support in ITV – at east among the major players – was that the ITV companies were far too small to play a significant role on the world media stage dominated increasingly by multinational players such as The News Corporation and Viacom. Consolidation in ITV was vital, Green believed. It was ludicrous to see ITV entirely in the UK context and insist, as the government was doing, that no less than ten of the fifteen regional ITV companies were 'large' and therefore could not take each other over.

By May 1993 National Heritage Secretary Peter Brooke had been persuaded to consider the case that ITV companies should be allowed to get bigger. But he was equally adamant that there should not be a free-for-all and, unlike Green, believed that competition issues in the media industries were different in character from those involved in the ownership of baked-beans manufacturers.

There was widespread lobbying, with Green bending, in particular, the ear of Michael Heseltine, the Trade and Industry Secretary, who was suspected by many of trying to muscle in on the affairs of National Heritage. When Heseltine arrived for a lunch at Carlton's headquarters, he explained that he would be able to stay for only forty minutes, because of an unexpected meeting. Green ploughed straight ahead and read from a typewritten piece of paper with five points on it. It was virtually a Green monologue. As Heseltine left the building he was heard muttering to his private secretary, 'Who does that man think he is?' Other ministers say bemusedly that they don't mind being lobbied, but they do find it unusual to be lobbied all the way to their cars after a lunch.

A meeting of chairmen and managing directors of the ITV system to discuss the ownership issue with Peter Brooke was held on 14 June in the conference room at the Department of National Heritage. The original plan – a dinner organized by Green – was seen as impractical, because Carlton's motives would be suspect. At the meeting, although there was a general consensus that change was probably inevitable, there were deep splits on what form it should take and when it should happen. The big companies wanted the freedom to launch more takeovers, but the smaller companies wanted to extend the moratorium on takeovers due to run out at the end of 1993. Lord Hollick, of Meridian, for example, was against piecemeal changes and thought the future of UK broadcasting should be looked at again during the renegotiation of the BBC's royal charter, which ran out at the end of 1996.

After the meeting, Green immediately issued a press release claiming a wide measure of agreement for his main propositions. 'The majority view – by my calculation a minimum of 70 per cent of ITV – stated that there was a need for change and the Secretary of State certainly heard this loud and clear. The minority are looking for protectionism which is always a short-term answer,' he said, with a deft sleight of hand. It was hardly surprising that the big companies, which controlled 70 per cent of the advertising revenue, wanted the freedom to take over smaller ITV companies. Green then used the skilled negotiator's trick of trying to impose his view of the meeting on the government, in a letter to Brooke. He wrote to suggest that there had been a unanimous view that changed circumstances – such as the rise of British Sky Broadcasting (BSkyB) following the merger of Sky and BSB – since the 1990 Broadcasting Act fully justified a re-examination of the legislation, and said he had been very impressed by the high level of agreement reached in the discussion.

The National Heritage Secretary was having none of it, and in a rather sharp reply dated 24 June wrote, 'I am afraid I did not detect the same level of agreement that you did.' But it was the handwritten note of warning at the bottom of the letter, explicitly linking Green's hopes to own more franchises with the current attempts to move *News at Ten*, that added the extra sting in the tail. 'Given the parliamentary dimension to all this [ownership], I hope the *News at Ten* move is not going to be counter-productive,' Brooke wrote.

Expanding Carlton's interests in ITV was Green's main preoccupation, but the Carlton chairman was always interested in any relevant media. A proposition came before the board of Reuters that the news and information group invest in TeleWest, the largest cable communications operator in the UK – a joint venture of Tele Communications Inc. (TCI), the US cable group, and US West, the American regional telephone company. The Reuters management decided that sinking cable in the ground was not their sort of investment, but Green was interested and approached TeleWest. He said he would be prepared to invest £500 million for a one-third stake in the company. Instead TeleWest chose to go for stock-exchange flotations in London and New York to establish the worth of the company – a process that valued it at £1.8 billion.

When the licence to run the National Lottery was advertised, Green wanted to be involved in that too. He correctly identified that the front runner was Camelot, a consortium that included Cadbury Schweppes, De La Rue and Racal, and he wanted to be part of it. Green had a meeting with Jeremy Marshall, the chief executive of De La Rue, the international security printers, and his director of communications, David Rigg, who was closely involved with the emerging Camelot consortium. Green argued that Camelot needed a television company in its consortium to help promote the National Lottery. Marshall and Rigg were fairly sure that if they won they could hire an independent production company to make a weekly lottery programme, or more probably deal directly with the BBC. The De La Rue executives were noncommittal. Within a few hours the Carlton chairman managed to convince them they were absolutely right to have had reservations. Marshall called Rigg up to his office to see something extraordinary. Green had sent round by taxi a case of fine wine and two large Carlton Television golf umbrellas. Carlton did not become part of Camelot. Instead Green joined the Great British Lottery Company, with companies such as Granada and Associated Newspapers – a consortium that didn't even get close to winning.

In July 1993 there was a small but significant change to the structure of Carlton Communications. With Charles Denton having recently left to become head of drama at the BBC, Zenith was finally sold to Portman Entertainment, one of the UK's most long-established independent production companies. It wasn't much of a deal, with only a swap of shares involved. Even Denton's management buy-out plan might have raised more money. Later that month Green turned down the opportunity to buy a slice of LWT – a stake that later went to Granada – on the grounds that the price was too high.

As Green pressed on to win the right to buy further ITV licences, the programmes broadcast by Carlton Television faced an unusual and near-universal barrage of criticism that often bordered on the vicious. Television critic James Saynor struck a low blow in the *Guardian* when he suggested that Carlton's reputation as a provider of quality television 'seems roughly on a par with the reputation of Ratner's as a provider of exquisitely crafted jewellery'. Allison Pearson in the *Independent on Sunday* said that Carlton had won its ratings by finding the lowest common denominator and then halving it. Comments on individual programmes were no kinder. *Head Over Heels* was described as 'a nice programme for illiterate 12–years-olds', and the weekly current-affairs programme *The Big Story* was denounced as 'tabloid froth'. But, in reply to the bile of the critics, Paul Jackson was able to point to regular market research in the London area showing that 70 per cent of the audience were happy with Carlton.

That autumn and winter there were at least some advantages to running the largest ITV company. On 16 November Michael and Tessa Green happily joined the line-up to be introduced to the Prince of Wales at the Royal Film performance of the Mel Gibson film *A Man Without A Face*. It was funded by Majestic RCS, a division of the Italian group that had taken a 5 per cent stake in Carlton Television. The Greens were there because Sir Paul Fox, as president of the Royal Television Society, had persuaded Carlton to televise the event.

Ahead of the Greens in the line-up to be introduced to Prince Charles were Guy East of Majestic and Paolo Glisenti of RCS, a member of the Carlton Television board. After the Prince had moved on down the line, Tessa was heard to say to her husband, 'Why on earth didn't we get Majestic?' Owning Majestic would have put the Greens at the head of the line.

That autumn, government decisions on ITV ownership were imminent and it was not at all clear how effective the Green lobbying effort had been. By concentrating on ministers, not all of whom have a detailed command of their many briefs, the Carlton chairman seemed oblivious to the more subtle and effective forms of lobbying: opening and maintaining a dialogue with senior officials, both in the relevant departments and in Downing Street – a route Peter Ibbotson very effectively opened up for him.

The debate on ownership had split three ways in the Cabinet committee looking into the issue. Ministers coming from both the right and the left of the Conservative Party thought market forces should be liberated, subject only to normal competition rules. Another group, including the Welsh Secretary John Redwood and the Scottish Secretary Ian Lang, wanted protection for their local ITV companies on nationalistic and cultural grounds. Peter Brooke found himself rather isolated in the middle. But in the end his stepped approach to liberalization – that outside London it should be possible to own two licences of any size – won Cabinet support. Important backing came from Jonathan Aitken, then a defence minister, who could draw on his knowledge of television from his days running TV-am at its troubled beginnings. Aitken thought that Brooke had got it right.

It was not so much the lobbying that convinced Brooke of the need for a measure of change. He worried mainly about the public reaction if media companies from other countries in the European Union were to snap up a leading British broadcaster, as they could do under the Broadcasting Act. If British broadcasters were bigger it would at least make them more difficult and expensive targets. Largely on practical political grounds, Brooke rejected the option of extending the existing moratorium on takeovers, as a number of the small and medium ITV companies wanted. It would have required only a single-clause bill, but the danger was that a host of amendments could have been attached to it – in effect reopening the debate over the 1990 act.

The National Heritage statement that came on 23 November 1993 was simplicity itself. The proposed relaxation from 1 January 1994, subject to the approval of both House of Parliament, 'would allow a company to hold any two regional licences (excluding the two London licences), a 20 per cent stake in a third company, and 5 per cent in any further licences'. It was just what Green wanted to hear. However, he had no intention of waiting for parliamentary approval or the 1 January deadline before making his move.

After Brooke's announcement, Green and the Carlton team – including Nigel Walmsley nursing a temperature of 104 – were quickly on their way by private jet to Dundee in freezing fog to persuade D. C. Thomson, the regional newspaper group and comic publisher, to sell its 19.3 per cent stake in Central. D. C. Thomson would have preferred to remain a Central shareholder, but it also stood to make an enormous profit. It had paid £5.5 million for its Central stake, but now sums of more than £130 million were being talked about. The directors of the Scottish publishers indicated that, although they wanted to hear the argument at a Central board meeting, they were prepared to consider selling. Leslie Hill and the Central managing director, Andy Allan, had already been to Dundee and argued that change was now inevitable in ITV because of the government support for consolidation of ownership.

The flight back from Dundee included a stopover at Birmingham to talk to the top Central management. For the meeting with Green and Walmsley, Hill booked a room at the Swallow Hotel – to ensure privacy and to avoid any appearance of conflict of interest. Green was only a minority shareholder in Central, and Hill and the rest of the Central board had a legal duty to do their best for all the company's shareholders and not just cave in to Carlton.

At the Swallow, Green made it clear he wanted to launch a bid for the Midlands ITV company, and sought management support. Hill, who had come out of the record industry – at EMI he had signed the notorious Sex Pistols – and was very much a commercial animal, had been arguing in public for years that ITV was too fragmented to compete in international television markets and that there should be no more than five or six ITV companies. Indeed he had once enraged most of ITV when he took advantage of a 'state visit' to Central by Mrs Thatcher to raise the issue very publicly with the Prime Minister. He could hardly now resist the principle of consolidation just because he was on the receiving end.

The Central chairman did, however, have two other plausible options that did not involve a meek surrender to Green. One was to bring in a new 20 per cent shareholder, and there had already been talks with TCI. The other was a merger with Anglia Television. Hill had been talking with Central's eastern neighbour for some time, and a bid was ready to go. Anglia was only a medium-sized company, but it broadcast to a region that was growing economically as it increasingly became a commuter region for London. It had an honourable programme record through wildlife series such as *Survival*. Hill and David McCall, the long-serving Anglia chief executive, also got on well. A Central takeover of Anglia would have created the largest ITV company at that time and also (something that appealed greatly to Hill) the largest 'pure' television company – devoted entirely to broadcasting and selling television programmes, without these having to compete at board level for attention and funds with projects such as motorway service stations, as at Granada, or film-processing laboratories, as with Carlton.

The Central board faced a difficult dilemma when it met on Friday 26 November. It was a company whose shares were rated highly on the Stock Exchange. If Central bid a price large enough to win Anglia – also a quoted company – the City might mark down the larger company's shares. Central's financial advisers advised that the most it could bid for Anglia without seriously damaging the Central share price was around £5 a share – £5.50 was absolutely the limit. This was unlikely to be high enough to be acceptable to Anglia. If the Central share price fell, Green would then almost certainly swoop in a hostile takeover – possibly getting the company for less than he might otherwise have had to pay. Because of the conflict of interest, Green was asked to leave the board meeting considering an Anglia bid – and he did so with good grace. Central then decided to put its bid plans for Anglia on ice and see what sort of deal Green was proposing. Hill and Allan travelled again to Dundee to suggest to D. C. Thomson directors that change in the ownership of Central was now probably inevitable.

The Carlton offer for Central had been prepared in advance, and a complex deal was spelled out to the Central board. The first offer was rejected and Green increased his price, but even then it was not a clear-cut decision. At a specially called board meeting at the Churchill Hotel, London, on Sunday 28 November some directors wanted to try to bring in TCI as a new minority shareholder, to help block the Carlton bid. Hill was reluctant, because if the plan had gone ahead it would have meant running the company with three strong 20 per cent shareholders – Carlton, D. C. Thomson and TCI – who might soon have been at loggerheads. He was also aware that, even if Central launched a bid for Anglia, Green might still push ahead with a hostile bid for Central. Green and Michael Sorkin of Hambros had also structured the Carlton offer cleverly. As well as cash, there were both shares and convertible preference shares. If the City liked the deal, its value could keep on rising as the Carlton share price increased. It was also made clear that Hill's position would be secure in any takeover: without even being asked, Green volunteered an undertaking, that Hill would remain executive chairman of Central. According to Hill's colleagues, the agreement was put in writing.

Just after midnight, in the early hours of Monday 29 November, less than a week after the government announcement, the Central board agreed to the terms. Green had a deal – subject to parliamentary approval of the ownership rules.

The deal announced later that same day, which valued Central at £758 million, meant that Central's shares were worth £26 each, compared with £7 only two years earlier. For the whole company Carlton was paying £204 million in cash, which came from its own resources, with the rest in Carlton shares and preference shares which together made up more than 18 per cent of the enlarged Carlton share capital. Shareholders could 'mix and match' between the various categories of payment. Green secured the agreement of D. C. Thomson, whose stake was worth £146 million at the offer price, and together with the 0.2 per cent held by Central management and its original 20 per cent stake Carlton had just under 39 per cent of the company. It amounted to a blocking vote, and it was very unlikely that anyone else would intervene.

The City liked the deal, and shares in Central rose by more than £4, to £25.73. This meant an instant profit on the day of more than £75,000 for Hill and his wife, Susan, who each had 9,400 Central shares. Fifty Central directors and executives also did well from an executive bonus scheme introduced the previous month. It produced £225,000 for Hill and £176,000 for Andy Allan.

The impact on the value of Carlton was immediate. The rise in the Central share price increased the value of Carlton's stake by more than £20 million, and Carlton's own share price jumped by 30p to 797p.

By buying Central, Michael Green was creating by far the largest ITV company, with an unprecedented 30 per cent share of ITV advertising and the ability to broadcast to 20 million people – 36 per cent of the UK population. 'We now have a platform to go all over the world,' said Green grandly as he sat contentedly in his office off Hanover Square, smoking a cigar, shoes as usual discarded under the desk.

It was the first big deal of the new era of British commercial television, but the man who now had the leading role in UK commercial television had no intention of appearing before the television cameras to discuss it. 'Should I do ITN?' he asked a visitor that morning. He was chairman, after all, and even he thought it might be a bit odd to turn down ITN's request for an interview. Yet that is exactly what he did. All day Green stayed resolutely out of the camera's eye, although he did talk to newspaper reporters. 'The last thing Tessa said to me as I left for the office this morning was, "Remember, you're a businessman not a show-business personality,"' he said.

The Carlton chairman did, however, watch the ITN lunchtime news intently, becoming exasperated as Labour politicians who had privately called to congratulate him on the boldness of the deal criticized its timing in ITN sound-bites. Green still found it difficult to accept that a politician could wish him well personally – and mean it – but later in the day contribute to political and parliamentary rituals in line with party policy. In a formal statement, Mo Mowlem, shadow National Heritage Secretary, accused Peter Brooke of being out of his depth and warned that 'companies are already making long-term decisions and announcing their intentions in anticipation that Parliament will approve these rule changes – that cannot be guaranteed'.

The Central deal was announced at the same time as Carlton's results for the year to September 1993. The annual results showed a 26 per cent increase in pre-tax profits, to £126.1 million on turnover up 56 per cent to £1.09 billion. And, most remarkable of all, nine months after going on air Carlton Television, which had involved an investment of around £90 million, had already made a £14.6 million contribution to operating profits. Green estimated to analysts that there would be at least £10 million a year in savings to be achieved by putting the two ITV companies together.

But, although overheads would be cut and jobs would inevitably be lost, Green insisted that Central's Nottingham studios would be preserved and might even become busier, making more programmes for Carlton Television. 'We are a major publisher-broadcaster while they are a big producer-broadcaster with huge production facilities. We both come to the business from different angles, and the fit is an excellent one,' he explained.

Two days later it was back to business as Green met Brooke again at Carlton Television, at a Disability Forum where television-industry executives met to consider how better to portray the disabled on television. Green, Walmsley and Jackson were all there at the door to welcome the National Heritage Secretary, who could stay for only part of the Forum. As the meeting progressed, big names from broadcasting concentrated on disability issues as if their lives depended on it – among them David Elstein, the former Thames executive, now director of programmes at BSkyB. 'The minister then has to go to another engagement. Green is out of the room within seconds. I have never seen him move so fast. Well, he was obviously seeing him off the premises,' says Elstein. Understandably Green was too busy to return to the meeting, even though some of the best work on television and disability was done in the hour that followed, Elstein notes.

Six days later, on 8 December, Green was in the Press Gallery in the House of Commons to see the affirmative resolution needed to change the ownership rules go through, although not without the usual last-minute panic. Peter Ibbotson had talked at length on the issue with Robin Corbett, Labour's shadow broadcasting minister, and Mo Mowlem, a former university politics lecturer. It was clear that Labour was slowly changing its view and accepting that there was a case for some consolidation in ITV. There would be a Labour vote against the resolution – partly because Green had moved before the wishes of Parliament had been determined, and also because the official Labour line was that the moratorium against takeovers should be extended to allow a more comprehensive look at the wider issues of cross-media ownership – but there would not be a very vigorous Labour attempt to block the change in the ownership rules. But earlier in the day Green rang Ibbotson and said, 'We failed. It's a failure! The Labour Party is going to vote against the resolution tonight. Mo Mowlem has lied to me. We've been naïve.' Green had missed the significance of the fact that Labour had put on only a two-line whip, as opposed to a three-line whip which would have made voting mandatory. A government victory was virtually assured, and indeed the measure passed the House by 144 votes to 106.

Green was 'very excited by the vote' but appalled by the ignorance of the subject displayed in the speeches. And, while waiting for the broadcasting motion to come before the Commons at 11.48 p.m. for an hour and a half debate, Green had sat through an earlier debate on Sunday trading and had been bemused as members spent an hour walking through the division lobbies in what seemed one unnecessary vote after another. 'Haven't they heard of electronic voting?' Green asked.

The final hurdle came on 13 December, in the House of Lords, where there was opposition from Labour peers such as Lord Hollick and the shadow Heritage spokesman Lord Donoughue. Both thought the ownership measure half-baked and incomplete and no substitute for a full review of the 'ludicrous' 1990 Broadcasting Act. Green could, of course, rely on the support of Lord Armstrong – a member of the Carlton Television board, who properly declared his interest – but he got more unexpected support from the investment banker Viscount Chandos, who has helped raise finance for a number of film and television companies and who made a rare visit to the Lords to speak in favour of the resolution. Chandos argued that, in television, profitability was not the enemy of quality but a condition for it, before commending the resolution to the House. Green loved the Chandos speech, and indeed as he wandered off to the Lords bar with a group that included Chandos, Mo Mowlem, and Katherine Pelly, the Kleinwort Benson media analyst, also there to hear the debate, Green joked to Chandos that his contribution had been a better speech than 'my man's [Lord Armstrong]' and 'I didn't have to pay you.'

The Central takeover was finalized in February, while Leslie Hill was away in the West Indies. A cricket enthusiast and former player, Hill had decided to take what was for him a rare winter holiday and watch England on tour. While he was away, it was announced that Hill would no longer be executive chairman of Central. In the interests of closer integration, Hill was to become non-executive chairman, Carlton said. Michael Green was now unambiguously in control of Central.

Chapter 15

'A Menacing Octopus'

By the spring of 1994 Michael Green was the most powerful man in British television. Carlton owned the two largest ITV franchises. He was chairman of ITN and, following the acquisition of Central, the Carlton stake in the news organization had doubled to 36 per cent. The Central acquisition also brought with it a 20 per cent slice of Meridian, while Carlton still owned 20 per cent of GMTV. Green's tentacles extended throughout the television industry, both through ownership and through assiduously cultivated contacts. But not many people knew what Green thought or believed. He rarely attended industry conferences and never appeared on television or gave speeches or lectures. Michael Grade was once mischievously reported as having told a would-be Michael Green interviewer, 'Ask him what he believes.'

On the evening of Tuesday 19 April 1994 Green walked out before the leadership of the British broadcasting industry and stood at the lectern in the Royal Institution in London's Albemarle Street. It was where Michael Faraday, the nineteenth-century scientist who discovered the induction of electric currents, had regularly lectured. Green was giving the 1994 Fleming Memorial Lecture – the most prestigious annual lecture in British broadcasting and the first public lecture he had ever given. The occasion of the lecture marked, as few other things could, Green's journey from unknown outsider to a man at the heart of the broadcasting industry whose opinions everyone wanted to hear.

As he gestured theatrically with his right hand and peered over his half-moon spectacles to the tiered seats arranged in a darkened semicircle around him, Green was speaking to the likes of Sir George Russell, chairman of the ITC, and Marmaduke Hussey, chairman of the BBC. Immediately in front of Green sat Tessa, who, in a mixture of pride and nervousness, never took her eyes off her husband during the hour-long lecture.

Green had been the first and obvious choice of the Royal Television Society to give the 1994 lecture in memory of Ambrose Fleming, the man who invented the thermionic valve, without which radio would not have been possible. He would be following John Birt, the BBC director-general, who had given the 1993 lecture. But it had not been easy to persuade Green to do it. Speaking in public, other than the essential work of trying to impress City analysts, had never had been his forte. The Carlton chairman could be physically ill at the prospect, and he had repeatedly turned down invitations to speak at forums such as the Institute of Directors.

A delegation made up of Michael Bunce, the director of the RTS, and Michael Grade went to his Carlton office to persuade him. He was virtually told he would have to do it because he was now such a powerful player in ITV. As part of the persuasion process Green was taken to the Royal Institution and shown where Faraday, a largely self-taught scientist who had been an apprentice bookbinder, had given his lectures. Green was quite taken with the idea of following in the footsteps of Faraday.

The actual speech was the work of several hands. A first draft was produced by Peter Ibbotson, and later Nigel Walmsley was also involved. But one part of the speech – in many ways the most interesting – was in Green's own words. He felt the need to explain where he had come from and why he had taken the route he had.

Green said he had been persuaded that, as he was chairman of one of the largest media groups in the UK, the industry had the right 'to have a look and a listen and perhaps to prod me though the bars of my cage'. He explained that he was first and foremost a businessman, but that people like him were 'the enablers for the creators'. He admitted that he had been a printer who had almost stumbled into the media business by accident, and that if his career now looked as if it had been a logical progression that was not how it had felt as it happened. Most of Carlton's smartest moves, he conceded, had been things it had not done – such as not getting into movie-making nor becoming highly leveraged, taking on a high ratio of debts to assets. 'If there has been a consistent strand in my own career it has been that, while obviously I wanted to make money, I wanted even more to make real things. But I am passionate about this business. And, even if I am not directly creating things myself, I love making it possible for those who do. That's not intended to sound like altruism – if you like, it's my kind of selfishness.'

Warming to his theme, Green went on to say how much satisfaction he got from being chairman of ITN, and asked who would want to retire at the age of forty-six to grow grapes in the south of France when they had a chance to play a significant part in reshaping ITV. Naturally he made no apology for arguing that consolidation in ITV must continue, and that companies – which of course would include Carlton – must be allowed to grow within the competition rules that applied to all businesses. 'I do not know if we shall ever see a one-company ITV. What I would like to see – and soon – is a clear division of responsibility between the regulation of licensed programme services on the one hand and the rules on media ownership on the other.'

In fact one ITV company was exactly what Green did want, with the clear implication that it should be Carlton. The need for a single ITV company was in the original text of the speech, but Lord Sharp had advised – wisely – that such an inflammatory statement might be going too far, and the words were deleted. Green also welcomed the ambitions of newspaper companies such as Associated Newspapers, United Newspapers, The Telegraph or The Mirror Group who were interested in buying into the television business, and he amused his audience with an explicit threat. 'If the *Daily Mail* wants to buy a slice of Carlton, I am delighted. I am certainly not frightened. I hope that no newspaper group would be frightened if Carlton wanted to buy a piece of them,' said Green, who added that he would have no complaint if ownership and competition issues were sorted out by the Monopolies and Mergers Commission, just like for any other industry.

The Carlton chairman even took a swipe at the successive British governments – although he had to be talking mainly about the Thatcher governments – who had conceded Rupert Murdoch's News International a scale of influence and reach which had consistently been denied to everyone else. It sounded very much like one would-be monopolist complaining about a monopolist who had already made it. In fact, stripped of all its grand phrases and personal revelation, the lecture said little more than that business values are good for television and it is in the national interest to allow Carlton to own more of the British media.

The lecture was reasonably well received. It had been rehearsed, even over-rehearsed, both in front of video cameras and at the Royal Institution under the gaze of a specialist trainer, Rowley Grimshaw. But the applause was more enthusiastic than mere politeness would have required. Whether they agreed with what he said or not – and probably most did not – the industry gave Michael Green, still a largely unknown quantity, credit for at least coming and presenting himself to his new peers.

As the crowd filed out of the auditorium, Richard Last, the long-serving television critic of the *Daily Telegraph*, on the verge of retirement, said that after listening to Green he was glad to be going. After digesting the Green message, with its emphasis on the need for business as well as creative values at the heart of the television industry, the distinguished television director Roger Graef, famous for his fly-on-the-wall documentaries, muttered that maybe it *was* time for him to go and grow grapes in the south of France.

Later, a dinner held at nearby Brown's Hotel turned out to be a Green family affair. Irene was there with her second husband, Willy Wilder, and so also was David Green. On Michael Green's table, Tessa was flanked by Lady Howe, the new chairman of the Broadcasting Standards Council – an organization that is anathema to broadcasters such as Michael Grade – and by the joint managing director of a small independent production company, Ardent Productions. The Ardent executive was on the guest list as Edward Windsor, although he is rather better known as Prince Edward. Also on the same table was Gerry Robinson of Granada.

As soon as the new broadcasting rules had been approved by Parliament, Robinson had on 16 December launched a hostile takeover bid for LWT. The LWT team fought hard to escape the clutches of Granada and explored alternatives such as involving Anglia in a three-way merger with Yorkshire-Tyne Tees under which Anglia would have taken the Tyne Tees licence and LWT the Yorkshire one. The deal unravelled when Anglia decided instead to go with Lord Hollick and MAI. Hollick had pounced just as the Granada-LWT battle was entering its final stages, with an agreed offer for Anglia worth £292 million, valuing the company at 637p a share. On 25 February 1994 Granada finally succeeded in winning control of LWT with an improved offer worth £765 million, and soon after Christopher Bland and Greg Dyke resigned. Bland took around £12 million and Dyke £8 million as a result of the management share scheme that created more than a dozen millionaires at the ITV company.

In three months ITV had been transformed, with three men – Green, Robinson and Hollick – controlling three-quarters of the ITV system in terms of both audience and advertising revenue. Of the three, Green was the most powerful – and the only one to have created his own company. The others were highly paid employees. The takeovers, which brought no new money to ITV programme production but which cost more than £50 million in bankers' and other professional fees, left one serious competition issue in its wake – the control it gave the new enlarged groups over advertising sales.

Traditionally, advertisers played one ITV company off against each other to get the best possible discounts. Now large ITV groupings were emerging with greater power to dictate television advertising rates. They could also drive hard bargains in the competition with Channel 4 for advertising revenue. It was a prospect that deeply concerned Grade at Channel 4, which by then had been selling in competition with ITV for fourteen months. In an article for the *Financial Times*, Grade argued that ownership of ITV companies was one thing – control of advertising sales another. If Carlton was allowed to sell advertising for Central as well as owning it, while keeping minority stakes in GMTV and

Meridian, 'we may well have a potential world player, but the government will also have created a menacing octopus whose tentacles will strangle home competition'. Grade wanted the existing rules that prevented any one company accounting for more than 25 per cent of ITV advertising to be upheld.

Asked if Green would not dislike such an article, Grade replied, 'Michael Green does not pay my salary.' There was later an extraordinary telephone row over the issue between the two men. 'The teddies were all over the pavement,' said Grade, who is not as close to Green as once he was.

The regulatory decision on advertising went Green's way in the end. The ITC decided to increase the limit to 25 per cent of *all* television advertising revenue, including that of Channel 4 and BSkyB rather than just ITV – a new limit that was generous enough to allow Carlton and Central's air time to be sold together. The liberalization followed the line adopted by the Office of Fair Trading, which decided that the big ITV takeovers would not be referred to the Monopolies and Mergers Commission for formal investigation as long as none of the sales houses accounted for more than 25 per cent of total television advertising sales by August 1995.

The inevitable reconstruction of the ITV sales houses that followed gave Green the chance to go for the man generally reckoned to be the best in the business, Tim Wootton, who with Dick Emery had set up Televising Sales and Marketing Services (TSMS) in 1989. It was the first of the stand-alone sales house set up to represent more than one ITV company. Central and Anglia each owned 40 per cent of TSMS, with 10 per cent each for Wootton, the director of sales at Anglia, and Emery, director of sales at Central. TSMS had made a success of selling the air time of Central, Anglia and Ulster Television – a success imitated by the creation of other sales houses.

Green badly wanted Wootton to sell the advertising time of the combined Carlton and Central. Carlton's existing sales director, Martin Bowley, would be offered the chance to work under Wootton.

Green was carefully briefed on his approach to Wootton, and was warned that this likeable, balding, middle-aged former public schoolboy – described by one friend as 'a Catholic puritan' – was not primarily motivated by money, partly because he was already wealthy. It is a concept that Green has difficulty with – that there are people who do not value wealth as much as he does.

Over a private lunch in early February 1994 in St George Street, Green spent more than two hours trying to find out how much Wootton would take for his minority stake in TSMS. Everyone has their price, Green believes, and the trick is to find out what it is and then knock a million or so off. Green seemed to have no interest in Wootton's senior staff – a large part of the reason for the success of TSMS. Wootton would simply be in charge of the enlarged Carlton-Central advertising sales team. Bizarrely, as part of the deal, Wootton was going to be allowed to keep Ulster Television's sales for himself, almost as a private fiefdom. Wootton was unimpressed.

Less than two weeks later Wootton met Lord Hollick, and the atmosphere was entirely different. The talk about money lasted fifteen seconds, and hardly went beyond promising a fair price for the TSMS shares. Hollick listened to what it was Wootton wanted, which included as much independence as possible and the right to bring key staff members with him. Hollick also encouraged Wootton and his team to walk around and talk freely with Meridian staff, to see if they liked the place. It was just the sort of approach that Wootton liked and, although it would mean less money than selling out to Green, he decided to join MAI.

Green made one more unsuccessful attempt to win the services of Wootton, in a meeting with Hollick where it was made clear that, as a 20 per cent shareholder in Meridian, Green could be very awkward unless he got what he wanted.

Green's anger and resentment at Hollick was reflected on the front page of the business section of the *Sunday Telegraph* on 27 February in a story by John Jay, who is usually well informed about Green's views. The story told of a bitter battle behind the scenes at Meridian between Hollick and powerful minority shareholders such as Green and Allan McKeown, of SelecTV, the independent production company that had a 15 per cent stake in Meridian. McKeown was genuinely angry because he felt he was not sharing in the benefits of the MAI-Anglia takeover. The takeover was carried out by Meridian's parent company, MAI, and therefore little extra direct value accrued to minority shareholders of Meridian like Anglia, a subsidiary of MAI. It was an issue that also irritated Green, but for him the row was as much about Wootton. 'There are dark mutterings in the industry that Carlton chairman Michael Green and McKeown will be rushing to their lawyers, claiming oppression of minority shareholder rights, unless Hollick offers concrete peace proposals. These could either involve an offer to buy out their shareholdings or an offer of shares in an enlarged Meridian-Anglia TV business,' the *Telegraph* article said.

Despite annoyances like the Wootton affair, the spring of 1994 was a vintage time for Green and Carlton Communications as the integration of Carlton Television and Central got under way. Before long the government would almost certainly decide on a further relaxation of the rules on cross-media ownership, which would allow Carlton to expand again. To help the process, Green could always speak to Michael Heseltine when he needed to, and he had also cultivated a social relationship with Viscount Astor, National Heritage minister in the House of Lords, a friend of Tessa Green. Green and Astor even went on a Scottish fishing holiday together. 'He went on holiday with me. I didn't go on holiday with him,' says Astor, who adds that Green caught a sea trout on his small Scottish river.

What is certain is that as a result of a large number of political contacts Green was usually well informed about the direction of government policy on the media. If the narrow rules on media ownership changed, Carlton might be able to buy a national newspaper group, such as United, and perhaps another ITV company.

Five weeks after delivering his Fleming Lecture, however, Green got a critical review he could not easily ignore, in the form of the ITC review of Carlton Television's performance during its first year on air. ITC criticized the ITV system generally for lacking adventure and courage. Although the network had taken a 43 per cent share of the audience, the general characteristic of ITV programming, the Commission judged, had been safety first. GMTV was given a formal warning that its service was inadequate and would have to improve in the current year, otherwise more severe penalties would follow. But among the other ITV companies it was Carlton that was singled out for the most stinging criticism.

The company's network performance had been well below expectations and, with some exceptions, its offerings had been neither distinctive nor of noticeable high quality. 'The ITC wishes to see a significant improvement in 1994 and beyond,' the judgement said. The Commission pointed out that only two of the drama projects in Carlton's licence application had actually been broadcast – *Frank Stubbs Promotes* and *Body and Soul*. *Frank Stubbs Promotes* and *The Good Sex Guide* were praised, but *Hollywood Women* – a series watched by an average of more than 10 million viewers – was denounced as glib and superficial. The ITC expressed a wide range of dissatisfactions with Carlton's output. Not only was the quality of network drama 'mixed', but network entertainment was 'uneven'. *The Big Story* was 'variable' in quality and covered no significant foreign stories.

The underlying ITC message was that it expected a lot from the biggest ITV company – the company that had displaced Thames – and that higher-quality programmes were wanted during the rest of the ten-year licence period. The ITC was demanding to see the standard of programmes promised in Carlton's application appear on screen, even though it was up to the Network Centre to decide what should be shown.

Labour's Mo Mowlem said the criticism heaped on selected ITV companies – she did not mention Carlton by name – 'is entirely justified after a year where commercial priorities have preoccupied the ITV debate'. To many newspapers which lavished large front-page headlines on the story next morning Carlton seemed to epitomize everything that was going wrong with ITV – money before quality, and ratings before everything. But Carlton and the other errant ITV companies did at least receive strident support from the *Sun*, which denounced the 'Telly Snobs' and asked 'Who's the best judge of what's on ITV. . . The elite few of a watchdog group or you, the viewers?'

Nevertheless, the critical report was an embarrassment to Carlton Television executives. At a two-and-a-half-hour meeting with the ITC on 1 March to review Carlton's performance, they had been given no indication of the weight of the criticism they were likely to face and therefore no opportunity to try to counter it. When the draft report arrived, two weeks before publication, it came as a shock. Andy Allan, the former managing director of Central, who was overseeing the combined broadcasting operation, wrote to the ITC to complain about the draft assessment. His letter accused the ITC of setting itself up as a television critic and making subjective judgements on programmes which in no way broke any of its codes and which the audience had liked.

Green did not like the ITC's draft comments any more than his broadcasters did. The Carlton chairman took the unusual step of calling Sir George Russell directly at the ITC to express 'disappointment' that the Commission felt the need to criticize the company in such terms. If the call was designed to get Russell to change his mind and water down the criticism it failed.

Inside Carlton Television there were disagreements about how to respond publicly to the ticking off. Nigel Walmsley's instinct was to accept the ITC's ruling and not bite back. The Commission had all the power. But Paul Jackson threatened to resign if an obsequious statement was issued, and after several attempts a press release was concocted that drew attention to the fact that the ITC review did not take account of more weighty Carlton programmes such as four films in Desmond Wilcox's series *The Visit* or a Thoi Nio documentary about contemporary Vietnam. 'Of course we shall pay heed to the ITC's comments,' said Walmsley in the official statement, but they should be seen in the context of the company's achievements, including the launching of forty-three new series and twenty individual programmes. Successes had far outweighed the failures, Walmsley claimed, although in fact in its first year Carlton Television had failed to produce a single unambiguous hit.

Carlton had legitimate complaints to make about the ITC criticisms. It was surely unreasonable for the ITC to attack Carlton for failing to persuade the Network Centre to use more of its programmes. Ironically, one of the main blocks standing in the way of Carlton's programme-making ambitions was Thames. The company was now the UK's largest independent producer and, after the usual negotiating threats to take its programmes to Sky Television or the BBC, a £40 million a year deal had been struck with ITV. Almost all the most popular Thames programmes, such as *The Bill* and *Wish You Were Here*, continued to flourish at the heart of the ITV schedule and in the ratings Top Ten. Naturally all the other most popular ITV programmes, such as *Coronation Street*, also continued to appear, so there were very few slots for new commissions, particularly for drama. If Carlton's ideas had been better, however, more might have been accepted.

By coincidence the ITC review was published on the day of the programme-awards dinner of the Royal Television Society at London's Grosvenor House Hotel. The fact that Carlton won two awards – *Old Bear Stories* won the children's award, and Margi Clarke was named best female presenter for *The Good Sex Guide* – lifted the mood at the Carlton table. As David Glencross of the ITC made his way through the dinner-jacketed crowd after the event, he felt the need to point out to a journalist that both programmes had been praised by the Commission, as if to justify singling out individual programmes such as *Hollywood Women* for criticism.

One of the most interesting interventions in the ensuing debate came from David Mellor, the man who had steered the 1990 Broadcasting Act through the Commons. ITV, he concluded in an article in the *Evening Standard*, was in general in fine shape, and the ITC would rightly jump on any ITV shortcomings. But, Mellor suggested, the Commission should keep its eye on the three emerging moguls of commercial television – Hollick, Robinson and Green. Hollick, Mellor said, was a tantalizing mixture of socialism and gold bars – a reference to the fact that some MAI employees had been paid in gold bars to minimize tax. Robinson was a hard-nosed businessman with more interest in catering than in TV and very different from his predecessor, David Plowright, who had been responsible for programmes such as *Jewel in the Crown*. 'As for Michael Green, he was the young pretender for so long, it's inevitable that now he has come into his kingdom, expectations will be high and scrutiny intense. He's an outstanding businessman who keeps a legendary close eye on the bottom line. He should be the last person to complain that the ITC needs to know that he's more than just a bean-counter of genius.'

During the summer of 1994, under the watchful eye of Green, plans were

produced to unite Carlton Television and Central, but the process was
surprisingly drawn-out. With most takeovers the winner quickly get to grips
with the business and chooses a new management team and creates a
combined structure within two or three months. Then those who have to go
receive their compensation and the pain and disruption are kept to a
minimum. Even though Green knew Central intimately and, as a director, had
been receiving monthly management accounts for years, five separate
committees were set up to plan the unification. Each committee was given
the task of finding savings to contribute to the minimum £10 million
promised for the first year of combined operations. There was a protracted
process in which managers had to work together on committees knowing that
some members were fighting for the same jobs. Paul Jackson, for example, sat
on a committee which included Jonathan Powell, who had become Carlton's
head of drama in 1993, and Mike Watts and Bob Southgate of Central, in the
certain knowledge that only two of their jobs would survive. In fact those
responsible insist it was a more complex task to unite Carlton Television and
Central than to run them as two separate companies.

When the details of the restructuring were finally announced, in
September, the two top jobs went to Carlton executives and the main
casualties were from Central. Jackson was to be in charge of the programme-
commissioning and production arms of Carlton and Central, which would
form Carlton UK Productions. The broadcasting operations of the two ITV
companies were to be run by Clive Jones, who had been in charge of the
London News Network, the joint venture between Carlton and LWT. Andy
Allan was chief executive in charge of the entire division – Carlton UK
Television. The two high-level casualties from Central were Mike Watts,
managing director of Central Productions, who was praised for the 'terrific
job' he had done in charge of programmes such as *Peak Practice*, *Sharpe* and
The Cook Report, and Jonathan Fellows, who had joined Central when it was
an unquoted company worth £25 million and had worked his way up to
finance director.

The merging of the two companies soon had an additional bonus for
Carlton, apart from saving money. Carlton, it was said, had at last produced a
top-quality series, *Kavanagh QC*, which was attracting more than 13 million
viewers for every episode. It was, of course, an idea developed and produced
by Central, but it now appeared under the Carlton UK brand. Just as Green
had in the past benefited greatly from putting the Carlton name on
programmes produced by Zenith and Action Time, so the Carlton UK
Television credit would now roll up at the end of a wide range of high-quality

programmes developed and produced by Central. In future it would be much harder for the ITC to criticise Carlton Television, holders of the London licence, because the Carlton name and ownership would be on nationally shown programmes that were indisputably top-class.

As the integration of Carlton's two ITV companies went ahead, the financial performance of the enlarged company was helped by the fact that advertising revenue was rising as the UK economy showed signs of life and new heavy users of ITV advertising, such as the National Lottery, pushed up the price of air time. This, combined with the savings from integration, provided an enormous financial boost to Green and Carlton.

In terms of prestige, however, Green was about to receive a second sharp reverse, and in an area where it mattered greatly to him – ITN. The *News at Ten* affair had strained the relationship between Green and David Gordon, the ITN chief executive, and several subsequent events aggravated the growing split between the two men. There were rows over issues such as openness and the extent to which staff and other directors should be kept in touch with the affairs of the organization. Green was enraged when Gordon sent a note about ITN profits to staff, and also seemed to resent that the ITN chief executive took very seriously the fact that Green, despite being chairman, was only one shareholder among others.

Gordon has told friends he did not enjoy working with Green. The ITN chairman would scream and shout about quite minor matters but remain totally uninvolved in others of far greater substance. Green in turn thought Gordon uncommercial and believed he had made the wrong choice of chief executive. Gordon was unlikely to remain chief executive of ITN indefinitely, yet it was Green's future as chairman of ITN that was to be questioned first.

Following the reconstruction of ITN there was a presumption that the chairmanship would rotate, although there are different views as to how firm this understanding was. One year after the reconstruction the issue was due to come up as a routine matter at an ITN board meeting that Robinson of Granada was unable to attend. Robinson had made it absolutely clear to Green before the meeting that he believed very strongly that the only way to run an organization with multiple powerful shareholders was to rotate the chairmanship. Green made it equally clear he did not like such an idea. Not only did he enjoy being chairman but surely it was his right to be chairman for a considerable time. He had not only saved ITN but had helped to turn it into a more efficient, profitable organization.

At the board meeting, Green argued that it was crazy to have the issue of the chairmanship coming up so soon. The new young company secretary,

Martyn Wheatley, suggested it would be possible to put through a resolution that Green should simply remain chairman *sine die*. Green thought that a splendid idea, although David McCall, the Anglia chief executive, was appalled at what he saw as the Carlton chairman's opportunism. There was a ferocious row afterwards with Robinson, who told Green it had been dishonourable for him to have behaved in such a way. The Granada chief executive warned that at the end of the second year he would do everything he could to ensure that the ITN chairmanship did indeed rotate. Robinson's tactics included pressing successfully for a second Granada director on the board, in the shape of the group's finance director, Henry Staunton, to strengthen his position. Robinson was determined to remove Green, and told colleagues that 'with Michael you either go along for the ride or you kick him in the head. There is no middle ground.'

The extent to which Green kept fellow board members informed of his activities as ITN chairman also became an issue. On at least one occasion Green got himself involved in negotiations that would significantly affect the future of ITN and have an impact on Reuters, yet neither board was formally told.

In the autumn of 1994 Green opened talks with Rupert Murdoch's News Corporation about the possibility of ITN providing Sky News, the twenty-four-hour satellite channel, with its entire service, under contract. The talks were serious enough to involve a meeting between Green and Murdoch. For ITN it would be a large new contract which would greatly expand its business. A deal would also mean that Sky News, which had always lost money, might be able to have a high-quality news service from ITN at a much lower price than the existing stand-alone operation. But it was a sensitive issue, because a large number of Sky News staff would lose their jobs, and Reuters, through Reuters Television, was a major supplier to Sky News. Green risked getting himself tangled in a web of conflicting interests.

News of the negotiations leaked to the *Financial Times*. That day, 11 November 1994, Green had been on a VIP Eurostar trip to France. The train had broken down in the middle of the Channel Tunnel and, to his horror, Green was out of mobile-telephone contact for a time. 'Steam was coming out of both ends of the tunnel,' Tessa joked. When he finally got out of the tunnel he tried to persuade the *FT* to hold the story, in return for a fuller article later, but the story was already on the front-page-news list for the next day. Green, wary of the government's reaction, rang Downing Street to explain about the story the *FT* was about to run. Downing Street rang Sue Tinson, the ITN associate editor, who is close to John Major, to see what ITN thought. She assured the Prime Minister's office that such a deal would offer ITN a significant opportunity, and was told that a positive note would go into Major's red box for overnight reading.

The *FT* story angered members of the ITN board who had not been informed. Reuters executives were furious for a similar reason. Murdoch, who thought – wrongly – that Green had leaked the story to put pressure on him, was dismissive. That day David Kogan, who ran Reuters' broadcasting interests, rang Sam Chisholm, the abrasive chief executive of BSkyB, to say Reuters could offer him a far better collaboration deal than ITN. The call ultimately led to a deal with ITN being dropped and a new, much closer, cooperation between Reuters and Sky being established. Reuters Television even managed to expand its interests into the USA with a news-supply agreement with Murdoch's Fox Television. 'Despite the fact that Reuters ended up getting the contract, there was a great feeling of resentment that this had been going on behind our backs. ITN can compete with us for any business. We recognize that and we don't mind that. But he [Green] had conflicts of interests because he was on two boards,' a Reuters director said. 'He was clearly trying to pull off the great Green coup, and because of short-term secretiveness he lost the lot.'

All that year Green's relationship with David Gordon had continued to deteriorate. As early as June 1994, when Gordon was away on a business trip to Asia, Green went to see Stewart Purvis, the ITN editor-in-chief, and admitted he didn't get on with Gordon and intended to get rid of him. 'Will I have to bring in an outside chief executive, or will you do the job?' Purvis was asked. Of course Purvis was interested. He admired what Green had achieved at the news organization. 'The key thing was that Green sensed that there was a business opportunity here when others were governed by a mind-set of disaster,' he says. As the man in charge of ITN journalism, he had also noted that Green had never once tried to interfere with the news content.

The affairs of ITN were, however, an irritating distraction from Green's biggest challenge that autumn and winter – trying to ensure that the government liberalized cross-media ownership rules and overturned the restriction preventing one company owning more than two large ITV licences. Green was so keen to get his views across that he agreed to a recorded interview for the *Today* programme on Radio 4. It was broadcast early on the morning of 27 December 1994, when most of the world were pulling their duvets around their ears and trying to get over Christmas. Green, who insisted that there were too many regulators and too much regulation of commercial television, was given an easy ride in what sounded a bit like a commercial for the Michael Green Party. 'You do realize', he said in his hectoring tone, 'that Carlton can have no significant presence in satellite – only 5 per cent? It can only have 20 per cent of Channel 5, and 15 per cent in an independent producer.' Britain needed big ITV companies to be able to expand around the world. 'It is an industry where big is beautiful. If you insist that all independent production companies must be small companies in Soho you are not going to get the best out of independent production in this country. We make no apology for saying you need to be large to take risks in programming and to sell programmes overseas.' Green's Christmas message to the nation was probably aimed at a few people in government – particularly the new National Heritage Secretary, Stephen Dorrell. It was therefore a pity that Dorrell was out of the country skiing at the time.

In January 1995 the issue of the chairmanship of ITN finally came to a head. Robinson did exactly what he had said he was going to do – ensure that the chairmanship of ITN rotated. McCall and Robinson had already decided there should be a new chairman, and they had the support of Reuters. With the executive directors standing aside, they had the necessary voting power to impose the change. Green pleaded and cajoled but accepted the inevitable when he knew he was going to lose. At the three-hour board meeting on 23 January 1995 he agreed without a vote to step down and be replaced by Robinson.

Green was, however, determined at least to resolve the Gordon 'problem'. Directors like Robinson saw no connection between the two issues, but Green asked Robinson to find out what Purvis thought of the ITN chief executive. The ITN editor was being given the dagger on a silver plate. He had only to plunge it in Gordon's back and the chief executive's job would almost certainly be his immediately. If Gordon survived another month or so, until Robinson took over as chairman, the ITN chief executive might be able to save himself.

When Robinson asked Purvis for his opinion of Gordon, he was told that he had been a very good chief executive who had been a breath of fresh air. People liked him, although the international side of the business had not grown as fast as Gordon had hoped. Yet Green went ahead and tried to fire Gordon.

Although Green had made his dissatisfaction with the ITN chief executive known to the board in general terms, ITN executives insist the attempted sacking had not been formally cleared with the board. Robinson was convinced that there was no operational reason why Gordon should go, and thought the man was not getting a fair hearing. Robinson was prepared to ight for Gordon, but the latter, after thinking about the issue overnight, decided that his position was untenable, because the relationship with Green had so poisoned the job for him and Green would remain a large ITN shareholder. Robinson, as chairman elect, then moved quickly and agreed a compensation package for Gordon in a single afternoon.

By then Robinson, the accountant who had never been involved in television before joining Granada as chief executive, and who had been denounced in a famous fax as 'an ignorant upstart caterer' by the actor and comedian John Cleese, was becoming a more and more powerful figure in the television industry. Just before Robinson managed to impose rotation on the ITN chairmanship and be elected chairman, Rupert Murdoch imposed similar rotation on the chairmanship of BSkyB. Frank Barlow of Pearson's stepped down as chairman, to be replaced by Robinson, who thus picked up two important television chairmanships in a matter of weeks.

Green tried to make it look as if the rotation of the ITN was completely normal and expected – almost as if he had thought of the idea himself. But, although he went on to accept his lesser role and to become an effective non-executive director of ITN, he was outraged at being outmanœuvred by Robinson.

Gordon also got his last word. He used his final, carefully worded, monthly chief executive's report in March 1995 to review the state of the company. ITN was well on the way to meeting and probably beating the budgeted £12.5 million profit available for shareholders for the year. This followed the previous year's profit of £11 million, and £7 million in 1993. Not only was the company profitable, with costs under control, but staff morale was now good. The report noted, however, that a climate of openness had been slow in taking root in ITN, and the roots needed continual watering and fertilizing. In his goodbye, Gordon told ITN directors that he was proud of his achievements in leading a great company to achieve more of its potential. Pointedly he added, 'I have enjoyed nearly every aspect of the job. I leave it in good hands and I will always remain a fan of the *News at Ten*.' No one needed to be told which bit of the job he hadn't enjoyed, or the reason for mentioning *News at Ten*.

ITN may have involved a few minor setbacks and embarrassments for Green, but in the venue where he is most happy to be judged – the performance of Carlton Communications – things were going very well indeed. In the six months to the end of March 1995 pre-tax profit rose by 64 per cent, to £120 million, and turnover increased by 22 per cent to £800.6 million. The company was by then worth £2.16 billion. The Broadcast

Television division, which three years earlier had scarcely existed, now
accounted for 42 per cent of group turnover and no less than 50 per cent of
group operating profits. Central, in particular, was already making a
significant contribution to profits, but its importance went beyond that. As
June de Moller put it rather shamelessly in her managing director's
assessment in Carlton's interim report, 'our contribution' to the successful
ITV schedule had included highly popular returning drama series such as
Peak Practice, *Sharpe* and *Soldier, Soldier*, and new dramas such as *Kavanagh
QC* and *She's Out*, a six-parter from award-winning writer Lynda La Plante.
The old and the new programmes worth boasting about had one thing in
common – with the exception of *She's Out*, they had all come from Central
and its talented retiring head of drama Ted Childs.

The results underlined the transformation of Carlton into a major
broadcaster. Analysts still, of course, argued that the results were flattered by
the acquisition of Central, and pointed out that underlying growth was less
exciting. Without further acquisitions the company's growth rate could slow
down further in future years, they warned. Luckily, three days earlier
Stephen Dorrell had provided a possible escape route with the publication of
Media Ownership: The Government's Proposals.

Dorrell, like Peter Brooke before him, had not bought the arguments of
partisan lobbyists such as Green that the media needed no special ownership
regulation beyond normal competition rules. He had been convinced, however, that converging computer and telecommunications technologies meant
that keeping rigid separation of ownership of different media such as
newspapers and commercial television – seen as vitally important only four
years earlier – was no longer desirable.

The government announced it would bring in legislation to allow
newspaper groups with less than 20 per cent of national circulation – that
ruled out Murdoch and the Mirror Group – to control television broadcasters
with up to 15 per cent of the total television audience. Terrestrial television,
satellite and cable broadcasters would be able to own each other for the first
time. Green was blocked from immediate expansion because the government
decided that two large ITV licences for one company would remain the
maximum. But when a new broadcasting bill was passed Carlton would be
able to own a cable network, a satellite-broadcasting group or a national
newspaper.

On the evening of 20 June 1995 Green was at one of those discreet private
dinners that leading merchant bankers hold for important industrial players.
This one was on the media, and it was presided over by Marcus Agius, a

senior banker at Lazard Brothers. The dinner was held in a plush house in Pont Street that Lazard uses for entertaining. The other guests included Greg Dyke, now chairman of Pearson Television, and Kelvin MacKenzie, the former editor of the *Sun*, who was in charge of the Mirror Group's move into television with the cable channel L!ve TV.

'Green had the glint of newspapers in his eye,' said MacKenzie, who felt at one stage that he was being interviewed by Green for a job. 'I told him, "Why don't you give the Tories £20 million for your peerage, instead of pissing £200 million up against a wall?" '

Chapter 16

The Business of Carlton

When Carlton Communications published its annual results for the year to September 1995, on 6 December, Michael Green made considerable efforts to draw attention to a change if not of direction then of emphasis. He had no choice, because there were no big deals to announce or even hint at.

The results were good, and certainly at the high end of analysts' expectations. The figures included the first full year's contribution from Central, and the effect was dramatic. The turnover of the Broadcast Television division had shot up from £496.7 million to £670.1 million, and operating profit had increased from £71.6 million to £122.8 million. Carlton was now primarily a television company. The second biggest division, Video Production and Distribution, had, by comparison, profits of £60.7 million. The profit at Film and Television Services rose modestly, from £38.1 million to £41.6 million, while Video and Sound Products – primarily Quantel and Solid State Logic – achieved a 43 per cent rise in profits, to £32.5 million.

In two years, thanks to winning the London licence and the takeover of Central, the profits from broadcast television had risen from 7 per cent of Carlton's total to 49 per cent. Overall Carlton had increased pre-tax profits by 30 per cent, to £248.5 million, on a turnover that was up 12 per cent to £1.6 billion. Carlton Communications was now a company employing more than 10,000 people. But on the day of the announcement Green felt the need to go beyond the very healthy profits to try to counteract the notion that Carlton was a company that was in danger of becoming boringly normal and competent.

Green reviewed Carlton's progress and set out his policy for the future. 'Carlton's strategy since the 1980s has reflected our faith in the power of broadcast television. While cable and satellite plainly have significant roles to play, we believe that, for the foreseeable future, Britain's television viewers will continue to look to broadcast channels for a large part of their entertainment and information. They are the bedrock on which our broadcasting interests are built and will continue to offer a firm platform for growth in existing markets and in the pursuit of new ones.'

As he kicked off his shoes and ordered a Diet Coke in his office after returning from a successful meeting with City media analysts, Green put more flesh on the bones of the tentative strategy. He was going to make more and more programmes for world markets. He was going to use the Carlton programme library to launch new cable channels, and perhaps buy a cable channel or two in the UK as soon as the legislation allowed. The telephone rang. It was Cyril Green ringing from his home in Spain to congratulate his son on the latest results. He had seen the story on Sky News. Typical, snorted Green – the Carlton story was on Sky but not on ITN. Presumably it was going out of its way to avoid being seen as showing favours to its large shareholder.

Returning to his theme, Green admitted that Carlton had changed and that perhaps City expectations for the company would have to change too. 'I accept that Carlton has become a bit boring. I don't think that's a bad thing. We understand the markets we are in. There are no fireworks. Don't mistake that for a lack of hard thought or lack of courage if the right proposition did come along. But you don't go out and do something for the sake of it,' Green insisted.

Whether or not Carlton was now boring and heading for a corporate plateau, its creation had been a remarkable business achievement. In the thirty years since its origins in J & D Stationers and then Tangent Systems, Carlton Communications had been turned into a company capitalized by then at £2.19 billion that combined growing international ambitions with being the largest single voice in British commercial television. And, although David Green's contribution was important in the early days, as were the Wolfson connection, Nigel Wray, Mike Luckwell and June de Moller, Carlton was mainly the creation of the driving ambition of one man – Michael Green.

There are few companies in the postwar business history of the UK that have matched Carlton's dramatic growth and survived. 'If he is not the most successful person of his generation I don't know who would be,' is the verdict of Maurice Saatchi, who has watched Green's developing business career from the outset. But even a comparison with Richard Branson's Virgin is hardly apposite. Virgin is a much more unorthodox achievement, based on extrovert marketing genius, whereas at Carlton the emphasis has always been on building a powerful and enduring public company. Branson did not care much for the disciplines imposed by the Stock Exchange and, after a brief and unsuccessful period as a quoted company, took Virgin private by buying back the shares sold to institutions. Green, by contrast, has always managed to win the support of both bankers and City analysts for the development of Carlton.

Michael Sorkin of Hambros had been impressed immediately by how practical and realistic Green was. 'I found him charming, pleasant and undoubtedly smart and intelligent. And he talked in basics – he is not an intellectual, which I find in many cases in business rather an advantage – and understands the temperature and the pulse of a business and what the ingredients are, on the ground, to make things happen. He could explain a business to you in the way that a ten-year-old would understand. And there would be fundamental truth in it,' Sorkin says.

Paula Shea, a media analyst at stockbrokers Kitkat Aitken, followed the affairs of Carlton Communications from soon after flotation. She visited not just Carlton but subsidiaries such as The Moving Picture Company and Abekas and found them well-run. She also noticed that Green never failed to make himself available to an analyst taking an interest in the company. 'I mean, he would actually say, "Well, you're a customer of ours in a way,"' she recalls, and she was often questioned by Green about how the City would react to a particular development. Green has also been able to maintain long-term relationships with important investment managers such as Stephen Zimmerman of MAM. Despite selling shares in 1989, MAM has since built its stake in Carlton back up to over 10 per cent again.

Yet the Carlton achievement goes beyond devotion to relationships with the City, personal charm, impressive cash flows, and the increasingly stylish glossy annual reports. An entrepreneurial company in the back-room of the television industry managed by the seat of one man's pants has gradually turned into something much more permanent and substantial with influence over other people's lives through the ownership of television franchises and its significant stake in ITN.

Carlton is still a long way from being the media equivalent of a GEC or an ICI, and the company remains very much the expression of the ambition of Michael Green. According to one Jewish media executive, despite the increasing size of Carlton and the arrival of non-executive directors, there are limits to how much has changed over the years. 'He runs it like a Jewish family business. He's the paterfamilias. He's allowed to scream and shout – and does – but on the other hand he knows they love him. June de Moller has worked for him for twenty-three years. Bernard Cragg and now Nigel Walmsley. He trusts them. They are all family. He listens to what they have to say.'

The eleven-strong Carlton Communications board now has three heavy-weight non-executive directors apart from the original 'family' and the more recent arrival of executive directors such as Walmsey and Tom Epley, the chief executive of Technicolor. Epley's stay was relatively brief, however. He joined the board in July 1993, but in April 1996 Carlton announced that he was relinquishing his role as chief executive at Technicolor, becoming non-executive chairman and leaving the Carlton board. Carlton had so reduced the head-office function in Hollywood that there was scarcely a job to do.

Sir Derek Birkin, chairman of the RTZ Corporation, the international mining group, joined the Carlton board in 1992 after previously giving Green informal advice – they first met at San Francisco Airport when a flight was delayed. Sir Sydney Lipworth QC, former chairman of the Monopolies and Mergers Commission, became a board member in 1993. Following the death of Lord Sharp in May 1994, Anthony Forbes, former joint senior partner at Cazenove, joined the Carlton board in July 1994 after he retired from the stockbroking house. None of the three non-executives could even remotely be considered ciphers, and all bring heavyweight experience to Carlton.

'I think the most fascinating thing about Carlton is that we are making the transition from the entrepreneurial, gutsy, feeling company – having got it right with a lot of luck – to now having depth of management and a real board of directors,' is how Green put it in 1994. It is a transition that has now largely been accomplished, although there is never any doubt who controls Carlton. Green says he believes in strong leadership and has no doubts about his role as chairman, and admits to feeling strongly about issues and having 'a huge influence' over the direction of the company. 'On the other hand when you have got Sir Derek Birkin on the board, who is no slouch in his own right . . . I have been stopped doing several things, and now I look back on it and think, "Jesus, they were right," ' he admits.

The history of his business career shows that Green has reinvented himself corporately at least five times. The first three business lives, in the guise of Tangent, saw a tiny office-supplies company, little different from hundreds of others around the country, transform itself into a direct-mail operation before moving into printing. Then, as the printing business began to look increasingly problematic, and just in time, the printing companies were isolated and eventually discarded, while the more promising bits and pieces – and they were hardly more than that – were merged with a more coherent financial-newsletter-publishing business. In the end hardly anything survived from the Tangent printing businesses. The fourth stage was represented by the move into television facilities and technology, and has in turn now largely dissolved into a future in broadcasting.

It is also noticeable that between flotation and 1992 Carlton had averaged a takeover or significant acquisition every eight months. This means that throughout almost all of its life as a public company there has not been a

single financial year, and very few half-year results, unaffected by a takeover
or a deal of some sort. Yet the deals were not haphazard. The ability to ensure
that Carlton evolved into related areas, when it has been absolutely necessary
to do so, has been one of the key characteristics of Michael Green the
businessman.

Throughout his career Green has also always been able to learn by example
from those more experienced than him or more knowledgeable about a
particular industry. 'In the 1980s Michael was single-minded about what he
wanted to do. He'd take advice, he'd pick brains and ask questions, but he
would form his own views and just get on with it,' one senior Carlton
executive remembers.

Apart from the Wolfsons, perhaps the most important business example of
all was provided by the Saatchis. Maurice Saatchi remembers playing snooker
with Green in his country house soon after the 1975 Saatchi reverse takeover
of the Garland-Compton advertising agency. In the middle of the game,
Green asked Saatchi whether Tangent should do the same thing. Where
outsiders see rivalry between the Greens and the Saatchis – particularly
between Charles Saatchi and Michael Green – Maurice Saatchi claims the
four were competitive against the world, not against each other. 'We have
always wished Michael well, and he has wished us well. We have never been
business rivals,' he insists. Maurice Saatchi believes that Michael Green was
greatly influenced by the growth strategy of Saatchi & Saatchi: 'Michael
watched the good things we did, and also the mistakes we made. He learned
all the lessons.'

An observer with no knowledge of Carlton turning the pages of the 1995
annual report could hardly fail to be impressed by the picture it portrays: of a
coherent collection of businesses, ranging from the manufacture of
sophisticated digital hardware for the television industry and the provision
of services to film and television, through to the making and broadcasting of
programmes. The company is split into four logical businesses, with the pride
of place going to Broadcast Television, a division that brings together Carlton
UK Television – the programme-commissioning, -making and -broadcasting
plus advertising sales of the two largest ITV franchises – with the stakes in
Meridian Broadcasting, GMTV, ITN and London News Network. Video
Production and Distribution includes both Technicolor's video-duplication
activities and Carlton Home Entertainment – the renamed Pickwick. Film
and Television Services unites the film-processing activities of Technicolor
and the remaining post-production businesses in Los Angeles and London:
The Moving Picture Company, Complete Post and TVi, now merged with

Video Time. There is little left in the Video and Sound Products division apart from the two main companies, Quantel and Solid State Logic.

Carlton now also provides much more financial information than in the past, and the figures show that Carlton is overwhelmingly an Anglo–American company in terms of sales and profits. In 1995, 56 per cent of profits came from the UK and 37 per cent from North America. Green has a long way to go to turn Carlton into a truly international company. Continental Europe produced just 4 per cent of group profits, Japan 1 per cent, and the rest of the world 2 per cent.

The straightforward nature of Carlton's accounts, and indeed its accounting methods, now stands up well to scrutiny. But a snapshot of Carlton at any particular moment tends to exaggerate the coherence of the company. The fact that Tangent and later Carlton were reinvented whenever it was necessary may ultimately be one of Green's greatest achievements as a businessman, but it is equally impossible to claim that Tangent and later Carlton were moving forward to a precise strategy. A careful reading of the small print in the Carlton accounts shows that the forward progress has been much messier than most people realize. Nevertheless there has been a rough line of policy, and, on the whole, the closer Green has stuck to it the more successful his many deals have been.

'He is very good on deals, but he does have vision – quite a big word, but he does have a kind of vision. He hasn't just done any deals: there has been a pattern to it. Quite clearly Carlton is a media company and has a strategy within media. It hasn't become a conglomerate,' says Nigel Wray. Carlton Communications is indeed very far from being a conglomerate, and the litter of little companies left over from fifteen years of takeovers and wheeling and dealing tends to emphasize just how focused the company has now become. In profit terms Carlton is overwhelmingly a publisher, duplicator and distributor of videocassettes, a broadcaster, and a processor of film. Little more than one-tenth of the company's profits now comes from the manufacture of broadcasting equipment.

The present success of Carlton is, to a disproportionate degree, dependent on two factors. The first is the cash consistently thrown off by Technicolor, which has turned out to be a very successful acquisition. The second is the success in the long, patient task of winning a broadcasting licence, followed by the instant acquisition of Central when the liberalization of the broadcasting ownership rules allowed.

By comparison the failures have all been modest and relatively inexpensive, and serve mainly to show that Green and Carlton have made their mistakes like anyone else. The mistakes, or at least the traces of them, nearly always dealt with by John Jeffrey, can be found in Companies House. There are more than fifty numbered inactive companies under the general title of Carltonco.

In some cases rights to a name have been preserved although the assets and business have long since been sold on for a nominal sum. Where the corporate losses were significant – as in the case of companies such as Skyscan, the satellite-dish company – they were retained within the group to offset against tax on company profits. Apart from Skyscan, the mistakes range from The Symmonds Drum & Percussion Company to Cambridge Computer Graphics, which, as the Carlton failures always do, simply disappeared from the list of operating companies without explanation.

Nothing much came of the purchase of Michael Cox Electronics, even though the proposed merger with Abekas which caused all the disagreements never did go ahead. In 1990, much to his amusement, Michael Cox was invited to a 'secret' lunch by John Jeffrey, playing his corporate-undertaker role. The company, then called Abekas Cox Electronics, was losing £100,000 a month and was on offer for a very reasonable price as long as the deal could be done quickly and without the usual formalities. Cox himself was not interested, but a company called Vistek, a manufacturer of picture monitors in which he had a stake, was. Vistek paid £500,000 for the loss-making company, which had initially cost Carlton £3.2 million. The price was made up of a down payment of £250,000 and, according to Cox, 'the rest when we saw them'. The only outward indication that anything had happened was the disappearance of the Abekas Cox name from the list of Carlton operating companies.

'So the guy's made a few cock-ups along the way. But isn't that the name of life in business: to get x per cent right and y per cent wrong and as long as you keep x essentially bigger than y you are OK? Michael has certainly kept x substantially bigger than y,' is the verdict of a senior Carlton executive.

But how good an investment has Carlton been over the years? Media analyst Katherine Pelly decided in 1993 to make a ten-year assessment of Carlton soon after joining stockbrokers Kleinwort Benson. Pelly, who has a chemistry doctorate from Oxford University and survived a stint working directly with Robert Maxwell on investor relations, wanted to form her own view of Green and Carlton. Rather as Bronwen Maddox had done before her, she went back to first principles and, after reviewing Carlton's annual reports, pulled all the available accounts of subsidiaries from Companies House.

'The one thing I found when I was looking at Carlton was that the City appeared to be divided very strongly into two camps, more than you usually find,' the media analyst says. In one camp were the older fund managers, who had experienced Green's share sale in 1990 at the top of the market and as a result 'just won't touch the company as an investment'; in the other camp were younger investors who focused more on the company's current potential.

Pelly found that, over the ten-year period she studied, Carlton's revenue had grown at a compound annual growth rate of 51 per cent, trading profit at 43 per cent, and pre-tax profit at 46 per cent – a good performance by any standards. However, when she looked at the return on capital employed – a measure that had infuriated Green when it had been used by Bronwen Maddox in 1989 – the figures turned out to be less impressive. Maddox, writing just after the acquisitions of Technicolor and UEI, had come up with a figure of 14 per cent – respectable but hardly spectacular. Pelly, looking at Carlton in September 1993, found that the return on capital employed – the measure of the total capital employed in the business, including the purchased goodwill – had fallen below 10 per cent in the years since 1989. In 1994 and 1995, she forecast, such returns would fall to a 'very poor' 5–6 per cent. Carlton's earnings per share, however, had shown a compound annual growth rate of 23 per cent over the five years to 1993, and dividend growth had been even better, at 29 per cent.

'The business has grown so much by acquisition, the question is, how has that capital been made to perform? And this is, in other words, the simple question: if I hadn't put my money in Carlton, would I have got it to work better elsewhere?' Pelly asked. For her the answer was an emphatic yes in those years.

Despite her astringent analysis, however, Pelly concluded that Carlton shares were 'a trading buy and a long-term hold'. But she warned that, although earnings per share would continue to grow, the company faced a period of slower organic growth rather than acquisitions.

American consultants Stern Stewart have applied a similar measure, market value added, to the top 500 companies in the UK. MVA measures the difference between the total capital that investors have put into a company and the money they could take out if the value of a company's shares and debts was realized. The survey put companies such as Shell, Glaxo Wellcome and Unilever at the top of the league table. Carlton was not the worst, but nor did it do very well. Between 1990 and 1995 Carlton rose from 255th place in the league to 203rd, with a market value added of £120 million. However, on another Stern Stewart measure, economic value added – after-tax net operating profit compared with the cost of capital, including the cost of equity

– Carlton produced a negative figure of £149 million over five years and a figure for return on capital employed of 7.4 per cent.

Green has preferred to focus on a different measure, return on operating assets, which in effect ignores history and what has been paid for companies and concentrates on how they are performing now. Here Carlton scores much better, with a 21–22 per cent return on operating assets in 1991 and 1992 – an indication that the Carlton businesses are managed tightly.

When, in 1992, Terry Smith wrote *Accounting for Growth* – an attack on what he saw as dubious, if not illegal, devices used to maximize stated profits in the corporate sector – Carlton came out of the analysis reasonably well. Some leading companies used as many as eight or nine of twelve devices that Smith saw as 'dubious'. Carlton made use of only two – extraordinary and exceptional items and the capitalization of costs.

In 1996, however, in a new edition of his controversial book, Smith was much more critical of Carlton Communications. The analyst concentrated on the fact that Carlton had written off £1.5 billion in goodwill from its string of acquisitions, and, using a similar argument to Katherine Pelly, Smith said that once goodwill was written back into the accounts Carlton had been a pedestrian performer. In 1995, for example, if all the accumulated goodwill was added back, the return on equity had fallen from 40 per cent to 8.5 per cent. Smith, who lost his job at the securities arm of the Swiss bank UBS when his book was first published, believed Carlton to be the most obvious 'sell' in the *FT*-SE 100 share index. In reply, Carlton finance director Bernard Cragg argued that shareholder value is a combination of the profits a company makes and its cash flow. 'For example, with Technicolor, which we bought for $780 in 1988, paying of the order of $600 million of goodwill, the majority of that investment has now been paid back, and yet it is continuing to deliver significant profits and clearly has real value,' Cragg argued. Anyway, goodwill was common when media companies were acquired and Carlton has always openly disclosed its extent.

The record suggests that Carlton paid a full price for its largest acquisitions but has been good at squeezing income from them. In particular it has been adept at monitoring and conserving cash.

Apart from his talent for oozing charm, and clinching deals, Michael Green's appetite for the company's cash is another of his most distinctive management characteristics. Requiring detailed monthly management accounts for headquarters is not just a hallmark of how Carlton is managed, it is also often one of the main methods of communication within a very devolved group. The managing directors of the Carlton divisions are set targets and have to make detailed, regular financial returns, so that their progress can be monitored, but are otherwise given an unusual degree of freedom. Contact with Green can amount to little more than 'state visits' once or twice a year. 'As long as you are carrying on and doing the best you can for your particular company you are left to our own devices,' says David Jeffers, managing director of The Moving Picture Company.

The sense of autonomy may also amount to a deliberate divide-and-rule policy by Carlton headquarters. According to one Carlton managing director, there is what amounts to a corporate philosophy of keeping divisional managers apart – which 'has been not something which has been particularly admired'. Unusually for a company of its size, there have been few formal get-togethers of the Carlton senior divisional managers over the years. The only exception was when Keith Edelman actively tried to bring the management from the different divisions together; the attempts ended when Edelman left to go to Storehouse. There are few meetings and indeed little socializing between Green and his top managers at the group level – and certainly no Christmas parties or champagne receptions. Anyone who runs a Carlton company has to run it as if it were their own, and that includes handling all socializing with staff. There is not even much socializing in Carlton headquarters. When Bernard Cragg celebrated his tenth year at Carlton, in 1995, Green took him out to lunch after the Carlton annual general meeting. The only previous time they had gone out to lunch together was on a trip to the USA years before.

In many Carlton companies Green would hardly be recognized if he walked unexpectedly through the door. Instead the Carlton chairman is like a spider at the centre of a large web, able to travel quickly to any outlying division should trouble break out. Jeffers believes that it is an approach which on balance is positive, because of the great freedom it gives managers. The business is, after all, successful and virtually debt-free, and, unlike so many of the 1980s entrepreneurs, Green has created in Carlton a substantial and lasting company. 'At the end of the day he has created a "for real" company. It doesn't just vaporize when you start to look between the pages. It's touchy, it's feely, it's for real,' says Jeffers.

Although little is organized at the Carlton corporate level, divisional managers do get to know each other informally over the years, and many friendships have been made. Willie Scullion, who runs Abekas UK, felt 'great friendship' between Abekas and other related companies in the group, such as Solid State Logic and Quantel. He also testifies to the lack of interference from Carlton headquarters as long as a company is performing. At Quantel itself, chairman Richard Taylor admires the fact that Green has the courage to leave things alone. He also acknowledges that during the height of the recession, in 1990, when Quantel was having a particularly tough time because few broadcasters were buying expensive new equipment, there were telephone calls from Green offering sympathy and encouragement rather than recrimination. 'He is obviously watching that he gets a large dividend cheque twice a year, and he watches the accounts unceasingly, but he has the confidence and wisdom to leave well alone. There are very few people like that in the City,' says Taylor.

When Green does visit Quantel, his passion for the business – for television – shines through, even though he would probably have difficulty telling one sophisticated Quantel digital editing system from another. Despite his lack of knowledge of the detail – Green has never been a hands-on manager – he is undisputed king in the world he has put together, Carlton Communications, and a huge and growing influence in British television.

There is no shortage of testimonials for Green the businessman. Sharp, fast, brilliant with numbers are the descriptions that occur again and again. Even experienced international consultants like Janice Hughes, who has seen many of the world leading industrialists at close quarters, are very complimentary. 'You can see the numbers just flicking through his mind and he is calculating and he is like a computer up there. He still has to be in terms of mental calibre amongst the highest that I have come across. Probably the top three, four or five that I have come across internationally,' says Hughes, who now runs her own consultancy, Spectrum, with Kip Meek of Coopers.

Green has also had the confidence and the patience to wait. In football terms, however, Carlton is still only an ambitious rising club in the First Division with ambitions to join the Premiership. Compared with media giants such as Time Warner, The News Corporation, TCI or Viacom, it is still a modest-sized company. But at least it is big and significant enough to enable Green to hobnob with the world-class media players. In July 1993, for example, Green was invited to the annual media conference at Sun Valley, Idaho, organized by the New York banker Herb Allen. The guest list at one of Herb Allen's summer conferences can include Bill Gates, Rupert Murdoch and John Malone, chief executive of TCI, as up to 100 of the most powerful media people in the world stay with their families at the Sun Valley Lodge hotel. In the mornings there are business presentations, but the afternoons are devoted to everything from white-water rafting and fly-fishing to heavy business schmoozing.

Frank Biondi, then of Viacom, remembers an exchange between Green and Malone over dinner with Herb Allen. Malone was waxing eloquent about the prospects for cable in the UK and claimed that there were 1.5 million subscribers at a time when the real figure was half that. Green challenged Malone's figures. 'It was very interesting, because people don't challenge John Malone too quickly,' said Biondi. The two men agreed to differ. But later Green got a note of apology from Malone, admitting that the Carlton chairman had indeed been right.

Green meets Murdoch about once a year, and the News Corporation chairman has become more impressed with the Carlton chairman since the early days of Sky. 'He's not a huge gambler. He takes a long time, and he plots it. But putting together London and Central was just a tremendous coup, and he has the power to go on. He's very, very able, and he has good people around him. He's definitely one to watch. Absolutely,' says Murdoch, who was, however, much less impressed by the Sky–ITN fiasco.

There is no doubt that Green has both the power and the determination to go on. It is less clear where he intends to go next, following Carlton's three big acquisitions – Technicolor, UEI and Central. Now, indeed, is the time of maximum danger for Green. Great things are expected of him in the hyperactive world of the media. Where will the next big takeover be and when will it come are the questions on the lips of the Carlton-watchers in the City and the national newspapers. If he listens to the advice of his friend Maurice Saatchi he will retain his sense of caution. 'My strong advice to him when he reads in the papers that Carlton is now "dull" is to ignore that – not to be goaded by people who say, "Where's your next trick?"'

Green continues to look at almost every opportunity that comes along in the media, and routinely tracks the trends and developments in the communications industry. His task now is to fashion the corporate future of Carlton, leaving June de Moller to be responsible for the existing operating companies, with Nigel Walmsley in charge of television and Bernard Cragg looking after finance and contributing to future strategy.

There have, however, been a number of sizeable initiatives that did not quite come off but which might have taken Carlton in new directions, as well as a number of smaller lost opportunities.

In 1991 Carlton was offered the possibility of taking a stake in TV4, the Swedish satellite channel, which was applying for a new conventional terrestrial-television licence in Sweden. The company wanted to attract a foreign strategic investor, and Carlton was offered a 20 per cent stake. It wasn't an easy decision. A fee had to be paid, and the regulations were changed halfway through the licensing process. Carlton made the mistake of turning down the deal, and TV4, the first commercial television channel in a country with one of the highest disposable incomes in the world, has turned out to be a licence to print kronor. Green would have had his money back five times over within a few years.

An opportunity to invest in the M6 channel in France was rejected. Carlton's attention was also drawn by Brian Wenham, a Carlton Television director, to the possibility of buying a stake in a new commercial channel in Poland, but little interest was shown and nothing happened. Green next rejected an offer to get involved in Vox, a heavily loss-making German channel controlled by Bertelsmann, the Germany media group. Murdoch took up the challenge and in July 1994 was given just under 50 per cent for £1 in return for trying to bring the channel into profit. By 1996 he was close to doing just that.

In 1995 Green became very excited about expanding into cinemas in the UK when Crédit Lyonnais, the troubled French bank, put the MGM cinema chain up for sale. Green was a serious and enthusiastic bidder, seeing cinemas as a logical extension of Carlton's media business and an additional regular cash-flow generator. Carlton also wanted to ensure that Rank – Technicolor's rival in the film-duplication business and another bidder for MGM cinemas – did not get its hands on the chain. This time Richard Branson got a little revenge over Green when Virgin and TPG, a US investment consortium, acquired MGM's 116–cinema circuit for £190 million. Virgin executives believe that Carlton made at least as high a bid for the chain, but that Green then tried to chisel out better terms and, as a result, exasperated the French owners so much that they decided to go elsewhere.

Carlton was also interested in expanding Carlton Books, a small company which produces illustrated books for the leisure and entertainment markets. Green went along to see Reed Elsevier, the Anglo-Dutch media and information group, when it put Reed Books up for sale. But the price was too high and Green walked away.

Carlton's attitude to Channel 5, the new fifth television channel that will be able to reach around three-quarters of the UK population, was also curious. However modest its viewing figures, the channel will compete for advertising revenue with Carlton television franchises. Possibly because of the threat of that competition, Green and his lieutenants consistently disparaged the proposed channel and suggested that, even if it happened, it would turn out to be financial disaster. Late in the day, when it became clear that the channel was indeed going to be launched, Green changed his mind and sought out Izzy Asper, the Canadian president of CanWest Global Communications, the company behind UKTV, the consortium that had bid the highest amount for Channel 5. Given the size of its bid, there was a good chance that UKTV would win. UKTV documents show that Carlton was listed as a potential investor. When asked about the volte-face Green replied, 'I am a good businessman because I can change my mind.'

But the Carlton chairman had backed the wrong horse. The ITC ruled out both UKTV and Virgin Television on the grounds that their programme plans did not pass the quality threshold, and the licence went to Channel 5 Broadcasting, a consortium put together by Lord Hollick of MAI. There will be no place in Channel 5 Broadcasting for Green. An assessment of the impact of Channel 5 by Neil Blackley, media analyst at stockbrokers Goldman Sachs, concluded that the new channel will knock £16 million off the profits of Carlton Communications in 1997, its first year of transmission. Green may have changed his mind about Channel 5 a little too late.

In June 1996 Green, in a joint venture with the Mirror Group, went head to head with Murdoch's British Sky Broadcasting to try to win the television rights for the English Premier League with a bid of £650 million for four years.

The presentation to the twenty League chairmen in a hotel near Coventry did not go well for Green – mainly because of the presence of Alan Sugar. Not only is Sugar chairman of Tottenham Hotspur, he is also the founder of Amstrad, the consumer-electronics company, and knows a great deal about satellite television. Sugar wanted to know whether Green and David Montgomery, the Mirror chief executive, had a satellite transponder to broadcast their football service if they won. Green replied that the consortium had a channel on the Eutelsat satellite system. Alone of the football-club chairmen, Sugar knew that Eutelsat largely broadcast to cable networks and that few in the UK could receive it direct through satellite dishes. When Green explained that, as part of the deal, they would fit special devices to dishes in more than 2.9 million homes, Sugar ridiculed the idea. Green lost his cool and told Sugar he had not come to be interrogated by him. 'You have come to bid for an important contract,' replied Sugar firmly.

Sam Chisholm of BSkyB won with a package worth £670 million.

The recent Carlton deals that have gone ahead give a clear indication of at least one strand of the company's future strategy – the long-delayed move into broadcasting markets around the world. Carlton plans to invest in television channels outside the UK – after previously passing up such opportunities – and, unusually for him, Green reluctantly accepts that it may have to be content with minority stakes, at least at the outset, to get a feel for new markets.

In July 1995 Carlton took a 28 per cent stake in France Télé Films, a satellite channel run by France Télévision, the leading French broadcaster. The channel, aimed at French cable networks, specializes in films and drama, and Carlton plans to offer series such as *Soldier, Soldier* and *Inspector Morse*. There have also been visits to the Far East by Green and Walmsley, although so far the only fruit has been a 31 per cent stake in KTV, a new music satellite channel based on karaoke and aimed at all of Asia. KTV has at least introduced Green to powerful Asian partners, Nanyang Press of Malaya and Pan Pacific Public Company. Even though the deal was small, Green flew to Singapore for the official signing. After all, the Carlton chairman emphasized, karaoke is very big in Asia.

Carlton has also tried to get into the Indian market. The first attempt was a dismal failure, with Carlton trying, unsuccessfully, to negotiate a deal with the powerful Modi family but choosing the wrong Modi brother by mistake. A Carlton Television executive, Robin Paxton, was then sent to India to try to find new potential partners to launch a satellite-television channel devoted to Indian films and drama.

While Murdoch spends hundreds of millions of pounds to establish digital satellite television in Asia, Latin America and Europe, Green, with characteristic caution, is getting to know a number of overseas markets through experienced local partners before committing himself to more ambitious investments. The investments are small, however, and there is a danger that he will increasingly be left behind.

For the first time in the history of Carlton Communications more than two years have passed since a significant deal has been negotiated – the November 1993 acquisition of Central. Has Green lost his touch? With every month that passes, staff wonder what is happening to a company which has largely depended on acquisitions to grow. One of his executives believes Green is in the process of missing the boat. 'None of us can understand why he isn't taking any of the satellite stuff. It's a fact of life that terrestrial broadcasting is off the road, isn't it? Terrestrial television in twenty years time, in my opinion, will be like the analogue telephone, like cranking the handle. Terrestrial television is *finito*. I am absolutely staggered that Michael has taken no part at all in satellite, and our view is that we assume it's got something to do with not rocking the boat. We can't believe it to be anything else, because the man isn't stupid,' said the executive.

It is a view supported by Lord Young, the former chairman of Cable & Wireless. 'If Michael recognizes the changes that are coming in the information and entertainment industries, in fifteen years' time Carlton could be one of the largest corporations in Europe. If he keeps only with broadcast television then Carlton will be a dinosaur,' said Young.

It is a concept of the future echoed by many, and indeed around the world billions of pounds are being spent on launching digital satellite systems that can broadcast 150 channels or more of television. Many television-industry specialists are talking about 500 channels of television being available in Europe by the end of the century. By comparison, four or five analogue channels broadcast from transmitters perched on hills seem ridiculous. And when video-on-demand – ordering the film you want when you want it, whether from a satellite, down a telephone line or along a cable network – is available will consumers still be willing to go out in the rain to the local video store? When a satellite can deliver a film in digital form simultaneously to every cinema in a continent, who needs vans carrying cans of film hundreds of miles to individual cinemas?

Over the past few years Carlton has put tremendous effort into assessing the impact of the latest technologies and concepts, ranging from the super-electronic highway, interactive television and digital terrestrial and digital satellite television to CD-Roms and the Internet. If the new digital technologies really do take off rapidly, Carlton's more traditional media businesses, based on film, videocassette and broadcast television, could indeed be seriously threatened. Green, however, is increasingly convinced that technologies such as video-on-demand are not about to sweep away the world of the traditional media. He will continue to track the latest developments, and is already producing CD-Roms in his Technicolor plants in the USA, but, as in the past, he will approach large investments in new technologies with caution.

Green is not alone in questioning how quickly consumers will actually take up most of the new offerings. Most of the video-on-demand experiments around the world have so far produced disappointing commercial results. There seem to be limits to how much people will pay for extra convenience and choice. Frank Biondi, a pioneer of satellite pay television in the USA, is one of the most knowledgeable executives on all aspects of the new media. Yet, with his backing, in 1995 Viacom bought a traditional Hollywood studio, Paramount, and Blockbuster Video, the video-rental chain.

In the UK the penetration rate for cable – the proportion of those subscribing as opposed to those who have cable in their neighbourhood – has stuck stubbornly at a disappointing 21.5 per cent. And even in those British homes which pay anything from £20 to £40 a month for the new television channels, whether delivered by cable or satellite, around two-thirds of viewing time is still spent with the traditional channels.

The current Carlton strategy – monitoring new developments closely, making modest investments in the new media to learn as much as possible, and building up programme libraries which will be valuable whatever delivery methods emerge on top – is sensible, but it is still not clear what the company's next big move will be. Even directors such as Nigel Wray are unsure about what Carlton should do now. 'Sometimes the most exciting thing about a company can be the next deal just around the corner that you don't even know about. Michael is capable of doing such a deal should it arise,' Wray emphasizes.

As the government dismantled the rules which prevent television companies owning newspapers, Green remained interested in buying newspapers. In the past there had been a number of informal conversations with Lord Stevens, chairman of United News and Media, publishers of the *Daily* and *Sunday Express*. 'To say that we have never looked at United would be wrong,' said Green, although he was talking at a time when potential predators such as Conrad Black were thinking of trying to acquire United and break it up. Carlton would have been interested in some of the pieces of the group – perhaps United's regional titles. The Carlton board still looks from time to time to see whether trying to buy a national newspaper would make sense. 'I wouldn't rule out that possibility,' the Carlton chairman said, although it seems increasingly less likely.

As Green ponders further expansion in the media, he insists he is still committed to companies such as Quantel and Solid State Logic, although the ties to the hardware and manufacturing side of his business seem less than total. In September 1995 Carlton unexpectedly announced the sale of Abekas Video Systems to the Scitex Corporation of Israel for $52 million. In the six months to the end of March 1995, Abekas had had revenues of $27.3 million and trading profits of only $400,000. It may have once been central to Carlton's success, but now it was not making serious money and the price offered was attractive.

Despite the uncertainty and speculation over Carlton's future direction, it would be foolish to write Green off. 'We've been there before with Michael. He keeps those inner thoughts private. And I'm sure that there were many occasions in the past twelve or fourteen years when we've thought, "What's he going to do now?" And suddenly he will come up with the rabbit,' says a long-time associate.

On Friday 15 December 1995 National Heritage Secretary Virginia Bottomley changed the nature of the game again with her long-awaited broadcasting bill. The expected changes included permitting ITV companies such as Carlton to own, for the first time, cable, radio stations and newspapers. But Mrs Bottomley went further. She also announced the government's intention to abolish the rule that no company can own more than two ITV licences. She had decided that the new barrier should be based on a maximum 15 per cent share of audience. It was a more robust and stable measure than advertising revenue, the government argued. 'Given the development of a more diverse media market with greater cross-media holdings, it is inappropriate to retain fixed licence limits. Market share is a more reliable measure of influence,' said Mrs Bottomley, who argued that further consolidation in ITV would help to strengthen the British challenge in world media markets.

Green could scarcely believe his luck. The National Heritage Secretary had adopted the policy that he had been arguing for. Green had even written Mrs Bottomley a personal letter lobbying for just such a change. Carlton Communications, through its two large ITV licences, accounted for only 9.4 per cent of total television viewing when the BBC audience was helpfully included and could now take over other ITV companies such as Scottish Television and HTV, the ITV company for Wales and the West – or even the larger MAI. Perhaps Mrs Bottomley has provided the rabbit that Green needed to push on to greater wealth, influence and power.

Planning on new takeovers began immediately, and a small £5.2 million acquisition announced in January 1996 suggested that Green would not hold back. Carlton Communications bought SelecTV, a channel transmitted to individual cable networks by satellite and featuring programmes such as *Birds of a Feather* and *Lovejoy*, together with dramas and comedies from the Yorkshire Television library. At the same time as Carlton bought the cable channel, Pearson bought the SelecTV production company and terrestrial television rights to its programme library, and MAI bought its 15 per cent stake of Meridian Broadcasting.

Technically, Green was not supposed to own such a satellite-delivered channel until the new rules came into force following successful passage of the Broadcasting Bill, which eventually took place in July 1996. But he found a way round such regulatory niceties with a device used initially to avoid the rules on ITN ownership.

In May 1995 the government had made it clear that it intended to keep the regulation that no one company could own more than 20 per cent of the television news organization. This presented a problem for both Carlton and Granada, which each owned 36 per cent following their respective acquisitions of Central and LWT, each of which held 18 per cent of ITN.

The ITC gave Carlton and Granada until 31 December to sell off their excess ITN shares. After failing to find a buyer for the shares at an acceptable price, Carlton set up a 'deadlocked company' to hold the surplus ITN shares. This was a new company, 50 per cent owned by Carlton and 50 per cent owned by a merchant bank acting on Carlton's behalf. Because no one had a majority, the company was 'deadlocked' and therefore legally no one had control of the shares. Green had breached the spirit of the legislation and exploited a loophole in the 1990 Broadcasting Act. The ITC expressed regret but said there was nothing it could do. The government will close the loophole to allow regulators to take account of de facto control as well as legal control, but could not do so before the new Broadcasting Bill became law and is implemented at the end of October 1996.

Green was able to use the device again to hold the SelecTV cable channel.

By the end of January 1996 Carlton programmes were already appearing on the SelecTV channel in more than 900,000 UK homes. 'Cable is going to be big in this country,' predicted Green, who has not ruled out buying a stake in a large cable operator – not to mention the prospect of Carlton owning an even larger slice of ITV.

It was Hollick, however, who pounced first, in February 1996, with an agreed £3 billion merger between MAI and United News and Media. Until the new Broadcasting Bill became law, United's Express Newspapers was held in yet another specially created deadlocked company. The deal, which took Green entirely by surprise – he was on holiday in the Caribbean at the time – simultaneously removed two possible Carlton bid targets. A horrified Green, who had been outwitted by Lord Hollick and Lord Stevens of United, interrupted his holiday and flew home. He went straight into meetings at Carlton's headquarters to see if anything could be done.

In the week that followed, Green planned a possible hostile bid for MAI to try to disrupt the merger of the two companies. Potential new brokers were approached, because Carlton's broker, Cazenove, also represented United, and preparations were begun to have an £2 billion bank facility in place. At Carlton's annual meeting, on 20 February, Green would say only that he was 'monitoring carefully' the MAI–United situation and Granada's decision to spend £50 million increasing its stake in Yorkshire-Tyne Tees from 14 to nearly 25 per cent.

In fact at a meeting at 9 a.m. on 18 February the Carlton board had already given Green its support to mount a hostile bid for MAI if he judged it to be the right thing to do. Nigel Wray advised Green 'go with your instincts. Its what you have got.'

The instincts of the Carlton chairman were cautious, and he remembered the advice of Maurice Saatchi. Michael Sorkin also warned of the dangers of overpaying for the non-television interests of MAI, such as its money-broking operations. If successful, there would also have been regulatory problems involved in holding two extra television licences before the new legislation had become effective. But Green decided against launching a hostile bid mainly because he was determined not to pay too much in case it undermined the Carlton share price. Lord Hollick had also promised there would be a robust counter-attack on Carlton's record in creating shareholder value if Green moved against him. Green was warned that he would be 'taken through the pain barrier' in terms of the price he would have to pay.

The decision was taken before the *Independent* reported on 22 February that Carlton was raising a £2 billion war chest to enable it to intervene in the United-MAI merger to try to scupper it. The effect of the story was immediate. The Carlton share dropped from a high of 466p to 419p. That morning Hambros was informed that the £2 billion was no longer needed. The City Takeover Panel asked Green for clarification of Carlton's intentions, and the company said, 'Carlton wishes to make clear that, in present circumstances, it does not intend to intervene in the proposed merger between United News and Media and MAI.'

For Carlton the takeover options in ITV were closing down before Green's eyes. It looked as if a takeover of a much smaller ITV company, such as HTV, might have to suffice, and that Green's search for a new rabbit to pull out of his hat might have to continue for a bit longer.

On 19 March there was at least a consolation prize. Carlton announced that it had joined with four partners – Pearson, the Hong Kong broadcaster TVB, the *Hindustan Times* and Schroder Capital Partners – to launch a channel in Hindi covering the Indian subcontinent. India has the fastest-growing television market in Asia, with the number of television sets expected to increase from 50 million to 100 million over the next four years. The channel was launched in June 1996 and could turn out to be a shrewd investment and the pattern for more to follow for Carlton Communications.

Despite the continuing absence of a huge deal, Green's profitable touch has not deserted him. In the six months to the end of March 1996 pre-tax profits were up by 19 per cent, to £143.3 million, with 'record programme sales, new and repeat commissions from ITV and proposals for a range of programmes for cable and satellite channels'. A five-for-two share split announced in January cut the price of a Carlton share and helped to make it more marketable for smaller investors. By June 1996 the market value of Carlton had reached £2.7 billion, excluding convertible shares which took it to the £3 billion mark. On 22 July 1996 Carlton paid £59 million for Cinema Media, the cinema advertising business owned for many years by Rank.

Whatever happens in future, Michael Green's business achievement and reputation are already secure. Green may never have been to a business school, but by never taking his eye off the cash, avoiding debt, sticking to a rough-and-ready strategy, and choosing able people to run his subsidiaries and letting them on the whole get on with it he has built an enduring company. Above all, his mistakes as a businessman have been relatively small ones and he has survived. Maurice Saatchi goes further and sums up Michael Green the businessman in the following way. 'If you landed from another planet and wanted to meet somebody who could rapidly explain how business worked on earth, Michael would be the perfect person.'

Chapter 17

Michael Who?

The most surprising thing about Michael Green is the extent to which the most powerful man in British television is not in any sense a public figure. Despite his influence and wealth, Green is almost completely unknown outside his circle of family and friends and his rarefied private network of high-level media, banking, business and political contacts. The chairman of Carlton Communications can walk down a street or dine in all but a few restaurants completely unrecognized.

While Lord Grade was happy to perform in public dispensing quips and waving his six-inch Montecristo cigars, and his nephew Michael Grade is willing to turn up on *Newsnight* to argue for Channel 4, defend the principles of public-service broadcasting or attack Rupert Murdoch, Green is nowhere to be seen.

Green may control a larger proportion of commercial television in the UK than anyone else, but he has never appeared live on television or given an interview for the cameras. There have been a number of on-the-record interviews for newspapers and magazines, and he also succumbed to two extended interviews which formed chapters in books devoted to the exploits of those under the age of forty who were already 'making it big' or were members of the new class of rising British entrepreneurs, but over the years such conversations have been few. His high-pitched voice, which rises ever higher the more excitedly he argues a case, has only occasionally been heard on radio, when he thought some public lobbying would be to his advantage. The RTS's Fleming Lecture remains Green's only public speech.

Green has not even been photographed very often, and there have been occasions when a reporter has been allowed into his third-floor St George Street office only to have the accompanying photographer sent brusquely away. When a profile of the Carlton chairman appeared in the *Birmingham Post* in 1995, describing him as the most powerful mogul in British television, it was accompanied by a large portrait of a podgy, balding figure who was quite another Michael Green.

Green remains the unknown tycoon, and is a virtual recluse compared to someone like Richard Branson. Green would never dream of crossing the

Michael Green

Atlantic in a hot-air balloon, no matter how much publicity it generated for
Carlton.

Given that Green is a very social man who enjoys company and sparkles
in it, and who can work his way around a party better than most
professional politicians, his lack of taste for publicity is an anomaly in need
of explanation.

What appears to be an almost neurotic reticence is partly explained by a
combination of genuine shyness, an equally genuine desire for privacy and a
realization that, as chairman of a public company, a few badly chosen words in
an interview or speech can send the company's share price crashing. His
friend Gerald Ratner's throw-away joke about one of his products being 'crap'
and the damage it did both Ratner and the company are unlikely to make
Green any less cautious.

Green's behaviour also suggests that, despite all he has achieved, there is
still a mixture of unease and fascination when faced by bright young things –
particularly women – with good degrees from universities such as Oxford or
Cambridge.

All this, however, amounts to something far more complex than a taste for
privacy, reticence or caution. Green wants to be able to dispense information
on his terms. He puts a great deal of effort into actively manipulating
information, and he certainly believes that the control over image and

perception that it has given him has been important in the development of Carlton.

The trick of remaining aloof publicly while working as hard as possible in private to generate positive images was learned from past masters of the art – the Saatchis and their former right-hand man Sir Tim Bell. It works. The further Green stays away from the flashbulbs, the greater the interest that is generated – a process intensified by the fact that he has chosen to enter the most high-profile business of all: the media. By limiting the flow of information, and relying on friends not to talk about him to the media, Green has been able, to a considerable extent, to control what appears in the media about him and, to a lesser extent, Carlton. He is, however, to a considerable degree a private and rather shy individual. 'I want and I will insist on keeping my private life private,' he says firmly.

Because information and the image of Carlton are so important to him, and because there is a growing media interest in everything he does, Green handles all important issues of investor and public relations personally. This leaves little room for those supposed to be doing those jobs in Carlton. And there have been a number of departures from those positions after short periods. The record for most rapid resignation so far is held by Jan Shawe, a very professional and experienced public-relations adviser who was director of communications at the much larger Reed Elsevier.

Shawe was approached by head-hunters representing Carlton soon after leaving Reed, following the ousting of her boss, Peter Davis, in a boardroom coup. To welcome her, Green in her first week virtually covered her basement office in bouquets of flowers. She resigned five weeks and two days later, on 6 December 1994. It was obvious the job was not working out because Green held all the essential information close to his own chest. She had not been shouted at herself, but she knew that would almost inevitably come. At the age of forty-five, she felt she did not need the irritation of working in an office where the talk among the courtiers was usually about what Green was doing and what his mood was on any particular day.

Journalists find Green equally difficult to deal with. Most do not get through at all: their calls are immediately transferred to the investor-relations department. The few he talks to are usually from the broadsheet newspapers, whose City or business pages can influence the Carlton share price. Many Carlton developments are, however, trailed in articles written by John Jay, the City journalist who in 1995 moved from the *Sunday Telegraph* to become City editor of the *Sunday Times*. Green has known Jay, another north-Londoner, for years.

As a journalist, it is difficult to talk to Green without getting trapped into some sort of deal or being forced to accept conditions in advance. The most banal comments are 'off the record', and even slightly sensitive information is for the deepest background only. Significant intelligence is passed over only on condition it is not for use – at least for now. When journalists get a story involving Carlton and call for comment, a typical Green tactic is to try to delay publication in return for the promise of help with a fuller story later.

Before the move to St George Street, Green from time to time used to invite a number of specially favoured journalists to lunch at Frederick's in Islington. At such individual lunches Green was solicitous, friendly and flattering. Richard Brooks, media editor of the *Observer*, formerly of the *Sunday Times*, was given the chauffeur-driven ride in the Bentley to Frederick's for lunch, but later the relationship cooled after he wrote a number of critical stories about Carlton. Years later, when Brooks was asking some tough questions about the progress of the Open College, its chairman rang the *Observer* out of the blue. Forget about the Open College story, suggested Green – he would give Brooks a terrific story about a leading media magnate. To find out what the media story was, however, the journalist would have to agree to drop the Open College story first. Brooks rejected the deal, although in the end the *Observer* was unable to confirm the Open College story anyway.

Press releases with handwritten notes by Green are sent to the editors of the *Financial Times*, the *Daily Telegraph* and *The Times*, but the manifestations of Green's almost obsessive interest in the media and how Carlton is portrayed are sometimes more sinister. Brenda Maddox, former home-affairs editor of *The Economist* and a distinguished media journalist and author, began writing a regular media column in the *Daily Telegraph* in 1987. Around Christmas 1994 Brenda received a pleasing letter from Max Hastings, the *Telegraph*'s editor. It encouraged her to continue writing her 'brilliant column' for the paper. Her first-ever telephone contact with Hastings came the following February. Hastings rang to say that he had just had Michael Green on the phone complaining that Maddox had been ordered to do a hatchet job on Carlton Television. Hastings, who knows Green socially and plays tennis with him, said he was very unhappy that anyone should have been given the impression that *Telegraph* journalists are told what to write. When Maddox denied that she was planning a hatchet job, Hastings persisted. How could such a thing have got round? Michael Green was very upset, he emphasized. Maddox confessed that she had asked a Carlton employee casually at a drinks party if they had any good news about Carlton

Television, because a *Telegraph* editorial executive had expressed interest in a 'robust' article. If that had been misinterpreted and got back to Green she was very sorry.

Maddox was asked for a full memo on what had happened and got a severe two-page reply saying that what she had done was contrary to how Hastings expected *Telegraph* staff to behave. She had compromised that most cherished thing, the editorial independence of the paper. The incident passed, and in April 1995 Maddox got a higher fee for her column. But at the end of May she received a letter from Hastings saying that more space was needed on the arts page for music reviews and he had decided to drop her column. It was true that there was pressure to find space for more music reviews, and her column, which was sometimes about the media as an industry, did sit a little uneasily on the arts pages, but Maddox still found it odd that no attempt was made to move her column, described as 'brilliant' less than six months earlier, to another part of the paper. It was immediately snapped up by *The Times*.

On Sunday 10 September 1995, when the story about Carlton's investment in the Asian karaoke channel appeared in the *Sunday Times*, Hastings was lunching with Green at his country home. Hastings called the *Telegraph* news desk to explain what a significant development it was. The duty reporter assigned to the story, Donald Cole, in his article quoted Green on the 'exciting new concept'. The piece had to be faxed to Hastings at Green's home for his approval.

To some on the *Telegraph* staff, Green appeared to take on the role of unofficial adviser on the media to the paper. 'Michael says . . .' was how Hastings often responded to any debate about media stories at the *Telegraph*'s morning news conference. But Hastings, now the editor of the *Evening Standard*, obviously protects the total independence of his television critics. On 3 July 1996, for example, the *Standard* critic Victor Lewis-Smith launched another ferocious attack on Carlton's programme standards in London and asked, 'Will the ITV authorities, if they have *any* scruples, renew Carlton Television's franchise next time round? No.'

But what, apart from being controlling and manipulative, is Michael Green actually like, and what motivates him?

Talk to enough people and you might think you are dealing with more than one Michael Green, so great is the contrast between the views expressed. Ask one person who has dealt with Green over the years what they think of him and without a moment's hesitation an unambiguous verdict is delivered: 'He's a total shit.' Others talk of his charm, his kindness, his humour, and the fact that he enlivens any gathering he joins, gliding effortlessly, as if on wheels, from person to person.

Conrad Black, who occasionally lunches with Green at his Berkshire country house, says of him, 'He is a delightful man. He is extremely charming, he has a splendid sense of humour, and he is very well informed not only by virtue of hearing a great many things but by making it his business to hear them through a constant nexus of people telling him things.' To the *Telegraph* chairman, Green is like a spider watching carefully over a series of interlocking webs.

There are also people who hold balanced views about Green, who can see his merits as well as his weaknesses and faults, but they are in a minority. Rather surprisingly, they include Sir Peter Michael. 'I have to say that over my career as a whole I have met now a range of business people that go from the shoddiest to those with the highest integrity. I put Michael Green in the sort of middling range. There are some really serious shits out there. And as one begins to work with the man one at least recognizes him for what he is.'

A former Carlton executive says of him, 'He is the most charming person, and he *is* a charming person, but he has these moments of extreme temper – you know, like a child.' The rows can be about quite trivial things, such as demanding to know why there are 'no bloody lights on the Carlton Christmas tree' – or who should push the timer button on his car. Every morning on his way to work Green used to push the timer button, to see how long the journey took. One morning he didn't, and his driver, thinking he was being helpful, reached over and pushed the button. 'I'd have put the timer on if I had wanted to,' said Green. 'I don't want you doing it.'

He can cut and cut at an employee who has fallen out of favour until their confidence is destroyed and defeat is acknowledged. Then decent compensation terms are agreed. He can shout and rage at everyone from secretaries to senior executives. Yet one senior executive, Keith Edelman, says he worked very well with Green and that the rows accounted for only 2 per cent of the time. 'OK, we had our disagreements – which you do in any business about certain things – but it would be wrong to say he was a tyrant. I would say he is a very strong manager and a very challenging man to work for. It would be wrong to say he was not kind. It would be wrong to say he is a megalomaniac. It is wrong to say that he is not very cautious,' says Edelman, who is now chief executive of Storehouse Group, whose interests include BhS stores.

To an unusual degree, Green divides people into those who love or admire him and those who loathe him and swear they will never work with him again under any circumstances. 'At the heart of it, and I suppose at the heart of my contempt for the man, is the fact that he is absolutely, totally, of the invincible religious belief that everybody and everything is grounded in cash. That there is nothing else that is more important. That anybody who attempts to pretend that human beings act from motives other than financial motives is just an idiot,' says Charles Denton.

Roy Moore, the former Superhire chairman, says he is still waiting for an apology over his summary dismissal. Green concedes that, although he wrote to Moore, it fell short of an apology. 'I didn't feel like apologizing at the time,' he says, and believes it would have been wrong for his young Superhire managing director to have been forced to leave under a cloud.

Moore, who was on one of the top tables at Green's second wedding, sitting next to Charles Saatchi, is still intransigent and insists he would never do business with Green again. And based on that single incident of the £100 payment to a Thames employee, which he believes involves an important point of principle, Moore delivers a harsh judgement on Michael Green. 'Well, my estimation, without any doubt at all, is that he is a man without honour. He sanctioned bribery and corruption. An honourable man doesn't do things like that,' he says.

Dorothy Berwin of the Jewish Film Festival acknowledges two sides to Green. 'He is such an attractive charming man, and he is also a complete monster. And he is totally split. He doesn't have a problem being very, very tough and not always being very respectable.'

The dichotomy between the two, or even more, versions of Michael Green is much more apparent than real. The opposing patterns of behaviour are all part of the same complex character, deployed in different circumstances and for different purposes.

Some of those who have worked closely with Green believe it is as if he has a charm button that can be switched on or off for effect, and rages can be deployed in a similar manner. It is probably impossible to know – even for Green himself – to what extent the charm is being used as a deliberate weapon: it is now completely integrated into if not his personality then his public performance. But both the charm and the rages when he does not get what he wants – and the utter determination never to give up – have been important drivers in the creation of Carlton.

'I think he is, in a business sense, that deadly combination of charm and ruthlessness. It's a lethal combination if you are at the wrong end of it. He does push things to the limit, almost. He really does. There is no question about that, in the sense of if he wants something he wants it and will go for it in every way – I am sure absolutely within the bounds of legality,' says Gerry

Robinson of Granada, who is enormously charming himself and who also does not flinch from tough business decisions that can end people's careers.

Another obvious characteristic is that Green likes women – a lot – and they find him handsome and attractive, even though his once jet-black hair is greying now and he increasingly peers over half-moon glasses to read. He has always been willing to promote able women employees, and indeed he married one of them. He is rich enough and suave enough to be able to attract almost any blonde show-business bimbo he might want. But that is not what interests him. He is drawn to strong, independent-minded woman of varying degrees of conventional beauty who usually have a much better formal education than he has. Janet, Jeananne and Tessa – not to mention other girlfriends over the years – mostly fit the pattern. Tessa Green is probably the most determined and tough-minded of them all. Although she will never want for anything in financial terms and need not work, she pushed herself to qualify as a barrister and now specializes in medical negligence cases.

Despite his remarriage Green still has a good relationship with the two daughters of his first marriage. He can sometimes be seen taking them to film screenings organized by his good friend Etienne de Villers, who runs the international operations of the Walt Disney Company from London, and then on to supper afterwards. On 1 December 1994 Michael Green was in the Disney preview cinema with Rebecca and Catherine to see *Miami Rhapsody*, a Jewish comedy directed by David Frankel. 'My people. Perfect in every detail,' said Green afterwards, with a proprietorial air. His son Theodore had just recently been born, and Green was showing snapshots of Tessa and her second child. Then Green climbed into the front seat of a small, very ordinary two-door saloon driven by his elder daughter, Rebecca, with Catherine in the back. Asked about the more usual Green Bentley, Rebecca explained that she wouldn't be seen dead in it.

Green also still keeps in touch with his former mother-in-law, Lady Wolfson, and discusses his latest businesses activities with her. 'After all, I'm the only mother-in-law he'll have,' she says, referring to the fact that Tessa's parents are both dead.

Green is besotted with his second family and his two young sons, Oliver and Theodore, except for one small, nagging reservation: they are not Jewish, because their mother is not Jewish. His Jewishness is important to Green, although much more in a cultural rather than a theological sense. It is his heritage, his sense of identity, and he rather despises those who try to bury their past and pretend they are something else because it might be more convenient to do so.

When Berwin was setting up the Jewish Film Foundation she approached Green for help, and it was instantly forthcoming. He has given his time for more than ten years, attended most of the board meetings, and financially underwrote a Jewish Film Festival at the National Film Theatre. Alan Yentob believes he and Green have a similar attitude to their common Jewishness – both are irreparably tied to that culturally rich and tragic past, unwilling to lose touch with it, but equally determined not to have their lives determined by its theological rigidities. 'Whatever his feelings about his background and his pride in it to some extent, about being an outsider in some ways, I don't think he would sacrifice his feelings or his instincts about who to spend his life with on that judgement. But I think it is still quite important to his beliefs, his life,' says Yentob.

Green was very close to Jeananne Crowley and he married Tessa Buckmaster even though practical and emotional difficulties inevitably flow from such relationships between Jews and Gentiles. The fact that Green 'married out' in his second marriage and that Tessa, an Anglo-Catholic, is not Jewish is a family issue. In September 1994 Tessa approached Jonathan Sacks, the Chief Rabbi, about the possibility of bringing up young Oliver Green as a Jew. It was explained to her that she could convert to Judaism, but that this was a long and difficult process and it still would not make her first-born Jewish. Oliver Green could become Jewish only by converting to the religion when he was old enough to understand the implications.

Green has, however, a sense of humour about his Jewishness. When Carlton executives wanted to negotiate the sale of ImMIX, a small part of the empire which had designed a digital video post-production workstation, to Scitex of Israel, Green told them they were wasting their time. 'They're Jews. They're Israelis. You'll never get a proper price,' he said. 'I left it to Bernard Cragg and June, and they got $21 million for a business we never made any money out of,' Green later explained with delight.

At the tenth anniversary in January 1995 of The Presidents Club – a largely Jewish organization that is a cross between Rotary International and the Variety Club of Great Britain and raises money for charity – Green was surprised to encounter a Gentile journalist. 'What are you doing here?' asked Green. 'Some of my best friends are Jewish,' said the journalist. 'Mine aren't,' replied Green.

Green the Jewish family man provides another key to his character as an individual and businessman. Unlike Rupert Murdoch, he is not a driven deal-maker in perpetual motion, a man without another life. There are many Friday afternoons soon after lunch when Green is already on his way either to his country home in Berkshire or to his more recently purchased house in France. Michael Green is no workaholic and is increasingly happy to set the strategic direction and leave the day-to-day running of Carlton to his small team. 'One of the things one has to admire about Michael is the way he has been able to protect his private life, the way he relishes recreation and enjoys his friends and family. He takes a great deal of pleasure in all of that, and it is a very fundamental part of his life – fundamental in the same way as the thing about ambition,' says Yentob, who, like Green, has young children and finds it very easy to relax and unwind in the company of the Greens at the weekend.

Green is interested in fishing, and has a stream running through his Berkshire grounds. He is a boxing fan, and was at the ringside in Las Vegas in March 1996 when Mike Tyson knocked out Frank Bruno in the third round. At the weekend he regularly plays tennis with Max Hastings. The games are intensely competitive, but Green usually wins. In the winter he sometimes skis with friends such as Yentob and Grade, but his enthusiasm is greater than his skill.

At Green's dinner table people from the world of television are entertained, but he is not just a star-gazer and is loyal to old friends who have suffered hard times or were never rich or famous in the first place. 'If you go to his house for dinner you meet sort of vague celebrities in the media, but you also meet people that he has known all the time. He doesn't drop them,' says Bob Gavron, the former printer. Opera has now largely superseded snooker and poker, although he does enjoy a rubber of bridge at the Portland Club in Piccadilly.

Above all, perhaps, Michael Green is an enthusiast – whether for fishing, bridge, chess or conversation – and indeed that aspect of his personality may also be one of his greatest assets as a businessman: his enthusiasm for business never flags.

Another of his lasting enthusiasms has been art – an interest absorbed both from his first wife, Janet, and from Charles Saatchi, one of the most influential collectors of contemporary art in the UK. Janet Green, now married to Gilbert de Botton, a banker who is head of Global Asset Management, was surrounded by her grandfather Isaac Wolfson's impressionist paintings as she grew up. Her own collection started in 1962 when she bought Andy Warhol's *Multiple Electric Chairs*, and includes conceptual and minimalist art. Janet, now on the board of Christies International, was the main initial influence on Michael Green's taste. But, as with many aspects of his development, Charles Saatchi was the mentor and often the model. But, although he has often inflicted his taste on staff at Carlton headquarters, Michael Green has never been a collector on the Saatchi scale.

Nicholas Serota, director of the Tate Gallery and a former school captain of Haberdashers' Aske's, has known the Greens since the late 1970s. He believes that Janet has always been a very serious collector of contemporary art and that Green, although interested too, always deferred to her judgement on art. 'I think his prime interest now is in earlier British art than in contemporary. In a way since he separated from Janet he has moved away from the contemporary field and has since found more of his own style and judgement,' Serota says.

Green can happily talk about paintings – but not with a fraction of the excitement he exudes if the word 'business' is mentioned. 'You could be talking about paintings and he is quite relaxed, but then start talking about business and his whole body posture changes,' says Alex Bernstein, now retired as chairman of Granada but a long-time partner in Waddington Galleries, where Green has bought a number of works.

Michael Green is much too impatient to spend too much time reading books. Jeananne Crowley has said that while she lived with him Green certainly read *The Economist* and *Investors' Chronicle* from cover to cover every week but she only ever persuaded him to read two books – Bob Geldof's autobiography and Tom Wolfe's *The Bonfire of the Vanities*.

Indeed, outside the sphere of business Green's achievements are modest, although there are rumours that more money goes out to charity through the Tangent Charitable Trust than is publicly realized or revealed. It is, however, difficult to know. The *Directory of Grant-Making Trusts* lists only that in 1986 the Trust had income of £20,500 and made grants of £6,350. The directory, which depends on information being supplied, has apparently received no information from Tangent since then. Yet when Green was asked if he could help Richard Freeman, the son of an unemployed former Thames Television security guard, to pursue a training course as a television technician, a cheque for £500 arrived from the Trust by return of post.

Green's one sally into public service, the chairmanship of the Open College, was not a great success. The College – marketing slogan 'Flexible Training That Works' – still exists, and since its foundation in 1987 it has helped to train more than 200,000 people. But it is little more than a distributor of training courses and backup materials, and has had much less impact than Lord Young hoped when he set it up. 'I don't think he [Green] did a good job of it. I don't know why. It just did not take off. The interesting thing about Michael Green is he is very reticent and dislikes personal

publicity. And you have got to have an element of the old ham – which I have,
I suspect – and sell an idea. So I think why it didn't go well was he didn't go
out there. You have got to persuade people,' says Young.

Michael Colenso, managing director of the Open College for part of
Green's time as chairman, is more charitable and would give him a beta-plus.
The real problem, Colenso believes, was the Treasury's insistence that the
College should be self-financing. 'He was punctilious in trying to find a place
for it where it could survive. Under no circumstances could it be said that he
shirked his responsibility,' Colenso believes. He adds, however, that at the end
of Green's five-year term 'he lost interest in it' and was pleased to be rid of it.

One critic – a senior executive in a television company – suggests that
Green has little grasp of 'public-interest' issues. 'Michael doesn't understand
these issues. His issue is solely "What's in it for me? What can I get out of it?"
He is not therefore an advocate for the [media] industry. He doesn't speak at
all on behalf of the industry. He is just too narrow, too narrowly focused,' says
the executive. When Hesseltine tried to drum up business support for the
Millennium Exhibition in Greenwich, it was Green who was sceptical. What
would he get for his money? They wouldn't own the land and the exhibition
would only last for a year.

The suggestion is that behind Green's intense interest in owning television
companies there is little more than the desire to increase profit margins. He
may say he is interested in producing high-quality programmes – and may
indeed believe it – but the reality is that the money comes first and that the
primacy of the bottom line in the Carlton culture militates against the
establishing of the creative atmosphere that could produce memorable
programmes of quality. One of the television executives hounded out of
office by Green suggests bleakly that if the Carlton chairman really does ever
want to produce high-quality programmes there would be few left in the
organization capable of doing it.

Has Green been a good thing for British television, or has television simply
been his business playground? He can hardly be blamed for the growing
competition and the resulting increasing commercialism of ITV. The
multichannel choice offered by cable and satellite has inevitably been driving
ITV in a more commercial and internationally minded direction. The days
when the network was almost a surrogate BBC which just happened to be
paid for by advertising were probably numbered anyway, and Green is as
much a symptom of change as its cause. Yet few have embraced such changes
so enthusiastically, played a greater role in speeding them up, or benefited so
much financially from them.

His old schoolfriend Dennis Marks of English National Opera delivers a tough verdict on Green's contributions to British television, despite, at the same time, believing him to be a devastatingly charming and extraordinary man. 'I think he has had, with the possible exception of Rupert Murdoch, more effect on the transatlanticization of British television than almost anyone else I can think of,' says Marks.

The ENO general director believes that one of Britain's greatest contributions to television is the idea that commercial television can also be public-service broadcasting, aspiring to the highest standards across the widest possible range of programmes – to more than producing slick game shows, soap operas, cop shows and popular drama. But, according to Marks – a former BBC television executive – even after just two years of Carlton Television ITV was already looking a lot less like public-service broadcasting. 'Michael's continuing lobby for deregulation, which I oppose viciously, is, I think, the single most dangerous thing happening in the media in Britain. What he is is a total supporter of a philosophy of broadcasting which will inevitably lead to the death of public-service broadcasting in this country. I have no doubt about that,' he says.

It is a verdict Green would reject totally. ITV audiences remain high, and the Carlton chairman could point to the fact that seven out of the ten most popular new dramas in 1995 were produced by Carlton UK Television – series such as *Bramwell* and *Kavanagh QC*. Carlton has improved considerably after its embarrassing first year on air – a judgement supported both by the doyenne of television critics, Nancy Banks-Smith of the *Guardian*, and by the ITC. In its review of the performance of the ITV companies in 1995, the Commission praised Carlton for the continuing improvement in its London franchise and said that Central had improved in quality in its first full year under Carlton ownership. The costume drama *Bramwell*, the ITC said, was arguably 'Carlton's first major success critically as well as with viewers'. The main regional news programme, *London Tonight*, was praised, as was the 'sharper investigative approach' of *The Big Story*.

There is also evidence that Green himself is beginning to pay more attention to Carlton's reputation as a producer of high-quality television – either for its own sake or because he realizes it will ultimately be good for business. Carlton's commercial-television business in the UK, Green now suggests, is so profitable that it will be possible to devote as much as £10 million a year to high-quality programmes that are not strictly necessary either to win audiences or to observe licence requirements. He points to the

£6 million animated version of *The Wind in the Willows* shown over Christmas 1995 as an example.

A telling sign that Green cared about Carlton's indifferent programme-making record at the beginning came in December 1995, when Paul Jackson, the founding director of programmes at Carlton Television and later managing director of Carlton UK Productions, was invited to resign. Asked why he had got rid of Jackson, Green simply pointed to the television set in his office. It was between programmes, and the screen was showing the Carlton Television logo. The implication was that Jackson, an important figure in winning the licence and getting Carlton on air, had not produced the goods – neither enormous hits nor enough programmes that had won critical acclaim. Green was also irritated about the third series of *The Good Sex Guide*, which he believed had descended into tackiness. Green said that, while he was no prude, there was no need for programmes which showed a lesbian workshop scene involving women wearing rubber gloves masturbating. If that was a factor in Jackson's removal it was a little unfair. As managing director of Carlton UK Productions, Jackson was responsible for the programme output, but the series was viewed in advance and cleared by his boss, Andy Allan. Jackson's departure further reduced the number of remaining executives who had helped to win the licence.

As he entered his fourth year as an owner of commercial-television franchises, Green was beginning to prove that he could create the corporate structures that might be able to produce programmes that are truly first-rate and go beyond the popular, slick and polished. Yet the Carlton chairman was still extraordinarily sensitive about the company's programme-making reputation. When the *Spectator* television critic James Delingpole in May 1996 attacked the costume drama *Sharpe* and asserted that Carlton programme-makers were interested only 'in appealing to the lowest common denominator', Green replied personally. The piece had been 'one of the most ill-informed, biased and frankly bigoted reviews I can remember reading'. It was all part of the British disease to attack anything 'new' in television, and particularly any 'new' company coming into the industry, he wrote.

Despite the number of programme awards won by Carlton, doubt remains over whether Green can grow to become a modern-day equivalent of Lord Bernstein or Lord Grade.

There is much less doubt that Green is now facing a more difficult patch in his business career than at any period since the 1990 share-price collapse. The political climate of the past decade and the high-level lobbying that was possible were very effective in enabling Green to realize many of his ambitions for Carlton. His best days as a lobbyist, and therefore as a wielder of industrial-political clout, are almost certainly over. They were at their height when Lord Young was in the Trade and Industry Department and Mrs Thatcher was in Downing Street. John Major's approach has always been less doctrinaire than Mrs Thatcher's, and a number of Major's ministers have found Green's style of lobbying too obvious and too relentless.

By comparison, Tony Blair will be polite, but little more. 'Michael is totally dedicated, neurotically driven to getting ahead and getting his own interests ahead of everybody else. Those are not values that will sit squarely with a Labour government. Michael is very much a creature of the eighties. He sits less comfortably in the world of John Major and, I think, of the world of Tony Blair. So far as John Major is concerned he is a supporter, so John Major has to listen to him. As far as Tony Blair is concerned, he doesn't have to listen to him,' a Labour peer commented.

Green's ability to reinvent himself should never be underestimated, but his close identification with the Conservative Party will be difficult to shrug off in a changed political climate. In 1996 he tried to open up a channel of communication with the Labour Party by persuading Baroness Jay, daughter of the former Labour leader Lord Callaghan, to become a director of Carlton Television. On 18 June he also held a dinner at his Mayfair home for two Labour politicians interested in broadcasting: Chris Smith, the former shadow National Heritage Secretary, and Alastair Campbell, press secretary to Tony Blair. But, at the very least, Green's chance of honours may be receding for the foreseeable future. He would very much like an honour to mark his arrival as a full member of the Establishment, although he is much more interested in a peerage than a knighthood.

There is a growing realization that Green tends to use people – a view that is held by a number of influential figures who in other ways admire his achievement. Jarvis Astaire notes Green's boyish, disarming personality and his infectious enthusiasm, but adds, 'The principal criticism I have heard about him is about using people, and I would not disagree with that. Although if people allow themselves to be used that is their prerogative. He is also one of the opportunistic Conservatives. He used Lord Young. Young appears to believe the telephone does not ring quite so often now he is out of office.'

Yet there is no unanimity about Green's character among those who know him well. Richard Taylor of Quantel acknowledges that there is a public perception of Green as a cold, uncaring businessman who is simply exploiting circumstances and people, but says, 'The image *we* see is someone who cares passionately about building a company, that loves to be associated with excellence.' Phil Bennett of Abekas emphasizes that Green has achieved his goals without lying and cheating and by doing what he said he would do rather than 'dancing around things a lot'.

Green has never broken the law to achieve his ambitions, although it is inconceivable that a £3 billion empire can be created in such a short time without treading on toes. He believes he is a businessman of integrity, and says to anyone who asks, 'I have nothing to hide. I am not a crook.' His judgement of what constitutes integrity is not a very sophisticated one, however, and his view of what is right is heavily coloured by what is considered acceptable business practice.

This is best encapsulated by an edgy disputation overheard between Michael Green and Bronwen Maddox, who had left Kleinwort Benson to become a *Financial Times* journalist, at another of John Birt's Christmas drinks parties in the Council Chamber of the BBC. Green was lecturing Maddox on the nature of integrity. The *Financial Times*, he said, had integrity, but should never have published the last line of its 1992 election-morning editorial supporting Labour – rather diffidently and with many qualifications. The editorial caused controversy and real anger in the paper's main City and industrial constituency. There were faxed calls for the resignation of the editor, Richard Lambert, and cancelled subscriptions. 'Commercial suicide,' Green told Maddox. 'You know that's integrity,' replied the young *FT* journalist. 'No, no – commercial suicide,' insisted Green, not apparently understanding the point that Maddox was making: that true integrity, particularly for a national newspaper, can lie in deliberately setting aside immediate commercial interests in favour of a higher idea such as editorial independence.

Yet as a media-owner Green has never tried to interfere in editorial decisions. His instincts are entirely those of a businessman, and it is as a businessman that he would ultimately want to be judged. Here the verdict is straightforward enough. Apart from his earliest days in business, Green has never run any of his companies in a day-to-day sense, but he has been a good – if sometimes expensive – deal-maker, with an acquisitive feel informed by a rough-and-ready strategic sense. He has also been able to find capable subordinates to run the Carlton subsidiaries, although at headquarters his unwillingness to cede power contributed to a series of high-level departures – from Mike Luckwell to Bob Phillis and Keith Edelman – until the problem was solved by the elevation of June de Moller to group managing director. 'I never thought he got the very best out of his staff,' is how Sir David Puttnam sees it.

Yet as Michael Green approaches fifty there are a number of unanswered questions. Why is he still running, still ambitious, still keen to make Carlton bigger and more successful? And what, if any, is the final destination? Why is he still interested in making more money? There are, after all, only so many Bentleys to be driven, so many expensive meals to be eaten and houses to be owned before they become more of a burden than a pleasure.

Ask Green why he is just as enthusiastic as ever to build the business and lift the share price and he will give the conventional answers of a businessman. Partly, of course, the money is a way of keeping the score and of measuring efficiency. But Green also believes passionately that it is as soon as businessmen start doing things for reasons other than profit and boosting share prices that 'companies go over the edge of a precipice'.

The answer, perhaps, is that there is no Michael Green mystery. For people like Green there is no final destination, no point of wealth or power or influence that will ever be enough. There will always be a new deal to do; a new place to expand to; other tycoons to compete against with bigger private jets, larger empires, greater visions than his. To Nigel Wray, his old partner and fellow board member, there is nothing surprising about, nor indeed any need to justify, the activities of a businessman who wants to do more deals. Wray does not think there is anything in the least odd about a rich businessman like Green, who is worth more than £100 million when all his assets are taken into account, being interested in making even more money. It is quite simply something that he does well, and there is nothing strange about wishing to enjoy the continued pleasure of winning. 'No one said to Sir Donald Bradman after he had scored a 100 against England, "Why do you want to score another one?" So why say to Michael Green, "You have made a million. Why do you need to score another million?"' says Wray.

Perhaps the desire to continue doing what he does well is motivation enough for Green the businessman. But many of those who know him best believe there is 'a monkey on his back' urging him on to greater effort, more obvious success. It is the Wolfsons – and Isaac Wolfson in particular. Michael Green is still, to some extent, the young man with the tiny business, unable to keep Janet Wolfson in tights, pressing his nose against the glass of one of the most famous Jewish business empires built from scratch – Great Universal Stores. To build something greater and grander and just as enduring as GUS and the achievement of Isaac Wolfson might finally be enough success. By May 1996 GUS was a company capitalized at £7 billion sitting on a cash pile of £1.3 billion. Carlton, capitalized at £3 billion and without much of a cash pile, has a long way to go to match that.

Yet if he ever surpasses GUS – and that must be entirely possible – then another mountain stretches ahead out of the foothills: Rupert Murdoch's News Corporation. Michael Green is not a Rupert Murdoch, and never will be. He is too cautious. Although he has been prepared to take risks, such as the purchase of Technicolor, they have never been risks on the Murdoch scale. Green has never been prepared to bet the entire shop on a single throw of the dice as Murdoch has done. He has been unwilling to pursue impossible, outrageous ventures like trying to persuade the Chinese that satellite television and the free flow of products of a Western culture would not really be a disruptive influence on a Communist society, or, against all conventional wisdom, challenging the three US networks with a fourth, Fox Television. Nor has he been prepared to tangle in the murky world of Italian politics to try, unsuccessfully, to persuade former Italian Prime Minister Silvio Berlusconi to sell his three national television networks to an Australian-American. And yet what Murdoch has created remains, at least in part, a target for Green.

Lord Young, believes that his former cousin by marriage still has a long way to go as a businessman – particularly if he reads correctly the fundamental changes now transforming the media industry on a global scale. 'Michael could be the modern equivalent of Simon Marks, who created Marks & Spencer, or another Isaac Wolfson,' says the former Trade and Industry Secretary.

Ask Michael Green what in the end he would like to achieve and he hardly hesitates. 'I would love to see a British – and I stress British – a British media company – a world-class one. I do think . . . I am shocked that we speak English, the world watches English-speaking programmes, films, television, software, and yet there are American, there are Australian, but there are no British companies that really do sell all over the world and have a product that everyone wants to watch. And I think we have a chance to do that,' he says.

In the end Michael Green the businessman will be judged not by whether he has been lucky. He is the first to admit that he has been. Nor even by whether he shouts at people sometimes, or uses them or is seen by some as too loud, crude and obvious. And the fact that he might not have made it on anything like his present scale without the Wolfson connection in the 1970s is now of no more than historic interest. Green will be judged by his creation, Carlton Communications – a company put together with patience and skill and which survived through the worst recession since the 1930s.

'Michael is practically the only person in this country with that . . . I don't quite know what the word is – it's a sort of character, personality, drive, all wrapped together with basic business skills and a healthy desire for the bottom line. He could actually bat on the world's stage,' is how Nigel Wray describes the Green phenomenon.

The ultimate verdict on Michael Green the businessman will turn on whether he can translate his simple vision into reality and create a major British production company making films and television programmes for the rest of the world. It will be a daunting challenge to take on the world-class media moguls at their own game. It would be foolish and premature to say that it is an achievement that is beyond Michael Green and Carlton Communications.

APPENDIX: Carlton Communications' Ten-Year Record

1 PROFIT AND LOSS ACCOUNT (£m)

	1986	1987	1988	1989*	1990*	1991*	1992*	1993*	1994	1995
Turnover	58.3	89.1	174.3	518.2	697.6	538.0	635.2	1,004.7	1,404.7	1,579.6
Operating profit	16.1	23.5	39.5	70.2	115.2	65.0	85.3	118.4	187.7	248.5
Profit before tax	18.8	33.7	43.6	83.7	103.1	79.2	100.2	126.1	190.2	246.7
Retained profit	17.9	18.1	22.4	31.3	32.1	18.3	29.2	46.1	66.6	96.0
Earnings per share	21.1p	30.6p	35.6p	34.3p	31.6p	25.4p	33.4p	42.0p	53.8p	65.3p
Total dividend per Ordinary share	4.0p	5.4p	7.5p	9.4p	14.1p	15.5p	17.0p	18.7p	20.65p	23.6p
Dividend cover (times covered)	5.3	5.7	4.7	3.7	2.2	1.6	2.0	2.2	2.2	2.6

2 BALANCE SHEET (£m)

	1986	1987	1988	1989	1990	1991	1992	1993	1994	1995
Fixed assets	25.0	50.0	65.6	205.6	178.6	170.3	213.9	268.2	290.5	295.6
Net current assets	32.7	45.5	67.0	109.5	247.1	283.3	336.7	356.9	351.8	442.0
Long term creditors and deferred taxation	(10.3)	(6.9)	(11.5)	(99.8)	(83.4)	(97.5)	(163.6)	(196.0)	(295.6)	(268.9)
Net assets	47.4	88.6	121.1	215.3	342.3	356.1	387.0	429.1	346.7	468.7

*Restated for FRS3.

Bibliography

Chaim Bermant, *Troubled Eden: An Anatomy of British Jewry* (1969)

Judi Bevan and John Jay, *The New Tycoons: Becoming Seriously Rich at 40*

Peter Chippindale and Suzanne Franks, *Dished! The Rise and Fall of British Satellite Broadcasting* (1991)

Andrew Davidson, *Under the Hammer*

Ivan Fallon, *The Brothers: The Rise and Fall of Saatchi & Saatchi*

Lloyd P. Gartner, *The Jewish Immigrant in England 1870–1914*

Paul Johnson, *A History of the Jews* (1995)

Michael Lewis, *Liars' Poker: Two Cities, True Greed* (1989)

Jeremy Potter, *Independent Television in Britain*, Volumes 3 (*Politics and Control 1968–80*) and 4 (*Companies and Programmes 1968–80*) (1988, 1990)

Jeffrey Robinson, *The Risk Takers: Portraits of Money, Ego and Power* (1985)

–*The Risk Takers Revisited*

Jack Tinker, *The Television Barons*

Lord Young, *The Enterprise Years: A Businessman in the Cabinet*

Index